Lovely Me...

"The best beach reading I can think of...
Lovely Me's author has created a character who
lives and breathes on its pages... Seaman is
a deft storyteller and she has a marvelous story
to tell here."

—**Joyce Maynard,** *Mademoiselle*

"Many of the readers who bought her novels
will be fascinated by this quality biography."

—**Mary Vespa,** *People*

"Shows skill, thoroughness, and affection.... It's
striking how much more readable the life
Jacqueline Susann lived herself turns out to be
than any of those she made up."

—**Jane Howard,** *Washington Post*

"Captivating... the best feet-up, girl-talk good
time of my life."

—**Florence King,** *Newsday*

"An intimate, illuminating dissection of an
American fantasy... brilliantly documented... a
far more satisfying book than any work turned
out by its subject."

—**Kiki Olson,** *Philadelphia Inquirer*

more...

CELEBRITY BIOGRAPHERS
AND BESTSELLING AUTHORS PRAISE
L★O★V★E★L★Y M★E

"A stunner! Her portrait of this gutsy, funny, determined maverick is a revelation. A bestselling book about a bestselling author."

—Barbara Gordon,
author of *I'm Dancing As Fast As I Can*

"A page-turner, with all the narrative drive of a Jacqueline Susann novel, yet incredibly enough a true story. Susann's life more than matched anything she wrote, however sensational. Barbara Seaman has done a terrific job: her research is fascinating, she omits nothing, and Jackie Susann for good or ill comes vividly alive."

—Gerold Frank,
author of *Judy*

"It's the mix of glitz and sadness that is so compelling."

—Betty Rollin,
author of *First You Cry*

"With its gossip and glitz, chuzpah and hoopla, *Lovely Me* is a delicious, satisfying read."

—Alix Kates Shulman,
author of *Memoirs of an Ex-Prom Queen*

"Barbara Seaman puts flesh on a fierce survivor and gives us an absorbing look inside the world of publishing. Better than lip-reading at the Russian Tea Room!"

—Gail Sheehy,
author of *Passages*

"Jacqueline Susann's own life makes her novels seem tame. Barbara Seaman's exceptional biography, well written and well researched, is wonderfully gossipy and a real page-turner."

—Barbara Taylor Bradford

Please turn this page for the spectacular acclaim
of the press for *LOVELY ME*.

Critics Rave Over

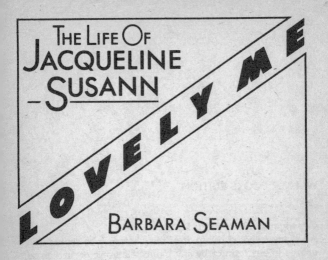

THE LIFE OF JACQUELINE SUSANN

LOVELY ME

BARBARA SEAMAN

WARNER BOOKS

A Warner Communications Company

Cover design by Fred Marcelino

Warner Books, Inc.
666 Fifth Avenue
New York, N.Y. 10103

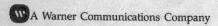 A Warner Communications Company

Printed in the United States of America

First Warner Books Printing: February, 1988

10 9 8 7 6 5 4 3 2 1

To my dear son,

Noah Samuel Seaman,

First reader and last,
whose wit and loving kindness
sustained me through this work.

A NOTE TO THE READER

"Jacqueline Susann" was not a stage name. Jackie's father, Robert Susan, spelled his name with one *n*. Her mother, Rose, a schoolteacher, added the second *n* professionally so that her pupils would pronounce it correctly, with the accent on the second syllable. Jackie was exceptional in that she married young, but then made a name for herself that was not her husband's. Susann was her father's name, amended by her mother.

Preface

Suddenly something reached out of a cage and touched my shoulder. . . . I asked the owner what it was. He said it was a poodle. . . . It seemed to have selected me.

—Jacqueline Susann in *Every Night, Josephine!*

*T*HE first question many people ask a biographer and many have asked me, is "How did you pick your subject?" Jackie seems to have selected me, much as her poodle Josephine selected her. It happened at a publishing lunch, in 1980, with Jerry Traum, my agent; Maria Guarnaschelli, my editor, and Sherry Arden, who was then vice president and associate publisher of William Morrow and Company. We were discussing a book about friendship that I thought I wanted to write, and Sherry mentioned a friend of hers, Jackie Susann. Someone asked me if I'd ever met her, and I said yes, at a doctor's office. She had seemed ill and extremely fragile, I recalled. Early the next

morning, I'd been stunned to see her on television, be
wigged and be-eyelashed, sassy, salty, and sharp. We al
chatted on, Sherry filling in more details about Jackie'
mental and physical indomitability. By the end of the
lunch, I was hooked on telling her story. The idea was to
focus on her discovery of breast cancer, in 1962, and he
remaining twelve years, during which she became the
best-selling novelist in the world.

For the book we had in mind I needed to talk to Jackie':
doctors and nurses, some of whom requested the consen
of her widower, Irving Mansfield. Sherry approached him
and he agreed to meet with me. He was staying in Los
Angeles, and I flew out. He asked to see an outline of my
book proposal. I spent weeks preparing it. Irving told me
tearfully that he loved it, and would gladly sign the
medical forms. Then he stalled. Although I had wanted to
zero in on the end of Jackie's life, I thought, Why not star
at the beginning, in Philadelphia, where she'd been born
My first visit there produced a shock. Within hours I wa:
given the names of three of Jackie's father's mistresses, al
of them still alive. Jackie had hardly grown up in a
conventional family. The book began to take on larger
dimensions, while Irving continued to string me along.
Eight months passed and then I had a second shock, in the
form of a telephone call from Irving's agent. He had
decided to write his own book, the agent said, and he
wanted to buy my research. I declined. Irving instructed
his friends to stop talking to me, which forced me to dig
deeper and go further afield, delving layer by layer into the
most hidden realms of Jackie's life.

The facts were entirely different from my early percep-
tions. Jackie's life was as colorful as her books, as
chock-full of gossip and scandal, drug addiction, obsessive
sexuality, and the compulsion for celebrity, or what Jackie
called mass love. Her books were almost anthropology.

They were her life, and the lives of her family and friends, with some enemies and rivals succulently tossed into the stew. And indeed, her final illness was her turning point, her transformation. Uneducated and insecure, Jackie had always used the casting couch to further her thwarted ambitions and to "stay in the game," as she put it. She could never muster the confidence for writing fiction until her mastectomy took her "out of the ring." Jackie is flogging *herself* when Anne declares to Jennifer in *Valley of the Dolls*, "You're the one who's been saying all along that you don't want to live for your body. Well, have some guts, some BELIEF IN YOURSELF—start proving it." Jackie was also as addicted to pills as many of her fictional heroines. It was the way of life in her circle before it became the way of life in the larger culture. Her lover, the film star Carole Landis, OD'd, and Jackie herself came close several times. Again, in *Valley*, it is the author's own memory speaking when Neely cries, "Hey, Jen, does it hurt before you die? Were you scared? Stay with me, Jen. . . . I'm gonna get some more pills—I'm gonna join you." Coming to fiction late and with urgency, Jackie didn't much cover her tracks. The very rawness and simplicity of her material made it seem "clichéd" to some readers, but compelling and true (as she intended) to others. Her work was so popular that in the years 1966–69 she became one of the richest self-made women in the United States.

As for my own book, what was to have been a two-year project burgeoned into six, but long before the end of that time I was able to answer a second, frequently asked question: "Do you like Jacqueline Susann?" The answer is yes, I love her. Loyal to her friends, malicious to her enemies, Jackie was outrageous, original, and brave. Her enemies thought her an outright liar; her friends understood that she dealt in illusion and flimflam—card tricks, as it were, or sleight of hand. What you seem to be might be what you become, as indeed Jackie did.

On the day I finished my own last chapter, my daughter Elana proposed a toast. "It only takes one year to have a birthday," she said, "and nine months to have a baby. *Lovely Me* is the equivalent of six birthdays and nine kids."

And so, my deepest gratitude to my loving and stalwart family: my children, Shira, Elana, and Noah, and my husband, Milton Forman. Thanks also to my sisters, Jeri Drucker, Elaine Rosner-Jeria, Celia Michaels; my stepmother, Ruth Gruber; my sister-in-law, Roslyn Weinrauch; my stepchildren, Daniel, Jo, William, and David Forman. Married as I was to Jackie, I stand guilty of a lot of neglect. At a party, if her name came up I tuned out everything else. Traveling in Europe with my family on vacation, I was interested only in tracking down her foreign publishers, noting details of the menus at the restaurants she'd dined in. And even in the Far East my obsession was to see how her books were selling in airports and hotels. Did they recognize her name in China? They did. They knew both *Valley of the Dolls* and, oddly, *Every Night, Josephine!* (I never got to Russia, where Andropov said that Jackie was his favorite American novelist, but I think I know the reason why. She revealed what he considered the "decadence" of our culture. Jackie would have been tickled that the Russians love John Steinbeck, for similar reasons.)

The folks at Morrow—Maria especially, as well as Sherry, Larry Hughes, and Al Marchioni—were patient and helpful beyond belief, while Lela Rolontz, Jim Landis, and Lori Ames also extended their assistance. Above all my wonderful agent, Jerry, deserves a medal, and my lawyer, Carol Rinzler, deserves another. And I truly could not have completed this book without my assistant, Chantal Dietemann, who stuck it out for three years longer than she planned, or without my photo researcher, Dan Starrer. Thanks also to researchers Julia Klein in Philadelphia, Angela Fox Dunn in Los Angeles, Karel Littman in New York, and Jean Rossner. No fewer than four copy editors worked on the manuscript under great time pressure. A special thank-you to Bruce Giffords, Joan Amico, Debbie Weiss, and Sonia Greenbaum; also to Harvey Hoffman in production, to Richard Oriolo, the designer, to Hearst attorneys Stanley Stempler and Richard Sugarman, and to Maria's assistants, Joy Warren and Peter Sims.

A number of colleagues gave me counsel and encouragement, made valuable suggestions, or provided important leads: Irwin Berg and Marisa Montecalvo, Michael Patrick Hearn, who at times gave Jackie more attention than he gave his own biography-in-progress of L. Frank Baum, Judy Feiffer, Joseph Amiel, Laura Foreman, Barbara Howell, Kitty Kelley, Kathy Brady, Helen Gurley Brown, Anne Roiphe, Sonia Nissenbaum, Ellen Dolganos, Patricia Bosworth, and the late Mel Arrighi, whom I miss.

Biography calls for a kind of courage or foolhardiness. To some it is the only valid history, the "stream of souls," as W. B. Yeats put it. Yet others deem it pernicious gossip, and Germaine Greer has called on its practitioners to "abandon biography and take up an honorable trade." What is remarkable—and I am grateful to Carolyn Heilbrun for pointing this out—is that, except for those with queens as their subject, precious few adult biographies of women have been written by women. There have been many female biographers of course, but why have they addressed themselves primarily to men? We may have the answer from Catherine Drinker Bowen, biographer of Tchaikovsky, Justice Oliver Wendell Holmes, John Adams, and Francis

Bacon: "To spend three years or five with a truly great man, reading what he said and wrote, observing him as he errs, stumbles, falls and rises again; to watch his talent grow if he is an artist, his wisdom develop if he is a statesman—this cannot but seize upon a writer, one might almost say transform him. One has climbed a hill, looked out and over, and the valley of one's own condition will be forever greener."

The lives of women worthy of biographies are rarely so uplifting. It seems the normal condition of men to want to compete and excel; competitive women historically were viewed as aberrations, and to some extent they still are. Their lives are not often pretty, which may be why other women have been reluctant to chronicle them. One of Jackie's obsessions was the exorbitant price women pay for success. "You've got to climb to the top of Mount Everest to reach the Valley of the Dolls. . . . The elements have left you battered, deafened, sightless—and too weary to enjoy your victory." Outstandingly successful women like Jackie are apt to come from backgrounds that are tragic or disturbed, and to reach adulthood and eminence in some way wounded. The reader of this book need not be a psychologist, as indeed the author is not, to grasp that Jackie's attachment to her father was near incestuous. At the same time, that relationship was her motor. She lived only to "show him what he missed," as she herself said.

I am grateful to Barnard College and to Oberlin College, for providing me with gifted, literate students for the endless transcribing and library research. Some of them did much more: Susan Roxas, Rosemary Byrne, Juliette Dickstein, Jackie Geller, Jeany Heller, Beth Pratta, Liz Skavish, Laura Yeager, David Zimmerman, Martha Aldridge, Eve Cagan. Thanks also to Lisa Terenzio and Ellen Houle-Dietemann; to Jonathan White, who kept my computer running, with additional help from Andy Brennerman, Bob Mullarky, and Mr. Rajan; to Francisco Richardson for servicing all the typewriters; to Vita Shapiro, who kept my back erect, and to Ada Tulloch.

Hundreds of sources provided information and photographs, and submitted to interviews. Most of them are listed at the end of the book. There is no way I can express my indebtedness for their thoughtfulness and generosity. Three individuals went to extraordinary trouble over a period of years: Robert Jelinek, Jackie's cousin, keeper of the family photographs and paintings—and certain skeletons; Don Preston, midwife to Jackie's success, and the victim of it; the incomparable Hildegarde, who still prays for Jackie every day, and who undertook the exhausting labor of locating every mention of Jackie in her own diaries. Special thanks also to Leah Appet, brilliant screenwriter, who shared her insights and knowledge; to Fran Wilderman Sacks, who, out of devotion to Rose Susann, took me to all the places of Jackie's childhood; and to Candy Jones Nebel, who dug out all those hours of tape recordings of Jackie on Long John's radio program. As always in such cases, I am beholden to many librarians, especially at the Lincoln Center Library and the Academy of Medicine Library in New York, the Library of Congress and the Copyright Office in Washington, the Jewish Archives of Philadelphia, the Pennsylvania Academy of Fine Arts, and above all the library at the University of Pennsylvania, where Susan Kallenbach did so much to set me walking. Calligrapher David Forman copied Jackie's horoscope from an original by Lynne Palmer.

A third question I am asked about Jackie is whether I like her work. Of course I respect it. How can you not respect an author who, in so few years and with so much illness, wrote three (or, including *Dolores*, four) novels that enthralled so many millions of readers? Do I equate Jackie with Emily Dickinson or Virginia Woolf? Certainly not, but how about Dreiser? His style was also clumsy and his characters contemptible. Like Jackie he believed he was exposing the corruption of his times. And like Jackie he had that certain something, that one-in-a-million narrative drive.

Valley of the Dolls, published in February, 1966, stands as an early storm signal of both the drug culture and the women's movement. Jackie had something to say and she said it, and if she did not say it artfully, she said it compellingly. But Jackie stands in literature for something more. Her manuscripts needed a lot of editing to be published, and a lot of hard selling to become popular. How she composed her novels and how she and her publishers launched them are the heart of this book, and I dedicate these sections to all writers everywhere.

Contents

1

Night Thoughts

One other dream besides Irving...

—Jacqueline Susann

CHRISTMAS Eve, 1962.

Of course she wouldn't sleep tonight. When things were going well she had a problem with insomnia, let alone when they were falling apart. Tonight her "dolls," her sleeping pills, had failed her, and so had the potent Nembutal suppositories she kept in her refrigerator for emergencies. Chasing sleep was a waste of time, and oh, how she hated to waste time! She had wasted months when they put her son, Guy, away; for months she hardly came out of her bedroom. Now she knew better. "Time," she reminded herself, "is life." She prowled the small apartment, searching for something to do. She watched the snowflakes drift down onto her beloved Central Park—

perhaps for the last time? "No," she promised herself, "it will *not* be the last time." If she did have cancer, she would lick it.

She wandered into the den and took a novel from her bookshelf, but it couldn't hold her. Drugged up as she was, she was still too tense to concentrate. She played solitaire. It was three-thirty in the morning when her eye fell on a small black looseleaf binder, the journal in which she'd so conscientiously entered a 227-page record of her recent trip to Israel and the Far East. She had dutifully escorted her mother, Rose, enduring for five full weeks a bunch of annoying old ladies. Her mother loved to travel, but wouldn't go without her; besides, since her heart attack and with her cataracts, Rose really could not go alone. The journal was to be a present for her mother, a memento of the trip, all typed up, cleaned up, grammar and spelling corrected, and with their many snapshots pasted in. The snapshots were revealing. In them Rose was always groomed and in a hat, even the day she took a ride on a camel's back, but Jackie looked exhausted.

When Jackie returned home, she'd added—in the original black looseleaf binder, and just for her own edification; certainly not for Rose's eyes—a summary of her thoughts on the art of aging gracefully. She entitled the page "Fight Against Old Age—What Not to Do in 1987!"

1. Be sure to stand tall.
2. Don't wear orthopedic shoes.
3. Don't talk too much.
4. Don't nag.
5. If you can't walk fast, DON'T—but don't hold others up.
6. Don't become helpless, and let others wait on you—open cab doors, pack, get into your coat.

7. Try to remember—someone young doesn't owe you anything—unless you've more than earned it.
8. Don't reminisce.
9. Listen.

Her own old age was not imminent. She was only forty-four. Still, she was all too aware that she was beyond the height of her beauty, and maybe beyond the best of her dreams as well. She was on the downhill slope. So be it, then. She'd face it. She'd age with dignity and flair—if of course, she got the chance to age at all.

She had been an angel on that trip, and look how God rewarded her. More lumps, specifically a lump in the breast. She'd had them before, but in the past they'd been nothing, and her gynecologist, Arthur Davids, had merely aspirated them, in a procedure she'd come to hate. She had discovered this latest lump in Japan, and though she'd returned home in November, she hadn't seen Dr. Davids until December 14. She had stalled, hoping it would go away when her period came, but it hadn't.

She liked Dr. Davids. So did Joyce, and some of her other women friends who went to him. She also knew him socially, mostly from parties at Billy Rose's mansion on East Ninety-third Street. The doctor was a jovial man, an excellent tennis player, a reader of good books. His office, off Fifth Avenue, was practical, not posh. The green and orange rug was industrial quality. A bulb was usually missing from the chandelier. The curtains were graying, and the beige linoleum in the foyer curled upward at the corners. It was an office to which mothers could bring their toddlers and where Jackie could—and often did—bring her poodle, Josephine.

On December 14 Davids had decided not to make Jackie wait. He had ushered her into his examining room and then left while she removed her old dog-walking slacks and her beige silk blouse. Jackie always dressed casually when she had a doctor's appointment—a habit she'd picked up from her mother, who thought that the doctors would charge less.

Stripped, she hopped up on the examining table while Josephine looked on. Davids returned, an avuncular, dapper, somewhat reassuring presence. "You know the procedure," he reminded her, brandishing a needle that was two inches long and tipped with yellow plastic. "If it's just a cyst, we're hoping it's going to collapse. This one could be a solid tumor, but don't panic. In most cases it would be benign."

She didn't want to watch. She scooped up Josephine, hugged her against her other breast, and shut her eyes. She made a deal with God that if the cyst collapsed she would *never* be unfaithful to Irving again. Never again.

The cyst did not collapse. "Okay," Arthur Davids told her, "now we have to take a biopsy, and let's not put it off."

Davids got Gerson Lesnick, a breast surgeon, on the telephone. Lesnick then tried to book the hospital room. Jackie almost laughed when she heard about it later. A hospital booking, it appeared, was as hard to get when you really needed it as a booking in the theater. Lesnick had tried for Mt. Sinai, but couldn't get her in. The best he could manage was Doctors Hospital, and the earliest available date was Christmas, nearly two weeks away.

Christmas was an awful time to schedule an operation, she knew. The staff, such as it was, would resent working, and half of them might be drunk. She remembered visiting her father in the hospital over Christmas, and it had been grim. She, her mother, and June, one of her father's mistresses, had stayed with him all day because you simply couldn't get a nurse. Other mistresses had popped in and out, but not a soul from the hospital.

Reluctantly Jackie had agreed to Christmas for her biopsy, but she was irritated—more than irritated, she was mad, furious, frustrated—and almost frightened to death. After she left Davids, she stormed into St. Patrick's Cathedral and marched directly to the statue of Saint Andrew, her appointed patron saint. "Do one thing for me before I die," she told him grimly. "Make me important enough to get a bed in a fucking hospital!"

But now, prowling her apartment, she knew that Christmas morning would soon dawn, the morning of her biopsy, and—reading between the lines of what the doctors had told her—quite possibly the morning of her mastectomy, too. Of course she couldn't sleep, and she really didn't want to. What if this *was* the last Christmas she'd see? Yes, she could fight cancer, but could she win? Dear God, she couldn't die yet. She was too young to die, and there was too much left to do—for herself, for others. Guy needed her. What if he ended up in Willowbrook or Creedmoor or some awful public funny farm? She had to protect her son. And Irving needed her, maybe now more than ever. She had to protect him, too, and to hold intact, for both their sakes, his image of her. He needed to adore her; she needed to be adored.

She prowled the apartment, but quietly, careful not to wake him. It would have been nice to turn to him for comfort, to share her fear with him—but not at the expense of smashing the icon he had made of her. He thought she was so strong. "My queen," he called her. If he knew the truth, "My Lady of the Sorrows" would be closer to the mark.

She would share with her diary instead. Writing in it was an old habit, and it always helped her collect herself, lift herself from despair. Her first diary had been a gift from her grandmother on Jackie's seventh birthday. It had been a lovely thing—real leather with a lock and key, and her initials stamped on the cover in gold to match the edges of the pages. "Sometimes you might feel sorry for yourself," Grandma had said, "and when you do, put it here, put it in your diary, and don't breathe a word." For all these years she had kept a diary. And she had kept her sorrows to herself.

But the diary she was using now was tucked away in a wig box in her bedroom, and she might wake Irving if she retrieved it. Her eye fell on the black notebook that chronicled her trip with Rose. There were still some blank pages in the back. She picked it up and settled herself with it in a chair, tucking her long legs beneath her, her thoughts still with her grandmother. Grandma Ida had expected great things of her. And now, a decade after the old woman's death, what of note had happened to her granddaughter? Nothing, except possibly breast cancer— that and a job doing idiotic television commercials that had made her something of a laughingstock. Jackie had dreamed of a career in the theater, but that was over. No one would give her a real acting job now.

Her current hopes for fame and fortune—slim hopes, to be sure—were pinned on a book about Josephine, a cute book based on the poodle stories that larded her letters to her friends and turned up often in her diary. She'd gotten an agent to take it, but not a publisher. It had been at Doubleday now for months.

On December 25, 1962, at 3:30 A.M., she opened her notebook and began to write:

> This is a bad Christmas. Irving has no job. I haven't heard from Doubleday. I am going to the hospital.
>
> But it is not the worst Christmas in the world. I am going to the hospital accompanied by a man who loves me. And I love him. I am not alone.

The only thing I have to do alone is die—or fight cancer if I have it. No one can help me with that. I don't think I have it. I have too much to accomplish. I can't die without leaving *something*— something big. Irving has already made his mark. He'll make it again. But I have to leave *something*.

I haven't left a child that can carry on! But I've got a brain and talent.

I'm Jackie—I have a dream.

I wanted to love more than my life. But that was not for me. A woman is dull if she lives for love.

End of dream.

I wanted to be the biggest star in the world. I skirted on the fringes.

End of dream.

I wanted a girl child.

End of dream.

I wanted a wonderful husband.

I got him.

I think I can write.

Let me live to make it!

One other dream besides Irving must come true!

PART ONE

THE EARLY YEARS—ORIGINS [1492–1918] AND CHILDHOOD [1918–1936]

2

Her Father

I never wanted to marry anyone like my father because I didn't think there could be anyone like him. Sometimes the daughter of a famous or successful man will marry a man that nobody else wants, so that she won't have her mother's problems. She wants the security of a man nobody will try to take away from her.

—Jacqueline Susann

*S*HE had always been an extravagant dreamer. By the time she could toddle through the rooms of her parents' house in Philadelphia, the dreams were already rich and thriving, nourished by her father. Even as a small child, Jackie sensed that Bob Susan belonged to a wider world than his household could encompass, and as she grew she would see his other world as glamorous and exciting and probably deliciously wicked.

The family came to America in 1889, leaving a land where they had enjoyed aristocratic privileges for one where, at best, their youngest son might serve the rich. Susan, an ancient and honored name, is derived from Shushan, the capital of Persia. By the fifteenth century the family had settled in Spain. A "de Suzanne" served as the financial adviser to Queen Isabella and personally raised most of the money for Christopher Columbus's first voyage. During the Inquisition most of the de Suzannes were killed. According to family stories, the survivors fled first to Holland and then to Vilna, in the duchy of Lithuania, and were established there by 1568, the year the Jews were required to register with the government and pay a poll tax. There, they were known by the name Susan.

For two hundred years, Bob's immediate ancestors leased and managed an enormous lumber estate, which produced a princely income and was famous for its smokehouse. The estate employed hundreds of serfs, of whom a dozen worked in the household of Lillian Gimsen Susan, Jackie's paternal grandmother. Shy and aesthetic, Lillian devoted herself to painting. Her husband, Benjamin, a scholarly man, entrusted the management of the estate to foremen. Lillian bore Benjamin seven children, three girls followed by four boys. Bob, born on April 15, 1887, was the baby.

His older siblings all enjoyed a taste of privilege in their childhood, but Bob was born to catastrophe. Eastern Europe's tidal flux of anti-Semitism crested in the very year of his birth: Benjamin was ordered off his land. Two years later the Susans emigrated to America and settled near distant cousins in Shamokin, a coal-mining town in central Pennsylvania. Benjamin opened a general store.

Benjamin had his religious faith to see him through the collapse of the family fortunes, but Lillian, with no such resource, fell into a deep depression. She knew little about child care or household management; the servants were supposed to see to that sort of thing. Now, there was only the poverty and filth of this grubby town. All her senses assaulted, Lillian took to her bed, leaving to her three daughters the chores of housekeeping and motherhood.

By far the most maternal of the lot was Rosa, the youngest and most energetic of the daughters. And by far her favorite among her brothers was Bob, nine years her junior. He was her *boychik*, and she gave him her unreserved adoration. Along with it, she probably gave the young boy a lot of inadvertent sexual stimulation. Bob shared her bed during the five years they spent in Shamokin, and she was constantly cuddling and petting him. In his infancy she fed him with a bottle, but, as though sensing this was somehow inadequate, she also encouraged him to suck on her budding breasts. It was all innocently meant, of course. Even as an adult Rosa probably never heard the term "incestoid behavior," which the "alienists" of her day were beginning to throw around.

Even so, she seems to have had some insight about her little brother, who, even as a toddler, appeared to realize that his best chance for survival lay in his charm. Rosa later swore that he'd been born with an uncanny sensitivity toward women. Bobby never cried, and he never interrupted. He made his needs felt by toddling over to Rosa and stroking her leg, or laying his head on her lap, or throwing his arms around her neck and kissing or licking her lightly. His only way of showing anger was to "make jokes," practical jokes that, in fact, expressed some cruelty, but that usually ended up with the victim being blamed as a spoilsport. He would hide his brothers' shoes in the morning when they were getting ready for school. One brother, Pete, had a violent temper and reacted by smashing furniture or pummeling Bob—acts for which Pete would be punished.

Rosa found Bobby's jokes clever and adorable. Her three other brothers were expected to do chores, but Bobby's time was protected so he could practice his drawing. Rosa always felt that she had failed with Bobby in only one respect: She never infected him with her pride in being a Jew from Vilna, and in being a Susan. Indeed, all his life Bob would underplay and even deny his Jewishness, so much so that some of his closest friends didn't know he was a Jew. Rosa blamed his "trying to pass" on the circumstances of his childhood. "Momma lay crying on the couch, and Poppa prayed," she said. "Bobby resented that he didn't get the attention."

Lillian Susan did rise from her couch long enough for one last, definitive pronouncement. She was living only to see her daughters properly married to good Jewish husbands, she said, and there were no suitable beaux in Shamokin. The family would have to move to Philadelphia. Remembering the famous Susan smokehouse back in Vilna, some friends in Philadelphia set Benjamin up as a butcher, but he failed at it. Nevertheless, the move was a success in Lillian's mind because all three girls married. When the last of them was safely ensconced in the home of a husband, Lillian died.

Rosa was twenty-two when she married Harris Potamkin on February 12, 1901. On her wedding day she looked less like a Jewish bride than an Irish one, with her broad, cheerful face and auburn hair. Slender at the time, Rosa had a talent for cooking that soon undid her own trim figure as well as the stocky, muscular frame of her husband. According to their daughter Flossie, "It looked like somebody took a pipe and blew them both up."

Back in the old country, it's doubtful Harris Potamkin ever would even have met Rosa Susan. He was a poor Russian Jew straight off the *shtetl*. As a boy he'd hidden in a cupboard in his native village of Gormel and watched while his mother was raped and murdered in a pogrom. He was only a teen-ager when he crossed the Atlantic by himself, arriving on the doorstep of a carpenter uncle in Philadelphia and announcing his intention to save what remained of his family in Russia from the tsar.

The Potamkins were a vigorous, rugged and determined lot, Harris even more so than the rest. With the first few dollars he earned at odd jobs he hired a tutor. He soon learned to read and write English. Declining his uncle's offer to teach him carpentry, he walked the streets of Philadelphia dreaming of a business that would make his fortune. Then one fateful day he heard a Jewish housewife complain that she could not get succulent fish, such as carp, for her Sabbath table.

Harris was inspired. He rented a horse and wagon for a dollar and drove the rig to a lake in southern New Jersey, where he bought a dollar's worth of fish. Back in Philadelphia he sold the fish on the streets for a nickel, a dime, or twenty cents, depending on the size. Within two years he was prosperous enough to buy a house at 718 South Fourth Street and took in boarders, figuring that they would provide a captive market for any leftover fish. He then sent home for his father and stepmother, his five brothers, his sister, and his stepbrother. He settled them in a big house in south central Philadelphia near the Delaware River and took them all into his business.

Only in his early twenties, Harris was a rich man and getting richer when the Susan family moved into his South Philadelphia boarding house and Rosa caught his eye. He was twenty-five when they married, and all his life he would remain awed and grateful that a commoner such as he had managed to snare such a princess.

Commoner or not, Harris turned out to be the salvation of the Susan family. Most of the Susans relied on him at one time or another for support. It was only because of

Harris that old Benjamin could give up his futile efforts to make a living and could spend his days in *shul* pursuing his beloved religious studies.

Harris traveled a lot on business. He expanded his operations into Wisconsin and South Dakota, where succulent fish abounded but were not popular with the natives. He solved the problem of how to convey the fish safely home to Philadelphia by inventing a kind of refrigerated boxcar, an arrangement of fish tanks with chimneys through which ice could be inserted every three or four hundred miles. Soon he was so preserving 80 percent of his Midwestern fish and fast becoming a millionaire, which gave him the resources to become seriously embattled with the railroads over the high cost of freight. Harris was a lifelong battler who would eventually die in court, while giving testimony.

With Harris off in Wisconsin, Rosa was left happily alone with Bobby. With Bobby around, she said, "you didn't need entertainment." Now in his teens, Bob already had the dark, Italianate good looks that would soon draw women to him, and he was already spending hours every day at his drawing. He and Rosa had mastered perfect English, and they often taunted Harris, who had not. "The longer you live here, the worse you talk," Rosa would mock, and she and Bob would mimic his thick accent.

Harris doted on the children Rosa bore him—first Belle, and then the twins, Flossie and Leon. When his daughters wrinkled their noses at the fishy smell that always clung to him, he would merely chuckle and bow as low as his girth permitted, declaring, "I was never too proud to bow to a lady." As for Rosa, he indulged her every whim. She liked diamonds, so he festooned her cushiony bosom with them and adorned her wrists and fingers and earlobes with more. According to Flossie, "When Father took Mother to the theater, she was so lit up you didn't need a searchlight. She looked like a Christmas tree when she went out.''

Harris also doted on Bob, his young brother-in-law and ward. Certain aspects of Bob's developing character troubled Harris as the years passed, but he was always proud of the boy's good looks, his breeding, and his talent. Besides, Harris admired people who dared to be "different," as well as people who were devoted to their work; and Bob, however exasperating, was both different and diligent. Sometimes Harris liked to tiptoe into Bobby's room and watch him at his easel, selecting colors as meticulously as Harris selected fish. At twilight one evening, Harris urged Bobby to come to dinner, noting that it was getting dark. Bobby explained that it wasn't dark, that in Philadelphia the evening mists over the marshes of Delaware produced a blue unlike any other in the world. Harris strained to see the subtle shadings in the sky and also captured on Bobby's canvas. After that, Harris walked home from work more slowly, cured of his homesickness for Gormel, and loving the Philadelphia dusk.

Admiration for Bob's sensibility was by no means confined to his own family, however. He attended the Pennsylvania Academy of Fine Art, where the faculty was sufficiently impressed to grant him scholarships to study in Europe in 1912 and again the following year. Bob visited Florence and Rome and Amsterdam—and, of course, Paris, a city pulsing with artistic experimentation and permissive mores. Bob loved that city. He returned to Philadelphia after his first trip with overflowing sketch pads. But the next year there was little more in his steamer trunks than the latest European toys for the Potamkin children, silver candelabra for Rosa, some colorful bow ties for Harris, and some new clothes for himself—including stylish knickers with matching silk knee socks.

Harris was disturbed by Bob's lack of work—and by

other, deeper, matters—but for a time he kept his feelings to himself. He decided to hope for the best and look for signs that the young man was taking on some semblance of adult responsibility. But all through 1914 there were few such signs. At one point Bob actually went to work at a department store to supplement his artist's earnings, declaring that he didn't need Harris's support anymore. It was only a brief rebellion.

Once Harris had broached the subject of the second trip, and Bobby had immediately launched into one of his lectures. "I observed and I listened, and I learned a great deal more," he said. "I studied hands, Harris. Long hands, fat hands, thin hands, square hands and tapering ones, all have their own story to tell. Your own hands, Harris, are the index of your character. They show you to be ambitious and nervous."

Nervous, Harris thought. So true—though he doubted Bobby knew how much he himself contributed to the condition. In his late twenties now, Bob was no *boychik* anymore. He was a wonderful artist, yes, but there was an underlying problem. The real trouble, Harris mused, was this . . . this sex thing.

Harris wondered if Rosa knew that her brother, Bob, simply couldn't keep his hands off women—and that women couldn't keep their hands off him. Harris had first noticed it when Bobby was around sixteen, and he had prayed it would be temporary. But it only got worse. Harris had caught Bobby with one servant girl after another. He caught him slipping off to waterfront whorehouses. He caught him with his daughter Belle's girl friend, and with his neighbor's wife. And Bobby was indiscriminate: The neighbor's wife was a pitiful-looking, sickly young woman, cross-eyed and flat-chested, with stringy hair.

Philadelphia had seven hundred churches and synagogues and about half that many whorehouses. As far as

Harris knew, Bob, who now styled himself a "devout atheist," hadn't set foot in a synagogue since his bar mitzvah. But he was a familiar figure in the bordellos, the low-down as well as the posh—a fact that astounded the practical-minded Harris. Why *pay* for women when so many were available to him free? Models at the art school clawed at each other for the privilege of "sitting" for him.

Harris worried not only for his errant young brother-in-law, but for his own blood kin. Most of the young Potamkin women had crushes on Bob, who was easily the most romantic man they knew. And one of them, Ethel Potamkin, had more than a crush. Ethel, the eldest daughter of Harris's brother Max, was tiny and delicate, with dark wavy hair. She suffered from a heart murmur and therefore clearly needed a strong, protective husband— something Bob would probably never be. But Ethel was attractive in her fragile way, and Bob paid a lot of attention to her. Certainly Harris wanted Bob to get married, and the sooner the better. The settling influence of a good woman might be his salvation. Married, yes—but not to Ethel Potamkin.

By 1915 Harris was beginning to lose patience. He decided the time had come for a serious talk, so he went again to Bobby's room. As usual, Bobby launched into a lecture on painting, though Harris wasn't listening. The boy could be so pedantic. Harris shut the door behind him, in case things should come up that Rosa shouldn't hear, and held up a hand to stem the flow of words.

"Excuse me," he said when Bobby paused, "but your sister and I are getting a little nervous. We were wondering if you have any plans to marry? Maybe that schoolteacher you've been seeing, the pretty one? You know, Boris Jans' older girl, Rose?"

3

Her Mother

*It all depends on whether the girl says she can't live
without him. There are girls who say, "If he just comes
home once a week, I'll take that rather than not at
all, because I care about him."*

—Jacqueline Susann

*T*HE exact details of their closed-door confrontation
can only be surmised, but it is reported that Bob,
then twenty-seven, argued that an artist, if he married at all, should wait till at least thirty. Harris supposedly
retorted that if Bob didn't mend his ways he'd be dead
before thirty, probably of venereal disease. Harris was
painfully aware that Bobby's friend Booth Tarkington had
used him as a model for the ladies' man in a short story.
He was also aware of at least one very real scandal,
involving Bob's attempted seduction of a Main Line matron whose portrait he was painting. The matron's husband

had run Bob off the estate, and Harris wondered if the story had circulated widely enough to affect future commissions. True, Bobby had won second prize in the Toppan Competition; still, how many men would send their wives or daughters to a painter whose reputation was so questionable?

However the conversation proceeded, it is known that Harris ended it by issuing an ultimatum: Bobby had six months to find a girl—other than Ethel Potamkin—and marry her. If he was married by July 4, Harris would help the newlyweds buy a house. If not, then Bobby had better be prepared to declare his own independence and move out. Furthermore, if Bob had no one better in mind, he might do worse than to consider Rose Jans. She was the belle of Philadelphia's Russo-Jewish community and she came from a good family. Besides, as a teacher with an income of her own she could afford the luxury of marrying an artist.

Indeed, while Bob Susan had been romping through foreign capitals and local whorehouses, Rose Jans had taught school and marked time. She was truly a belle, yet at the same time she was a breath away from being an old maid. Exquisite as she was, almost every eligible man who saw her wanted her. The problem was that the one man she wanted hadn't asked her.

Like Bob, Rose Jans came from a background of affluence. She was descended from merchant princes of Kiev, who were an elite, as the Susans had been in Vilna. In Kiev a man named Kahalofsky, Jacqueline Susann's maternal great-grandfather, was a manufacturer of fine chocolates and an officer in his synagogue. His second child, his daughter Yuccha, was born in 1867 in a home that resembled a small palace. She was beautiful and she was also exceptionally bright. As soon as she could write she began keeping a diary. But what Yuccha truly loved and excelled in was science. She hoped to go to medical school like her older brother. There were few if any women doctors in Russia, but that didn't bother her or her parents. They all believed in education for women, and, more to the point, they all believed in Yuccha.

But when she was fourteen, Yuccha's sheltered world was shattered. Tsar Alexander was assassinated on March 1, 1881, and his successor, Alexander III, was aggressively anti-Semitic. In May the Kahalofsky house was burned to the ground, along with most of the rest of the ghetto. For some three months the family scrambled for survival. Then, in later summer, Kahalofsky received an amazing communication from the Quakers of the city of Philadelphia in the United States. The Quakers said they "stood aghast at the atrocities against Kiev's Jews," and that, to mark the bicentennial of Philadelphia's founding by William Penn, they would send a ship to bring 350 Jewish refugees to Philadelphia. Kahalofsky felt he had to decline. He was a leader; his responsibility was to stay. But it was decided that his children and one of his brothers should go.

On February 23, 1882, the steamship *Illinois* docked in Philadelphia. Yuccha and her fellow passengers were met by a delegation of Quakers, led through customs, and then put on a train bound for Market Street Station, where they would stay until they found homes. The cavernous old depot had been made into a makeshift hotel, and the refugees were provided with food and fresh clothing. Yuccha's brother presented his professional credentials to Dr. T. J. Ellinger, head of the volunteer medical team caring for the newcomers. Impressed with the young man's excellent English, Ellinger enlisted him as an interpreter. At the same time, he suggested that Kahalofsky change his name to something more American, like Kaye.

Ellinger couldn't pronounce Yuccha at all, so he called her Ida, the name she adopted and used thereafter.

Many of the refugees were bewildered or even terrified by their new surroundings, but Ida was already demonstrating the adaptability that would characterize her life. She kept herself busy comforting the other refugees. Sometimes she would sit quietly for hours at a time, holding the hand of a young woman whose baby had died during the ocean crossing. What time she had left for herself she spent with a certain Mr. Rubin, a handsome twenty-one-year-old she'd met on the ship. Mr. Rubin was a hot topic in the new diary or "sentiment book" that Ida was now laboriously keeping in English. He was from Warsaw, where Jews had recently suffered a pogrom even bloodier than the one in Kiev. Mr. Rubin's parents had been killed and he was both orphaned and penniless, but Ida didn't care. They were in love. As it turned out, Mr. Rubin was not only Ida's first love, but also her last. When he failed to find work in Philadelphia, he set out to seek his fortune in Oklahoma, taking only a backpack and ten dollars the Kayes had loaned him for needles and thread to sell along the way for living expenses. He promised to send for Ida, and, eventually, he did, decades later. They were married when she was in her seventies, after she had buried her first husband and divorced her second.

As the days passed, Ida remained more excited than daunted by the prospect of living in America, but there was one thing bothering her. The Quakers were wonderfully kind, and so were the other Christians who had welcomed them. But where were Philadelphia's Jews? They couldn't be unaware of the *Illinois*'s arrival or of her passengers; the story had been in all the newspapers.

The one Philadelphia Jew who did visit during the first week at the train station was a Mr. Shiffman, a reporter covering the story for the *Philadelphia Record*. He had taken a liking to the Kayes, who looked much more "westernized" than most of the others, and he had a feeling they would make it in America. A doctor could always get work, and Ida was certainly pretty enough to find a good husband. But the others . . . they looked so worn, so *Jewish*. Shiffman decided he would serve the Kayes best by telling them the truth, harsh as it was. He began instructing them on Philadelphia's caste system.

The Sephardic Jews had arrived first, coming from Portugal and Spain to settle in Philadelphia before the American Revolution. In Philadelphia if your wealth dated back to the colonies it didn't matter if you were Episcopalian, Quaker, or Jew. You were acceptable. When some fifteen hundred German Jews immigrated to the city in the 1850's, the Sephardim were not unkind to them, but neither were they especially warm. Nevertheless, the German Jews made money. They produced respected professionals and cultural leaders—and they were very protective of the social status they'd attained. These new Jews—these odd-looking, Talmudized, *foreign* Jews—were an acute embarrassment to Philadelphia's Jewish establishment. Shiffman, a German Jew himself, had heard several other German Jews remark that they wished the Quakers weren't such damned do-gooders.

Shiffman was blunt, but he was accurate. The Kayes and their traveling companions eventually settled, very much on their own, in an area called Little Russia south of Pine Street near the Delaware River. The Kayes themselves fared reasonably well. Ida enrolled in school. Her brother found work as a hospital orderly and studied to become an American doctor. The uncle sold off some gemstones he had brought from Kiev. But the Kayes were not typical. On July 14, 1882, more than half the families who had crossed on the *Illinois* boarded another ship to take them back to Russia, their tickets home paid for by established Philadelphia Jews.

The story of the well-meaning Quakers and the snobbish Jews became a great favorite of Ida's, and she would tell it often to her granddaughter. And Jacqueline Susann would never forget it. It was one reason for her lifelong ambiguity about her own Jewishness.

Ida Kaye eventually found herself a good husband, an extremely handsome, blond, mustachioed fellow Kiev emigré named Boris Jans. Boris was "beneath" Ida socially in much the same way Harris Potamkin was beneath Rosa Susan. Though a Kiev Jew, Boris was only a tailor. Still, like Rosa, Ida fared well in her marriage. Boris's trade might have been a comparatively lowly one, but he was an acknowledged artist at it.

The Jans family was never wealthy in the sense that the Potamkins were, but Boris kept his family financially comfortable and secure. And by all accounts he and Ida had a good marriage. They thought alike in most things, seldom fought, and pulled together for the family's good. They were respected in their community, widely admired for their bearing and style. In their stable household Ida would produce for Boris, and rear with a strong hand, two daughters: first Rose, on January 15, 1892; then, more than a decade later, Isabel, on March 26, 1903.

All the Jans women were strong, though the strength would manifest itself in different ways. In Ida it would show as independence and durability, in her daughter Rose as an imposing dignity, and in Rose's daughter Jacqueline as a relentless tenacity and drive. Each of them would be a leader. Each would be especially supportive of other women and would gather into her orbit a close and admiring circle of female satellites. And each would be, in her own way, a little out of step with her times.

Ida, for instance, could be surprisingly non-Victorian.

When her seventeen-year-old Irish servant girl got herself pregnant, Ida knew that young Annie Adair had fallen through innocence more than lust, so she set about marrying her off to a good man and equipping her to be a model wife. Ida taught Annie good posture, good grooming, good table manners, how to entertain graciously and behave with dignity—and, of course, how to keep a diary. She taught her own daughters all that she taught Annie Adair, and more besides. Among her principles: A woman should never be seen at less than her best, but she should see to her looks efficiently—only a certain number of minutes a day on hair, nails, wardrobe—and no lolling around in beauty parlors. Every woman should play a musical instrument or do something artistic. And, emphatically, every woman should have a profession.

From the time she was first allowed to date, Rose had been besieged by suitors. Apart from her beauty and elegance, there was a self-sufficiency about her that belied her years. It drew men to her, but at the same time it kept them at a certain distance. And she was elusive. Around the time she started teaching she was seeing a lot of a childhood friend, Isaac Witkin, who had gone off to Harvard but still made regular pilgrimages home to see her. But the match, favored by Rose's parents, failed to materialize. One by one her beaux, rejected or simply baffled, went on to new alliances, while Rose, now nearing twenty-three, waited, as though for some destined event.

Rose saw Bob Susan one night across a room at a party, and she said to a friend, "That man is special." She loved his walk, his "impressive bearing," and she sensed some "mystery" in him. She would tell him later that she felt some "hidden part" in each of them matched a corresponding part in the other. "Only I can see that in you," she would say, "and only you can see that in me."

Bob was intrigued by Rose, too, though probably less

romantically besotted than she. He took her out. He went to her family's home and gathered with them around the piano to sing while Rose or Ida played. But he made no commitment and offered no proposal. There were other women, after all—and Rose was certainly aware of at least some of them. She knew, for instance, of his dalliance with Ethel Potamkin, whom she would avoid for the rest of her life. But even if she sensed then that he would probably not be faithful, and even knowing that he might never earn a living either, still she waited. He was the only man she wanted.

She was still waiting on the day that Harris Potamkin decided it was time for that showdown with his brother-in-law. But Harris's arguments must have been persuasive, because Bob proposed to Rose within weeks of that confrontation. And, despite a fainting spell on the fateful morning, Bob Susan married Rose Jans on July 4, 1915. It is said that Harris marched Bob to the altar with a threat that would turn out to be strangely prophetic: "Be a good husband to her," he commanded. And then, perhaps remembering the womanizer in Booth Tarkington's story, he added, "And behave, or someday someone will put you in a really *filthy* book."

4

Her Birth

*My mother? She's lovely, she's a lady. People wonder
how she ever had a husband like my father or a
daughter like me.... My father? He was divine.
He looked exactly like Rudolph Valentino. The great
thing about him was that he could make everybody
like him. Most artists, like my father, are selfish—
charming but completely selfish. Most men are,
aren't they?*

——Jacqueline Susann

*T*RUE to her heritage, Jacqueline Susann was born to
catastrophe. It was a wretched summer to begin
with. Bob and Rose had moved from a small apartment in South Philadelphia to a spacious, three-story home
on the corner of Sixty-first Street and Latona, in a pleasant
West Philadelphia neighborhood. But even the high ceil-
ings and breezy ventilation of their new house were no

defense against the record-breaking heat wave that had settled itself on the city.

Trapped in this inferno, Rose was all the more miserable because she was struggling through a difficult pregnancy with little help from her husband. Bob had not wanted to be a father, but he had wanted to be a soldier even less. With the draft hanging over his head he had agreed to start a family, to put one child's worth of distance between himself and the grasp of the Selective Service System. However, having done his part by impregnating his wife, Bob was content to leave the rest of the project to her. The hardships of Rose's pregnancy gave him the vapors.

With no support from Bob, Rose relied heavily on her mother, and Ida, as always, was a rock. When Rose got cold sweats, Ida made her a strong tea of boneset, red pepper, and morphine. When she suffered from agonizing leg cramps, Ida worked on one leg while Rose's sister, Isabel, worked on the other. There were times toward the end of the pregnancy when Rose, sweating and aching, would scream that she wanted to tear the baby out of her womb. Ida, or sometimes Isabel, would stroke her forehead, soothe her, tell her it would all be over soon.

Jacqueline was born on August 20, 1918, as the Americans were making a bloody incursion into France. In Philadelphia it was a fine evening, a little cooler at last. Bob managed to make it to Lankenau Hospital for his daughter's birth, though he quickly regretted it. The baby was healthy enough, weighing almost seven pounds, but she was long and scrawny, and her face and body were threaded with coarse black *hairs*! He was appalled, and as he stared at the ugly child he grew dizzy and fell into a faint.

Rosa Potamkin took him home with her and cared for him, ministering to the new father in ways surprisingly like those Ida had used for the expectant mother. She

removed his clothes and sponged him down with water and
spirits of camphor. She massaged his head with a vinegar
solution and applied poultices of mustard to his hands and
feet. Nevertheless, ten days later, when Rose and Jacqueline
were discharged from Lankenau, he was still too weak and
distraught to go home to them.

Bob discussed his ugly daughter with his sister. He told
Rosa he didn't think the child could carry a name like
Jacqueline. It would be ludicrous, such an ugly kid with
such a glamorous name. Rosa soothed him. Her own
daughter Flossie had been an ugly baby and a sickly one to
boot, and she had turned out to be adorable. Maybe it
would be the same with Jacqueline. At least little Jackie
was thriving, and those awful hairs were falling out, more
every day. And Jackie was the brightest, liveliest baby in
the whole nursery. Rosa knew, because she had visited the
hospital daily, bearing presents for her sister-in-law and her
new niece. She'd given Jackie a string of baby pearls from
Caldwell's, Philadelphia's premier jeweler. They were
lovely, and outrageously over-priced. "Forty percent was
for the box," Rosa announced proudly, displaying the
pearls for Rose's inspection.

With every visit Rosa became more certain that Jacqueline
was, in fact, going to look like Bob, and she must have
convinced her brother. He did eventually go home, and in
no time at all he was utterly enchanted with his new
daughter.

The vast sprawl of neighborhoods that was Philadelphia
in 1918 was home to nearly two million people and
temporary home to another 300,000, who were in town for
war-related jobs. Many of the temporaries worked in the
huge Philadelphia Navy Yard, and it was there, early in the
fall, that one of the laborers began complaining of chills
and fever. He felt hot and cold at the same time. He ached

in every joint and muscle, and he felt as though his skin were trying to crawl off his body. On September 12 he became the city's first reported case of Spanish influenza.

One week later the *Philadelphia Inquirer* carried a story headlined SPANISH INFLUENZA SENDS 600 SAILORS TO HOSPITAL HERE. The story, pushed aside by the war news, was not prominently displayed. Two days later the Philadelphia Board of Health issued orders to hospitals that flu patients were to be strictly isolated. Hospital personnel were to wear gauze masks, and caps and gowns. All bed linens and utensils that came into contact with flu patients were to be boiled.

But if health officials were alarmed, the general public was not. Then, on September 28, more than a million patriotic citizens massed in Philadelphia to watch the fourth Liberty Loan Parade in support of the war effort. And the epidemic exploded.

The Spanish flu was, in fact, pandemic. It killed millions worldwide. Exactly how many millions is uncertain, since victims died faster than their corpses could be accurately counted. But it was, by any count, the deadliest plague the world had seen since the Black Death decimated Europe in the Middle Ages.

Philadelphia was one of the hardest-hit cities in the world, and certainly the worst hit in the United States. People died faster than they could be buried. At some city morgues bodies were piled three and four deep, covered with dirty, bloodstained sheets. They were not embalmed and there was no ice, so the corpses themselves became a health hazard. Hundreds of caskets piled up in funeral homes and cemeteries. Theological students and convicts were among the groups who volunteered in the emergency, and they worked side by side as gravediggers. Boris Jans was among the tailors who volunteered their labor sewing shrouds.

The corner of Sixty-first Street and Latona, in front of the Susan home, was a collection place for corpses, as was the drugstore run by Henry, Bob's pharmacist brother. Some of Henry's customers were even carried into his store in their final hours by relatives who hoped their beloved "Doc" might have a miracle remedy. Most of Rose's colleagues gallantly returned to teaching until they themselves were infected or their schools were again closed. But Rose could not teach or even join the volunteers. She had her baby to think about. She was terrified for her baby, and for herself.

In the fall of 1918, with the epidemic at its height, Ida and Boris offered to send them away, and she could hardly refuse. Rose took two-month-old Jackie to the New Jersey coast and rented an apartment in Atlantic City. She wheeled the baby up and down the Boardwalk, making sure Jacqueline got maximum benefit from the salubrious sea air, whose protective powers Ida firmly believed in. Rose shared the belief, and she pushed her baby carriage five or six hours every day, even when the winter brought subfreezing temperatures. Boris made her a cape with a fur hood and a fur blanket and carriage liner for Jackie, while Isabel knitted booties and mittens for the baby and scarves for Rose. Rose wrote her thanks, adding that she hoped Boris's soft fur would "compensate his granddaughter for her mother's chapped and scratchy hands."

Rose's nipples, too, became roughened from the powerful soaps and disinfectants she now used, and nursing became an ordeal. Worse than the physical discomfort was the heartache she felt when she glimpsed herself in the mirror, a strange figure in her flu mask. "Our poor little Jacqueline," she wrote to Ida from the Margate Avenue boardinghouse. "I must look so grotesque to her. I can't even kiss her, and she never sees me smile. And my hands are so scratchy, not gentle like a mother's hands are supposed to be. She winces when I dress her." Ida advised that Rose try to communicate with her eyes, which were known for their expressiveness.

Before the epidemic Rose and Ida had had some disagreements about baby care, but they had agreed about the disinfectants and sterilization. Both had worn gauze masks when they handled the baby, and both had scrubbed their hands in alcohol before feeding or changing diapers. The baby's environment was literally sterile, peopled by masked creatures who held her at arm's length and dared not cuddle her.

Rose stayed on in the boardinghouse through the winter, along with other refugees from Philadelphia. On some weekends Bob visited, and he climbed the fire escape to peer through windows at his infant daughter, whom he was forbidden to touch. Bob was becoming increasingly interested in his "little monkey," now that she was responding more actively to the world around her. He swore she came to recognize him out there on that fire escape, his teeth chattering in the winter winds.

By February, 1919, the flu had pretty well vanished from Philadelphia, though it would rage on in parts of the world for many more months and would kill some twenty-two million people by 1920—in contrast to World War I, which claimed eight and a half million lives. Bob had been working on the Latona house over the winter, with help from various relatives, to ready it for his family's return. He had even completed his portrait of Rose in the costume of a Spanish dancer—what she called her "monkey suit" —and hung it over the fireplace.

The house was finally shaping up for the family's reunion, though it would never really satisfy Bob's artistic sensibility. Despite the view of the park, the house was dark and filled with strange nooks and crannies that broke up the space and ruined the symmetry. Bob dreamed of

major renovations that would let in light and open up
space, and a few years later he even drew up plans, with
help from his new brother-in-law, Sidney Jelinek, who was
an architect. Sidney was also a world-class athlete and the
only Jew on the 1924 U. S. Olympic rowing team, feats
that impressed Bob even more than the architectural exper-
tise. The work was never done, but the plans remained in
Bob's safe deposit box until his death.

The one thing the house did have, however, was bedrooms—
enough of them so that the new Susan could not only have
her own bedroom but her own parlor as well, reached via a
private staircase in the rear of the house. This became
"Jackie's Secret Staircase," while the bedroom overlooking
the park became "Jackie's parlor."

When Rose returned from Atlantic City, she was so
proud of her trim figure that she brought her husband a
most unusual and uncharacteristic gift. It was a "dance
costume" she had fallen in love with in the window of an
Atlantic City shop, a frivolous froth of green satin with a
partially open midriff and a skirt of transparent chiffon,
bedecked with floral appliqués, through which green satin
panties were partially visible. She had bought the costume,
and then she had done an even more remarkable thing: She
had slipped into Scott's Photographic Studio and had an
"art" photo taken, as a present for Bob's thirty-second
birthday. Jackie never saw the photo, and it is likely that
she never guessed the fires of passion hidden behind her
mother's cool and regal exterior.

Bob welcomed his wife and daughter home from Atlantic
City with genuine enthusiasm. He had especially missed
his daughter, who came to interest him more and more as
she, in turn, grew more interested in the world around her.
By her first birthday she was still no beauty, but she was so
precocious, so bright. She was already speaking, babbling

to her dolls and to the stray kittens that were already becoming a part of the family.

For her second birthday, Boris made Jackie a dress and pantaloon suit trimmed with a white collar and cuffs, and enhanced with embroidery and a matching floppy hat. Rose had a formal picture taken as a thank-you gift to her parents, and in it Jackie peers forth from beneath long, uneven bangs that emphasize her wide-set eyes. Later that year Boris made yet another outfit, a gorgeous yellow *peau de soie* dress with a high beruffled neck and twenty-four tiny covered buttons, which she would wear as a flower girl in her nineteen-year-old cousin Belle Potamkin's wedding. This event, described by one of the bridesmaids as "a lavish and nightclubby affair," was planned by Bob and featured attendants in short, somewhat décolleté evening gowns with yards and yards of tulle. It was held on Christmas day, and Jackie would later recall it as "my theatrical debut."

Her performance was one of the wedding's more memorable features. Wearing a chaplet of yellow flowers on her head and her Aunt Rosa's pearls around her neck, she walked down the aisle of the hushed ballroom ahead of the procession, concentrating intently on distributing the flower petals uniformly while not tripping on her long skirt. She had been warned not to throw all the petals out at once, so she sprinkled them sparingly down the aisle. But when she arrived at the altar she discovered she had been *too* sparing, and the basket was still half full. She stood for a moment, pondering, then came up with the solution. While the orchestra paused and Belle waited on Harris's arm, the two-year-old marched back up the aisle distributing the remaining petals, then triumphantly held the empty basket aloft so the crowd could see how well she had done. There was thunderous applause, which had to be quieted so the wedding could continue.

* * *

If Rose watched her daughter's development with pride,
she no doubt viewed the rest of her domestic situation with
some alarm. Not only was her husband away much of the
time, coming home late or sometimes not at all, but he
was also perpetually short of cash. He was getting plenty
of commissions, but he was also spending generously on
himself—playing the horses, betting on the fights, buying
every new game and phonograph record that appeared.
And she also suspected that he was splitting his commissions with some of the more established artists who sent
work his way, and perhaps with some of the down-at-heel
socialites who directed their friends to him.

In any case, Bob was hard pressed to make the mort-
gage payments on the house, and the rest of the family's
expenses were beyond him. Rose decided to reclaim her
teaching job. Besides, she admitted that she was getting
bored with housework, and that she missed the challenge
of teaching. So in the fall of 1920 she became a part of a
very tiny minority of American professional women who
were also mothers of preschool children. She hired a
teen-age girl named Flossie to stay with Jackie, and she
returned to the job she would keep throughout the years of
her daughter's childhood and adolescence.

5

Her Childhood

*I could have had all the women whose portraits I
painted, plus all their mothers and all their daughters.*

——Robert Susan

ONE of her earliest memories was of the fighting.
Her father usually came home too late for dinner,
but when he was home he and Rose often argued.
They argued about the Prohibition amendment, and about
Bob's home-brewed alcoholic beverages, which Rose felt
would teach the baby a disrespect for the law. They argued
over movies, which Bob loved and Rose had come to scorn
as trivial or outright immoral. They argued over his devotion
to sports, especially boxing, which Rose considered bar-
baric. They even argued over food, when Bob adopted a
faddish raw-vegetable diet recommended by M. O. Bircher-
Benner in a book called *The Fundaments of Our Nutrition.*

How could he have a healthy diet while drinking "bathtub whiskey"? she wanted to know.

On New Year's Day in 1922, when Jackie was three and a half, her parents argued over the Mummers' parade. An old and curious Philadelphia custom that had originated in the ethnic neighborhoods, the parade featured groups of men, most of them wearing gaudy and often bizarre costumes. It was too garish and vulgar, Rose said, inappropriate fare for a small child. Besides it was too cold for Jacqueline to spend the whole day out of doors. Bob replied that the kid would love it. He put her snowsuit on her and started out the door, but Rose grabbed her sleeve and held on, still arguing. They tugged on her for a while, one on each arm, until Bob managed to jerk her free. He hoisted her onto his shoulders and marched out the door, slamming it on Rose's objections.

She loved the parade, as Bob has predicted, but when she finally went to sleep that night she had a nightmare that would repeat itself, with diminishing frequency, until the year her father died. The dream had none of the startling monsters of the Mummers' Parade, however. Instead, it replayed the scene of earlier that day, with her mother tugging on one arm and her father on the other until she stretched between them and began to tear in half. That's when she woke, crying, her shoulders and arms aching and so heavy she could hardly lift them.

The fighting was confusing, because she knew her mother and daddy really loved each other. Mother was always touching him, and they even had pet names for each other. He called her Suzy, and she called him Mookie. Jackie couldn't understand the anger, and she couldn't understand why Daddy stayed away so much of the time if he loved her. But when she asked, her mother would be evasive. Or she would lie, telling Jackie her daddy had gone to a ball game when she had heard him say he was going to his studio to work with Doris. And who *was* Doris? She knew her father painted pictures of Doris, but why did her mother sound so hateful when she said the woman's name?

Confused by the lies and arguments, she retired more and more to her own fantasies, building imaginary kingdoms with her dolls in which she ruled in happy harmony. Her mother dismissed her stories of this make-believe world, but Bob was charmed by them, as he was by most of her inventions. He was an artist, after all, and artists lived by creating things. And by *seeing* things, such as the way some people looked like certain animals. He often played a game with her, identifying passersby with the animals they resembled.

They took walks together, playing the game, and sometimes he took her to his studio, which was near the middle of town. She loved to go there, to look around in the big room filled with Bob's paintings. She loved to touch the soft brushes and to climb up on the stand where the models posed and to rummage in the small dressing room where they could change clothes. She was fascinated with the costumes that were kept there, and she loved to feel the strange fabrics and sometimes even to try them on, pretending she was a grownup lady on the way to a fancy party. There was a cabinet of heavy, carved oak, but it was always locked because that was where he kept the liquor. Big old armchairs stood about on a rug with a design of faded flowers, and in the middle of it all was a large couch covered in crushed velvet the color of raspberries, a gift from Aunt Rosa Potamkin. It was all like a make-believe world, with a happy, casual clutter never found in their home.

She had not visited the studio without her father, though, so when she told Flossie she wanted to go there the girl was unsure about it. Though only a teen-ager herself,

Flossie had a feeling Bob Susan lived a strange, separate life in his studio, and she wasn't at all sure he'd welcome unexpected visitors. But Jackie was bored and restless, and she insisted her father would want to give her the watercolors he'd bought for her but forgotten to bring home. They could go downtown and get them, she pleaded, and probably Bob would invite them to stay awhile. She'd show Flossie the bathroom down the hall, which you had to have a key to open and which had a roll of paper towels you could unroll right down to the floor. Finally, reluctantly, Flossie agreed to take her.

When they got to the studio Jackie ran up to the door first and pushed on it. It was unlocked. As it swung open she saw her father, lying on the couch in a funny position. She yelled "Daddy!" before she even realized that he didn't have any clothes on.

The woman who was lying underneath him looked at her and screamed, "My God, Robert, it's your daughter!"

Jackie slammed the door and ran back to Flossie. "I want to go home," she said. And that's all she would say all the way back to the house. She wouldn't talk about "the incident," as she later came to call it, but from then on when she went to visit her father's studio she was careful to make noise on the stairs and to yell out "Daddy, I'm here" before she entered.

The picture of her father and that woman remained with Jackie forever, and she could never get over how grotesque he had looked "all humped over" like that. "Humping" was the word she would use for sexual intercourse throughout the rest of her life. It is doubtful that "the incident" changed Bob's habits very much, though perhaps it at least taught him a lesson about locking doors before he led his latest conquest to that red velvet couch.

* * *

In truth, it almost seemed that the twenties had been made to order for Bob Susan. He thrived on the morally anarchic spirit of that flaming era, the contests, the flappers, the stock market speculation, the speakeasies and jazz joints, the big cars, even the rackets that were to be Prohibition's bloody legacy. He followed all the fads—the flagpole sitting and marathon dancing and crossword puzzles that everyone spent hours trying to work—and the sports figures whose exploits fascinated him. But most of all he loved the sexual freedom.

His circle was the most "bohemian" in the city, yet even among such unconventional people there was disapproval of his bragging, his constant and very public infidelities, and the kick he seemed to get out of betraying women who loved him. One friend, a fellow painter, is still convinced that the constant womanizing took its toll on Bob's personal life, and that it also affected his professional standing. "There were a lot of men who wouldn't let him get anywhere near their wives or daughters," he remembers. "I got some commissions that would have gone to him except for his sexual notoriety."

He recalls that Bob was a gifted portraitist who became more commercial in his attitude toward his art as the years went by. "He'd use a beautiful young model who was maybe size eight to sit for the torso of a portly middle-aged matron," he says, recounting instances of Bob's catering to the customer's vanity. He tells of a woman who had her portrait altered repeatedly to accommodate ever-larger strands of pearls, and another who insisted that Bob redo her hair color when she dyed it. "He was annoyed, but he said, 'What the hell, it's a big commission.'"

After "the incident," four-year-old Jackie developed an almost obsessive curiosity about the mechanics of sex. She experimented with her dolls and stuffed animals, modeling penises from clay and attaching them to her Hans Brinker doll and her teddy bear. She had seen her father's penis often when they'd showered together, to Rose's consternation, and she was aware of how his "sissy" differed from her own. But what did it mean?

She then turned to her girl dolls, using scissors to make slits between their legs from which the sawdust filling oozed out. Rose, ever the fussy housekeeper, noticed the trails of sawdust and investigated. "Why are you doing this?" she asked Jackie, holding one of the dolls before her accusingly.

"I wanted to see if her sissy would fall out," she explained. That was not exactly true, but then she didn't really know why she *was* doing it, or what she was trying to learn. And she knew instinctively that what she had seen in her father's studio was not something she would discuss with her mother. Or with her father, either.

In desperation Rose wrote to her uncle Dr. Kaye, who was now living in Waukegan, Illinois, and who was interested in the field of child development. In her letter she described the strange behavior of "one of my students" with her dolls, and asked her uncle's advice. Dr. Kaye replied that he considered doll play highly significant in revealing traumatic events. If a child is hurt in an accident, he said, she will often use her dolls to re-create the accident in an effort to control the event and calm her fears. He wondered if Rose's student might not have had some sexual trauma—little boys pulling her pants off in the park or some such. He advised that the child be taken for a physical examination.

Rose took his advice and made an appointment with her own doctor, but the examination was not very helpful. Jackie's hymen was intact, and there was no evidence of any sort of trauma. In fact, the only result of the medical examination seemed to be an increase in Jackie's anxiety. The doll play continued, as if she was determined to understand something that puzzled and disturbed her. Flossie warned her that she was upsetting her mother, but it did no good. Finally, in desperation, Flossie began to patrol the doll collection with a needle and thread, sewing up the latest slits before Rose discovered them. She also collected all the household's hand mirrors, which Jackie was using in an attempt to examine her own pubic area, and returned them to their proper bureaus. Flossie worried that the child might injure herself in these self-examinations and tried to find a way to discuss it with Rose, but the opportunity never seemed to arise. And in a few weeks the examinations ceased. Either Jackie had figured out the mechanics to her satisfaction, or she had given up trying to understand. Flossie was never sure which.

The dreams, however, continued, nightmares of wild beasts that tried to dismember her, or people who suddenly turned into animals and came after her. She told her grandma she was afraid of the night-time creatures that were trying to tear her apart, but Ida said she should not worry. In Russia all the little children were chased in their sleep by wolves and bears, she said, but no harm ever came to them, because the animals in children's dreams were *always* chained to the walls.

Rose, too, was concerned, and she tried to find only pleasant stories to read at bedtime. But one of her favorite poems was also a favorite of Jackie's, and since it was by Edna St. Vincent Millay—a poet Rose considered to be among the world's great writers—she refused to believe it could be harmful. It was called "The Ballad of the Harp-Weaver," and it told of a poor widow who is forced to sell all her possessions except ". . . a chair we couldn't break/And the harp with a woman's head/Nobody would take/For song or pity's sake." On Christmas Eve the mother sits on the single chair all night, weaving "the clothes of a king's son" on the harp, presumably from her own flesh. On Christmas morning the woman is found dead among these wonderful presents. Ida was horrified and warned that such gruesome stuff was probably fueling the nightmares, but Rose would not be moved. She often read ''Vincent's'' poetry to her students, and she was firmly convinced great poetry could not possibly be harmful. After all, she pointed out, Millay had just won a Pulitzer Prize for the book that featured this very poem.

Harmful or not, the poetry did inspire Jackie to make up little verses of her own, all of which her mother pretended to admire. Her father admired the poems too, but without the enthusiasm he had always shown for her drawings. Only her beloved ''Aunt Esther'' seemed to take the verses seriously enough to discuss them and say which ones she really liked, and why. But then Esther Weinrott always had a way of listening and talking that was different from the others. She and her husband, Judge Leo Weinrott, were friends of her parents, and she knew the judge was a very important man because he always insisted that everyone call him Judge—even his own family. But it was Aunt Esther who read books to her and encouraged her poetry and stories.

Jackie loved to hear Aunt Esther read, especially books with sad endings. They both loved George MacDonald's *The Princess and the Goblin* and Charles Kingsley's *The Water Babies*. Esther gave the characters different voices and accents, so listening to her was almost like seeing a play. And Esther was interested in plays herself, often describing one she might one day write. To Jackie, being a ''play writer'' seemed a wonderful thing, and she once told her mother quite seriously that she had been ''bitten by Aunt Esther's theatrical bug.''

Jackie learned to roller-skate with her friend from next door, Selma Rosinsky. Many of the neighborhood children wouldn't play with her, but Selma followed her through many childhood adventures, sledding in Cobbs Creek Park and venturing into forbidden places and acting out "plays" with the toys and dolls in her upstairs rooms. Selma recalls that others in the neighborhood considered Jackie a snob, always boasting about her father and his society friends, whose names were often in the newspaper in what she thought were called the "sock-it-tee" pages. But to Selma she seemed daring and adventurous, very grown up for her years.

She had little chance to play with boys in her neighborhood, and even less opportunity to meet Irish children, since the Irish were often hostile toward the Jews. But she did get to know one Irish boy, a strange child a few years older than Jackie who walked with a limp and therefore was left out of the neighborhood games. His name was Jimmy, and she met him in the park on the special "wishing hill" where she liked to sit among the wildflowers— especially the yellow daisylike blossoms Flossie called "black-eyed Sus-*anns*," pronouncing it like their name. Jimmy was there often, and he told her stories about the baby Jesus, who grew up to be mankind's savior and who was nailed to a cross by the Jews. He told her that Jews would all go to hell unless they became Catholics, but he said he liked her and hoped she would convert and go to heaven.

She liked Jimmy, too, and even liked hearing about Jesus and heaven and hell, which were not the sort of subjects her family was given to discussing. In fact, except for a few lessons in Sunday school with her mother's friend Mildred Berkowitz, she rarely heard about religion at all. Aunt Esther seemed to have some vague notion of "something out there," and Flossie went around humming hymns as she worked, but Jimmy was the first person in Jackie's life who seemed really interested in God. He even said he wanted to be a priest when he grew up. But then one day he told her he was moving away and wouldn't see her anymore. He gave her a going-away present, but he warned her that she probably oughtn't to tell her parents about it. It was a silver chain with crystal beads spaced out along it and with a silver medal at the bottom on which the Virgin Mary held her baby, Jesus. It was called a rosary, he told her. She thought it was beautiful and she kept it—hidden, as he had advised—for many years, a secret treasure she would remember often in her later life.

That fall she started school, and thoughts of Jesus gave way to new problems, and new adventures. Even getting to the Harrity School, which was nearly a mile from her house, was both a problem and an adventure. She flatly refused to let Rose or Flossie take her, and insisted that she and Selma could go alone, like big girls. A compromise was finally arranged in which Selma's older sister Sylvia accompanied them and took their hands crossing streets, though even that indignity was protested by Jackie.

School was a mixed blessing. The teacher complained to Rose that Jackie was ''lax,'' that she would get caught up in daydreams and not pay attention. She was aggressive on the playground, trying to outdo the boys, who weren't pleased and often fought with her. She had some talent for drawing, and she showed imagination in making up stories— too much imagination, some thought. She complained to Rose that the children in her class didn't like her, and that she was lonely.

Rose tried to help by importing playmates from among her own pupils and the children of friends. But that was rarely satisfactory. One of her friends from Normal School moved into their neighborhood, though, and brought a child with her who would turn out to be one of Jackie's closest chums, even though Jackie was two and a half years older and considerably bolder. The new girl's name was Thelma Schonholz, and she was a shy child with pale skin and dirty blond, straight hair. Dissimilar though they were, the two took to each other at once.

Early on Jackie told her, "I'm going to be famous," and Thelma never doubted it. "I was always trying to catch up to Jackie and I never did," she remembers. "She was always better than I was at everything, and that would get to me. No matter how fast I could run, she could run faster. She would hide in the alcove in the living room and jump out, and laugh because I would scream. But I loved her. She was a complete daredevil. My childhood would have been pallid without her."

They slept over at Jackie's house on weekends, often using Rose and Bob's antique double bed and trying on all of Rose's jewelry, which Jackie swore her mother had promised to give her when she grew up. They stayed out of the living room most of the time, as Thelma remembers: "It was like a museum, because of the antique furniture, the baby grand, all those paintings." They played imaginary games with the dolls, and Jackie made up plays for them to perform. And they drew, constantly, with crayons and encouragement supplied by Bob. "When I was six years old, Bob used to take my hand and bow from the waist and say, 'Good morning, Miss Schonholz.' I would turn beet red and want to die."

Thelma recalls that when they visited Bob's studio Jackie would do her tramping act. "She whistled and sang and made lots of noise to announce our arrival, and she would leer at me dramatically and say, 'Who knows what's going on?'" They ventured into places they had been told to stay away from, Jackie leading and Thelma protesting. "She would do anything," Thelma recalls. "If you weren't allowed to do it, that made it attractive." Jackie's flair for the dramatic nearly cost Thelma her life at one point. It happened the summer Jackie was seven, when their mothers had rented cottages on the grounds of a boys' camp called Rockydale. The children were allowed to play in the nearby creek so long as they wore their inflated water wings, but splashing around like babies in a bathtub was far too tame for Jackie. "She went around the bend where you couldn't see her," Thelma remembers. "She let her water wings go and screamed, 'I'm drowning,' and she wanted me to come in and save her. I tried to save her but I couldn't swim, and I lost my own water wings. Then I screamed for my mother." Jackie made it to the bank by herself, but Thelma had to be pulled out, thoroughly frightened.

One day they were invited to watch a play the camp boys were putting on. Jackie was impressed. "That's when she decided to write her own play," Thelma says. "A little three-year-old girl was the wife. Jackie was the husband as she was the tallest and I, believe it or not, was 'the other woman.' I said, 'I'm not going to do this; you can't make me,' but she persuaded me. . . . Jackie did all the talking for all the parts. I can still remember the horrors of going on the stage . . . but my embarrassment was nothing compared to what Rose Susan felt. She almost died of mortification—but yet she let Jackie do it."

At seven Jackie made another discovery: babies. The family next door to Thelma had a baby girl, and Jackie fell in love at first sight. She would rush over to Thelma's after school and say, "Let's go see if Lela is awake." And, since Lela's mother was part of Rose's Mah-Jongg circle and one of her admirers, she was even persuaded to let Jackie "take care" of the baby—under her own watchful eye. Entranced, Jackie told Thelma she intended to have a daughter herself when she grew up. She even had the name picked out: Gillian. Or maybe she'd just call her baby Jill, so they'd be Jackie and Jill.

Her fascination with babies would persist through her

childhood and teen years, and indeed even through her adult life. Little Lela was followed by little Allen Rosinsky two years later, and this time Jackie had a real "in" with the family. Not only was Selma one of her best friends, but Selma's Aunt Mary had been the woman picked by Rose to marry Bob's handsome brother Henry, the pharmacist. With all these family connections, Selma's mother could hardly refuse to let Jackie babysit with little Allan. Besides, she was around much of the time anyway, playing with Selma. Mrs. Rosinsky thought Jackie was an intense little girl, and sometimes she told stories that weren't strictly true, but she seemed bright enough and even pretty, though she didn't smile very much since she'd broken her tooth.

That had happened when Jackie was eight, and once again it had resulted from her daredevil nature. Bob had bought her a two-wheeler and she had insisted she could ride it, though Rose had protested that she was too young. Bob, as usual, had taken Jackie's side, and off she had gone—only to go sprawling, and to get up with a noticeable chunk missing from one of her front teeth. Rose had been angry, and she had ruled that the damage couldn't be repaired until Jackie was older and had stopped growing. Jackie was embarrassed by the jagged look she had when she opened her mouth, so she rarely smiled now, even when Bob tried his best to catch her off guard with something funny.

The stories that weren't true weren't really lies, though. She was just exercising her imagination, the way her father had encouraged her to do. She'd played a game with him, describing what she'd seen on the way home from school, and of course she had embellished things a bit and sometimes made things up altogether. That made it more fun. And of course she continued to read, especially the fantastic novels of Edgar Rice Burroughs and H. G. Wells.

"When I was nine I thought of myself as the female Tarzán," she remembered years later. "I broke three shoe racks swinging from them."

Making things up seemed natural to her, and so did writing them down, which she did almost every day in her diary. She was still writing her little poems, too, and one of them had even been published in a children's magazine. Her writing never satisfied Rose, who was a stickler for proper grammar, but it must have impressed at least one of her teachers. As Jackie recalled in later years, "When I was nine or ten a schoolteacher predicted, 'Jacqueline should be a writer. She breaks all the rules, but it works.'"

Bob had taken her to visit Shamokin, the dreadful little town where he had spent part of his childhood and where he still had some cousins. She had enjoyed the picnics they had there, but she really preferred the movies Bob sneaked her into, over Rose's objections. She'd seen *The Jazz Singer*, the first movie in which the people actually talked, and she'd even seen Greta Garbo in *Flesh and the Devil*, which certainly was not proper fare for children, as her mother would have insisted if she'd known. Garbo had been so beautiful that Jackie could hardly stand it. She got a picture of Garbo to tack up on her bedroom wall, along with other actresses and actors she loved, and even some athletes, like the handsome swimmer Johnny Weissmuller. She had a crush on him, too. In fact, it was hard to decide who were more beautiful—theater people or athletes, women or men?

Nearing her teens, she was beginning to develop breasts, and her interest in the stage and movies was growing stronger than her interest in books. In the fifth grade she'd gotten the highest score of anyone in the whole school on an IQ test, to the amazement of her teachers. But movies and sports and even politics were beginning to seem much more interesting than her school studies. She read the papers, and when a long interview with her father appeared she read that too, though she didn't quite see what there was about it that seemed to upset her mother so. She supposed it was because there was so much in the story about Bob's favorite model, Doris Le Savoy, whose hands he described to the reporter as "the most beautiful hands in Philadelphia." Rose always got upset about any mention of Doris, and Jackie had come to understand that Doris was "the other woman" even before the newspaper story practically said so. Whenever she wanted to get even with her mother for something, she knew that all she had to do was ask innocently if Daddy was coming home tonight or staying in his studio with Doris.

When she was eleven she made a new friend, Evelyn Arnold, a slender, pretty girl who was in Rose's art class at the Lea School, and who remembers that Rose kept talking about her daughter and suggesting that Jackie would be a good person for Evelyn to meet. By then Rose had added a second *n* to the family name for the benefit of the students, so they would pronounce it correctly with the second syllable accented. She impressed Evelyn as "a perfect lady who even came to breakfast looking like she was going to a party." The two girls stayed over at Jackie's often, since Evelyn's family lived in rather cramped quarters, and together they frequently journeyed to Aunt Rosa Potamkin's apartment at Garden Court for snacks after school or visited Jackie's Aunt Isabel and Uncle Sidney Jelinek.

At about this time Aunt Isabel gave birth to a son, Robert, apparently named after Bob Susan. In later years, when Jackie had left home, the boy, called "Little Bob," would become like a son to her father and something of an after-the-fact rival for his love.

That same year Jackie met Rose's chief rival, Doris Le Savoy, and maybe now she understood a little why Bob seemed so interested in the woman. Beautiful women, beautifully dressed and made up, were important to him. She often found herself watching them and wishing that she, too, could look like that. She knew her father's affairs were painful to her mother, especially the very public one with Doris, but she still found the women intriguing. (The newspaper story would remain in her mind, however, and years later she would have the heroine of *Valley of the Dolls* discover her husband's affair through a gossip column item.)

The death of her grandfather Boris Jans had a deep effect on Jackie. Boris had always doted on her and made her lovely clothes, and she'd been sure he was the best-looking grandfather anyone ever had. Once when he had picked her up after a matinee at the Forrest Theater, a woman had confused him with the star and asked for his autograph. He'd died so suddenly, too, and her Grandmother Ida's grief and shock were so great they transmitted themselves like electricity as she clutched Jackie's hand.

Boris had been relatively young and still quite handsome, so they'd decided to have the coffin open for the funeral. But that proved to be a mistake; the embalmer had not been able to conceal the look of agony and surprise on Boris's face, and the effect was grotesque. When Ida went forward to view her husband for the last time, she trembled so that she seemed near collapse, and her grip on Jackie's hand was hard enough to hurt.

But then, suddenly, there was a change in Ida that surprised Jackie. Her grandmother seemed to steady herself by an effort of will, and she let go of Jackie's hand, drawing herself up tall. Staring into her husband's contorted face, she raised her hand slowly to the velvet lapel of her black mourning dress. She fingered the material for a moment, as if remembering all the wonderful clothes he had made for her, and then with a violent jerk she ripped the dress open to the waist, the sound loud in the quiet room.

As Jackie watched, wide-eyed, Rose followed her mother's lead, tearing open the front of her own dress. And the others followed suit, Aunt Isabel ripping at her clothes and Uncle Sidney and her father tearing the lapels of their coats. Jackie, too, tore her dress. She ripped it open across her budding breasts, then clutched at it to keep it from gaping as she stood there beside the coffin, among the now-silent mourners.

Later, when her grandfather was in the ground and the period of mourning had passed, she asked her grandmother about the tearing of the clothes. "It's an old custom," Ida told her. "A thing we used to do in Russia, as part of our grieving." She stopped to think about it, then asked, "Have you ever heard the saying 'I won't take that lying down'?"

Jackie nodded.

"Well, that's Jewish law. You must always stand up when you tear your dress, to show that you'll never knuckle under. That's what it means to be a Jew, to stand up tall even while your heart is breaking."

Jackie hardly felt Jewish, though she knew her family was. Her father never talked about it, and she knew he often told people he was from Holland. In fact, it often seemed that her parents were determined to forget their background. But she would always remember the image of her grandmother, standing tall and proud beside her grandfather's coffin and defiantly ripping open the black dress of her grief.

6

Coming of Age

I'm very Philadelphia in my thought. . . . A Philadelphia girl is much more inclined to feel her roots than a New York girl. Philadelphia is a state of mind she doesn't ever quite escape.

——Jacqueline Susann

*P*HILADELPHIA had always been different from New York or Chicago. "The City of Brotherly Love," or sometimes "the City with a Country Heart," in the early decades of the century it was also often referred to as "a city of homes." Sprawling over 130 square miles, with the 7,000 acres of Fairmount Park cutting a diagonal swath across it, it was not known for its restaurants or theaters, or for public ostentation. It was a city of rather uniform row houses within which families led quietly conservative lives. Boston and New York might tolerate eccentricity and worship genius, but Philadelphia expected its geniuses to conform.

Many of its artists, feeling the cramp of the city's small-town morality, moved on. Even the wildly nonconforming Bob Susan admitted, in a later interview, that he would do things differently if given a second chance at his early career. "I would certainly study at the Academy again," he told the reporter, "but I should like to spend more time abroad. And I don't think I would stay in Philadelphia. There are more opportunities in New York and Chicago. We are an older city with a more staid background."

As Jackie entered adolescence, the country plunged into the worst economic disaster of its history. The Great Depression brought much of America to the edge of poverty, but the Susan household, buttressed by Rose's teaching salary, felt little of the pinch. Bob continued to get commissions to paint the wealthy and the politically powerful, many of them through his pals Charlie Berwind and Judge Leo Weinrott, with whom he was believed to have split some of the lucrative fees. His male friends were helpful, and to show his gratitude he often served cocktails in his studio, inviting his beautiful young models to help with the entertainment.

But if he hustled the rich men in his circle and catered to the whims of the wealthy matrons he painted, he seems to have balanced the scales when dealing with students, who remember him as a kind and patient teacher. One, Pearl Sklaroff, recalls that "nobody taught like Bob. He wanted to show you everything he knew. He even told you how to mix paints, and it was fascinating to see how he got his skin tones. He was a very good-hearted person, and he charged his students almost nothing."

The Susans often summered in Atlantic City at the Ritz Hotel or the Villa D'Este, but in 1931 Rose went off to

Europe with a group of teachers and left thirteen-year-old
Jackie in Bob's care. It was a lovely, adventurous time for
her, being squired to prizefights and wrestling matches and
baseball games by her handsome father. She had started
wearing makeup and tweezing her eyebrows, and she was
allowed to buy some clothes her mother would have vetoed
as inappropriate. The flapper look, which Jackie had long
admired and aspired to, was giving way to the sultrier,
sexier "siren" style, which she liked less. She swung
between the two, but at heart she remained a flapper and
would through much of her adult life, delighting in jazzy
clothes and shocking language.

Bob took her to movies, too. They saw *Emil and the
Detectives*, which was based on a book she had read and
loved. They also saw the exciting *Front Page* and Chaplin's
new silent film, *City Lights*, which Bob admired even
though most Hollywood films were now talkies. Rose
would have disapproved if she had known, since she
considered Chaplin's personal life immoral. But then Rose
disapproved of many things permitted by Bob. Even Jackie's
whistling, which she had raised to a high level of skill with
Bob's approval, drove Rose crazy. It was not proper, she
protested in vain, quoting the adage about whistling girls
and cackling hens coming to no good end. Still the
tweeting and trilling continued, to Bob's amusement.

Bob even took her to the racetrack and to some of the
city's livelier "restaurants." They visited the Broadaxe,
the Fortside, the Bluebell, and the Embassy Club, speakeasies
whose patrons often drank too much of the still-illegal
booze that flowed freely, and slipped away to private
rooms upstairs with their girl friends. Bob introduced her
as his daughter, but he seemed to get a kick out of the
disbelieving looks that produced from some of the other
men.

When she wasn't with her father, she was often sneaking into theater matinees or movies with girl friends, who were also dragged along in pursuit of autographs from any star who happened to be appearing. She would later be commissioned by Bob to relay the plots of movies to him, so he could claim to have been there with her instead of partying with one of his mistresses.

And she continued to read voraciously, progressing from such childhood favorites as *Little Women* and *Rebecca of Sunnybrook Farm* to the wilder novels of Jules Verne and H. G. Wells and even Edgar Rice Burroughs, whose interplanetary "tits and swords" fantasies appealed to her even more than his Tarzan stories had. She loved stories of death and the supernatural and was endlessly fascinated by sexual betrayal and scandal, but it was the world of speculative and fantastic fiction that truly held her.

The following spring she graduated from the Harrity School, revealing a surprising talent for handiwork and sewing the prettiest graduation dress in her class. That summer it was decided that Jackie should go to camp, and to a Jewish camp at that. The one chosen was in the Bucks County, Pennsylvania, town of Pipersville, and was run by the Workmen's Circle as a place to promote health, fitness, and a sense of Jewish cultural identification. It was coed, simple, and unpretentious, with about two hundred campers housed in ten large bungalows built around a creek. It featured the usual summer-camp activities—hiking, tennis, volleyball, basket weaving, evening bonfires—plus Sunday shows put on by the campers. Thelma had gone there the year before, and was back again this year, too, though she and Jackie were less close now. Jackie was entering puberty with a vengeance.

A new friend appeared to take Thelma's place in the camp high jinks Jackie began to stir up. Her name was Tybie Marder, and her recollections of that summer are sharp a half century later. She especially remembers those

Sunday shows, which would have been just Jackie's meat except for one small detail—they were in Yiddish, which she had never learned. But she didn't let that stop her. "It was hilarious hearing Jackie speak the words in Yiddish," Tybie says. "But she pulled it off. She was such a mimic, and her memory was excellent.

"Jackie was in a rebellious mood and didn't want to conform," Tybie remembers, ". . . and she really stirred me up. I was a very docile but willing accomplice in all her tricks. I don't think the camp had ever had to deal with anyone like Jackie. Our friendship was an embarrassment to my mother, who happened to be the camp cook. We all wore shorts and blouses, but Jackie managed to take some nips and tucks in them, and leave some buttons open or shorten her shorts and make them seductive. Glamour had become extremely important to her.

"She was very inventive when it came to escapades. We would prowl at night and paint people with Mercurochrome. . . . Both of us would creep into people's bunks and paint their faces as they slept. It worked very well. Very few people awoke. Mercurochrome is very hard to get off."

They also short-sheeted beds and dreamed up a stream of annoying pranks for which they were punished severely and often, yet Tybie recalls the summer with fondness. "Jackie wrote a play that we appeared in," she remembers. "It was very bad but she did it, and it was produced." Jackie also talked frequently about her favorite actress, June Knight, whose pictures she had all over her walls at home, along with Margalo Gillmore's photo in what today's sexual underground would recognize as a "dominatrix" pose, complete with high polished boots and riding crop.

That summer Jackie also acquired another photo for that bedroom wall, though this one was not of a famous

actress. It was a snapshot of the camp's dance counselor, a
happy and shapely twenty-year-old named Molly Tabachnik
whom Tybie describes as "an early hippie, fifty years
ahead of her time." Molly played the piano and sang as
well as danced.

Jackie was smitten with an adolescent crush that bordered
on outright adoration. She followed Molly around, moon-
struck, and confessed to friends that she was confused
about her deep feelings for the woman. Sometimes she felt
she wanted to be exactly like Molly, but other times she
wanted the woman, the way men wanted women in the
books she had read. When she thought of Molly she got
twinges "down there," she said—twinges she had never
felt about a boy. She even acquired one of Molly's cast-off
sandals, which she kept under her pillow and took out
often to hold and stroke. (She would always cherish
intimate mementos of those she loved, and in time would
even find a use for this eccentricity in her novels. In *The
Love Machine* Amanda carries Robin Stone's soiled towels
around in her purse.)

She worried that summer about her feelings for Molly,
and when she got home she rushed to the Cobbs Creek
library to look up "lesbian," which she suspected was
what she was. She told her diary about it, though she
wasn't sure just what these women actually did together.
And she even discussed it with Grandma Ida, who told her
that many girls her age got crushes on women and that it
didn't mean a thing. But it did mean something to Jackie,
and she continued to have those twinges when she stared at
Molly's snapshot on her wall, or at the photos of Margalo
Gillmore and June Knight.

In the fall Jackie began high school, still "a tall and
gangly fourteen-year-old with lank, dark hair and a broken
front tooth, though she was already arching her eyebrows," as Tybie recalls. Jackie and Evelyn entered West

Philadelphia High, an ugly brick building built in the style of a square prison, the building extending from curb to curb with little surrounding grass. The school was a melting pot, with black and Jewish students as well as Irish and several other ethnic groups in the mix, but it was considered a "nice school," with no muggings or purse snatchings or attacks on teachers in the 1930's. It was, however, crowded, its grounds rimmed with Quonset huts that had been added to provide extra classrooms. It was to be her second home for the next three years, but she never liked the place and always yearned to leave it.

She and Evelyn were dating now, often with boys who were older and more experienced. Five years later in a newspaper interview Jackie described one of those dates, when a college boy took her to her first nightclub, the old Club Seville in the Stephen Girard Hotel:

> It was my first real date and the boy was a junior at Penn. I thought "Gee, he could have asked a senior girl!" And I was thrilled. I had some beautiful dresses and mother laid out a plain one for me. But she had gone out for the evening with my father.
>
> I went into her closet and got out a black dress of hers and wore it. With high-heeled slippers. It was too big, but I sort of bunched it up. I looked terrible, of course, but I thought I was swell.
>
> Mother had told me to drink only water and orangeade, but she said I could smoke to look like the others. It was the first time I had been allowed to smoke in public. I used a lot of cigarettes, too, because I couldn't dance and I got all over the poor boy's feet.

The boy hadn't known I was only 14. I was tall
and when he met me I kept my mouth shut. But
he found out.

Smoking in public may have been forbidden, but she
was puffing Camels steadily by now, later moving on to
Luckies. She and Evelyn got into trouble with school
authorities when they were caught "smoking cigarettes
and who knows what" on the fire escapes, a favorite
hideout for the rebellious. The "who knows what" came to
include an occasional "reefer," which she claimed helped
to calm her down and offset the effects of the Dexedrine
pills she was taking to aid in her various diets.* She was
thicker in the waist than she wanted to be, and would
remain so all her life. She ate Tic Tac mints with the
"dexies," explaining to Evelyn that you needed a little
sugar to make the pills work. She even got Evelyn to try
one, but it almost caused her to faint and thoroughly
frightened both of them. After that Evelyn stuck to cigarettes on the fire escapes.

When she wasn't dieting Jackie binged on sweets,
making up huge batches of candy with Evelyn's help or
dropping by Aunt Rosa's apartment for generous helpings
of the cupcakes she adored. When Prohibition was repealed
the former speakeasies her father had taken her to became
legitimate restaurants, though some still maintained those
upstairs rooms for their customers' amorous pursuits. Bob
still took her out from time to time, but now she had
boyfriends to squire her about. One, Herman Robinson,
was even persuaded to take her all the way to Atlantic City
for wrestling matches featuring the three Dusek brothers,
on whom she had a collective crush. Herman was a student
at a military academy, and he had a mother who approved

*Jackie probably got the pills from one of Bob's models.

of Jackie so enthusiastically it worried her. Mrs. Robinson would smile fondly, twisting the huge diamond ring she always wore, and would say, "Someday this could be yours, you know."

Jackie was not very popular with the high school faculty, but her English teacher, Mr. Anthony, sensed a talent in her the others couldn't see. He encouraged her to write, and he often picked her to read her compositions before the class. A believer in dramatic opening sentences, he often cited the well-worn example " 'Hell,' said the duchess, as she lit another cigar." Jackie liked him and tried to follow his instructions, so when she presented an essay on her father she opened it with the memorable line "When my father was in Sing Sing Prison . . ."

What happened next is remembered by a classmate, Marvin Weiss, who joined the rest of the class in hoots of laughter. "The more we laughed the more she screamed at us," he says. "And the more she screamed the more we laughed. And she kept screaming, 'My father is a famous artist and he was up there giving demonstrations for the welfare of the prisoners!' "

Perhaps if Jackie had been better liked, it would have been forgotten. But as Weiss recalls, she was never part of the crowd. "She was aloof," he says, "the kind of person to whom you'd say, 'You wanna do this?' and she'd say no. She was constantly standoffish. And most of the Jewish kids had their little cliques. Jackie was not a member. She was not a Jewish type. She was considered an opinionated snob. You used to hear so much about her famous father, and never even knew she had a mother. Before I met Jackie I never heard of Robert Susan, and after I met Jackie that's all I heard about. . . . My brother thought that Jackie was attractive but I didn't feel that way. She was sort of skinny and gaunt and bony. She was probably taller than I was."

The Sing Sing story would haunt her for most of her high school years, especially after kids learned that they could make her furious by asking innocently, "Hey, is your father still in prison?" She lost interest in writing and became much more concerned with her appearance. She had her low hairline raised with electrolysis, much to Rose's chagrin, and she grew adept at styling her hair, setting it every night in rag curlers. Once, staying overnight in Evelyn's small apartment, she became so frustrated with the lack of rags for curlers that she got a pair of scissors and cut up Mrs. Arnold's best pillowcases.

She and Evelyn continued to double-date, sometimes with college boys who would take them to nice places. "In those years you went dancing," Evelyn recalls. "Those were the years of the big bands. You drove to places like Pottstown. Philadelphia was not like New York. There was nothing much to do in Philadelphia, very few places to go out. Entertaining was all done at your club, if you belonged to one, or in your home. There was no dating during the week, only Friday or Saturday night." She remembers that Jackie was not a good dancer but that she liked to watch people on the dance floor, trying to imagine what they were thinking about and what they would say to each other when they got home.

Jackie's interest in the theater, which had remained constant, began to focus on one particular show during the early years of high school. It was a radio program called *The Children's Hour*, which was aired Sunday mornings on WCAU, sponsored by Horn and Hardart. The show would be the training ground for an astonishing number of stars, including Ezra Stone, Eddie Fisher, Joey Bishop, Bernadette Peters, and Frankie Avalon. It had begun in the late twenties and would run for thirty years, in time even finding an audience in New York City and broadcasting from there on alternate weekends. But in the early thirties it was *the* Sunday event in Philadelphia, preempting nearly all other activities for the hundreds of thousands who sat glued to their radios. Jackie, of course, was one of them.

It was a family show in one sense, presided over by Esther Broza, its talent coordinator and reigning genius, and emceed by her husband, who was also the station's program director. Their son Elliot (later known as Elliot Lawrence) had a little band in which he played the drums. There were singers and musicians, and there were plays and sketches stressing "good behavior, patriotism, and decency," most of them written by Esther. They were constructed around "certain outstanding children who attracted an audience," Esther remembers. "We looked for talent, and when we found someone who was promising we tried to develop the child."

One of the children she developed was Kitty Kallen, who went on to become a popular vocalist. "You would come in every Saturday and Esther Broza would tell you what songs you were going to do and whether you were going to be on," she recalls. "There weren't any stars as such, but there were certain favorites who got on every week. And we'd get a free meal—three tickets for free meals at Horn and Hardart's, that was our pay. But I must say, as a result of the show I had a following. I felt like the sweetheart of Philadelphia, and when I was seventeen I left home and joined a band."

For Jackie, already somewhat stagestruck, the show soon became more than just entertainment. She decided she wanted to be a part of it, and again she was lucky in her family connections. Esther Broza was the aunt of little Lela Rolontz, the first baby Jackie had loved to carry around, and Lela's mother was part of Rose's circle of friends. Through them Jackie was able to arrange an audition in which she sang some of the popular songs of the day: "Three Little Words," "Goodnight, Sweetheart,"

"Body and Soul." Unfortunately, she could barely carry a tune, and Esther had to send her away with very little encouragement.

The next week she was back, this time with a sketch she had written. It, too, was wrong for the show, and again Esther had to say no. But Jackie refused to quit, and in the months and years that followed she kept returning to auditions and submitting new sketches, though she and her scripts were passed over time after time. Nevertheless, she made an impression. "She had so much personality, she was so ambitious, she had such verve," Esther Broza remembers. "I told her that she was tough enough for New York, that she was strong, and that she should go there."

Jackie was no doubt flattered, but still she wasn't on the show, and she began to sense that she might never be on it unless she came up with something novel. She came upon her opportunity in the form of another aspiring performer, a beautiful, slender, blue-eyed young dancer and sometime model named Judy Shinn. Judy was as hungry for show business as Jackie, and was spending every spare dime on dance lessons—tap, ballet, even modern dance. Jackie was impressed with the girl's determination, and together the two worked out some simple tap routines, though Jackie admitted she was "definitely a klutz" and therefore had to follow Judy's lead.

Still, it was a different angle, and they spent hours rehearsing a tap dance to the hit song of the day, "Who's Afraid of the Big Bad Wolf?" She hoped that it was a novel enough notion to attract Esther Broza's attention, but even so she was surprised when Esther went for it. Not long after, Jackie made her theatrical debut, with Judy, doing a tap dance double—on a radio show. In the years that followed Esther would continue to use her from time to time, sometimes in tap routines and occasionally in a dramatic sketch that included a brief adult part of the sort her voice and delivery suited. And Esther kept encouraging her to write, even though the sort of urbane dialogue Jackie favored was inappropriate for that show. "I didn't think much of her acting talent, and her singing was zero," Esther recalls, "but I remember telling Jackie that she was born to write, even though her subject matter was too mature for us."

Jackie was unconvinced. Whether because of the glamorous women who surrounded her father or because of her unpleasant experience with the Sing Sing story, she had made up her mind to be a performer. "Acting is glamour," she declared, "but writing is hard work!"

More and more, as the high school years dragged past, she began to think of New York City, the home of all that was glamorous and exciting in the theater world. College began to seem less and less appealing, and her college-oriented academic curriculum seemed a waste of effort. Rose, however, was adamant: Her daughter *must* go to college, must pursue a more substantial and less glittery—and less dangerous—career than the theater. Besides, she was convinced the talent just wasn't there, and that Jackie would be doomed to disappointment. As Jackie's determination grew, so did Rose's.

And Rose was no mean adversary, as her daughter well knew. The "duchess" of the Lea School, revered by the rest of the faculty, Rose was a dynamic, forceful, strikingly attractive woman who is remembered as resembling movie star Norma Talmadge in both looks and peppy style. She loved being in front of great crowds, often leading assemblies of several hundred kids. And she valued dramatic effect, waiting until the assembly bell rang and then tripping across the schoolyard, dressed to the hilt and bejeweled with beads and earrings, to make her entrance. She taught most subjects during her career, but specialized in music, English, and art. And her standards were formidably high, as her colleagues and students—and her daughter—were well aware. Jackie would later write of a fictional mother: "I understand about my mother. I have no complexes there. . . . Mother believes it is her duty to break down false vanity and make one rely on one's true merits, namely, one's mind and creative ability. God help those who weren't blessed with these sterling qualities. Mother had no time for them."

Mother and daughter had clashed on many things and Jackie had often had her way, but on this matter of higher education Rose held firm. Jackie wanted permission to switch to a nonacademic home economics course; Rose remained stubbornly opposed, and refused her permission. The impasse was resolved in typical Jackie fashion: She forged her mother's signature on the permission forms and entered the less demanding nonacademic course she wanted. By the time Rose realized what had happened it was too late to change back. Through guile, and with quiet encouragement from Bob, Jackie had won.

Meanwhile, there was still the rest of high school to be gotten through, with the help of her friends and the various boys she dated. One of these was Richard Allman, whom she had first met in dancing class when she was very young, barely into her teens. A product of private schools, the Hill School and Yale, Allman was the scion of an "upper-crust" Jewish family who lived on Rittenhouse Square and belonged to the exclusive Philmont Country Club and the Locust Club in the city. The family business, the largest wallpaper firm in the country, had been started in 1840, making the Allmans distinctly "old money" and far above the Susans socially.

Richard took Jackie to parties and movies, and he remembers her as "dark and good-looking, slim, a very pretty young girl, very striking, dressed older than her age.

She was the life-of-the-party type, very vivacious, a wisecracker, but not a loudmouth by any means.'' In spite of the good times, however, Allman was very much aware of Bob's reputation, and of the Susans' lower social standing. People of the Allmans' status socialized with the German Jews or the Portuguese Sephardim, such as the Mastbaum brothers, who owned every movie theater in town. But Bob Susan was known as a ''gallivanteer,'' and the family was of Russian Jewish origin. ''Socially my mother never had anything to do with them,'' he says, recalling those days. ''And my father would never permit a Russian Jew in the house.''

Whether because of these social barriers or as a natural result of the gap in their ages (Allman was four years older than Jackie), in time he stopped calling her. There were other boys always available, including the faithful Herman Robinson, who stood forever ready to go anywhere or do anything she wanted. But Allman had been something of a catch, athletic and handsome and affluent, from a background she couldn't help envying. It hurt when he dropped her, especially since she knew his family had always considered her inferior.

Along with dates and school and experimentation with the ''reefers'' and ''bennies'' that were becoming ever more prevalent in her crowd, there was the theater and her growing desire to be a part of it. She and her friend Evelyn followed the fan magazines avidly, studying the changing styles in hair and clothing and comparing notes on figures, measuring themselves against the actresses whose pictures they clipped and tacked to her wall. Evelyn was pretty and she had a nearly perfect figure, but she lacked the dramatic effect Jackie could somehow create. ''She had a very finely shaped oval face set on a long, graceful neck. She had funny bazooms, ovallike and long—she couldn't wear a gown without a built-in bra, but with a bra she looked terrific. She had broad shoulders, and her big problem was that her waist wasn't small, but because of her narrow hips if she dressed properly you didn't notice. . . . When she entered a room every man would be stunned, and just drop everything and look at her."

She was still dropping by Bob's studio whenever she got a chance, often taking friends along to meet her handsome father and his models. The visits to the studio produced one curious aftermath that would have devastated Jackie if she had known about it. Samuel Heller, a fellow painter who had a studio next door to Bob's, recalls the incident well:

"I remember that one day Jackie brought this friend of hers—a beautiful girl, not Jewish—and Bob slipped her a note to come back, and she came back. And I guess the whole thing was a great adventure to her, but then Bob confided that he got her pregnant. He was desperate. He had to get her an abortion. He asked all the guys in the building to help him find one. He threatened to kill himself; he was terrified. It was his daughter's friend."

Presumably the abortion was arranged, but the experience sobered Bob considerably. And when a newspaper story lauded his "unusual services in behalf of the youth of Philadelphia," the other artists in his building had a good laugh at his expense.

One welcome by-product of her change from academic to home economics courses was that she now needed fewer credits to graduate. As a result she finished in midyear, with her graduation slated for the evening of January 30, 1936, in the University of Pennsylvania's Irvine Auditorium. As an indifferent student who was not even college bound, she would not ordinarily have been featured in the graduation ceremony at all. Jackie had "torn up her ticket to college" by switching courses, a thing Rose's friends on the high school faculty knew pained her deeply. To soften the blow for her, the friends came up with a clever idea to get Jackie into the ceremony.

Jackie had done nothing to warrant being honored, but each year a girl was selected to write the presentation speech, and another girl was picked to give it during the ceremony. Those two were chosen in advance, and when the names were announced Jackie's classmates were astonished to learn that she had been selected—by a committee of two teachers—to deliver the presentation address.

Her speech may have been a proud moment for Rose, but for Jackie herself, facing the stone wall of resentment from her classmates, it must have been unpleasant. Everyone knew that in truth she had specialized mostly in cutting classes to sneak off to matinees or to smoke cigarettes on the fire escapes. And everyone, it seemed, was upset about it. She knew they were making insulting remarks behind her back, but she bluffed it through.

And then it was over, and she was free to head for New York. And yet she wasn't quite free, it turned out. Again, Rose was adamant: Jackie was too young to go off alone, and she would have to wait at least till after her eighteenth birthday, in August. Six whole months more of Philadelphia!

She had just about given up reading books altogether by now, but she found things to fill her time, some of them even useful things for a would-be actress. She took singing lessons, got her clothes ready, attended classes at the Bessie V. Hicks School of Drama, and looked over her high school yearbook, which quoted her as saying that her ambition was to own a mink coat. She joined the Theater League of Philadelphia, an amateur group directed by Jasper Deeter of the Hedgerow Repertory Company, where she made another friend named Hana Karol, who would later follow her to New York.

There was one bright spot in the spring, when she entered a contest conducted by Earl Carroll to pick the most beautiful girl in Philadelphia. The competition had been announced in March, in a brief newspaper story that listed a panel of judges to be headed by local portrait painter Robert Susan. There was more publicity over the next few weeks, but by the time the pageant was actually held, on April 16, the "panel of judges" had shrunk to two: Earl Carroll, the eminent review producer, and Samuel Saxe, production chief of Warner Brothers studios, which would screen-test the winner. Bob's name had mysteriously disappeared from the list.

There were thirty-one finalists on the day of judgment, all supposedly selected from theater audiences during the previous week. The two judges, with or without Bob's help, then narrowed the field to four. What happened after that was so confusing that reporters covering the event never did get it straight: The *Record* said: "Brown-eyed, black-haired Jacqueline (Jackie) Susan, daughter of Robert Susan, noted portrait painter, is the prettiest girl in Philadelphia. That's the verdict of Earl Carroll, beauty picker par excellence. . . . 'Jackie' and three runners-up will be given screen tests in New York—and so on to Hollywood perhaps. She is 17, a graduate of West Philadelphia High School. She dances, sings, but does not sew. Her measurements? Well, 34 bust, 27-waist, 35 hip, weight 128, height 5 feet 7 inches."

The *Inquirer* told a different story. Under the headline EARL CARROLL SEEKS PHILA. BEAUTY QUEEN AND DISCOVERS FOUR, the story explained that "Philadelphia girls are so beautiful . . . Carroll simply couldn't decide on one only. . . ." The four winners were named, with Jackie's name appearing first. The story then continued with the curious line: "A silver cup which Carroll was to give to the beauty selected was presented to Miss Susan."

Whatever the circumstances, Jackie did end up with the cup, which she proudly displayed for the photographers. But once again there were sour notes in her triumph. There were people who swore they had seen her grab the silver cup from Mr. Carroll, and there were others who said that Bob had remained a judge but persuaded the reporters not to use his name. Bob shrugged it off, telling her not to worry and adding, "This contest isn't worth a damn but it's a good-sounding credit." And, of course, there was that screen test awaiting her in New York—yet another reason she had to go, she pointed out to Rose.

She waited, taking her lessons and doing what she could to pass the time through the hot Philadelphia summer, until at last her eighteenth birthday rolled around, followed by the promised day of her release. Bob had offered to drive her to New York but she refused, certain that her mother would want to come along and that the arguments between her parents would continue throughout the trip. Rose had given in, but she was still protesting that Jackie was too young to live alone in such a big, wicked city. Besides, she argued, there were thousands of pretty girls who sang and danced better than she did.

Jackie tuned it all out and carefully packed for the train trip she was sure would change her life forever.

PART TWO

THE CITY
[1936–1947]

7

City Lights

*I love New York. Before I came to New York I was
nothing. I was dead. When I came to New York it
was like a veil lifting. For the first time I felt I was
alive, breathing.*

——Jacqueline Susann IN *Valley of the Dolls*

IT was hot, so hot that Jackie had sweated through her
linen travel suit—yellow, her lucky color—well before
they got to the train station. Not Rose. In her white
summer dress and black accessories Rose looked perfect,
as always.

"Don't you perspire like ordinary people, Mother?"
Jackie asked.

"*Ladies* don't perspire," Bob retorted with a wink. "If
you were a lady like your mother, you wouldn't either.
Unluckily, you inherited my genes—and I've never been
accused of being a gentleman."

Rose didn't say a word. It was true that she rarely perspired anymore—not since her pregnancy eighteen years before. It had wrung her dry, she suspected, exhausted her sweat glands permanently. She didn't cry much either, but now she was perilously close to tears; closer than she'd been since the day she'd seen Boris in his coffin. It would be lonely with Jackie gone. Raising a daughter was over so *fast*, and it seemed never to turn out the way one expected. This child—and she *was* still a child, with all her smudged mascara, siren outfits, and sophisticated patter—was hardly prepared to live alone in New York. She was still a dreamer, and she still hadn't learned to distinguish her dreams from reality. Rose still shuddered when she remembered that terrifying summer afternoon, not so long ago, when Jackie and Thelma had almost drowned. *Water Babies*. How absurdly had Jackie *believed* in that book.

And how she had believed in Ernie Dusek, that silly wrestler. There were three of them, the Dusek brothers, and all of their pictures were pinned up on Jackie's wall. Bob was a fan, and Jackie, naturally, had had a crush on each of the Duseks in turn. And Ernie Dusek *was* handsome, even Rose had to admit—blond and with a moustache, almost like a muscle-bound Boris Jans. One August night, the summer she turned fifteen, Jackie had sneaked out to see Ernie—pitted that evening against the Red Devil—in the Convention Hall at Atlantic City. Ernie was being badly beaten, it seemed, and the Red Devil was jumping on him. Jackie started to curse, loudly, and when the Red Devil kicked Ernie she picked up a folding chair and threw it into the ring. The Red Devil ignored the chair and started to gouge out Ernie's eyes. Jackie went berserk. She hurled herself into the center of the ring, grabbed the Red Devil by the hair, clawed and kicked him violently and refused to let go. The police had to pull her off the man, and then they had to literally drag her off to jail, where she spent the better part of the night.

Rose was beside herself, but Jackie tossed it off as an experience that would help her with her acting, especially meeting a couple of real live prostitutes and a genuine gangster. Predictably, Bob had found the episode hilarious and had bragged to his pal Charlie Berwind that Jackie was the "ultimate fan." Fan, indeed! The child could easily have been crushed to death right there in the Convention Hall. Rose could forgive Bobby his crimes against *her*, but not for the crazy ideas he had put into Jackie's head. Never would she forgive him, even if as a result of it all Jackie became a star.

Rose snapped her black patent-leather purse open and handed her daughter an envelope, reminding her to open a bank account as soon as she arrived. "Never carry more than twenty-five dollars in cash, Jacqueline." (She pronounced it "Jak-wah-leen.") "And never leave cash in your room. At the end of the year you'll come back and get your academic diploma. The money's all saved, and we won't touch it, never fear."

Jackie exchanged an amused glance with her father, who hoisted her suitcases up on the train. The suitcases were sleazy looking, cardboard—"Leatherette," it was called. Bob had wanted to get her the best, had even made the rare gesture of offering to pay for them out of his own money, but Rose had said, "No, not yet." It just seemed too *final*. Next year, when Jackie went to college, they would buy her good leather luggage with her monogram.

Jackie jumped aboard and rushed to find a window seat so she could wave good-bye. "Don't forget to call the Witkins," Rose shouted to her. Jackie smiled and nodded, but there was something almost harsh about that smile, something . . . well, theatrical. Jackie didn't cry, either, which hurt a little. Didn't most girls cry when they left their parents for a new life? Not Jacqueline. If anything, her jaw appeared even more prominent, more stubborn.

"Hey, Suzy," Bob said to her as they walked, hand in hand, toward the car. "That's some lovely daughter you've got there."

"No, Mookie," she told him, her voice resigned. "She's not my daughter, she's yours."

Jackie took a room at Kenmore Hall, a women's residence club on Twenty-third Street. Thirty years later she would describe it in *Valley of the Dolls:* "not much of a room, but the ceiling is high and it kind of stirs the air." And of the lumpy studio bed: "Sometimes she wondered how many people had slept on it—hundreds, perhaps. The small battered nighttable crisscrossed with scratches and old cigarette burns; the bureau with the three drawers that had to be left slightly open because they stuck if they were closed, and if you pulled too hard the knobs came off; and the pregnant easy chair, its lowered belly bulging with springs that just longed to burst through."

When Jackie arrived in New York in the late summer of 1936, there was not yet a television industry. Radio was important, but half of it originated in Chicago. Movies were made in Hollywood. In New York theater was king. The greatest hits of 1936 were Richard Rodgers and Lorenz Hart's *On Your Toes*, George S. Kaufman and Moss Hart's *You Can't Take It with You*, Robert Sherwood's *Idiot's Delight*, and *Bury the Dead*, by a twenty-three-year-old wunderkind named Irwin Shaw who had set Broadway on its ear. In November, two months after Jackie's arrival, Eugene O'Neill would win the Nobel Prize, bolstering everyone's conviction that New York now had the greatest theater in the world.

You could take a screen test in New York, though, and Jackie did. She had "won" it along with her Earl Carroll beauty contest the previous year. But even while she was taking it, she knew better than to raise her hopes.

The makeup woman rubbed gobs and gobs of pancake on Jackie's face. "Honey, you got a great shape and a be-you-ti-ful face," the woman told her. "If I had your looks I'd head straight for a modeling agency."

"Modeling? But I'm an actress."

"Listen, honey, you don't have to be an *actress* to get a movie contract. You need small paws."

"Paws?" Jackie was startled. She held up her hands and looked at them.

The makeup woman chuckled. "Naw, paws! Like the paws on your *skin*. You got big paws, honey. They could never use you in a close-up. I don't care if you got the talent of Katharine Cornell, you ain't gonna pass the close-up in the screen test. They magnify your skin at least a hundred times. You got to have small paws!"

Jackie was taking the test with a dozen other hopefuls. She sat for an hour, fanning herself, watching her makeup run and trying to repair it. She was called around four o'clock, and she was finished by three minutes after. She thought she had been pretty good, but as she was leaving the set a cameraman called her. "Hey, cutie. Too bad about your paws. Got a date tonight? You wanna have dinner?"

Jackie declined and hurried home to the Kenmore. She wanted to talk to Elfie, her new friend. An orphan, Elfie had been in vaudeville since she was six or seven and was therefore an expert on show business. She was Jackie's age, and though she had lived out of trunks and never attended school, she was an authority on who was sleeping with whom. She shocked Jackie with gossip about the great Katharine Cornell's *ménage à trois* with her husband, Guthrie McClintic, and a woman songwriter. She told how Tallulah Bankhead alternated between young actors and actresses on her country weekends, and how J.J. Shubert, the powerful producer, regarded his chorus girls as a harem and often took the whole corps to dinner, with no other men allowed.

Shubert's casting director was a different story, Elfie said. A flaming homosexual who wore a shawl, "Ma" Simmons demanded a free hand in choosing chorus boys—and he expected them to show their gratitude. Elfie said J.J. liked to hire homosexuals the way one hired eunuchs in a real harem, but that he was also impressed with Ma Simmons's friends at the Metropolitan Opera and his knack for hiring away singers who didn't quite make it there. She said the chorus boys in Shubert productions were known around Broadway as "Ma's girlfriends," or simply "Les Girls."

Jackie found Elfie as adorable as she was informative, a true Broadway sophisticate and yet an all-American kid, with her snub nose, freckles, and mop of brown curls. She seemed wonderfully open, but her source of income was a little bit unclear, as was the source of her gorgeous silver fox jacket, which she urged Jackie to borrow when it got cold.

Not that Elfie was extravagant. She showed Jackie how to stretch her food budget in New York, at the Automat on Broadway between Forty-sixth and Forty-seventh streets and the Mayflower Doughnut Shop at Broadway and Forty-fifth. She introduced her to several of the kindlier theater ushers and box office agents, those who were inclined to let pretty young actresses see a show for free when the house wasn't full. And she took Jackie to the two hangouts most frequented by theatrical hopefuls—the café in the RCA Building at Radio City and the Walgreen's drugstore at Forty-fourth and Broadway. "Walgreen's is . . . well, it's like the Broadway switchboard,'' Elfie explained. ''It's like an agency for show business people who don't have their own agent yet. And real agents come by, too, and so do producers when they're looking for new talent.''

''And so do wolves?'' Jackie asked.

''Yes.'' Elfie giggled. ''And so do wolves.''

The high point of Elfie's tour was a stop at the famous Friars Club, where established performers, even stars, went to drown their sorrows and swap shady stories when they were ''at liberty.'' Jackie and Elfie got all dressed up to go there, but when Jackie peered around she didn't see a single familiar face.

One man did catch her eye, though. He was slight of build, not much taller than Jackie, and decidedly dapper, with a made-to-order conservatively cut suit, an impressive silk polka-dot tie, and a heavy gold ring. He was somewhere in his early thirties, had a pixie, elfin face and a California tan that only partially concealed a terrible scar on his cheek.

Jackie learned his name, Joe Lewis, which confused her. Wasn't that the Negro boxer, the ''Brown Bomber'' that Bob had lost so much money on a few months ago, when Lewis was defeated by Max Schmeling for the world heavyweight crown?

''This one's a comic,'' Elfie explained.* ''He used to be in vaudeville and burlesque. They say he made it big in nightclubs in Chicago and L.A., but he's a nobody here.''

''He seems to have a lot of friends.''

''Oh, yeah. He's what they call a comic's comic. They say that Sophie Tucker used to have a thing for him. Jolson

---

*Joe Lewis, the comic, would soon take the middle initial ''E.'' to distinguish himself from the boxer. His friends, including Jackie, would thereafter call him ''Joe E.''

and all—they felt sorry for him after he was slashed up by gangsters in Chicago. Lived off of benefits for years before he got his voice back, they say."

Jackie moved a little closer to Joe, so she could eavesdrop. His voice *was* hoarse and raspy, like sandpaper. She couldn't imagine how a man with a voice like that could ever perform. As she listened, someone was telling him a hard-luck story, and he kept nodding sympathetically. He reached into his pocket and pulled out an enormous wad of bills, peeled off several of them, and pressed them into the fellow's hand. Someone else said, "Hey, sport, you ain't even got a job yet. Maybe you betta go easy with the handouts."

"Aw, I figure he wouldn't ask me if he didn't need it more than me," Joe said. "Besides, I'm goin' to the track tonight. Got a date with a surefire filly."

"How come you quit the Trocadero out in Hollywood?" someone asked. "Fifty-nine straight weeks! I read in *Variety* where you broke all the records."

"Yeah." Joe grinned happily, and Jackie thought it was one of the most enchanting smiles she'd ever seen. "Maybe I should see a psychiatrist. But the Sunset Strip ain't Broadway, and you know what Cohan says. 'Everything west of Broadway is Bridgeport.'"

But Joe didn't say "psychiatrist." He said "psychiatwist." And he didn't say "Bridgeport." He said "Bwidgeport." As Jackie would learn later, after the gangland beating in 1927 Joe had remained speechless for almost two years. Three hoodlums had pushed their way into his room at the Commonwealth Hotel in Chicago, hammered his skull until he was unconscious, and then ripped his throat open, delivering twelve gashes with a hunting knife. They had left him for dead, and when he crawled out of his room and down the corridor to the elevator, he was first taken to the morgue. But the hoodlums had miscalculated, missing his jugular by the breadth of a hair. A six-hour operation had saved his life, and then an English teacher at Notre Dame, Father Heitzer, had patiently taught him to speak again.

Jackie was intrigued by the story, and by Joey's grit. He had been paralyzed when the hoodlums left him, blinded, and bleeding ferociously. How did he get out of his room and go for help? "I'm a Capricorn" was all he would say when people pressed him. "We're stubborn." And it was his stubbornness that had provoked the attack, she learned. He had moved from one Chicago nightspot, the Green Mill Café, to a competitor called the New Rendezvous. And he had taken all the customers with him. The Green Mill's owners had not been pleased.

Jackie and Elfie would leave the Kenmore in the morning, after tossing a coin to decide where to have their lunch. They would stroll up Broadway and then, depending on who had won the toss, stop at either the Mayflower or the Automat. Elfie, who had a sweet tooth, loved the Mayflower doughnuts, while Jackie preferred the Automat because it was next to the Palace Theatre. In front of the Palace, at 1564 Broadway, was where, by some undecreed custom, the comedians and vaudevillians would hang out, swapping routines and jokes. Jackie was hoping to see Joe again. She looked for him every day, in fact.

Finally she did see him, briefly. He was singing a slightly off-color song to the tune of a hymn called "Lord, You Made the Night Too Long." He was singing it right there on the sidewalk, in his unforgettable raspy voice:

> *You made the coat and vest fit the best,*
> *You even made the lining strong.*
> *But, Sam, you made the pants too long.*
>
> *I wear a belt and I wear suspenders.*

I figure what can I lose?
But what good is a belt and what good are suspenders
If my pants hang over my shoes?

I get the damndest breeze through my BVD's,
My fly is where my tie belongs.
Sam, you made the pants too long.

He got an enormous hand from his fellow comics, and after he was finished, someone asked, "Joey, is it true L. B. Mayer wanted you to do that song in a movie?"

"Yeah, it's true," Joe replied. "But so much of it was left on the cutting room floor I still get fan mail from the janitors."

Joe began getting work, and Jackie always went to see him. He emceed a vaudeville review at Loews State. It was reviewed as "far from the best this house has played." In other words, a flop. With all his talent, Joe's voice wasn't really big enough to carry in a large theater and he would never recover 100 percent. But then he opened at the Frolics, a new supper club atop the Winter Garden, and although the money wasn't great, he soon began filling the room. One of his regular fans was Beatrice Lillie, who talked him up to the columnists. New York was discovering Joe—to whom Jackie had still not been introduced.

But when would New York discover Jacqueline Susann? For weeks she went from audition to audition without any luck, and before she knew it summer had turned into autumn. If she hadn't had Elfie's cheerful smile to bolster her, the discouragement would have begun to hurt.

8

The Women

When I was eight years old my father said, "There will be no one to carry on the name of Susann." I said, "I'll carry it on, Daddy. I'm going to be an actress." And he smiled and said, "Well, if you're going to be an actress be a good actress. Be a people watcher."

——Jacqueline Susann

B Y October, when the weather changed, Elfie was still Jackie's only girl friend. Rose said she was a *louche* character, a girl one does not take out in public. And poor Elfie tried so hard to be elegant. When Jackie had taken her home to Philadelphia, Elfie had worn her best fall outfit, a purple taffeta dress and a black coat with a red fox fur collar. Rose had gasped visibly when she met them at the train. "Geez, I'm glad to meet you," Elfie had proclaimed warmly, while Rose eyed her in disbelief. "Hey, I just gotta tell you your daughter's a doozie."

Jackie missed Evelyn terribly. Now she had only Elfie with whom to laugh and shed tears, and gossip, and share her highs and her lows. But Elfie had some surprising facets to her character, Jackie thought. The girl was an omnivorous reader and hungry for an education. Her room was Kenmore Hall's unofficial lending library, for she always had the new bestsellers and was happy to share them after she was done.

On the train ride home from Philadelphia, Elfie took her nose out of John Gunther's *Inside Europe* long enough to say, "Geez, Jackie, you got parents who woulda picked up the freight for collitch, and you nixed it. How come?"

"College is a time waster," Jackie declared, with more confidence than she really felt. "Look at you, Elfie. Aren't you educating yourself?"

"Yeah," Elfie replied. "I'm tryin'. But if I had a family like you do, I'd grab the free ride."

After ten weeks of rejections, Jackie started to ask herself if Elfie could be right. Dear God, she hoped it wouldn't take her as long to become a star as it had taken Ruth Gordon, who, at thirty-nine, had only this year become the new toast of Broadway, playing Mattie Silver in *Ethan Frome*. Jackie made rounds every day, stopping by the offices of all the agents and producers who might have an ingenue part, or a walk-on, or *anything*. She left her photographs, with her meager acting credits listed on the back. She never got past the reception desk at the good places. The only encouragement she had was from an agent named LeRoi LeFevre, a small man who bristled and who looked like . . . no, not a weasel, exactly. She tried to think what animal Bob would have seen in his face. Aha, a raccoon! LeFevre looked amazingly like a raccoon!

LeFevre wasn't successful enough to have his own office. He only had desk space with some other minor agents on West Forty-sixth Street. But he did handle one or two featured players, and some showgirls and dancers—"ponies" and "gypsies," as they were known in the trade. He always greeted Jackie warmly, and if he was free he asked her to sit down and shoot the breeze with him. Now and then, as she told her diary, she fancied that she'd caught him looking down her blouse or up her skirt. But no, he was much too old to be interested in her *that* way.

Jackie asked LeFevre if he would be her agent, and he said that he couldn't sign her until she got a part. She started weeping. "Do they do this to make young actresses crazy?" she asked him. "You can't get an agent until you have a part, but you can't get a part until you have an agent to send you out."

LeFevre said he saw her point. He couldn't sign her yet, but he would give her some leads. She might go over to Ma Simmons, who was casting a road company for the Shuberts. Then, if Ma liked her...

Ma didn't like her, but J. J. Shubert did, although he couldn't offer her a part. She wasn't quite a showgirl type, or at least not the type for this production, and she couldn't dance or sing. But he wanted her to stay in touch. LeFevre told Jackie that it sounded as if J.J. might use her eventually, although he usually let Ma prevail on the first go-round. LeFevre added that he was encouraged by J.J.'s interest, and he told her to come back to his office the following day. There was a possible role he wanted to discuss.

The next day she worried that LeFevre might be missing his lunch in order to audition her, so she stopped at the Mayfair and bought a bag of jelly doughnuts. When she arrived, the office was empty. The place was dustier than she had realized, and seemed a little bit sleazy. In a few minutes LeFevre arrived, and they ate their doughnuts together. He thanked Jackie and brushed the crumbs off his suit, then stood up and said, ''Okay, my beauty, let's start the audition right now.''

Jackie didn't understand, but she stood up obediently, towering over the man. As she started to ask what she should do first, he grabbed her and thrust his tongue into her mouth.

She wrenched away from him.

''What are you afraid of?'' he asked.

''I'm afraid I'll vomit,'' she told him, picking up her purse and the folder containing her photo composites. She raced out of the office, slamming the door, then stopped in the hallway to take several deep breaths and count to twenty-five, as Grandma had instructed her.

As her nausea and anxiety receded, that weird and awful feeling that her body would break into pieces—the feeling that always came with her dream—slowly went away. It was immediately replaced by anger. She swept back into the office to find LeFevre grinning smugly.

''Forget something?'' he asked.

''Yes,'' she said. ''This.'' She punched him hard in the mouth, hard enough to send him reeling.

Elfie was horrified, as much at Jackie's behavior as at LeFevre's.

''Geez, Jackie,'' she exclaimed, ''that's a sure way to make enemies, belting a guy in the kisser.''

''You expect me to stand there and let him paw me? It was disgusting. I wouldn't even let Herman Robinson do that, and Herman's in *love* with me. And he's the right age, too, and he's rich.''

''Sayin' no is one thing. Losin' your temper with the only agent who gives you the time of day is somethin' else. Dale Carnegie says, 'If you want to gather honey don't knock over the beehive.' "

"Who's Dale Carnegie?"

"Who's Dale Carnegie! He's the author of this great book, *How to Win Friends and Influence People*. I got my copy all marked up, but you can have it. You need it as bad as me. Worse."

Jackie took the book to her room and settled down to find out what had impressed Elfie so much. In an hour she was back at Elfie's door.

"You're right," she said. "I need a way to get rid of guys without hurting their feelings. But the book doesn't seem to go into that."

Elfie thought for a minute. "Tell 'em you're engaged. Like they do in the movies."

"But that would be lying."

"So what? Pretend to yourself you're engaged to Herman Whatshisname. Your mother would like that. And maybe it's not a lie. Maybe you will go home someday and marry Herman."

Jackie practiced pretending she was engaged to Herman Robinson. And then she went on to Carnegie's six ways to make people like you:

1. Become interested in other people.
2. Smile.
3. Remember names.
4. Be a good listener.
5. Talk in terms of the other person's interest.
6. Make the other person feel important.

This shouldn't be too difficult. In fact, most of it was advice she'd been hearing all her life anyway. Take Rose. Rose always said it was important to greet people respectfully, by name. Rose always told her to smile, too, and

even Bob tried to make her laugh by being funny, especially when she wouldn't because of her broken front tooth.
And being interested in other people was practically Grandma's motto. She said it helps you to forget your own
troubles. Everyone *loved* Grandma.

Feeling a little sheepish, Jackie returned the book to
Elfie. "I didn't really have to read this. It's what they've
been telling me all my life. But now I'll try a little harder
to *do* it."

As if to reward her, Bob phoned with good news. His
pal Charlie Berwind had asked after Jackie, and Bob had
said she was looking for work in the theater. Charlie said
that Max Gordon, a producer he knew, was casting a play
called *The Women*, with thirty-five female parts. Charlie
said she should go to Gordon's office and use his name.
And she might mention his late Uncle Edward, a wealthy
man who had invested in several Gordon productions.

Jackie knew it was like an omen. Maybe God had
picked her out for something special. And maybe He
would help her make a good impression on Max Gordon.
God and Dale Carnegie.

She practiced remembering the name of Charlie's uncle.
She practiced smiling—just a little, so her teeth wouldn't
show too much. She practiced saying, "Yes, Mr. Gordon.
Thank you, Mr. Gordon." She practiced not interrupting,
no matter how excited she might get. And, just in case,
she practiced saying, "I think you're swell, Mr. Gordon,
but I'm engaged to Herman Robinson back home."

She went to Max Gordon's office with trepidation, but
Berwind's name got her right past the receptionist and into
the inner sanctum.

"So," Gordon said. "You're from Philadelphia and
you're a friend of Charlie Berwind."

Jackie thought he eyed her suspiciously. Did he doubt

she knew Charlie, or did he think that maybe she was one of Charlie's girl friends?

"Aunt Ellen and Uncle Charlie are fine, Mr. Gordon," she replied demurely. "They're my parents' friends." Rose had never met Ellen Berwind and neither had Jackie, but Carnegie didn't say not to lie.

"And how is Charlie taking his uncle's death?" Gordon asked her.

"Oh, he's very sad about Uncle Edward's passing, Mr. Gordon. He says that the thirty million he was left doesn't mean a thing. He's throwing himself into his charity work, especially with the Big Brothers."

Gordon nodded sympathetically. "Well," he said, "let's look at you. There's one small part in *The Women* that we haven't cast yet, a chic French maid named Hélène." He explained that her bit opened Act Three, which took place in an elegant black marble bathroom. The villainess is relaxing in a bubble bath, smoking and reading a magazine. Hélène is scrubbing her back. "She has only three lines, so we thought that someone already in the cast could double up in the part. But no one who looks right seems to speak French. I assume that if your folks run with the Berwind crowd you've been to finishing school and all that. You've probably got the accent."

"*Mais oui*, Monsieur Gordon," Jackie said. She didn't know a word of French beyond that phrase, but she was a good mimic—surely she could fake three lines.

"First rehearsal is tomorrow at eleven," he told her. He gave her a script to read and promised a contract by Friday, at twenty-five a week. "Welcome aboard. And say hello to your Uncle Charlie."

Elfie rehearsed her, sitting in the bathtub and puffing on a cigarette while Jackie practiced scrubbing her back and speaking her lines.

"Mademoiselle Mary has just feenished ze sooper viz her daddy," she said, scrubbing away.

Elfie shook her head. "Jackie, your scrubbing is fine. You do that real good. But . . ."

"I know. My accent stinks."

"I wouldn't say it *stinks*, Jackie, but it doesn't sound like real French to me. It sounds more like vaudeville French."

Jackie left Elfie in the tub and went for her coat. "I have to see if Janet of France is still open. Maybe she can help me."

"It's two in the morning!"

"I know, but she told me that sometimes she stays open late."

Jackie ran most of the mile and a half to Janet's midtown restaurant. The Manhattan streets were scary so late at night, deserted except for a few dog walkers and drunks, but she wasn't nearly as scared of being harmed as she was of blowing her first Broadway part because she had lied about knowing French.

The place was closed. Gloomily she trudged home.

She tried to sleep but couldn't. At dawn she got up and set her hair. What to wear? The show would provide costumes once they were in production, but she wanted to look right *today*. She checked the telephone book for a store that sold servants' uniforms. At five feet six and a half and 132 pounds, with a waist that was on the thick side, she usually looked best in a size 12. She found a size 10 maid's uniform in the first store and decided that the tight fit across the breasts was sexy. After practicing bending down in it—which she could just barely manage— she bought it, along with a frilly apron and cap. Then she hurried over to the Ethel Barrymore Theater.

* * *

He was in his mid-thirties and was one of the most attractive and distinguished-looking men she'd ever seen— even more attractive than Bob Susan, if that was possible. She recognized him from his newspaper photographs: Leland Hayward, the legendary theatrical agent who was conducting bicoastal romances with Katharine Hepburn in Hollywood and Margaret Sullavan in New York.

Hayward was sitting with his client Clare Boothe, the play's author. Thin, blond, chic, and gorgeous, she was someone Jackie had read about, too.

Clare had left school at seventeen to do factory work and dream of writing. She had talked her way into a job at *Vogue*, doing picture captions, and then moved on to *Vanity Fair*, where she became managing editor in 1933. She ran with celebrities and was courted by Bernard Baruch, the famed financier and Roosevelt adviser. Clare was credited with coining the term "Café Society," of which she was a leader. Her business suits were gorgeous, sexy, and numerous, her style more from the twenties—smart set, flapperesque—than from the thirties. And yet there was something very feminine and even romantic about her.

In the thick of the action—cultural, social, and political— she still somehow carved out time from her hectic life to write plays. *The Women,* which followed the entangled marital and extramarital affairs of several fictional members of the author's social set, was her second, and was already predicted to be a surefire hit. Advance excitement had been fueled by Broadway rumors that George S. Kaufman was "the man under the bed" whom Clare had consulted while she was writing it, but Kaufman had announced that if he'd written the play he would have signed it—and taken the money.

Jackie stopped staring and went to join the cast, which had assembled on stage for a pep talk from the director, Robert B. Sinclair. "Ladies, I'd like you all to meet our star," he told them. "Miss Margalo Gillmore, who will play Mary Haines."

Jackie tried to remain calm. *The* Margalo Gillmore! It was almost too much to believe that she, Jacqueline Susann, would be working with the woman she'd had a crush on for years. When Jackie was thirteen years old she had seen Margalo play Henrietta in *The Barretts of Wimpole Street*. After that she prevailed on Bob to take her to New York every time Margalo appeared in a play. Jackie clipped every article, interview, and photograph she could lay her hands on.

While Jackie was still staring at her idol, the director was introducing Ilka Chase, who was to play the part of the bitchy Sylvia Fowler. Unlike Margalo, who had attempted a Hollywood career without success, the thirty-one-year-old Ilka was featured in two current movies, *The Lady Consents* and *Soak the Rich*. And now she had returned to Broadway, to assume what would prove to be her most memorable role.

Jackie would soon feel as if she were eavesdropping at the Algonquin Hotel's famous round table, where all the wits and fashionable writers met. Clare was one of the wittiest writers in New York—the script of *The Women* proved it—but in conversation it was Ilka who kept everyone in stitches. When someone commented that *The Women*, which drew a laugh about every thirty seconds, would probably make Dorothy Parker livid, Ilka retorted, "Clare is quickwitted on paper, but I would not say that in conversation she tosses off witticisms at the rate of Dorothy Parker. I wouldn't say that of Dorothy Parker either."

Jackie was glad she didn't look like Ilka, who had an enormous mouth and was what Jackie's Uncle Harris Potamkin would have called a *mieskite*, or ugly girl. But oh how Jackie envied Ilka's nimble wit. And what a marvelous character actress and comedienne she was.

Jackie was so overwhelmed to find herself among these extraordinary women—*and* Leland Hayward—that she had forgotten her problems with the elusive French accent. But the first read-through, the opening of Act Three, made the problem painfully clear—to everyone. Her line, "Madame has been soaking an hour," came out in a language that certainly wasn't English, but neither was it remotely French. The actress who was in the scene with her was so non-plussed she forgot to retort, "So what?" She just gaped at Jackie, and so, it seemed, did Clare and Leland and Margalo and Ilka. Robert Sinclair called a hurried conference with Max Gordon.

Backstage, no one said a word to her, and only one girl even acknowledged her existence with a friendly nod. The girl was maybe a couple of years older than Jackie. She was blond and slender and very beautiful, as aristocratic looking as Clare though less vivacious. She was almost as tall as Jackie. In her black cashmere sweater, black skirt, and rope pearls, she was perhaps a little overdressed for a morning rehearsal, but Jackie felt that she understood why. The girl's part called for a state of extreme undress from which she probably wanted to dissociate her real self. She played a corset model.

"Don't I know you from Walgreen's?" Jackie asked.

The girl nodded again. "Walgreen's is practically my home."

"You were terrific. How did you get your part?"

"It was a fluke. I was hired to go on the road with *Boy Meets Girl*, but then one of the actors wouldn't go without his wife so I got bumped. That's fair, I guess, because I was the last person to be hired, but I was brokenhearted. And somebody in the cast took pity on me and gave me a tip about this play. So I went and read for Mr. Gordon, and here I am."

The girl's voice was really lovely, her speech quite

cultivated. Jackie had a sudden inspiration. "I think Mr. Sinclair wants to fire me," she said. "Can you help me with my French accent?"

"I can try," the girl said.

Her name was Beatrice Cole, Jackie learned, and she came from Winthrop, Massachusetts. She was actually a product of the sort of education that Max Gordon thought Jackie had. At nine she had attended the Roseneck School near the Swiss city of Lausanne, and at fifteen she'd spent a year in France. In between she'd studied at Fieldston, a prestigious private school in New York, where Clifton Fadiman had been her English teacher. "I was thirteen and madly in love with him," she told Jackie later. "When I found out he was married I spent the next three months writing long, bitter essays against the shackles of matrimony." More recently she'd worked as a fashion model for John Robert Powers.

Patiently, in the alley outside the theater, Bea coached Jackie and rehearsed her, and by the final reading, at eight in the evening, she showed definite improvement. By then everyone seemed exhausted except Jackie herself, who told Bea she was headed for Janet's restaurant to get more coaching.

The following day Jackie was so improved that Bea was impressed. "You've really got it down," she exclaimed. "You're a marvelous mimic." But when the actors were dismissed for the day, Sinclair called Jackie down front, and Bea could tell from their expressions that it was all over.

Bea waited outside the theater. "Would you like to come to my apartment for some tea?" she asked when a stony-faced Jackie finally appeared.

"No, thank you, Bea. I have to head downtown. I'm expected for dinner at some friends of my parents. The Witkins. They—" She gulped and took a deep breath.

"They invited me over to celebrate my first Broadway part. But . . . I'll see you soon."

Jackie was grateful to Bea for turning and hurrying off. She knew that Bea knew she was about to cry.

9

Enter Irving

I was fascinated the minute I met him. It was simple. If I knew he was going to be at an opening at the Copa I would sit at a table near him. If I knew he was going to be invited to a party I made sure I was invited.

—Jacqueline Susann

THE Women opened on December 26, 1936, with Arlene Francis playing Héléne, the French maid, as well as Princess Tamara, a model. The play was a controversial hit, although the powerful critic of *The New York Times*, Brooks Atkinson, called it "Clare Boothe's kettle of venom."

Jackie made friends with the guard at the stage door. She returned for almost every performance and watched from the wings. After a while she knew the script as well as the actual performers did. Her friendship with Bea blossomed, and so did her infatuation with Margalo. Sometimes, anticipating a particularly moving scene, Jackie would burst into tears while Margalo was waiting to make an entrance. Margalo was aware of the girl's attention, but she chose not to acknowledge it. "I never discussed it with her," she recalled in 1985. "I wanted to keep it on an even level. She was very young. I think she had a childish crush on me. She did everything she could to endear herself to people she had crushes on."

A backstage visitor to *The Women* might well have been startled to find Jackie weeping while another actress stood near her, Bible in hand, drowning out Jackie's sobs with a loud chanting of Psalms. It was forty-six-year-old Marjorie Main, a minister's daughter and self-styled evangelist, who played Lucy, a cook. Jackie tried to ignore her, as did most of the cast.

Jackie continued to make her rounds, unsuccessfully. Bea tried to help her get work as a model, but the Powers Agency wouldn't take her. She was too curvaceous, too large-boned—she just wasn't the right type. For two months they worked together doing demonstrations for Lux dishwashing lotion. They received thirty dollars a week, but they had to go to West Forty-fifth Street and perform three times daily, soaking one hand in Lux and the other in Brand X, which Jackie began to suspect contained carbolic acid. In order to keep the job they began sneaking a little preventive lotion on the hand that would be exposed to Brand X, but even so it made their hands red and blotchy and ate away at their fingernails. Some nights their left hands looked so awful that they were reduced to ordering chicken à la king, which didn't require a knife, for dinner. Together they tried ballet lessons and acting lessons, the latter with Madame Ouspenskaya, a student of Stanislavsky, the inventor of "Method" acting. Madame Ouspenskaya ordered Jackie to describe a figure eight with her hands while reciting the alphabet backward. "Maybe we're not ready for this," she giggled to Bea. Shortly after, she left the class.

Although she'd been fired from it, *The Women* was her life. She felt as though she belonged in that play, and she told Bea she knew that in time she would get a part. Someone would leave the cast, and she'd be waiting. She tried to hate Arlene Francis but she couldn't. Arlene was so bright and friendly, and she had such a rich voice, such a hearty laugh, such incredible vivacity. And her accents, as both Hélène and Princess Tamara, were perfect.

Like Bea, Arlene had grown up just outside of Boston and like Ilka she had attended convent schools. Jackie was amazed that those convent schools turned out graduates of so much wit and sophistication. She began to pretend to herself that she'd gone to a convent school, and she often thought of Jimmy, the boy in Cobbs Creek Park who'd given her the rosary beads so long ago. Despite herself, she came to feel a kinship with Arlene, who seemed to be as hungry for approval as Jackie was herself. "I want to be appreciated," Arlene admitted frankly, "and I don't care where or by whom." She also told Jackie to think of life as "the best party to which you'll ever be invited."

And in between other activities, Jackie continued to spend hours at Walgreen's, along with many other performers who were "in between jobs." The place was a Broadway hangout, with pay phones that had become virtually an office for people chasing parts. One of the regulars was not a performer. He was a slender, dark-haired man, only slightly taller than she was, with a round, animated face. Someone had told her he was a press agent, that he got paid for getting people publicity. It seemed a strange way to make a living, but she filed the fact away for future reference.

Then one day she watched one of the phone booths anxiously, hoping for a return call from an agent to whom she'd given that number. The phone had been tied up for a long time, and she was beginning to get alarmed. Then the door opened and the press agent came out, walking toward her. Immediately the phone rang. Both of them ran for it, but he stopped when he saw her determined look. "I'm sure it's for me," she told him. "I'm expecting a call."

She grabbed the phone and said hello breathlessly. And then she turned back to him, the look of expectation fading. "You wouldn't be Irving, would you?" she asked.

He nodded and took the phone from her, but he watched as she walked back to her stool at the counter. And when he was finished with his call, Irving Mansfield went to join her.

"Good news?" she asked as he sat down beside her.

"Yes," he said. "Can I buy you lunch, to celebrate?"

They went to Dave's Blue Room, and over a lunch she could not have afforded he told her a funny story about his meeting at "21" with a man named Alexander Woollcott, of whom she had heard. He had gone to be interviewed by Woollcott, who was thinking of hiring him as a personal press agent, and had joined the famous journalist in a martini, Woollcott's favorite drink. They were double martinis, in fact, and then there were two more, and then two more, and Irving had felt himself growing stiff and numb.

"And the last thing I remember is smiling and smiling as I slid off the chair," he told her. The friend who had arranged the meeting had helped carry him to the men's room and revived him, and he'd somehow got himself home.

"Gee, that's too bad," Jackie said. "I guess he'd have been a good client."

Irving smiled. "What do you mean, 'would have been'? He *is* my client."

After that she saw Irving often, and they began to go out together, though when he found out she was only eighteen he seemed to become more brotherly toward her. But he was a great storyteller and he seemed to know all the show business gossip, so she enjoyed their evenings together even if they weren't romantic. Besides, he took her to all the best restaurants, and he seemed to know everybody. He knew Walter Winchell and often got items about his clients into Winchell's columns. Sometimes he even rode around Manhattan with Winchell, listening to the famous columnist's special police radio and racing with him to the scene of a crime. He pointed out celebrities wherever they went, and even introduced her to some of them.

Irving had a way with words that amused her, though she wasn't sure whether some of his turns of phrase— "figurines of speech," as he called them—were intentional or not. When he told her about getting mad at someone and "unbraiding him a little," she wasn't sure if she should smile. She discovered that he twitched a bit when he lied and that he was color-blind, often wearing clothes that clashed. She began to feel that he needed someone to take care of him.

He was very obviously Jewish, in ways that her own family was not, and he told her that his "maiden name" had been Mandelbaum and that he went to dinner with his parents in Brooklyn every Friday night. He was a little evasive about his age and so was she, but eventually he admitted that he had been born on July 23, 1908, which made him ten years and one month older than she was. His age didn't bother her nearly as much as hers seemed to disturb him, however. He was a perfect gentleman around her, though she had heard that he kept company with some pretty oddball types, including a number of rather shady ladies. She sensed that he might be tiring of this free and easy life and looking for a more solid kind of relationship.

Irving lived in a Manhattan hotel in the middle of the clubs and restaurants that were his "beat." He often dined with his clients, including the bandleader Richard Himber, who was also a personal friend and sometime roommate. Himber, who looked somewhat like a giant teddy bear, was an inveterate practical joker, and after one of their dinners he had whipped out a pair of handcuffs and shackled Irving to his chair. He then left for a movie, while Irving thrashed around furiously. Eventually a police lieutenant was summoned and Irving was released. "Himber wouldn't hurt a fly," Irving said as he told Jackie the story. "I wish he felt the same way about human beings."

On Irving's arm Jackie learned that the social life of a true Broadwayite was centered at Lindy's. Leo Lindy was your adoptive father once you became a regular at his place. Dave's Blue Room was the other hangout, but it was favored by too many chorus girls and singers who seemed to know Irving. Jackie thought that Lindy's was more fun. She could relax there, and she loved it when Leo or his wife greeted her by name, or when Irving traded quips with the comedians. Someone was always dropping by the table, often someone whose name she recognized.

One night a small, slender man came toward them carrying a saxophone. He was Irving's age, but he was much more boyish looking, with dimples and a warm, engaging smile. He put down his saxophone case and held his hand out to Irving.

Jackie looked at the saxophone case, then at the man, whose name was Joey Nash. "But . . . aren't you the singer? The one with the Ritz-Carlton Orchestra?"

"Sure I am. Or rather I was. I'm really a saxophone

player, but I sang with Rich Himber's band for a while.
That's how I met your friend here.

"In 1933 we're playing the Capitol Theater, and one
night when I come out the stage door there's Irving
waiting for me. He's with his buddy Kenny Lyons. Irving
asks would I be interested in a press agent, and I say
truthfully I don't see it. And Irving says, 'I'll make you a
household name. Just give me a chance.' And I say, 'What
do you mean by a chance?' and Irving says, 'Well, I'll
work the first week free, and I'll show you the press
clippings I can get.' I was quite bemused, so I say, 'Go
ahead.'

"Well, it took about twenty-four hours, and there's a
headline in Nick Kenny's column. And then I'm in Winchell's
column and all over. Irving just makes things up, like he
says that Janet Gaynor heard me sing and she's taking me
back to Hollywood for a screen test. I'm in Nick Kenny's
column all the time—the guy loves Irving. The columnists, they generally expect payoffs from the press agents,
at least a bottle of scotch, but Nick uses anything Irving
gives him.

"Then one miserable winter night around ten o'clock my
bell rings. There's Irving with a girl, a short little runt, and
they come in and Irving says, 'Joey, this lady doesn't
believe that I'm George Gershwin and that I wrote "Rhapsody
in Blue." You've still got a piano here, don't you? I want
to play it for her.' Irving knows I've never had a piano, but
I say, 'No, we don't have a piano anymore.'

"And then later on I get a mastoid infection. Irving got
me pretty good publicity, that I was a hero, performing
with this serious condition. But then Irving goes too far.
He goes to the radio editor of the *Journal-American* and
gives him the story that I am going deaf, and that I'm
going to hire an airplane to go over Floyd Bennett airfield
and make a parachute jump to cure my deafness. And that

got on the first page of the newspaper! I said, 'Irving, you're a terrible liar,' and he said, 'A liar, maybe, but never a bore.' ''

Jackie admitted that she wasn't really attracted sexually to Irving—not the way she was to the comedian Joe E. Lewis, or even to Margalo. She had a weakness for people who were either beautiful or charismatic performers, and Irving was neither. Still, she came more and more to rely on him, and to look forward to their dates.

Evelyn came from Philadelphia for a visit. Jackie was delighted; then she discovered that neither of them had enough money to pay for dinner at a nice restaurant. Jackie wanted their first dinner together in New York to be something special.

''I know,'' she told Evelyn. ''There's a man in this town who is crazy about me, and he eats every night in the same place. We'll go by and tap on the window, and he'll ask us to join him. But we mustn't make pigs of ourselves. We'll just order the soup and eat the free rolls.''

The ploy worked, and later Evelyn told Jackie she thought Irving was a ''superior man,'' and that he made up in devotion what he lacked in physical appeal. Jackie was inclined to agree on both counts. Certainly Irving seemed like a man she might be able to manage, in a way Rose had never managed Bob. And he was more than just casually interested in her, she was certain.

His parents, Jacob and Anna (Schiff) Mandelbaum, were simple folk, his father a hardware salesman. The first time Annie Mandelbaum met Jackie, she whispered to her, ''Don't make sin.'' One of Irving's uncles was considered a *meshuggener* like her own Uncle Pete, the wild redheaded dentist. Another uncle, the star of the family, was Samuel Mandelbaum, a federal judge. Uncle Sam had been assemblyman and then state senator from the Lower

East Side of Manhattan, and had served in Franklin
Roosevelt's "Turkey Cabinet" when he was governor of
New York. He and Roosevelt became good friends, perhaps because Sam also had a paralytic condition of his
legs. He often told Jackie, "I have a terrible affliction
which the Lord has smothered with his blessing."

Like Jackie, Irving was an only child, although Jackie
felt she "almost had a sister" in Bea. She was fond of
Elfie, too, but the girl's odd life worried her a little. Elfie
was still "at liberty" from her vaudeville act, still living
with no visible means of support, and evidently not much
concerned about it. At least not until the day Jackie
returned to Kenmore Hall to find her friend, in tears,
surrounded by policemen and a sizable collection of jewelry and fur coats.

Jackie tried to charm the policemen into letting Elfie go,
but she soon saw it was hopeless. The girl had a long
record of shoplifting arrests, they informed her.

"Elfie, the books, too?" Jackie asked as they were
leading her friend away. "All those books you had me read
were stolen?"

Elfie hung her head, for once silent.

A few weeks later Elfie phoned Jackie to meet her at the
Mayflower Doughnut Shop. She had escaped from the
laundry room of the Women's House of Detention, she
told Jackie and Bea, and now she needed cash and some
clothes so she could leave town. They gave her what they
could and she left them, but she reappeared a few hours
later with a handsome fur jacket. She told Jackie she
thought it would look really nice on Bea.

Jackie told Bea about the jacket and pleaded with her to
buy it, but this time Bea was adamant. "I don't want to be
a spoilsport," she said, "but I really think we should
forget about Elfie for the time being. You have to consider
your parents. Next time the police may pick *us* up, too."

Jackie reluctantly agreed, though she never quite got Elfie out of her mind. Years later she might pause in a conversation with Bea and say, "I wish I knew Elfie was all right."

Jackie didn't just hang out at the Ethel Barrymore Theater, where *The Women* was playing to standing room. She also haunted Gordon's office, and in May he told her that Beryl Wallace had given notice that she was leaving to marry Earl Carroll. By popular acclaim Jackie could be first to audition for the part, which was that of another model (*"A handsome wench in a slinky negligee"*). A saleswoman tells the model that she must lead with her stomach when she walks, and the girl replies, "I'll try, Miss Shapiro. (*Tearfully*) But if you had my appendix!" At the end of the scene, after the lead character's confrontation with her husband's lover the negligee model comments, "She should have kept her mouth shut. Now she's in the soup."

Jackie entered the cast of *The Women* on June 2, 1937. She handled the tummy-forward slouch and the appendix line very nicely, and to her delight, she wheedled a bigger laugh out of her first-night audience than Beryl Wallace had ever got with the line. This partially mollified Rose, who wasn't delighted with Jackie's negligee. But even Rose had to preen a little when she and Bob rushed backstage after the final curtain to find Margalo, and even Clare Boothe herself, congratulating Jackie.

Jackie made introductions, and Margalo stopped to chat for a moment with Rose. "We're all so delighted that Jackie finally got a part," she said. "She's been like a member of the family here, and she's volunteered to help me with my Equity work. She's very bright and interesting for one so young, and very nice."

"Thank you," Rose said modestly.

"Yes," Margalo continued, "and she's awfully determined. In fact, I think she may be the most determined person I've ever met in my life!''

Rose was on the verge of asking Jackie what *that* was all about when Bob interrupted. He had noticed two newspaper clippings—head shots of Jackie—taped up on the mirror of her dressing table. Once was from the *Mirror* and the other from the *Daily News*, both announcing that Jackie was entering the cast as if she had a major part. Jackie explained that her friend Irving had arranged them, and that he had also sent her to Murray Korman to have the right kind of photographs taken.

Bob was especially proud that his girl was almost earning a living wage: twenty-five dollars a week, the junior Actors Equity minimum. "To tell you the truth," Jackie said, "if I had to, I'd pay them." Still, she was grateful to Equity. She had never thought much about unions and strikes before she'd met Margalo, but now she was all for them. Margalo's proudest possession was the Equity card her father had issued her when she was in her teens—Number Three.

Jackie adopted some of Margalo's manners of speech— she used the word "Pie" for people who didn't meet her standards of dash—and she carefully put in her diary every word Margalo uttered about acting. Margalo said that "you should never press a point," and that "you should hold the line of your character firmly in hand." When Jackie doubled as an extra in the final nightclub scene, she tried to be so different from the lingerie model that no one would suspect it was the same actress.

Jackie and Bea left the cast of *The Women* in June, 1938, shortly before it closed. They went off to spend the summer in Cohasset, Massachusetts, at the Marshfield Hills Playhouse. Inspired by what she'd learned about dialogue from Clare Boothe, Jackie took a crack at improving some lines in a Noel Coward play, though it isn't known whether any of her revisions were actually used.

In her diary she rated 1937 as an in-between year and 1938 as a great one. She had no reviews to show for her months in *The Women*, but she had gotten her name and picture in the papers, thanks to Irving. And she was meeting some fascinating people through him, show business types like Al Jolson and Vincent Lopez, who was a client of Irving's. He was handling the Andrews Sisters, too, and the Savoy Ballroom in Harlem, and even such heavyweights as Dorothy Thompson, the famous correspondent.

Looking back on her time in New York so far, she felt certain that college would have been a pallid alternative. She was learning a lot about the *real* world, the one she hoped to succeed in, although she was grateful to Elfie's books, too. She'd read a lot when she was younger, but without Elfie she might well have given up books altogether. And that wouldn't do. She mustn't appear ignorant to Clare Boothe and Ilka Chase, or any of the other fascinating people she was likely to meet.

Decades later Jackie would recall that 1938, '39, and '40 made up the greatest three-year interval she ever had. She was getting work, and it appeared that she was also getting married. On November 5, 1938, her picture appeared in the *New York Daily News* under an item that announced, "Jacqueline Susann, featured in 'The Girl From Wyoming' at the American Music Hall, will wed Irving Mansfield, theatrical publicist, next month."

As often happened after good news, "God took away with the other hand." She got word that Bob Susan had had a heart attack, and that he was in an oxygen tent at Mount Sinai Hospital in critical condition. She boarded the next train for Philadelphia to be with him.

Jackie had learned a trick or two from Irving, so she

was able to mine some personal publicity from even this family crisis. On December 10 a long feature story appeared in the Philadelphia *Record* under the headline GIRL QUITS BROADWAY SHOW TO BE NEAR DYING FATHER. The subhead went on to announce, JACQUELINE SUSAN, 20, TAKES DANCE JOB HERE, HOPES AGAINST HOPE FOR PAINTER'S RECOVERY, and the text noted that "Jacqueline, disobeying his last order to her, chucked a job as a lead in a current Broadway success, and came here to dance until the oxygen tent is folded."

There was one sour note that even Irving, consummate press agent and man-about-Lindy's, could not have foreseen. The *Record*, searching its library for a photo, came up with the one taken two years before, when Jackie had won the Earl Carroll beauty contest. In it she stares at the camera through dark, sunken eyes while her mouth is spread in a broad, pasted-on smile outlined in thick lipstick. Under this ghoulish picture the caption read: "Jacqueline Susann . . . awaits father's death."

10

From Cow Belles to Cantor

[Philip] Roth wrote about the son of the strong mother. I'm interested in the daughter of the strong father, like I had. . . . The girl is looking for the big man. Oh, I think she finds him many times until she finds the one who is not at all like her father. . . .

—Jacqueline Susann

*T*HE Girl from Wyoming, the show Jackie left to be near Bob, opened on October 29, 1938, at New York's American Music Hall. It wasn't exactly a play, and the theater wasn't exactly a theater. And Jackie didn't exactly have a featured role. There were ten speaking parts, a chorus of sixteen singing cowgirls and cowboys, and then—for decoration—six showgirl waitresses who neither spoke nor sang and who were listed in the program as "Cow Belles." Jackie was a Cow Belle.

The show, a burlesque spoof of Western melodrama,

concerned "a noble cowgirl who defends a Harvard man."
The American Music Hall was a converted church on
Fifty-fifth serving drinks in an atmosphere more like nightclub than theater. Burns Mantle, the *Daily News* critic,
described it vividly: "The American Music Hall continues
to be the one place of synthetic amusement in New York in
which the audience can be absolutely depended upon to
entertain itself. Probably the show on the stage is important to a few. It cannot be important to many. . . . With a
drink on the table and a loud song ringing clear this is a
happy audience. The less entertainment the more drink.
The more entertainment the less drink. And so it goes.
This may be the bar's best season."

This was the show Jackie was forced to leave in late
November, when Bob took ill. By December 10 she had a
new job as a dancer in a nightclub, though she admitted
that she was inexperienced. As she told the *Record* reporter: "I went to see Joe Sully, the agent, and said, 'I want a
job on the Walton Roof in Philadelphia.' He said, 'Yeah, I
want to be president, too.' I said, 'I know, Mr. Sully, and
I'm not very pretty. I know that. And I'm too tall. But
honest, I'm not so bad in greasepaint.' " She got the
job.

Despite the newspaper's dire predictions, Bob began the
slow road to recovery. The Latona house was sold, and
when he left the hospital it was to their new home, a
"bohemian and stylish" double apartment at 1702-04
Walnut Street, at the corner of Eighteenth. Bob's studio
occupied the front part of the floor-through and the rear
section was their home, though the entire premises could
be opened dramatically if the occasion demanded. As
Jackie's friend Thelma recalls: "You came up in an elevator which opened into a fancy, open foyer. You could look
through and see the studio with the beautiful windows in
front and the apartment, with the grand piano, to the rear."

One occasion for which the place would be opened up was Jackie's wedding, which was now scheduled for April 2, 1939. Bob and Rose had met Irving and had not been overwhelmed, but if this was what their daughter wanted they would not stand in her way. After all, as Rose told her girl friends, she had married a man her own parents opposed. Who was she to argue with her daughter's selection? It did seem strange, though, that Rose—an eminently practical woman—had married for love, while Jackie—who was hopelessly impractical in most things— seemed to have chosen for other reasons. She admitted that she might not be truly in love with Irving, but he was a "catch" in their circles. Everyone knew him around Lindy's and Dave's Blue Room, and he was very smart about getting her picture in the papers.

Bob understood that, of course, but he sensed nonetheless that some chemistry was missing between his daughter and her fiancé, and it saddened him. Still, it was clear that Irving was enormously proud of the prize he had captured. "Isn't she the most beautiful thing you ever saw?" he would ask when Jackie appeared dressed for an evening out. It reminded Bob of Harris Potamkin's attitude toward Rosa, a glow of pride mixed with disbelief at his good fortune. And like Harris, Irving came from a less-cultured background than their own, though he too appeared to be doing quite well financially. Bob still wasn't entirely sure what a "theatrical publicist" was, but at least it seemed to pay well. For Bob, his daughter's marriage was another reminder of his increasing age, along with the graying hair, which he sometimes colored, and the glasses he had to wear for reading and painting. At fifty-two the irrepressible reprobate was reluctantly giving way to the conservative middle-aged man who wore gray suits, starched white shirts, and neckties even at work.

The wedding was an afternoon affair but formal, as

Thelma recalls, and she was "horrified" when she saw Jackie's bridal gown. "It was pearl-gray," she says, "sheer and lacy, very pretty—but gray. Jackie was always different. We giggled when the rabbi said that Jackie would make a good Jewish home and be a good Jewish wife." She retains no impression of Irving at the wedding, though she does recall that the Mandelbaums seemed "so much more Jewish" than Jackie's family.

The rabbi, Dr. Simon Greenberg of the Har Zion Temple, one of the largest conservative synagogues in the country, recalls the wedding well. "I said, as I always do, that I hoped the home Jackie and Irving established would be a proud link in the great chain of Jewish tradition." He could not have known that the "home" Jackie and Irving would establish would, in fact, be a series of hotel suites. After her marriage Jackie would put her home economics training firmly behind her. Years later Irving would say that they had lived in one hotel apartment four years before she discovered it had a kitchen. However, he always added, "If I'd wanted a cook, I'd have married one."

Irving's mother, Annie, a good-hearted, simple woman, wandered teary-eyed among the guests declaring, "Mine son and mine daughter should live and be well. . . . Such a beautiful daughter God sent me." She meant it. She would be a good friend to Jackie, and Jackie would try to be generous toward her. In her old age Jackie and Irving would send a weekly check, but Annie would bank every dime of it and leave it all to them in her will.

The wedding was noted in the *New York Sunday News*, again with Jackie's picture: "Lovely Jacqueline Susann, who played in *The Women* and *The Girl From Wyoming*, will become the bride of Irving Mansfield, Broadway publicist, in Philadelphia today. Jacqueline is the daughter of Robert Susann, noted portrait painter.'' (Irving would actually list his occupation as ''writer'' on their wedding license, perhaps in deference to Jackie's parents. He would also list his parents' Brooklyn address as his home and his retired father as Jacob Mansfield, though his parents had not changed their family name. Jackie, too, varnished the truth, giving Holland as her father's birthplace though she was well aware of the family's glory years in Vilna. Like their new Mr. and Mrs. towels, ''His'' and ''Hers'' matching fibs.)

Few of Irving's pals made it down for the wedding, though Goodman Ace was there with his wife and radio co-star, Jane. Their wedding present to Jackie was one that would be both inspirational and prophetic: a portable typewriter. There were many other wedding presents, of course, but the two Irving would remember best in later years were that typewriter and the check from his uncle Judge Mandelbaum, for whom the whole fancy wedding and the rabbi had been arranged. It was for one hundred dollars.

The newlyweds returned to New York, to a sublet apartment near the East River at 433 East Fifty-first Street, which was also Margalo Gillmore's building. Margalo would recall, many years later, that although she had been charmed at first by Jackie's devotion, having the girl move in on her ''was a little much.'' More important, they returned to Irving's world of Broadway bistros and the celebrities who frequented them, some of them clients and other potential clients to be wooed and possibly won. Among the latter was Eddie Cantor, the comic whose high-powered radio career had been cut short after a speech at the 1939 World's Fair attacking certain public figures as fascists.

Irving's own credentials must have appealed to Cantor.

As press agent for columnist Dorothy Thompson, Irving
had accompanied her to a German-American friendship
rally at Madison Square Garden in February of that year.
Miss Thompson laughed out loud at an anti-Semitic dia-
tribe, and the two of them were escorted from the Garden
by police. Irving saw to it that the episode was front-page
news and was written up in *The New Yorker*'s "Talk of the
Town" column.

The same World's Fair that heard Cantor's speech also
introduced Irving and Jackie to Billy Rose, producer of the
Aquacade, who would become a lifelong friend. And, of
course, there was Irving's client Dovita, the stripper who was
the sensation of the midway. Jackie and Irving took her
parents to see the act, in which a large number of trained
doves flew off with various pieces of Dovita's costume.

Bob, the old roué, was appalled, and in June he expressed
his outrage to an *Inquirer* reporter: "What impressed me
most was the way people stampeded to see midway attrac-
tions which featured girls wearing next to nothing while
they neglected the truly great exhibitions of artistic and
scientific progress," he pronounced. "American girls are the
best looking women in all the world, but to commercialize
them in this manner is to give a wrong impression. . . .
Distinctly, it is a retrogression, a mere vulgar display.
Nudity exhibits at the World's Fair are unworthy of
America. . . ."

Irving was quite successful by now, due in part to the
celebrity hustle he and Jackie were perfecting. For all his
wit and storytelling gifts, Irving had a flat and almost drab
persona, so Jackie began to function as a kind of lure. She
did what wives were expected to do for their husbands—
charm the clients and bring in business—but her seductive
and aggressive manner gave ammunition to the Mansfields'
future enemies, who would later quite erroneously suggest
that Irving "pimped" for Jackie to gain his own ends. As

a friend points out, with a nod to Jackie's allure, "Jackie didn't need anyone to pimp for her!"

Irving had perfected his own solo version of the hustle years ago, as described by his first client, Joey Nash: "Irving's the best namedropper I ever met. Nobody compares to him. And another thing I learned from him, the big celebrities don't want to offend, so they'll say hello to anyone. You can go up to someone like Al Jolson and say, 'Hello, Al, how are you?' and he'll say, 'Hi there,' in return, as if you were his oldest buddy. And the person you're with will be very impressed." And if it worked alone, it worked even better with a glamorous woman on your arm.

The press agent's world is colorful but chancy, as the legendary Eddie Jaffe explains in Studs Terkel's book *Working*. "Being a publicity man is a confession of a weakness," he says. "It's for people who don't have the guts to get attention for themselves. You spend your whole life telling the world how great somebody else is."

But if the Mansfields' public life was glamorous, their private affairs were somewhat less satisfying. Jackie was disappointed in the physical side of her marriage. Irving was nice, but "it just didn't happen," she complained to a friend. "Jackie said that sex with Irving was 'vacant,' although she enjoyed cuddling and body warmth," the friend remembers. "And she liked oral sex, but it didn't ever culminate, as she told it to me. I mean she never really had an orgasm. Later she said it didn't matter to her whether she had an orgasm, as long as she was in bed and had body warmth from a guy. That was what she needed. And she could go on with oral sex for hours and hours; she enjoyed that. She liked to swallow semen. She believed it had vitamins and minerals that were beneficial to her."

She didn't like any man to see her nude, a shyness that Irving blamed on Rose. But Rose was only part of it,

Jackie told her girl friends. The truth was, she didn't think her body was beautiful. She knew how to make it *appear* beautiful in clothes, even very revealing ones. But naked, her breasts hung down too much and her waist was too big.

Besides, sex itself just wasn't pleasant for her much of the time. As Irving admitted many years later, their wedding night was a failure. He wasn't able to penetrate, and, when he finally did on the second night, "There was this ocean of blood. Jackie had to change all the sheets. She was mortified. It was three years before she let me see her undressed."

Jackie was still following the travels of Joe E. Lewis, and whenever he was in town she dragged Evelyn out to see him perform. Evelyn was unimpressed. "I think he's ugly and a flat-out drunk," she told Jackie. Jackie couldn't deny either charge, but she told her friend she "was sick for Jewish comedians." It was a weakness she would indulge more actively in the years to come, but for now she remained only a loyal fan. And she was also loyal to Irving, who considered his wife and himself to be the perfect Broadway couple as they worked the clubs of his "beat." They were both always dressed in the latest fashion, though actress Mary Hunter, who played Marge on Goody Ace's popular radio show, remembers them as "a little too much so."

Jackie was still pursuing her dream of acting success. In December she got a part in a four-act melodrama, first produced in 1913 as *Little Lost Sister*. It was revived in 1939 as *She Gave Him All She Had*, and Jackie had a small speaking part. One reviewer said: "With due respect to Westbrook Pegler, whose father coauthored the original, it stinks beautifully. . . ."

Produced in a "slightly converted restaurant" called Uncle Sam's Music Hall on West Forty-eighth Street, the play was part of an evening's entertainment that was a bargain even by Depression standards. For a top admission of $1.65, the customer got free beer and pretzels as well as a ham sandwich and coffee, and between acts the audience was treated to "four snappy acrobatic acts [including both a high-wire act and ice skaters], a tap dancer, a singer-comedian, and a pretty chorus." After the show there was a community sing, and customers could dance on the stage. No wonder Jackie's performance went unnoticed.

After this gem, Jackie had little luck in her endless rounds until early in 1941, when she got the part of Miss Grumley in a real Broadway play called *My Fair Ladies*, which opened at the Hudson Theater on March 23. Although it starred two gifted actresses, Celeste Holm and Betty Furness, the story of two showgirls pretending to be titled Britons was, in the words of critic Burns Mantle, "that type of comedy that experienced playgoers know is a dud ten minutes after the curtain is up." The kindest comment was that it afforded "some good actors employment— at least temporarily." Jackie was not mentioned as one of the good actors. Despite the offer of free admission to servicemen in uniform, the play closed after thirty-two performances.

After five years of trying to storm Broadway, Jackie didn't even have a scrapbook of reviews to show. Disgusted with the progress of her acting career, she got out Goody Ace's wedding present, the portable typewriter. She took the telephone off the receiver, and she grumbled at Irving to go entertain himself. She finished her first full-length play in five exhausting days and took the manuscript to Margalo Gillmore, who agreed to read it. "This is a very bad play," Margalo told her. "But it's a start. Keep trying. Just don't show this to anyone."

Jackie took her advice. She put the play away. And then she put her typewriter back in the closet.

* * *

Jackie's lack of success in both acting and writing set her to thinking about her marriage and Irving's career. She thought about Rose, who had managed to be a professional "artist's wife" without losing her own identity or profession. Rose had lent her dignified presence to countless social occasions, maintaining her poise even in the face of Bob's flamboyant misbehaviors. The latest of these had occurred at a du Pont–Roosevelt wedding in Wilmington, where Bob was commissioned to do a family portrait. Rose got locked into one of the mansion's thirteen bathrooms, and the entire wedding party searched for her. Later she and Bob both told their friends that it was Bob who had locked her in that bathroom, but none of the du Ponts or Roosevelts ever guessed it. Whether because of the attention the incident got him or in spite of it, Bob got further Wilmington commissions.

Jackie decided that she, too, could be the loyal and helpful wife. She knew that Irving, like most press agents, dreamed of creating a star and then having that star take care of him. Well, Cantor was already a star, but his reputation was tarnished. Given the chance, Irving could set him glowing again in show business. She tried at first to befriend Eddie's wife, but Ida was too simple for her taste. So she decided to charm Eddie instead.

There isn't any doubt she had an affair with him because for the rest of her life she replayed it, almost compulsively, with certain of her friends. It was her first adultery, and she never stopped hating the man who had led her into it and then dropped her. In 1950, with the assistance of her loyal friend Bea, she wrote a three-act play about the experience, and characters clearly based on him recur in her novels. In *The Love Machine* he is amalgamated, along with other comics, into the pathetic Christy Lane. In later years she would keep long lists of those who were with her or against her, but Cantor would always occupy a special place on her hate list. At twenty-two she had tried to play Rose's game and Bob's game at the same time. It backfired.

Broadway legend has it that Jackie and Irving plotted together to snare Cantor, that Irving later came upon them in bed together and quietly excused himself. The story appears to have no basis in reality, and Irving himself has stated, "I was faithful to her through the thirty-five years of our marriage and I believe she was faithful to me."

Margie Hart, a woman who would become one of Jackie's intimate friends, recalls another explanation of how Irving might have discovered the affair: "She told me how Irving found her diary—it was stashed away under a hatbox in the closet—and how she handled it by saying that she had faked the whole thing because she was suspicious of his nosiness and she planted it there. She said he believed it." Then Margie adds, "He might have pretended to believe it because he was, you know, so deeply involved with her."

In any case, both Mansfields were deeply involved with Eddie, whose position as self-appointed "holy evangelist of the American way" required some delicate press relations. As a "one-man nationalist movement," Cantor often made public gibes at fascist and Nazi leaders, with whom the United States was not yet at war. When their diplomats and ambassadors issued howls of protest, Irving responded, through the press, that Eddie asked for no more freedom of speech than was granted the Nazi sympathizers in this country, who were ranting about the "Jewish conspiracy."

Jackie and Irving moved into the Essex House, where Cantor stayed while in New York, and they often accompanied him to the theater or dinner. Marilyn Cantor, the fourth of Eddie's five famous daughters, recalls that "Jackie, who was always dieting, would sometimes skip dinner to take a massage. She'd have her hour-long massage while everyone else ate.'' Marilyn still remembers Jackie as ''the most ambitious person that I ever knew in my life, and in fact my father used to say, 'I've never seen such ambition. Why can't you be that ambitious?' Nothing could deter her from becoming famous.... When Jackie saw Gertrude Lawrence in *Lady in the Dark*, she said, 'I'm going to be the Gertrude Lawrence of my day.' Irving said, 'Honey, you don't sing.' She said, 'Okay, I'll be the Helen Hayes of my day.' ''

Cantor, who was an orphan, liked to ''shmooze'' about his impoverished childhood spent with his grandmother in a basement apartment on New York's Lower East Side. A grammar school dropout, he sang on the streets for pennies, entered amateur contests, and got his first real job when he was seventeen as a singing waiter in a Coney Island saloon. He developed an act with a large-nosed piano player. The two improvised comedic songs to titles suggested by customers. A customer would shout, ''My brother-in-law's mother fell in a sewer,'' and the piano player would improvise a melody while Cantor invented verses to go with it. The piano player was a homely kid named Jimmy Durante, later to become famous as ''The Shnozzola.''

Cantor next went on the vaudeville circuit in a blackface act, and one night when it fell his turn to warm up the audience he was so nervous that he rushed toward the footlights at a frenzied pace, rolled his bulging eyes, clapped his hands, bobbed up and down, and practically shouted a song called ''Rag-Time Violin'' by an unknown East Side neighbor named Irving Berlin. There was thunderous applause. On that night, as a result of a stage fright he would never fully conquer, the patented Cantor style was born.

By 1914, when Cantor was in his early twenties, he had

saved enough to marry the immortal Ida ("sweet as apple ci-i-i-dah"), and in 1915 the first of the five immortal daughters arrived. By 1917 he was starring in Flo Ziegfeld's *Follies*, his first Broadway show, and by 1929's stock market crash he had made and lost two million dollars in vaudeville, Broadway shows, and Hollywood movies. In 1928, with writer David Freedman, he co-authored a best-selling rags-to-riches autobiography called *My Life Is in Your Hands*. The two collaborated on further articles and books, including a Wall Street satire titled *Caught Short*, which H. L. Mencken said "did more to take people's minds off the tragedy of the Depression than any other tonic."

And then there were the endless charities, the patriotic and political causes, the citations, plaques, and honorary degrees that poured in, literally by the hundreds. In a typical year Cantor would serve as New York chairman and national vice-chairman of Brotherhood Week, vice-chairman of the National Conference of Christians and Jews, and grand marshal of the parade for the March of Dimes, which he helped originate in 1936. He raised enormous sums for a number of causes and was active in Actors Equity, whose 1919 strike parade he had led down Broadway, along with the Barrymores, W. C. Fields, Fanny Brice, and Will Rogers. Though not all his causes were popular, by 1941, when America entered the war, he had become an authentic folk hero.

But there were rumors of a dark side, too. Some said the constant charitable works, all highly publicized, were nothing more than an artful form of self-promotion. And there was the matter of his personal finances, where signs of a mean streak often appeared. One writer, Andras Michael, charged that a story he'd submitted was pirated for a Cantor movie, *Ali Baba Goes to Town*. In 1934 David Freedman, the writer who had worked closely with Cantor since the late twenties, sued him for $250,000, claiming that Cantor had reneged on a 1931 contract providing that Freedman be paid 10 percent of the comedian's gross radio income. The trial was highly publicized, with Freedman's lawyer claiming that his client had been "the all-important man in the background of much of the defendant's success."

Freedman had a heart attack and died during the trial, leaving a widow and several small children. According to his son, an eminent religious scholar and author, the Freedmans were plunged into poverty after his father's death and were forced to auction off their furniture. Cantor, freed from a quarter-million-dollar lawsuit, gave the widow a present to help out—twenty-five hundred dollars!

In 1941 Cantor, whose radio career had suffered, announced that he would return to Broadway in a musical called *Banjo Eyes*. He'd appeared on Broadway several times between 1918 and 1927, in the Ziegfeld *Follies* and Shubert productions, but since then he'd concentrated entirely on movies and radio. *Banjo Eyes*, based on a comedy called *Three Men on a Horse*, would be a personal comeback celebrating his twenty-five years in the theater. And Jackie had a small speaking part.

Her role offstage was somewhat larger, though, as recalled by Kate Witkin, a dancer in the show and also a daughter-in-law of the Susans' friends, "It was an Eddie Cantor show. It might have been called 'The Eddie Cantor Story,' or 'The Eddie Cantor Story with Jackie'. . . . Jackie behaved so unprofessionally. It was obvious to everyone why she was in the show. She was not a singer or dancer, and not really a showgirl either. But . . . she was in the opening scene, and in rehearsal when her scene came everybody had to wait, everyone would have to go looking for Jackie. I don't know where she was, she may have been off with Cantor, who was obviously one of her special people. We all felt very antagonistic since we knew she was a special friend of Cantor's."

It seems odd that a star so much in the public eye—and so publicly married—would flaunt his affair with Jackie in front of the cast, yet David Freedman's widow, Beatrice, says that Cantor often had such casual affairs with young girls. And his dressing room may well have been the only private place he had, according to one reporter's description of his hotel life: "Inasmuch as he is always accompanied by his staff and Ida and the five famous daughters, his comings and goings resemble nothing less than a tribal migration. When interviewed the other day, Eddie's entourage already occupied most of a floor, served by four elevators, in a hotel on Central Park South. There were suites for the various members of the family, a large office and four kitchens, and what with an office staff of six, hotel servants and a resident masseur and his wife parading in and out of the rooms, Eddie's life was almost literally an open book."

Banjo Eyes tried out in Philadelphia (with photos of Eddie and Jackie in the papers), then opened in New York's huge Hollywood Theater on Christmas, 1941, just after America had entered the war. It was a lavish production with elaborate moving sets and a huge cast of showgirls, singers, and dancers "hand picked for the ultra in physical attractiveness." The critics were warm to Cantor and called *Banjo Eyes* "the biggest show of the season," noting that Eddie's standards like "If You Knew Susie," "Makin' Whoopee," and "Margie" brought down the house. The show was a success, despite its large investment of $140,000.

But all was not well. Eddie had not been happy even during rehearsals and had wondered publicly why he'd ever returned to the stage. *Banjo Eyes* ran for sixteen weeks and then, after the April 12, 1942, performance,

Eddie had "an emergency minor operation" in his doctor's office. Subsequently he was moved to Sydenham Hospital, though he promised he would return to the show by April 16. Then it was suspended for two to four weeks. Cantor was criticized because he continued to do his radio program from his hospital bed even during *Banjo Eyes'* suspension, and while his unpaid cast was waiting for him to return. Cantor's doctor defended the decision, pointing out that his Broadway role required the fifty-year-old to run a mile during every performance. Cantor released a statement explaining: "I had been in intense pain for ten days prior to surgery. Afterwards complications set in which required a second operation." However, on April 27 Ed Sullivan snidely reported: "Eddie Cantor around town and showing no signs of the medico's recent excavations." What Sullivan omitted as unfit for print in a family newspaper was the story of Ida's discovery of Eddie and Jackie in a hotel room. One of the daughters had tracked them down there, and ran back to fetch her mother and another sister. A daughter climbed up on somebody's shoulders, and tried to squeeze through the transom, frantically waving her arms. Jackie was hiding and missed a lot of details, but she heard Ida scream, "The jig is up." She gave Eddie an ultimatum—close *Banjo Eyes*, get out of New York and away from Jackie . . . or divorce.

Jackie was twenty-three. She later said she found it amusing that in nineteen years she had come full circle, from being the child who discovered her father to being the mistress who was caught, the "other woman." It wasn't so funny at the time.

On May 10, with *Banjo Eyes* suspended for good, Cantor left for Palm Springs. Kate Witkin remembers bitterly, "It was time for Eddie's vacation, and everybody was out on their asses without a day's notice, and off he went into the sunshine leaving two hundred people out of work.'' Those two hundred people received only one-half week's pay, and over $50,000 in advance ticket sales had to be returned. Backers lost close to $100,000 on a show that had seemed a certain money-maker.

With *Banjo Eyes* closed and Eddie basking in the sunshine, among Ida and the girls, Jackie was once again unemployed. And once again, she didn't even have a good review to show for the experience.

—————11—————

Cry Havoc

*With women, you see, it's not just the sex they desire,
as men do, but it's as applause to an actor—it's
approval they want.*

—Jacqueline Susann

WHEN *Banjo Eyes* closed so unexpectedly, Jackie
went home to Philadelphia to lick her wounds.
Theater people were gossiping about her and
Eddie, and everyone knew someone connected to the show
who was now out of work. None of them were friendly
toward her, and their resentment stung. She would list
1941 and 1942 in her diary as bad years, perhaps the worst
she ever had back to back.

She was nervous and thin, too thin to suit either Irving
or Bob, who called her Skinnybones and warned her that
the diet pills and cigarettes were beginning to show on her
face. She was down to 109 pounds and was smoking

constantly, four packs or so a day, Pall Malls when she could get them but any of the wartime brands such as Wings or Spuds when her favorites weren't available. She had begun to harden and some gray was already showing in her hair, though she was artful with makeup and with the falls she had begun to wear. The affair with Cantor—which Bob had divined at once—seemed to have taken its toll on her. Bob felt twinges of guilt, wondering if the example he'd set in her childhood was responsible for her lack of constancy now. She had a husband who seemed devoted to her, yet she had been blithely untrue to him—and with a man her own father's age. "Don't throw love away," he advised her in one of their infrequent personal talks. But why should she listen to him, of all people? Even though he, of all people, might have warned her about men like Cantor, men who played around but always returned to their wives.

And her career seemed to be going nowhere. What little work she got was usually through Irving, bit parts on his friend Goodman Ace's radio show, *Easy Aces*, or through clients such as Fred Allen. She'd had small parts in road company productions and other minor shows, but after six years she seemed to be no closer to real success. She'd tried praying, first in a synogogue where she'd never felt at home, then in private, on a hill in Central Park. She tried to converse with God, even offered Him deals, but it was never satisfying. No one had taught her how to pray, but she kept restlessly seeking something, even if she couldn't say what.

The war was making life difficult. New York's nightclubs and restaurants were filled with uniformed servicemen, who got the best tables at special rates, and many stage and screen stars were deeply involved in USO activities at home and abroad. An amusing item about Joe E. Lewis said that on a USO tour he'd tried to avoid the fifty-five-

pound weight limitation by carrying two suitcases, one
containing his clothes and the other his liquor. Told he'd
have to leave one behind, he left his clothes.

Yet Jackie seemed not to have been affected very much
by the war, at least not directly. She was filled with stories
of the social life she and Irving led in New York, of nights
out with the Aces or with Irving's clients, who hung
around in Lindy's or whatever other restaurants were
favored at the moment, telling stories and cracking endless
jokes. Fred Allen was even funnier offstage than on. His
mock feud with Jack Benny amused millions on the air,
but his very real twenty-year offstage feud with J. J.
Shubert was truly hilarious. J.J. had gotten so angry at
Allen he had forbidden the comic the use of "Shubert
Alley," the privately owned passageway that many used as
a shortcut between Forty-fourth and Forty-fifth streets. The
ban was lifted after Allen, who discovered that half the
alley was owned by the Astor estate, began hopping
through on one foot, yelling to Shubert that he was only
using Astor's half.

Jackie was making friends of her own, too, she assured
her parents. She'd gotten to know the wonderful actress
Jessie Royce Landis, during a brief tour in *Watch on the
Rhine*. She was learning as much about acting from Landis
as she had earlier from Margalo. She'd also made friends
with the *Hollywood Reporter* columnist Radie Harris, who
hobnobbed with Hollywood and Broadway stars. And
she'd gotten to know Rosemary Wilson, wife of Earl
Wilson, whose column covered the nightclub beat and
often used stories about Irving's clients. She'd met Rosemary at Florence Lustig's dress shop, where both bought
the glittery, décolleté outfits they thought suitable for the
Broadway night life. (Another friend, recalling Jackie's
Lustig costumes, describes them as "plastic dresses cut

down to her navel," adding that "her style was bizarre, and I don't mean *Harper's*.")

Bob didn't doubt his daughter's stories, but he couldn't help noticing how forced her gaiety seemed as she told them. He told Rose he feared Jackie was giving up on herself and her career, living vicariously through her celebrity friends. To cheer her up, Rose took Jackie to speak at a Lea School assembly, introducing her as "my daughter, the eminent stage actress."

For Bob, life had undergone some changes since his heart problems. He lived quietly now, rarely appearing in public with his bachelor friends or his mistresses. He went to the fights with his young nephew, Bob Jelinek, and spent time with his young protégé and assistant, Charlie Diletto, who had begun to work with him in 1940 and who would continue, with undiminished loyalty, until Bob's death. He had a separate studio again and was back at work, painting the portraits of politicians that were his bread and butter, often giving them Diletto's torso, regardless of their height or build. He spoke of Diletto and Jelinek as "the sons I never had," and when he died, years later, he left Diletto his brushes, along with the cherished oak cabinet in which he always hid his liquor supply.

Bob and Rose had visited Jackie and Irving in their Essex House hotel apartment, and were struck by how few homey touches they saw there. True, Jackie had always said that the two most important words a bride could learn were "room service," and certainly she had never shown any desire to keep house. Even so, it seemed that the only personal possession in sight was Bob's portrait of teenaged Jackie, and even that wasn't actually hung, but was leaning against a living room wall. Even the refrigerator was bare, except for some prescription drug and a jar of olives. It was as if no one lived in the place, and Bob found it depressing.

So did Rose. She stared into the refrigerator, studying that jar of olives. Then, shaking her head, she said, "Well, I guess Mr. Cantor drinks martinis when he's in town." There was a sharp edge of sarcasm in her tone that would have cut Jackie if she had heard.

As 1942 drew to a close, Irving Mansfield was waiting for his draft notice, and Jackie was still waiting for her first substantial part, becoming more glum with every passing month. Bob grew increasingly worried. What would she do when Irving was drafted? She could never live on a private's salary, yet what kind of real job might she find?

"She could be a telephone operator," Rose suggested. "She has beautiful diction, after all. It isn't what she wants, but if she has to do it, she'll do it." As it turned out, Rose's "telephone operator" remark had a weird kind of prescience about it. In February Jackie arrived for a surprise visit, without Irving, looking more radiant and happy than she had since her opening night in *The Women*. She had just gotten a part in producer John Wildberg's road company version of *Proof Through the Night*, now retitled *Cry Havoc* and due to open in Chicago the first of March. She was to play a telephone operator, one of several women who are acting as volunteer army nurses in a bomb shelter on Bataan. It was an all-female cast once again, like *The Women*, but this time she had a significant part. She had quite a few lines, and she even got to sing one song, a wartime pepper-upper to the tune of "Hinky Dinky, Parley-Voo."

"And do you know one of the main reasons I got the part?" she asked, giving Rose an odd smile. "Well, it was because I also have to whistle part of the song. And I'm a good whistler. Remember?''

Cry Havoc had had a strange history. Written by Allan Kenward, a director at MGM, it had run successfully in California, had been sold to the movies, and had opened in New York under the Shubert banner. There was considerable advance publicity, but there was also disagreement and dissension between Shubert and Kenward. As a result, the play closed on January 2, 1943, after only ten performances at the Morosco Theater. John Wildberg, who had produced such successes as *Porgy and Bess* and *One Touch of Venus*, was in that closing-night audience. He described it in a newspaper story: "The 13 girls in the revised version of the West coast hit took their curtains with tears streaming down their faces. The audience applauded and cheered and cried with the girls. And I sat there knowing darned well I was going to reproduce that show, put it on the road and call it by its original name, *Cry Havoc*."

Wildberg moved fast. Only two of the original cast were willing to go on the road, and none of the stars. He would need someone to bring in the audiences in the towns outside New York, someone who would capture attention. But who?

He found his attention-grabber in the unlikely person of Margie Hart, the famous vaudeville stripper, who came forward to take the part of Grace, an ex–burlesque queen who is trapped in the shelter with the other volunteers.

Jackie always referred to the play as "a Theatre Guild production." In actual fact it was not a production mounted by the Theatre Guild but rather an independent effort sold by the guild to fill out its subscription quota. The tour was to last for several months including dates in Detroit, Columbus, Toronto, Baltimore, Boston, Newark, Brooklyn, and Harlem, then known as "Upper Manhattan." It did well on the road, garnering enthusiastic audiences and some mixed reviews, most of them more appreciative of the cast than of the play itself. New York critic Ward Morehouse journeyed to Boston and wrote: "*Cry Havoc* wasn't a good play in New York. It isn't here, and I wonder if it ever was. But the project has given employment to some attractive people . . . I suspect, too, that with its all-female cast it will be taken up here and there by the summer theaters." Unfortunately for Jackie, most of the review attention focused on Flora Campbell and the surprisingly talented Margie Hart, though one Chicago critic did note that "Jacqueline Susann, the switchboard operator," was "excellent." It would be one of the very few critical mentions Jackie had gotten for *any* performance.

Jackie was enjoying herself. She got to room with the redoubtable Margie Hart, and in Chicago she discovered that Joe E. Lewis was appearing at the Chez Paree. She left a message at his hotel, signing it Mrs. Irving Mansfield, and got an immediate reply, inviting her and any others of the cast to see his show.

Jackie and another actress jumped out of their army nurse uniforms and into something more appropriate—which in Jackie's case was her most clinging and lowest-cut red dress. They hustled to the packed nightclub and were shown to a ringside table, where a chilled bottle of Dom Pérignon awaited them.

The lights dimmed and Joe E. sauntered out into the spot, tanned and dapper, and began to speak in that well-known gravelly voice. Drink in hand, he introduced his piano player, Austin Mack ("Austin plays a pretty good piano. I think it's a Steinway"), then took a healthy slug from his glass.

"Some people say I drink too much," he told the audience. "And I resent it. I don't deny it, I just resent it.

My doctor says not to drink, it cuts down your years. Maybe, but looking around I see more old drunks than old doctors."

The show was vintage Lewis, and the audience loved it. Wandering around the room, he explained that he wanted to have fun now, "not when I'm old and wrinkled, but while I'm young and wrinkled," and assured them that he was in great shape, and that "every artery is hard as a rock." He noticed a man who appeared to be snoozing and told him, "I don't mind when you fall asleep, but it hurts me when you don't say good night." And of course there was the trademark line: "You know, they say you only live once. But if you play your cards right, once is enough."

He kidded Austin ("When Vladimir Horowitz came here last week and heard him play, he stood up and shouted, 'Waiter, my check!' ") and then segued into some of his "special material," songs laced with sexual innuendo for which he was famous. One concerned the plight of a bridegroom who found his wedding hall so crowded that, as the refrain repeated, "the groom couldn't get in." ("A tenor got in, a soprano got in, even Vincent Lopez and his goddamn piano got it—but no room for the groom!")

Jackie prayed he would stop by their table when his act was over, and she had already prepared a note she would try to give him if he did. It read: "Could be I'm prejudiced. Seems to me your groom didn't *want* to get in."

To her delight he did stop by, and she managed to hand the note to him during the introductions. He glanced at it and slipped it into his pocket, then gave her a long, speculative look. She smiled back, boldly, wondering if she'd shocked him.

At last he smiled, too, and said, "Listen, why don't you have supper with me in my suite. Both of you, I mean," he added quickly.

Jackie accepted instantly, but her girl friend, who could

sense the sparks flying between Joe E. and Jackie, begged off. What happened after that is remembered with amusement by Margie Hart: "It was like having a room alone in Chicago. The first morning when Jackie came home to change her clothes, she told me all about Joe E. and how funny he was, and what they did the night before. They stayed up until four in the morning doing joints. She told me how they ordered breakfast, and then she said, 'He dumps his toast in the eggs, and when I looked at him strangely he said, "How else can you eat eggs?"' She never said that he was a great lover, only that he was 'a love.' But she was hot and heavy for him."

Another cast member, Maxine Stuart, also remembers that Jackie would often look at her watch during a scene, "to see how many minutes were left until she could go and meet Joe E." She adds, "Joe E. was obviously crazy about her, but I'd think he'd be the worst lover material. He was a pretty good drinker." Jackie gave Joe E. a diamond-studded cigarette case inscribed with all her love, and later, when the play moved on to Detroit, she commuted back and forth as often as she could. She even informed Joe E. that she intended to ask Irving for a divorce. After all, he was going into the army and wouldn't be around for a while.

Irving had in fact received his draft notice not long after she'd left for Chicago. He was due to report soon to Fort Dix, New Jersey, which would leave their Essex House apartment untenanted. Before he left, he lugged Jackie's clothes to Bea Cole's apartment at the Royalton Hotel, a favorite theatrical hangout on West Forty-fourth Street near the Algonquin.

Joe E. was dubious about the marriage. A confirmed bachelor at forty-one, he was, in the words of his biographer Art Cohn, "a gay, gregarious, carefree Villon who lived without restraint, leaping from bar to bookie to boudoir. . . ." He lived out of trunks, forever on the move. How long could Jackie take his kind of life, Joe E. asked her, sleeping all day and staying up all night in smoky clubs, drinking, listening to his same jokes and songs every night of the year? Jackie was undeterred. She was determined to marry him, and she was going to ask Irving for a divorce immediately.

The method she chose for doing that is well remembered by Margie Hart, Maxine Stuart, and probably all other cast members who were present that day. As Margie recalls it: "Irving was in the army, stationed in New Jersey. She wrote him a Dear John letter which she read aloud, at full blast, to the entire cast. It said, 'Irving, when we were at the Essex House and I had room service and I could buy all my Florence Lustig dresses, I found that I loved you very much, but now that you're in the army and getting fifty-six dollars a month, I feel that my love has waned.' It was very funny but it was serious, and they did split. When she got back to New York she moved into the Royalton with Bea, where her clothes were."

Jackie's letter may have seemed funny to the cast of *Cry Havoc*, but it isn't hard to imagine how amused Irving must have been when he got it. As for Joe E., love was mixed with a large measure of pure fear. He had heard enough of Jackie's background to know it was far more lofty than his own. She told him she had gone to Bryn Mawr, and her parents ran with Philadelphia society. People like that would surely disapprove of him and the way he lived.

In a panic he got on the phone to the USO and begged for an assignment that would take him "to the other side of the world." They sent him to an advance base of the Fifth Air Force somewhere in New Guinea.

───── 12 ─────

Daddy's Girl

*Jackie once said to me, "No matter who a woman sleeps
with, or how many people, she only thinks of one man."*

—————John Wingate

*A*FTER Joe E. decamped, Jackie went somewhat
crazy. As Margie Hart recalls: "It was whoever,
wherever—whoever the local comedian was, that's
who she was having the affairs with. . . . She had no guilt
about it. It was fun. . . . I think her comedians were more
for laughs. . . . She never did say anything about *anyone*
being a great lover." She remembers a photo Jackie
autographed years later: "I one time accused her of having
a complex, that she had to prove something with all those
guys. On the picture she wrote, 'So I have an inferiority
complex. . . .'"

As the play moved from city to city and Jackie moved
from comic to comic, Irving was also on the move. After a

brief stint in New Jersey he'd gone to Atlantic City to complete basic training, but as usual he was looking for a way to improve his situation. He asked Fred Allen to put in a word with the head of the special services division, pointing out how Irving's show business contacts might be of use. The result was an assignment to assist the well-known agent "Swifty" Lazar in casting an upcoming air force musical to be called *Winged Victory*. The job involved considerable travel, so perhaps the sting of the Dear John letter was soothed by the hectic activity.

Jackie was still in *Cry Havoc*, at least in body. As Maxine Stuart recalls: "She had a good part and she was okay in it, but acting was not really her thing. She had a wonderful sense of humor about herself as an actor. She would say marvelously funny things in rehearsal, and sitting around on stage before the curtain would go up. But she had absolutely no concentration in terms of acting. *None*. She would play with her hair during a scene, it was like that. . . . She was also a little knock-kneed, and it made her walk a little funny. . . . I really don't think she was motivated enough. She had stage presence, yes, because she was beautiful, great to look at, and she had the kind of humor that can be more important than any of the other stuff, so I'm sure that from the front you looked at her a lot."

The beauty that impressed Maxine Stuart was hardly an accident of nature. Jackie was becoming an expert with makeup, as Margie Hart remembers: "She had beautiful eyes. No makeup at all she still had pretty eyes. Aside from that, her features were a little heavy, a little coarser than her mom's. Rose was closer to being a genuine beauty but Jackie was dark like her mother, dark hair. She helped it along by making it even darker. . . . She was the first one to get me to wear a fall. She used to get them on expertly. She was terrific at makeup, too. But I remember

her looking particularly tired one night, and she said,
'Look at these circles. You watch how I can make them
disappear.' So she used the lighter base under her eyes,
and then she blended rouge in clear up to her eyes to
take away that tired look. She used to get a fantastic
makeup. She could do it very expertly and very quickly.'' But her appearance was not her most memorable
quality, Margie recalls. ''What I liked most about Jackie
was her gutsiness and her self-confidence. She was full
of that.''

In Boston Jackie's self-confidence would be put to the
test, at least in the love department. There, in her pursuit
of Jewish comics, she became involved with Georgie
Jessel. A friend of both Cantor and Lewis, Jessel may have
represented a special sort of triumph for Jackie—one
laced, perhaps, with a touch of revenge.

Jessel was well into his forties then and at least two
decades older than Jackie. He'd been a child performer,
first in a youthful singing trio that had included Walter
Winchell and later in a vaudeville partnership with Cantor,
who played a blackface butler while Jessel wore a powdered
wig. He'd had a stormy marriage to Norma Talmadge,
which had ended when he'd found her with another man
and fired a .45 revolver at him. (The bullet missed, but hit
a gardener in the rump two blocks away.) The next bride
was a sixteen-year-old, Lois Andrews, from whom he was
in the process of getting a divorce at the time. ''My
mother was thirty years my father's junior but they were in
love,'' he told Jackie. ''What was good enough for my
father is good enough for me.'' When Jessel married Lois,
Cantor had quipped to a nightclub audience, ''George
was to be here tonight but he couldn't make it. His
wife is teething.'' At twenty-four Jackie felt over the
hill.

Jackie liked Jessel's stories, particularly the ones about

Joe E. and Eddie, but he was always complaining about how broke he was because of all his problems with women. Years later at sixty-three, Jessel would lose a $200,000 paternity suit brought by a young actress. Still, he was amusing. And more important, he seemed to be going places. In fact, Jessel was heading for Hollywood in June, 1943, on a seven-year contract to produce movies for Darryl Zanuck. Surely there would be parts for her.

Back in New York, *Cry Havoc* made a ring around Broadway on the "Subway Circuit," beginning with Brooklyn's Flatbush Theater on June 2. Subway Circuit theaters were essentially neighborhood vaudeville houses, but sometimes they booked musicals and plays. Margie Hart attracted more stage-door Johnnys than Jackie had ever seen but, when the show played the Bronx, Jackie acquired a fan of her own. Nicknamed Jackie's "stage-door Joan," she was a plump, conventional-looking housewife in her thirties who attended every performance, bringing Jackie little gifts—flowers or vegetables from her Victory garden or homemade preserves. Jackie decided to chat with the woman who said she envied the way Jackie could keep her voice low and sexy while still somehow projecting it into the balcony. She was trying to model her own voice on Jackie's, she said.

Jackie was feeling remorse about the Dear John letter to Irving. And her public affairs with the Jewish comics were almost part of the Broadway folklore. One wag suggested a revolving door on her bedroom, with maybe a hatcheck concession in the hall. And what had it all got her? She was feeling used and abandoned, even by Joe E. Lewis, the one among them she had cared for.

She might have felt less humiliated if she had known that Joe E., risking his life in New Guinea, thought of her constantly. He told his piano player that for once he was really in love, and that he would probably marry Jackie after all. He even decided to write to her, though he didn't know where to send the letter or what to say in it. Finally he sent her a postcard care of "Actors Equity, New York City, U.S.A." On it he wrote: "This war is making me so damned patriotic I get up every morning with red, white and blue eyes." It may have been the closest thing to a love letter Joe E. Lewis ever wrote, but by the time it reached Jackie, months later, it was already too late.

Jackie was beginning to miss Irving. He'd been very good to her, working to get her name and picture in the papers and leaning on everyone he knew to get her auditions and parts. And she couldn't cook, couldn't even make decent coffee. Irving got up first and went out for containers from the coffee shop. He brought it to her in bed, and he fought to get her awake and going on mornings when she'd taken too many pills.

Thinking of what she had done, she felt ashamed. All their money—which wasn't much because they lived so high—was still in her name. She gathered up their bankbooks and returned them to Irving.

Having done that, she felt less guilty about her next move: a frontal assault on J. J. Shubert, the temperamental producer who had been encouraging to her when she first came to New York. He was easy enough to find. When he wasn't in his office he was either at his front table at Sardi's with the ladies of his current harem or at one of his famous "soirees" in his penthouse apartment upstairs. Then in his middle sixties, J.J. led an unconventional domestic life, spending evenings and weekends with his faithful companion, Muriel Knowles, but lunching with other ladies by the dozen. Muriel did not concern herself with J.J.'s lunches, or his afternoon dalliances. She often helped entertain the harem at dinner, and favorite girls were invited to spend the weekend with J.J. and Muriel at their home in Mamaroneck, New York. These girls, including Jackie, learned that if you wanted to join J.J.'s inner circle, you had to bring your wartime ration book along and give some of the stamps to J.J.'s cook.

Jackie was invited to Mamaroneck several weekends that summer, and sometimes she brought Margie Hart. It was obvious that Jackie was that summer's special pet. J.J., or "Jake," was clearly charmed by her humor, her deadpan skill at poker, and her cleverness at Monopoly or almost any other board game. In August he offered her the featured role of Greta, a comic maid, in the fifth New York revival of his favorite production, *Blossom Time*. Her name would appear sixth in the billing, in letters far larger than she'd ever had before.

In the operetta's ridiculous plot composer Franz Schubert, in love with Mitzi, writes "Song of Love" for her and than asks his best friend to sing it. Mitzi falls in love with the friend, who has a beautiful tenor voice, and a heartbroken Schubert composes the "Unfinished Symphony" to express his pain. Finally, at death's door, he writes the "Ave Maria." Curtain. The story was awful but Sigmund Romberg's score was based on Schubert's own melodies. The result was something of a classic, with songs that moved many to tears.

The original production opened at the Ambassador Theater on September 29, 1921, and ran for two years, spawning innumerable road companies and revivals all over the world. It had been playing continuously somewhere ever since and had been the source of staggering profits. It didn't require stars, so that Ma Simmons found plenty of able singers who would work for a pittance. The period costumes, which were recycled until the colors faded into a uniform brown, permitted décolleté but otherwise covered the actresses' bodies, which meant that expensive "Class A" showgirls were not required. According to Jerry Stagg, author of *The Brothers Shubert*, the many companies of *Blossom Time* became known as sanctuaries for "amateurs and would-be's, never-was's and old-line retainers." The revivals always played the Ambassador, and often J.J. would drop a road company into the theater for one night so he could truthfully advertise it as "direct from New York."

The fifth revival opened there on Saturday, September 4, 1943. J.J. gave Jackie bigger billing than her part really called for, but once again she was ignored by the critics. J.J. had ordered her picture sent to the papers and the *Herald Tribune* ran the photo with its review, but without comment.

The Times complained that "it is the comedy of *Blossom Time* which approaches the frightful. Its humors are heavy handed and dull." This comment was a special blow to Jackie because J.J. had allowed her to add new bits of dialogue, including a reference to the meat shortage and rationing as "a concession to 1943."

Jackie had the good fortune to share her dressing room with Helen Harris, the understudy to the lead. Helen did not become as close as Bea or Margie had, but she remembers Jackie very fondly. Indeed, forty-three years later she still treasures an unusual souvenir—a one-piece undergarment, a lightweight but effective "corsellete" that Jackie bought for her because it left no lines or ridges under a tight-fitting dress. "It was most unusual for those days," Helen says, "because it wasn't bulky. You could take it off and slip it into your purse. And it cost twenty-five dollars, almost a week's salary for Jackie."

Helen detested "Jake" Shubert, whose "car was there for Jackie night after night. . . . He was gross and fat and dirty, and I never saw him without his one dirty tweed suit. . . . Once Jackie was very late and she kept the whole cast waiting. The director yelled at her in front of every-

one: 'Susann—you come in here late just one more time
and you'll be back walking the streets again.' Jackie just
laughed, but I was mortified for her.''

Helen did not meet Irving, who was still away, but she
was privy to many stories about Jackie's other beaux. The
theater was dark on Sundays, and one weekend Jackie
dashed off to Philadelphia to meet Joe E., who was back
from New Guinea. The next weekend she got a telegram
from Cantor, which she showed to Helen, before their
rendezvous. But, much as she loved her comics, Jackie
was also seeing some Hollywood types that fall. She met
Walter Pidgeon at a party and flirted with him, after which
he showed up at her hotel apartment. ''He knocked on the
door,'' Jackie told Helen, rolling her large brown eyes in
delighted mischief, ''and what do you suppose he wanted?''
Jackie had interesting girl friends too, including Renee, the
Sardi's hatcheck girl who did legwork for Winchell and
who often dropped backstage to collect gossip.

On opening night during first intermission Jackie heard
someone screaming and cursing out on the street. She
rushed out in her long gown and bonnet to find J.J.,
apoplectic and quivering, in the throes of a temper tantrum
as violent as those of her own infamous Uncle Pete. The
object of his wrath was a critic named Louis Kronenberger,
who had savaged recent Shubert productions. J.J. had
barred Kronenberger from all his theaters, but this time the
critic slipped in. He was taking notes for a review that
would complain, ''The Shuberts have put their faith in
Model T,'' when J.J. discovered him and had him ejected.

J.J. was not the only producer on whom Jackie set her
sights. Another was the tall, lean, distinguished Vinton
Freedley, from a Main Line Philadelphia family. Freedley
had a high squeaky voice that belied his looks. She'd
heard much about him from her girl friend Radie Harris.

Radie was in love with Vinton and had been his lover for several years.

One of the most extraordinary producers in the world, Vinton had produced such hits as *Lady Be Good, Girl Crazy, Anything Goes, Funny Face,* and *Cabin in the Sky.* He had a phenomenal eye for talent, having either discovered or developed such stars as Nanette Fabray, Fred and Adele Astaire, Carol Channing, Ginger Rogers, Bert Lahr, Bob Hope, Mary Martin, Jeanette MacDonald, Jimmy Durante, and Danny Kaye. He'd also discovered Ethel Agnes Zimmerman, a stenographer who'd been moonlighting in a stage show at the Brooklyn Paramount when he'd put her in Gershwin's 1930 *Girl Crazy.* Gershwin, hearing her sing, told her, "You've got talent. You'll be a star. But never, never take any singing lessons." Miss Zimmerman, who changed her name to Ethel Merman, took his advice.

Vinton Freedley was married and had children, but he and his wife had an "understanding." So that posed no problem for Jackie, at least. But how to meet him? She could hardly ask Radie to introduce them, so she turned instead to his buddy Ward Morehouse, who had come up to Boston to review *Cry Havoc.* He'd told her he liked her work, but then he'd failed even to mention her in the review. Maybe he would feel he owed her. And the two men did hang out together a lot, at Sherman Billingsley's Stork Club and at "21."

She went for a massage and a facial (a tricky operation that involved ironing her face with wax, resorted to only in do-or-die situations), put on her prettiest fall and her latest Florence Lustig, and set out for "21" at cocktail hour. She spotted them at Freedley's customary table and wandered over, greeting Morehouse warmly and hanging around just long enough to be invited for a drink. When she left an hour later she and Freedley were on a first-name basis and he had said he hoped to see her again. And she believed him, because he'd been flirting outrageously.

Jackie's affair with Vinton surprised Margie Hart, mainly because "Radie and Jackie remained good friends, and Jackie used to talk to Radie about her crush on him. I don't know how long it lasted. It was kind of a serious thing at the time." Serious or not, they saw each other frequently, and Vinton hinted that he might have a part for her soon.

They were still seeing each other that November, when Irving reappeared in New York. A few weeks before *Winged Victory* was to have its grand opening he'd been ordered to report for a physical and was found to have a duodenal ulcer, not surprising considering the state of his marriage. Released from the army because of his medical problems, Irving shed the uniform in favor of a blue suit and his old job as Fred Allen's publicist. He attended *Winged Victory*'s triumphant opening in New York on November 20, though he was no longer associated with the production.

On January 13, 1944, Vinton Freedley's new musical comedy *Jackpot* opened at the Alvin Theater, starring Nanette Fabray and Betty Garrett, along with the popular singer Allan Jones and comics Benny Baker and Jerry Lester. Jackie, who wasn't mentioned in the reviews, played Edna, one of the seven ex-wives of a Tommy Manville playboy type. Critics hated the libretto, co-authored by Guy Bolton, Sidney Sheldon (later to become a best-selling novelist), and Ben Roberts. One remarked that, "It hardly seems possible, but according to the program it took three men to write the book of *Jackpot*."

And Jackie's hand was almost in it, too. She said she had "smelled disaster" in the out-of-town tryouts, and in Washington she had holed up for a thirty-six-hour session of solitary rewrite in an effort to salvage the play. Instead of being pleased, Vinton was offended. He stormed out of her hotel room, pausing for a parting shot. "Write your own play, Jackie," he squeaked, "and then I'll look at it."

Early expectations for a new Freedley musical had generated large advance sales, so the play limped along at the Alvin for sixty-seven performances before closing on March 11. Marion Lulling, a dancer in the show, recalls a lot of backstage camaraderie. "I never thought Jackie would write a book," she says. "But she was a very nice girl. She was always busy running out for her date, and once she invited me out for a blind date but I couldn't go. I recall she was dating Irving, her future husband, at the time. But I didn't think they were married."

No one remembers exactly when Jackie and Irving reconciled, but it appears to have happened either during *Jackpot*'s New York run or not long after. Margie Hart says, "Irving had ulcers or something. He got out of the service and Jackie really wanted to get him back. By now he was working again and making good money, and she had kicked around a while. She got him to take her out one night for dinner, then she kind of lured him up to the room and he took her to bed and then he got up and put his clothes on and said, 'That's it.' She called me the next morning to tell me she was mortified, but apparently it worked because ultimately she did get him back. That was the only time I ever saw her really down—when she thought she'd lost Irving. He was her provider."

——————————13——————————

Year of the Woman

> *There's a certain type of girl, usually blonde, who tend
> to get killed off. Look at Monroe, Harlow, Carole Landis,
> Jayne Mansfield. They seemed to fulfill a death wish.*
>
> —Jacqueline Susann

*I*N her later ranking of the years of her life, 1944 was
classed as an in-between year. She got Irving back, she
found a dentist who could properly cap those teeth she
had always hated, and she discovered a masseuse who
could help straighten out her posture and improve her
awkward walk.

In the spring, not long after *Jackpot* closed, Jackie's
most ardent and embarrassing admirer caught up with her
again. It happened at a war bond rally where Jackie and
five other actresses were being auctioned off to the highest
bidder. They, along with singer Allan Jones from the
show—the sole male in the group—would be escorted to

the various Broadway night spots by whoever bid highest
for each of them in the auction.

When the bidding opened on Jackie, a voice shouted
out, "One hundred dollars!" The auctioneer, surprised
that the voice was clearly female, said, "Ma'am, I
think you want Allan Jones. You're bidding on Jacqueline
Susann."

"That's who I came to bid on," the woman replied.

"But you can't go to the Stork Club with Miss Susann,"
the auctioneer argued.

"Oh, I've never been to the Stork Club," the woman
said. "I'd love that." She went on to point out that, since
Miss Susann was a married woman, it would not be proper
for her to go out on the town with a man.

As a reporter later recounted, "The authorities attempted
by every means possible to dissuade her, but the more they
argued, the more she insisted. Jacqueline Susann, the
beautiful actress, was escorted on a tour of the Broadway
nightspots by a chubby housewife from the Bronx."

The lady, of course, was Jackie's "stage-door Joan,"
who had taken her life savings from the bank, embarked
on her first long subway ride to Manhattan, and bid twenty-
five hundred dollars for an evening with her idol. And with
that curious night on the town Jackie not only gained a lifelong admirer, but a free clipping service as well. For years
thereafter every New York review and column mention
would arrive in the mail a few days later, neatly clipped
and underlined, in an envelope from the Bronx. And the
housewife sent everything, including the unfavorable reviews Irving often tried to keep her from seeing. If they
were really bad they often had consoling notes attached,
such as "What a jerk!" or "This guy needs glasses" or
"Seems they're jealous of your well-deserved success."

The column mentions were frequent and Jackie made
use of them to send messages to Vinton Freedley, to twit

Irving—or, in one Earl Wilson column, to do both: "Irving Mansfield, after seeing the best-dressed Vinton Freedley at the Stork Club, complained to his wife Jacqueline Susann that he wears good clothes but he never looks as well. 'Maybe he takes his clothes off when he goes to bed,' Jacqueline suggested." But Irving gave as good as he got, as witness another Wilson item shortly after, a tongue-in-cheek reminder of just who her provider really was: "Not knowing that her husband, Irving Mansfield, Fred Allen's press agent, puts nothing before a good gag, actress Jacqueline Susann recently supplied his name as a reference for a checking account. . . . He wrote to the bank that he had known her 'since her startling escape from Bedford Reformatory,' that she 'no longer had kleptomania,' and was 'pinup girl of three thousand police stations and one thousand post offices' and was 'well-informed, being able to tell at a moment's notice where to get opium or how to open a stubborn lock.' P.S. The bank may recognize kidding but she didn't get the account."

Some of the column mentions were provided by Radie Harris, whose friendship Jackie had managed to hold on to even during her off-and-on affair with Vinton. Radie, too, had dreamed of a career on the stage, but after a teen-age riding accident cost her a leg she turned to chronicling the escapades of actors for the *Hollywood Reporter*. Now successful, she gave herself star-studded late-October birthday parties that included on the all-woman guest list such names as Mary Martin, Wendy Barrie, Martha Scott, Ethel Merman, Jessie Royce Landis, Annabella, and Gertrude Lawrence, who was herself a former lover of Vinton's.

Another of Radie's guests was "The Incomparable Hildegarde," the highly paid chanteuse who was then the darling of café society and Jackie's latest idol. She attended all of the singer's openings at the Plaza Hotel's Persian Room, awed by Hildegarde's fabulous gowns and the dramatic style with which she performed her theme song, "Darling, Je Vous Aime Beaucoup." Jackie was so smitten that she even became a blonde, briefly and unsuccessfully, in emulation of Hildegarde's gleaming upswept hairdo. She seemed the epitome of glamour, from her shoulder-length white gloves to her off-the-shoulder gowns, which earned her the nickname Miss Armpits, to her handmade lace handkerchiefs—she had over a hundred of them—and the red roses she handed out to members of the audience.

In truth, Hildegarde was a cultured, somewhat shy, and deeply religious woman, a strong supporter of many charities and the Catholic Church. In 1950 she would swear a vow of chastity and become a lay Carmelite nun, leading to her later investiture as a lady of the Equestrian Order of the Holy Sepulchre of Jerusalem, the highest papal honor bestowed on a lay person.

Hildegarde's late-night soirees, held after her performances in the large Plaza suite she shared with her producer-partner, Anna Sosenko, may well have been the most prestigious parties in all of browned-out wartime Manhattan. Their guests included Nobel laureates, artists, musicians, writers, members of Roosevelt's cabinet, admirals, generals, possibly even a stray cardinal or two. Jackie longed for an invitation, and Radie lent her support to the campaign, constantly observing "Jacqueline Susann at the Persian Room" in her columns. It took more than a year. The earliest mention of Jackie in Hildegarde's meticulous diary occurs on October 1, 1945, when she notes that Jackie and Irving attended a soiree. Mentions of Jackie would be frequent thereafter.

Meanwhile, in early 1944 Jackie was marking time, enjoying her reconciliation with Irving and their Broadway social life but getting nowhere professionally. Then, in June, she got a part in the road company of *Let's Face It*, a Cole Porter musical that had run successfully on Broadway in 1941 and again in 1942, with Danny Kaye in the lead. When the touring company opened in Chicago it featured Benny Rubin in Kaye's role, with Jackie as one of three matrons who, believing that their husbands are philandering, seek revenge by inviting three GI's to spend a weekend with them. Critics agreed that Rubin was no Danny Kaye, but they were kind to Jackie. One wrote: "Jacqueline Susann, who made such a hit recently in *Cry Havoc*, shows her versatility in a comedy song and dance part as one of the matrons on the loose." Another called her "excellent," and as she pasted the reviews in her scrapbook (carefully omitting sources and dates, so a casting director might get the impression these were New York reviews) she scribbled, "Am I any nearer to success?" Later she added, "Slightly," and still later, "Seems around the corner." But another scribble after that adds, "Oh, yeah!"

The Broadway version of *Let's Face It* was produced by Vinton, who introduced Jackie to his drinking buddies Richard Krakeur and W. Horace Schmidlapp, the road-company producers. A young Princeton graduate, Schmidlapp was "affluent in no small way." He backed race cars, Broadway productions, and a mile-a-minute lifestyle when he wasn't off duck shooting on his Southern estate.

Schmidlapp became friendly with Jackie and was thrilled for her when, on the road, she received an accolade in the August issue of *Esquire*. The critic George Jean Nathan had compiled a list of "the most appealing ladies who graced the stage of the New York Theatre during 1943–4." Jackie was on it! As Greta in *Blossom Time*, Nathan wrote, Jackie ended the servant problem for the men in the audience.

After the brief tour she returned to New York and Irving, and to good times at the clubs. Those days are vividly recalled by Betty Bartholomew, then the teen-aged sister of Jackie's neighbor and intimate friend Jean Bigelow, later wife of the composer David Rose: "Jackie and Irving and my sister and her husband Joe and Margie [Hart] and some others, they all went to Toots Shor's a lot; that was their hangout. They were all very close friends and they used to play poker in our apartment. [Eddy] Duchin and [Joe] DiMaggio would come, and sometimes Toots if he could get away from the restaurant. And sometimes Artie Hershkowitz, the Mansfields' attorney who was also Fred Allen's brother-in-law. Jackie was a good card player, a very intelligent person and a wonderful gift of gab. . . . Jackie was so glamorous in my eyes, as a child looking up at her. From morning till night she was fixed up beautifully, and she was a wonderful storyteller. . . . Jackie loved beautiful clothes; she loved furs and she loved jewelry. . . . She was just wonderful, good-hearted; she was always giving or loaning something to someone; she was just a fabulous woman. . . . If she loved somebody she gave of herself.

"Irving was Irving," she remembers. "He and Jackie were very mutually interested in a lot of the same things, and I think that's what held the marriage together. When we were out with them Irving told stories and he was always kind of the center of attention. . . . His whole life was talking, thinking, eating show business, and he always knew the inside of everything." Then she adds, "But Jackie with the girls, that's when she would light up and really be funny and do her thing."

One of Irving's favorite stories concerned "a turnip-eared gent named Sonny Reardon" who ran a couple of dubious nightclubs in 1934. Reardon, impressed with Irving's college education, hired him to ghost weekly love poems to an Earl Carroll dancer who had great legs and a literary mind. Since the job paid fifty dollars a week, Irving jumped at it, and for the next two months he delivered the weekly poem to Reardon every Friday promptly at five.

Memorable lines: "My heart is a chasm of deepest despair/ On account of because your love isn't there." Then one Friday he forgot. On Saturday a frantic Reardon phoned, demanding the poem he'd promised his girl. Dashing to catch a New Haven opening, Irving cribbed a few lines from Shakespeare and dropped them off.

On Monday a friend located Irving at Lindy's. White-faced, the man advised Irving to get out of town fast. Seems Reardon had taken his girl friend and her mother to Katharine Cornell's *Romeo and Juliet*, and they had recognized the latest lines of poetry in a second-act speech. As Irving told it, he hid out with a friend in Connecticut, where he would probably be hiding yet if his erstwhile employer had not been picked up on a concealed-weapons charge, nailed for an old homicide, and sentenced to thirty years in Sing Sing.

Was the story true? Were any of Irving's stories true? Perhaps an answer lies in one of his favorite lines, planted in a column as Goodman Ace's quip but actually his own: "I caught Irving Mansfield in a truth the other day." Irving and Jackie lived in a world of storytellers, the same world chronicled by that famous observer of Broadway, Damon Runyon, at whose table they often sat. For Runyon, and for others gathered during the days at Lindy's, "Mindy's" in his tales, or nights at the Stork Club, a good story was always the main thing, and mere facts should never be allowed to get in the way.

Though Runyon was by then well past his prime, having lost his larynx and trachea to throat cancer a few years before, he was still to be a major influence on Jackie. She, too, hoped someday to write about the Broadway scene, though she would naturally do it from the "dolls'" point of view and in dialogue that came from the real speech of the show business people she knew, rather than the street slang of Runyon's hustlers and horse players. For a while, though, she adopted some of his favorite phrases: "on the Erie" for eavesdropping, "monkey business," "drop dead," "cheaters" for glasses, "dukes" for fists, "knock" for criticize, and "croak" for die. Mainly she was fascinated with how this fourth-grade dropout had made a fortune writing of the world he knew, and she often saved the sheets from the notepad he used to communicate. And it was because of his losing battle with cancer that she began her own lifelong struggle with her cigarette addiction. When Irving complained about her growing dependence on pills, she would argue that cutting down on cigarettes was more important. After all, did he want her to "croak" like Runyon, with tubes in her throat?

Runyon was dating a girl friend of Jackie's, a singer named Dorothy Dennis, who was often mistaken for Dorothy Lamour. Dennis had another beau, a multimillionaire named Al Strelsin, whom she married soon after Runyon died in December, 1946. Jackie encouraged Dorothy to set her cap for Strelsin, and she helped her to plot and plan and juggle the two relationships. "Women only own the world when they are very young," Jackie said. "A girl has to make the most of those years." Yet Jackie, who could herself have courted a millionaire, Schmidlapp the wealthy playboy-producer, didn't want him. "I'm different from some of my girl friends," she acknowledged later. "I don't want to live through a man or spend my life shopping."

If 1944 had been a so-so year, it ended on the upswing, thanks to J. J. Shubert. This time it was a featured part in a play called *A Lady Says Yes*, a vehicle for the Hollywood pinup queen Carole Landis, but billed as featuring "thirty lovely ladies of fashion and passion." Chief among them were Jackie, who played a somewhat obtuse girl named Hildegarde, and an amusing Ziegfeld stripper named Christine Ayers, who when asked if she ever posed in the nude replied that she "always had something on even if it was only a string of pearls and a dark light."

Jackie and Christine had the two major supporting roles, and even though the script was dreadful, Jackie loved every minute of the December previews in Boston and Philadelphia. In her hometown, where the press was usually kind, her character was described as "a dim-witted damsel given to hard puns, but still not hard to look at." Those quips were relentless, including such lines as "Do you like Kipling?" "I don't know, I never kippled."

It seemed for a time that the play might succeed on glamour alone, but the New York opening at the Broadhurst on January 10, 1945, once again drew heavy fire from the critics. John Chapman, noting the play's title, added: "The critic says no." He was less negative about Carole Landis's famous sweater-girl figure, which he described as "something of a national monument in human architecture. Even in repose she always looks as though she has just taken a deep breath." It was noted that the script was the pseudonymous work of a plastic surgeon, bringing forth the inevitable "No amount of facelifting can save it." And the Arthur Gershwin score drew equally predictable comparisons with those of his famous brothers, one critic observing that it "proved without much question that musical talent does not necessarily run in the family." Once again Jackie was ignored by the New York critics, though Earl Wilson did run her picture with the caption "Jacqueline Susann who plays the dumb doll in *A Lady Says Yes* is really the smarty pants Mrs. Irving Mansfield of saloon society." The play closed on March 25, after eighty-seven performances.

For Jackie the months with *A Lady Says Yes* were doubly rewarding, despite the play's dismal reception by the press. Not only was her role a major featured part in a Broadway play but her association with Carole Landis turned into one of the most intense relationships of her life. Carole fell in love with Jackie and was not reticent about showing it. She sent flowers, followed by a tiny pair of perfect pearl drop earrings, even tried to present a mink coat from her personal wardrobe. And Jackie, no doubt flattered, reciprocated, later describing to her girl friends how sensual it had been when she and Carole had stroked and kissed each other's breasts.

The two were contemporaries, only a few months apart in age, and they found they had much in common. Both had dreamed of stardom; both had won early beauty contests; both had even tried an adolescent dance act with a female partner; and both had had early marriages to men named Irving, though Carole's had not lasted. As Jackie headed for New York, Carole was tackling California, where the movies quickly found a place for her ample physical charms. Her big break came in a Hal Roach, Sr., film called *One Million B.C.*, a part she supposedly got because she ran more athletically than the other candidates.

By 1945, when she and Jackie had their encounter, Carole had been married three times (or four, if you count two teen-age marriages to the same man). Later that year Jackie fixed her up with Schmidlapp, but that marriage too would end less than three years later, when Carole fell in love with Rex Harrison.

The depth of Jackie's feeling for Carole, and the nature of their physical relationship, can be surmised from the tender lesbian affair described in *Valley of the Dolls*. In it, Jennifer North, the blond beauty based at least in part on Landis, has the only truly satisfying love of her life with a woman—a brunette like Jackie. It is echoed in the affair between Judith and Karla in *Once Is Not Enough* and in the posthumously published interplanetary fantasy *Yargo*, whose heroine admires the title character's male attractiveness yet has her only deeply emotional relationship with another woman, soothing her grief with kisses and caresses.

Though the Landis affair was not to last, it may have had an interesting by-product: On February 2, Radie Harris's column announced that Jackie was "a sight for sore eyes in her new mink coat." Irving had presented it to her, thus fulfilling her high-school-yearbook ambition. The coat cost over three thousand dollars and involved monthly payments for a year, but according to Irving, Jackie was so smitten with it that she could hardly be persuaded to let go when time for summer storage came. A second gift was a three-room apartment Irving had managed to sublet at the Hotel Navarro on Central Park South, just a few steps east of the Essex House and Eddie Cantor, and one block west of Hildegarde's Plaza suite. The Navarro (now the Ritz) then housed famous transients, including Richard Burton when he was in town, as well as long-term residents, though the Mansfields' twenty-six-year sojourn may have set some kind of record.

However, when *A Lady Says Yes* closed in March, Jackie was once again out of work, and again in some doubt about her future as an actress. Now, with time on her hands and Damon Runyon's stories as inspiration, she again turned to Goodman Ace's wedding gift, that typewriter languishing in her closet. Inspired by Runyon's tales of Broadway "dolls" who dreamed and schemed about marrying rich, as well as the dreams and schemes of some of her own girl friends, she came up with what she considered a really bright idea for a play. Based on the somewhat oddball life of a Navarro neighbor named Lya Lys, the play would follow the adventures of a lovable but untalented former movie actress in her attempts to marry a rich man, a plan complicated by constant reappearances of various ex-husbands. One ploy involved the acquisition of a fancy dog, which the heroine hopes to use as bait to catch the dog-loving rich man's attention and whet his interest.

Jackie described the general plot to her friend Bea Cole, whose acting career was limping as badly as Jackie's. Bea thought it sounded terrific and suggested Jackie write it. Jackie, perhaps remembering her earlier attempt, had a countersuggestion: "Why don't we do it together," she said. Bea agreed, and Jackie instantly called Goodman Ace and asked him to give Bea a typewriter, too.

Jackie began calling Bea "Moss," after playwright Moss Hart. Bea retaliated by calling Jackie "George," after George S. Kaufman And thus rechristened, "George" and "Moss" sat down at the typewriters, inserted paper, and typed: "Act One. Scene One." Bea remembers vividly what happened next: "We stared at those four words for three hours and then got hysterical. We had a hundred twenty pages to go."

Nevertheless, the two persevered. "We wrote it in three and one half weeks," Jackie said later. "Then we went up to Bea's mother's home in Mahopac. Mrs. Cole gave us a room and we shut ourselves up for ten days and revised our script. Walks were forbidden." In fact, Bea was so concerned about Jackie taking "the first hitch home" that she convinced her they should remove their makeup and smear their faces with lanolin—"bear oil," they called it—while they worked. It was guaranteed to keep them from straying, and it was good for their skin.

Rewrites and revisions went on through the summer and into the fall, interrupted by Jackie's late-summer appearance in a Toronto revival of Philip Barry's *Animal Kingdom*. Jackie picked up the best reviews she'd ever had, including one that called her acting "subtle and sensitive," and declared herself indebted to Robert Henderson, the director. She would remember that debt and repay it more than twenty years later.

Back from Toronto, Jackie showed the finished script, now titled *The Temporary Mrs. Smith*, to Vinton Freedley, no doubt reminding him of his promise to look at her play. Freedley was impressed, so impressed that—as one newspaper report put it—"he gave them a fat check, and guaranteed production before April." Jackie and Irving next went to work on their friendly columnists. In the following months mentions of the play appeared in Radie's column and also in those of Earl Wilson, Ward Morehouse, and even Winchell. It was described as hilarious, a "brilliant lampoon." Jackie screwed up her courage and wrote to Sam Zolotow, drama editor of the stately *New York Times*. She asked him to run an item about the play, which "they hope to have ready for production within the new year." To her delight, a couple of mentions did appear in the *Times*.

While she awaited the play's production, Jackie brought her home economics training to bear on her wardrobe, sewing hundreds of tiny sequins on a gown by hand and—as her friends recall—leaving a trail of them wherever she went. But that, too, paid off. A Radie Harris column described Jackie at one of Hildegarde's Plaza openings wearing "a sextacular midriff gown of white sequins," adding that she was "the most sensational femme on the dance floor, who had all the wolves howling."

One distressing note in all this was her constant recollection of a phone call she had gotten from Carole on V-J Day in Toronto. Her friend had been seriously depressed, wondering what would happen to her now that she would no longer be needed to entertain the troops and raise war bond money. Carole explained that she was getting too old for the sexpot roles but that no one would give her a chance to act, and she had told Jackie how lucky she was to be so smart, because maybe she could make it as a writer.

Maybe so, Jackie hoped as she waited for Freedley to
get the show rolling. All in all it had been a very good
year, she thought. There had been better parts, a flattering
notice or two, not to mention the affair with Carole,
however brief. There were the much-sought-after invitations to Hildegarde's parties. There was even the Navarro
apartment, with her beloved room service always at hand,
a dream come true in itself. And, of course, there was her
play. She could hardly wait to see it on the Great White
Way.

—————14—————

The Temporary Mrs. Smith

My measure of success is money. I have no interest in artistic triumphs that are financial losers. I would like to have an artistic success that also made money, of course, but if I had to make a choice between the two, I would take the dough.

——Damon Runyon

WAITING for Freedley to cast *The Temporary Mrs. Smith*, Jackie remembered a promise she'd made to Irving: If a producer took the play, she would throw away her diaphragm. All their parents wanted a grandchild, Irving wanted to be a father, and she herself had dreamed of having a daughter since she was seven years old.

Money shouldn't be a problem. With a lot of prodding from her, Irving was making use of his experience with *Winged Victory* to break into the production end of show

business. He was already earning $600 a week as a radio
producer, and his prospects in the business looked good.
Even though their Navarro apartment was expensive—$650
a month—they could certainly handle the expenses of a
child. They had room, too: In addition to their good-sized
living room and bedroom, there was a small study that
could be converted to a nursery.

Jackie loved the apartment. It wasn't grand—the high
rent was for the location, but it was large enough for them,
and it had a lovely view of Central Park where she had a
new "wishing hill" for her private musings about life and
her infrequent "bargains" with God. The apartment's
kitchen was a makeshift arrangement in a closet, but the
hotel had excellent room service and a good steakhouse,
which meant she didn't have to cook anyway. It would do
for fixing bottles and baby food.

Jackie tried to create an atmosphere that was "sexy
and glamorous, but not vulgar." She bought a bar for
entertaining, a long black couch set off by lipstick-red
pillows and chairs, black lamp bases shaped like human
torsos topped with red and gold shades, a vermilion
upholstered swivel chair, and a spinet piano over which
hung a large Robert Susan nude. (Framed photos of
Jackie and Irving with various celebrities would be
added over the years.)

The closets, however, were far too small for the wardrobe
she was accumulating—or wardrobes, to be more accurate.
She was compiling a daytime collection of Rosalind Russell–
style suits and dresses to suit her playwright image, but her
after-dark wardrobe still featured what she called her
"sireen" dresses and colorful, glittery "fuck me" shoes.
And for Sunday night dinners or lunches out with the
ladies, there were all her stylish hats from such designers
as John Fredericks, Sally Victory, Walter Ferrell, and Lily
Dache. Jackie and Margie and Rosemary Wilson had a

competition going over hats. Jackie was sewing again and got good at making turbans. At a restaurant Van Johnson tried to buy one right off her head to give to his wife. Jackie depended on Irving to rein in her excesses. "When I dress too fussy or too young, Irving starts singing 'On the Good Ship Lollipop' à la Shirley Temple, and I go change."

Pills were a part of Jackie's way of life; she rarely gave them a second thought. Booze was dangerous—it could ruin careers—but sleeping pills got you a good night's sleep and "dexies" put pep in your step in the morning. Jackie took both a red and a yellow pill at bedtime; one worked faster, the other longer. Like many theater people in her crowd, she kept a list of midtown doctors who gave prescriptions with no questions asked. Another nice thing about pills was that they ended arguments with Irving. Jackie often told her friends that pills were the way to close a discussion with a man. Swallow them right in front of him, and go to sleep. What can he do?

Hildegarde had insomnia, too, but she didn't like to rely on chemicals. Prayers helped her sometimes, and exercise. They disagreed on pills but Jackie admired Hildegarde, and asked her to be godmother to her baby.

Though the two women were quite different in personality and outlook, Jackie greatly respected the self-possessed, quietly spiritual Hildegarde. The singer became Jackie's confidante and religious adviser, a person to whom she could come for talks about her moral dilemmas, her pain at the human condition as she watched Runyon die, her "deals" with God. Hildegarde took her to mass, bought her Catholic medals, gave her a prayer book, heard Jackie's "confessions" about her earlier sexual affairs and even some that were to follow. Jackie's fascination with her latest idol ran deep, and it came to include far more than an admiration of Hildegarde's beauty or talent or flair for glamorous clothes, on which she spent a reported ten thousand dollars a year.

Deep down, it may well have been Hildegarde's independent spirit that Jackie admired most, as she often had admired women who relied on more than good looks or male support for sustenance. Audiences "crave the bright-eyed girl," she once said bitterly, but the truly gifted—people like Margalo, Clare Boothe, Hildegarde, even Rose Susann—could always earn their own way and take care of themselves.

Runyon's public deterioration and imminent death were something of a turning point for Jackie, and she discussed his condition compulsively with her friends. She told Hildegarde she had promised God she would give up liquor if he survived, but she must have known it was a bargain she would not likely be held to. Would a *woman* in Runyon's condition dare appear in public at all, she wondered? And if she did, wouldn't she more probably be shunned than lionized? Just growing old could be catastrophic for a woman, as it seemed to be for Carole Landis and others whose very existence depended on youthful sex appeal. Better to have a deeper talent, and maybe better yet to have a husband and child to support and nourish your life.

Yet appearance was still of utmost importance to her. She heard producers and critics speak of this actress's flabby thighs or that one's spreading hips, and the sagging chin that seemed to affect most women (flange, it was called) became a constant fear that sent her to the mirror daily. Her masseuse, Margaret Roberts—or Roberta, as Jackie called her—became her adviser of physical conditioning, first as part of Bonwit Teller's staff and then through a private arrangement that brought the masseuse to the Navarro, and later to the Mansfields' apartment at 200

Central Park West. To Roberta she always remained a heroine, even when tragedy had hardened her and success toughened her in the eyes of many others. "She was a very beautiful person," Roberta says now. "I never heard her say anything nasty about anyone."

Slowly but surely, despite her sexy clothes and man-grabbing reputation, Jackie was becoming a "woman's woman," the center of a circle of friends who would later be described, in a *New York Times* article by Marylin Bender, as "dramatic-looking, clothes-conscious and talked about." Most of her friends were in show business, and most of them recall the Jackie of that period as gracious and considerate, loyal and warmly supportive. Although she later admitted to Evelyn, her high school sidekick, that she cultivated some people who were "good for business," her loyalty to many of her women friends has never been questioned.

Dorothy Dennis Strelsin recalls those days vividly: "I never heard of ladies' lunches before I met Jackie. She would have us to the Navarro for lunch or tea. She would order up from room service, or get cold cuts. We would sit around and gab and gossip . . . and she had a wonderful quality about herself. She was like a mother confessor. Everybody who had problems would always go to Jackie, and she would be right there to help everybody out. . . . She was always there for them. That was a great quality of hers."

One of the girls for whom Jackie "would always be there" was the blond actress-showgirl Joyce Mathews, then married to Milton Berle. The two women had seen each other around, but Joyce remembers that they had their first real conversation in the ladies' room of Bill Miller's Riviera, a nightclub across the river in New Jersey. Joyce was flamboyantly good-looking, "like a vanilla ice cream cone" (in Berle's words), and Jackie was aware that together they were traffic stoppers, often referring to the two of them as Rose Red and Snow White. As they became closer they began to share each other's wardrobes and jewelry, even though Joyce was two inches shorter and somewhat rounder than Jackie. "We wore exactly the same size," Joyce remembers. "We lived the same lifestyle. We had lunch at '21' all the time. We shopped at Wilma on Fifty-seventh Street. It was sort of like Florence Lustig. Jackie always had to watch her weight with salads and no big desserts, but I didn't watch mine." And Joyce, too, was heavily involved with pills.

The daughter of a legendary stockbroker, Joyce was herself a legendary shopper, a woman Berle describes as the only person he knew who "went to Tiffany's with a shopping list." He adds that "she tossed money around as if it were confetti. I was making big money, but between me and my horses and Joyce and her shopping sprees, I was always in hock." Their six-year marriage would end in divorce in 1947, though they would remarry in 1949 and redivorce in 1950. After that, Joyce would have two marriages to Billy Rose, in 1956–59 and 1961–63, prompting Jackie to refer to her friend as "Joyce Joyce Berle Berle Rose Rose."*

Joyce remembers that Jackie helped in her marriages to Billy Rose, who was very fond of the Mansfields, and that Jackie often served as a go-between when she and Billy quarreled. Milton Berle tells a different story, blaming the breakup of his earlier marriages to Joyce on the girl friends, including Jackie: "Joyce, instead of working out

---

*Actually there had been yet another marriage, an unhappy youthful fling with the exiled son of a Venezuelan dictator. This nasty experience Jackie would later adapt and bestow on the Jennifer character in *Valley of the Dolls*.

her own problems, was a great one for asking advice, and whoever got in the last word, that was whom Joyce listened to. We might have had a minor blowup at breakfast. By lunchtime she had just about forgotten it, unless she happened to mention it to one of the girls, who said, 'What do you mean you're going to forget about it? I wouldn't take that from him!' Joyce came home all steamed up again."

But whether wise and supportive, as Joyce and others recall her, or meddlesome and manipulative as some have claimed, there is no doubt that Jackie presided over a lively and attractive female conclave that included Joyce, Dorothy Dennis Strelsin, Bea Cole, Navarro neighbor Jean Bigelow and her younger sister Betty, Margie Hart, and many others who came and went. "Irving was always behind her," Dorothy adds, "backing her up a hundred percent in anything she wanted to do."

One thing she wanted to do was to become pregnant, a project Irving approached with some enthusiasm. His performance was to be examined from unusual angles, as it turned out, because Jackie celebrated her first check from Freedley by purchasing a large stand-up mirror and experimenting with different positions from which to view the act, much as she had experimented after the "incident" when she was four years old. "It was such a wonderful moment in my life, I wanted to watch the miracle of conception," she later explained to interviewer Claire Safran. "I wanted to be aware in every possible way."

As 1946 began, Jackie and Bea, "two Cinderellas of the theater," were having a great time with the press. Bea described their play as "a synthesis of Broadway, Hollywood, Cafe Society, and everything we laugh at and hate—and envy." Jackie added modestly, "George Bernard Shaw doesn't have to worry about us." She also reminded

reporters that she was still an actress first, and that she
would take a good part if it was offered.

Almost instantly one was. She got an offer again from
the director who had allowed her to collect her first really
good reviews. Robert Henderson, recalling Toronto and
perhaps encouraged by all the publicity she was getting as
a budding playwright, asked her to audition for the lead in
a new comedy he had lined up, *Between the Covers*. A
cynical look at the world of book publishing, it had been
written by Charles Raddock, a frustrated novelist whose
serious book had been turned down by a New York
publisher who then brought out a potboiler penned by a
striptease artist. Jackie signed on January 21 to play Fudge
Farrell, the stripper modeled after Gypsy Rose Lee, who
writes a bestseller. *Between the Covers* was set to preview
in Wilmington in late February, and then to tour Cleveland,
Detroit, and Chicago, reaching St. Louis in March.

The weeks of rehearsal were a time of high spirits for
Jackie, despite bewildering developments reported from
Freedley's office. His top choices to direct *The Temporary
Mrs. Smith* had declined, so Billy Gilbert had been hired
instead. (He would later be replaced by Thomas Mitchell,
then rehired when Mitchell backed out.) And Luba Malina,
the musical comedy star who had just finished a successful
run in *Marinka*, was being coy about her availability.
Freedley and Jackie both thought her a natural for the
leading role, but Malina couldn't seem to make up her own
mind about it. She said yes in January and changed her
mind in February—a mere taste of the flipflops she would
perform in the months to come.

Jackie enjoyed the rehearsals of *Between the Covers*, the
clippings, the nights on the town or performing before the
mirrors with Irving, even the vicissitudes of her play,
which Freedley continued to find difficult to mount but
which Jackie found easy to publicize. On February 14, a

columnist described how a Latin Quarter customer "laughed so hard and applauded so much that Jacqueline Susann, a few tables away, sent over a note, and asked, 'Will you please sit between critics George Jean Nathan and Louis Kronenberger at the opening of my play, *The Temporary Mrs. Smith*? The seats are on me!' " Jackie was so excited by all her activity that some days she would take a pill or gulp a scotch on the rocks to bring her down from the morning dexie.

Then she discovered she had gained almost five pounds, all in her waist as usual. With the skin-tight costumes she would be wearing in *Between the Covers* she could not afford extra poundage, so she went on a near-starvation diet of nothing but the pills and an afternoon scotch until dinner, which was just a steak and salad. By the third afternoon she was so shaky that a ringing telephone made her drop the highball glass, which broke and covered her scrapbook with scotch and particles of crystal. She took the mess to her new wishing hill across in Central Park, hoping the sun would dry it and bake out the smell before Irving got home. Shaken, she promised God she would give up pills, if she was pregnant, "until Jill is born." A few days later her period came, leaving her disappointed but a bit relieved that she could continue her diet of pills and booze.

In late February and early March, as the road company of *Between the Covers* moved through Wilmington and several other cities toward St. Louis, the script was almost universally panned. Jackie and her costumes seemed to be the only items of interest to the critics, one of whom said: "Jacqueline Susann caught what laughs exist with a bold sexy travesty on strip-tease queens. Her brief costumes are eye-stunners and this gal has plenty to reveal."

The costumes led to some bitter disputes between Jackie and playwright Charles Raddock, who charged that she was "overplaying her part" with her gyrations and seminudity, and complained that playwriting was "difficult enough without dirty politics, upstaging and downstaging." He was particularly incensed by the very brief bathing suit she wore in one scene, and finally he appeared with a white beach robe and demanded she wear it on stage. She did, but artfully managed to let the robe fall open. The audience loved it. Raddock did not.

The reviews didn't help Raddock's mood. In Cleveland a critic wrote: "The only striking lines in *Between the Covers* belong to Jacqueline Susann, and they're the shapely kind. A dress she wears in Act II drew a collective gasp on opening night. It has a split skirt, bare midriff and a halter neck and fits like the skin of a grape." Jackie put the clippings in her scrapbook alongside the cheesecake publicity shots, one of which shows her bending forward in a low-cut gown, her bosom almost entirely exposed. In another she sits on a table top, wearing a seductive smile, high-heeled shoes with bow ties at the ankles, and a dark dress with a white belt. The dress is sedate enough, but Jackie was twisted so that the camera looked straight up her crotch, a shocking photo for a newspaper to print in 1946. With some coaching from veteran model Christine Ayers, Jackie was learning to sizzle for the photographers.

The newspapers followed the feud between her and Raddock with growing fascination. On March 17, Robert Sylvester noted in the *Daily News*: "That $265 bathing suit which designer Florence Lustig fashioned for Jackie Susann in the touring *Between the Covers* and which disappeared from the show with Miss Susann in it, continues to be a point of bitter dissension." Sylvester next reported that Jackie had been fired out of town, but a telegram from her corrected him: "I wasn't fired. I am fleeing for my life."

Jackie returned to New York in a good mood. *She* had

gotten flattering reviews and a few fat paychecks in the starring role, and Freedley seemed to be making some progress with her own play, having at last persuaded Luba Malina to sign a contract. News from Philadelphia was not so good—Bob's heath was failing again, and so was Grandma Ida's—but the mirror act at the Navarro seemed to have paid off. In March she missed her period and her breasts began to tingle, and by April 11 Hildegarde was noting in her diary that "Jackie thinks she's pregnant." Indeed she was, as her bouts of nausea and her insatiable craving for sweets confirmed—along with her doctor. To celebrate their seventh anniversary, Irving gave her a gorgeous stone-marten stole to add to her growing fur collection.

The news from Freedley's office began to turn somewhat sour. Luba had "remembered" an earlier commitment and was again withdrawing. For a time only Freedley's associate Richard Krakeur would take Jackie's calls, though she did manage to persuade them to consider Millard Mitchell, the great character actor who had appeared with her in *Between the Covers*, for a major supporting role as one of the heroine's ex-husbands. He was signed in May. Luba was persuaded to stay on once again, but people were beginning to wonder why Freedley, who had produced so many successful extravaganzas was having so much trouble with a small-cast one-set comedy.

In June the movie funnyman Mischa Auer was signed for his first Broadway role as another of the ex-husbands, and in July Billy Gilbert was replaced as director by veteran actor Thomas Mitchell. This brought another resignation from Luba Malina, who complained that Mitchell was "an actor, not a director." Freedley threatened to file breach-of-contract charges against the Russian-born actress, but he had to back down.

In August the play went into rehearsal, with Francine

Larrimore in Luba Malina's role. A road tour was set, beginning at the Playhouse in Wilmington, Delaware, on September 13.

Freedley was still dissatisfied with the play as the Wilmington opening approached, and he was especially uncertain about Francine Larrimore, a former star who had not appeared on Broadway since 1934. The actor Arthur Siegel remembers the somewhat strained train ride to Wilmington: "Jackie carried big when she was pregnant. She didn't hide it much. And Freedley was upset. He was always very well dressed, a fashion plate, a man of distinction—but on the day we got on the train to Wilmington, we got on the club car, and he had two different-colored socks on. . . . We thought this was so funny—Jackie, too." Siegel recalls that on Yom Kippur he asked Jackie if she fasted on the holy day. "She said, 'I'm not Jewish,' and I was shocked. I said, 'Oh, really?' and she said, 'But I've got a little Jew in me now,' and she pointed to her belly."

The Wilmington opening drew mixed reviews, although *Billboard* predicted the play would be a box-office winner. The plot was described as revolving around the efforts of a fading screen star (Larrimore) to marry a rich man, after having married several times for love. One of her ex-husbands is a former flagpole sitter (Auer) and another is a theatrical press agent (Mitchell) who has spent endless years on the road with *The Student Prince* and *Blossom Time*. Both men keep reappearing, with Auer using Mrs. Smith's apartment to practice his new act, sawing a girl in half. There are bits with the heroine's young daughter, her teen-aged best friend, a tough-talking neighbor lady, and a number of dogs, since one of the heroine's plots to attract her would-be husband involves acquiring a puppy and joining the "Tailbumpers," her intended's organization of dog-lovers.

After two nights in Wilmington the company moved on

to its week in Washington, where the critics were negative, while the week in Baltimore drew the following comment: "*The Temporary Mrs. Smith* is a good idea gone wrong: not very far wrong, but just far enough to make the difference between success and failure."

There was real doubt about whether or not the play would ever reopen after it was closed for "repairs." Washington reviewer Richard Coe had pretty much summed up the general feeling of ambivalence: "This first comedy from the joint efforts of Jacqueline Susann and Beatrice Cole falls all over itself in attempts to be funny. And sometimes it is funny indeed. But watching a play fall over itself can be painful, and very often the playwrights are pretty transparent with what they're trying to do to you. . . . With more playing and cutting it will remain a slight whiff of a farce . . . yet it certainly has its moments and laughter in a theater is welcome and infectious." Arthur Siegel didn't expect Freedley to go on with it, but Bea and Jackie thought he might—if Luba Malina came through. As they closed in Baltimore, Bea vividly remembers feeling Francine Larrimore's heartbreak: "That last performance, I thought she was wonderful, but she knew and we all knew that her comeback had failed."

15

Lovely Me

How could this happen to lovely me?

—Jacqueline Susann

VINTON Freedley had a problem. An Actors Equity rule required an eight-week hiatus after the firing of a lead performer, and Francine Larrimore had been the lead until the play closed in Baltimore. He requested that an exception be made so he could reopen sooner, but Equity refused. On October 30 the *Herald-Tribune* carried a notice that "rehearsals will begin again on Monday with Luba Malina in the title role, and the show will open Nov. 25 in Philadelphia." The same item noted: "Jessie Royce Landis has been engaged to direct the revised version" of the show, replacing Billy Gilbert.

Jackie was delighted with the new director, whom she had known since her road tour of *Watch on the Rhine* in

1942. Landis was a veteran actress, having appeared in dozens of Broadway productions including the long-running *Kiss and Tell*, but she was then in a career slump. In later years she would make a comeback via Hollywood and Alfred Hitchcock, playing Grace Kelly's mother in *To Catch a Thief* and Cary Grant's mother in *North by Northwest*.

Jackie was in the late stages of her pregnancy by now, but she was not about to miss her play's reopening in her own hometown, where she had always been able to stir up publicity in the local papers. Irving had misgivings about the trip, but he knew argument was useless. Besides, her parents were there, and Bea would be with her in case of problems. The baby wasn't expected till late December anyway. He was as last persuaded that Jackie and Bea would be quite comfortable in their rooms at the Ritz Hotel, where they could work on any last-minute revisions that might be needed.

She lost no time in wooing the press. In one interview she "bubbles with enthusiasm" about the portrait being painted of her by her famous father and is also enthusiastic about the signing of Luba Malina in the lead, as "a Russian who adopts the name of Smith because, as she explains in a thick accent, she wouldn't want to be typed as a foreigner." Another reason for her good humor, she added, was the expected holiday arrival of the stork, who would be bringing them a girl, "so I can name her Jill. It would be so nice to have a Jackie and a Jill in the family."

Between Baltimore and Philadelphia Jackie was still working on revisions, even though she was now enormously pregnant. At one point shortly after the Baltimore closing she was talking with Arthur Siegel and she happened to glance at her profile in a full-length mirror. "How could this happen to lovely me?" she asked plaintively, a turn of phrase Siegel found so charming he wrote a song based on it for Luba Malina to sing in the show. A comedy number, it featured such lines as "Who makes stormy days seem sunny, dear/Who'll help you spend your money, dear/Who'll laugh though your jokes ain't funny, dear/Lovely me."*

The show opened on November 25 as scheduled, though Freedley was still dissatisfied with the first act. But if Jackie had expected an array of friendly hometown reviews, she was disappointed. Linton Martin of the *Inquirer* noted that both Jackie and Freedley were natives and therefore due some local pride and patriotism, but he went on to report that it "is a pretty attenuated and talky little tale that spread over an entire evening makes for tedium." Luba Malina's "typical night club song, with all the acrobatics, writhing, contortions and grimaces that are indigenous to the lively forms of floor show entertainment," were well received, as were her "eight different gowns, one without a visible means of support." But Luba was unhappy that changes she wanted were not being made. She was so displeased, in fact, that she confronted Jackie and Bea in Lew Tendler's restaurant and started yelling that she had to knock herself out to get the laughs. "If it weren't for me and Mischa, your play would go right down the toilet," she screamed. However, Vinton decided to book the play into Toronto for an opening on December 9. This was good news to Jackie, who had not known from day to day if the show would live or die, but she was to miss the Canadian tour entirely. On December 5 she woke up in her Ritz hotel room wet, her water having broken during the night. She phoned a local doctor, who advised

---

*Siegel, who still performs the song, says, "People ask me for copies of it, especially girl singers who are putting together an act."

her to return to New York immediately. "First babies always take their time," he explained.

The advice to undertake a ninety-minute train ride must have been somewhat astonishing even to a novice at pregnancy, but Jackie did as she was told, rushing off in the early morning with a hotel towel clamped between her legs. Irving met the train at Penn Station with a wheelchair and whisked Jackie off to nearby French Hospital, where she went into extended labor. The baby was born at four A.M. on December 6, weighing six pounds seven ounces. There was a bruise on his forehead, caused by the "mid-B forceps delivery" necessitated by the "dry birth." But to Jackie her new son was beautiful, and she named him Guy Hildy Mansfield—Hildy for her friend and idol Hildegarde; Guy because, as she told friends, he was "just some guy" and not the daughter she had so confidently predicted. Irving, evidently somewhat giddy from new fatherhood, sent out a birth announcement that added two pounds to the baby's weight, then had to send corrections to the columnists.

With Jackie still in the hospital, Vinton and the cast moved on to Toronto to prepare for the December 9 opening. An Earl Wilson column noted that Freedley had phoned Jackie in her hospital room to discuss further script changes and had been told that "the only changes that I can talk about now are the baby's." But even in her postnatal high, the uncertainty about the play's future must have been working on her nervous system. Each newspaper brought a new bit of indecision from Freedley, who hoped for a Broadway opening one day and talked of folding the next.

The situation was frustrating and a bit perplexing to Jackie, because the audiences seemed to love the play despite the reviewers' generally negative reactions in all four cities they had toured. This odd dichotomy was even commented on in the press while the play was in Washington, when a columnist wrote: "I had the best time watching the antics in *The Temporary Mrs. Smith* at the National Monday night. The next morning when I read the papers, I find I am a moron or something. It wasn't funny at all, say the critics." The play had got big laughs every night—even more now with Luba Malina in the lead role—yet critics kept saying it wasn't funny.

The Temporary Mrs. Smith was a hit in Toronto. On December 17 *Variety* noted: "Play had a splendid press here, particularly on Luba Malina." Unfortunately, the same item reported that Freedley was dropping out. "Producer spent final week with the show. The Shuberts and Jules Leventhal also had representatives present, sizing it up."

That same day brought more frustration, reflected in Robert Sylvester's column in the *Daily News*: "Vinton Freedley earned some sort of a medal for his booking of *The Temporary Mrs. Smith*," the item noted. "He did two different productions of the comedy, took it on two road tours, and then forgot to hire a New York theatre. Meanwhile, the cast is in town. Just sitting around waiting for some place to go."

The cast did not sit around very long. Within days a new backer and a new producer were announced. The backer was Jules Leventhal, who must have liked the reports from Toronto, and the new producer was David Lowe, a recently discharged air force lieutenant whose last production had been in 1943 and who wished to make his return known. The show had been retitled *Lovely Me*, after Luba's show-stopping number, and it was now billed as "A Gay Comedy with Songs." It was to open at the Adelphi Theatre on Christmas Eve, but on some reconsideration the date was changed to Christmas Day.

The Adelphi had become available when Ray Bolger's illness forced the early closing of *Three to Make Ready*, but the announcements noted that the theater was already committed to a musical version of *Street Scene* on January 9. That meant *Lovely Me* had two weeks on Broadway, and after that it would either have to find another theater or close down. The reviews would have a lot to do with its continued run, but in this case the availability of another theater was a further complication. Jackie, still settling in with her new baby, was under constant tension as the opening neared. Irving tried to cheer her, reminding her of how many friends they had in the New York press. Several of the columnists would surely be on their side, he assured her, and besides, he'd heard that Douglas Watt would be reviewing the play. Watt was a member of the old lunch crowd at Toots Shor's, and Irving knew him well. "Jackie, baby, we have nothing to worry about from the *Daily News*," he assured her.

For once Irving was wrong on all counts. The December 26 reviews were uniformly disastrous, including the one in the *Daily News*. As Douglas Watt recalls it: "If my mother had written a play I didn't like I'd say so. So in the case of *Lovely Me*, during the intermission I could see Irving trying to wind his way toward me, and I went out to smoke a cigarette or something. And I'd avoid him by going around the crowd the opposite way. And then I went back, and with three reviews we had limited space, so I wrote as tersely as I could. A terse and, I suppose, a deadly review. Supposedly when Jackie and Irving got home and they got the reviews, Jackie threw an ashtray in Irving's face and said, 'You and your friggin' friends.'"

Jackie was somewhat inured to bad reviews by now, but to be savaged by a *friend* was just too painful. She fumed and stewed about this betrayal for months, and eventually ran into Watt. As he remembers the incident: "A year passed and I'm sitting at Sardi's with a couple of press agents. I got up to leave. At that time Sardi's had a men's room and a women's room on the ground floor, separated from the restaurant by a six-foot partition. I left the men's room, and there was this woman standing in the bend with a white turban and a very dark complexion who could have been a variant on Lena Horne, and she had these flashing white teeth. And she said, 'Are you Douglas Watt?' and I said, 'Yes,' and she hauled off and smacked me in the face as hard as she could. She hit me with the flat of her hand. She didn't loosen any teeth or anything, but it was a smarting blow. She had been waiting for me for a year, waiting for this opportunity." Walter Winchell reported, somewhat inaccurately, that after the great blow had been struck Watt said, "Gee, she is pretty, isn't she?" and Jackie said, "I hated to slug him because he looked like such a nice guy." In any case, Watt recalls that years later he and the Mansfields were thrown into a cab together, and that the incident was never mentioned but that Jackie "went out of her way to be friendly."

Douglas Watt was certainly not alone in his negative reaction, Jackie's ire notwithstanding. The *New York Times* review, like most of the notices, had applause for the performers but little good to say about the play itself: "There are some funny passages and a few bright lines in *Lovely Me*, but it does not quite make up its mind what it is to be—comedy, farce, or just a sentimental escapade. Most of the situations are unreal and the humor is wrung out forcibly." The *Sun* thought the play was "pleasant" and "might make the grade in summer stock." The *Journal-American*'s Robert Garland was vicious: "On excellent authority Jacqueline Susann and Beatrice Cole are said to have gone off to the country and written *Lovely Me* in two weeks' time. At the Adelphi Saturday night I was wondering what on earth they could have done to fill out that fortnight!" And *Variety* delivered the coup de grâce, noting that "the actors tried heroically," but "the whole thing is rather a mistake."

However, amid the jeers a familiar observation was beginning to reappear. A reviewer for the racetrack newspaper the *Morning Telegraph*, had little good to say about the play, but added: "The first night audience, apparently made up of family and friends, thought it was hugely funny." The *New York Post* agreed: "All in all, the comedy is loosely written, with a series of stock gags and situations, all of which were kindly received by the Christmas Night audience."

In truth, the play was turning into what Bea Cole calls "an audience play." Arthur Siegel says, "The audience was building with theater parties. I remember a lot of people came with blocks of tickets from certain offices, and they loved it. I never heard such laughs in the theater." Even some of the later critics confirmed that this was so, as did William Hawkins in the *World Telegram* on December 30: "*Lovely Me* . . . is a rowdy, bawdy farce that stops at nothing for a laugh. . . . This is the sort of show for which you had better leave your inhibitions at home. . . . Apparently there are plenty of people in that state of mind for the holidays. Saturday the audience did a good deal of bellowing and it made frequent remarks in intermissions to the effect that critics did not know what they were talking about."

Meanwhile, the need for a new theater loomed—if the play was to continue. On January 3, 1947, Sam Zolotow of the *Times* was reporting that the play would move to the Coronet, "encouraged by the New Year's Eve windfall," but would be able to remain there for only three weeks and would have to make way for Arthur Miller's *All My Sons* on January 29.

Lowe made every effort to obtain a third theater, and a columnist noted: "A bit groggy by his attempts to find another house, the indefatigable Mr. Lowe is still in there battling.'' He almost got the Playhouse, but the deal fell through. When *Lovely Me* closed, after thirty-seven performances, it was playing to sell-out crowds.

The experience must have been draining for Jackie, and the outcome bitterly disappointing. She had gotten her play all the way to Broadway, survived dreadful reviews, and then watched it close to enthusiastic standing-room-only audiences. Still, to have had a play on Broadway at all was an achievement. As she pasted the notices in her scrapbook, she must have winced a little at a Philadelphia interview that quoted her as saying, ''Bea and I wrote the play because we are fans of the great American dollar.'' In truth, she and Bea had barely earned enough to pay for their travel expenses during the road tours. At three hundred dollars a week in ''reduced royalties,'' a long run might have put them in the black, but thanks to the critics—those ''nine great men'' of the New York press especially—there had just been too little momentum to overcome the theater problem. But she would save the reviews. Or some of them, anyway. Not the hatchet job from that yellow-bellied Douglas Watt, though. That one went into her zebra-striped wastebasket.

She was glad that at least *Lovely Me* had not soured her relationship with her Navarro neighbor Lya Lys. As Jackie's cousin Bob Jelinek remembers, when he came to New York shortly after, Jackie fixed him up with Lya's daughter.

PART THREE
THREE

THE SCHIFFLI GIRL [1947-1963]

16

Albert and Lola

*I plan to concentrate on a program for Jackie. I don't
know exactly the kind of format we'll use, but I do
know that I'm going to build a show for her.*

———Irving Mansfield

FOR a time Jackie had hopes that Lowe might take
Lovely Me to Chicago after it was forced to close
in New York, but that was not to be either. It was
upsetting, of course, but less than it might have been if she
had not had a new baby to occupy her. They had hired a
nurse on a full-time basis, over Rose's surprising objections but on Irving's insistence. As he explained later:
"The mother stuffs farina down the baby's throat, stuff it
doesn't want, The mother disciplines the kid. Then the
father comes home, smelling of nice perfume or shaving
lotion and says, 'How is my little darling?' The kid thinks
the father is great. The mother is always the heavy, except

187

in families where they have nurses. Then the nurse is the heavy, and the mother—when she has time—plays with the baby and does all the nice things with the father. They both participate."

The nurse slept in on a cot in the study, which was now a nursery, and took charge of Guy all the time until *Lovely Me* closed, except on her midweek day off. Then Jackie took over herself, wheeling Guy to Central Park proudly. He was a beautiful baby, now that the bruise from the forceps was fading. Evelyn came to visit, and she remembers that he was "gorgeous, like Jackie, with enormous eyes." And Hildegarde, who had agreed to be his godmother, sent a blanket. Jackie had him photographed on it and sent the singer a copy, inscribed: "Here he is resplendent on your beautiful blue blanket." Guy looks almost ethereal in the picture, the shape of his face and his features nearly identical to Jackie's, a resemblance that would become even more pronounced in later childhood photographs. But his fingers are oddly contorted and splayed even in this early shot, as they would be in other photographs.

Rose was not pleased with the nurse Jackie had hired. The woman was too cold and professional, she felt. Little babies need a lot of warmth and cuddling, Rose insisted. She had always regretted that the flu epidemic had kept her from cuddling Jackie as much as she would have liked, because she was convinced it was important. And it was important that the mother be there to do it, she argued, not some no-nonsense, rigid hired person. Just *look* at the baby, she told Jackie. He was crankier than seemed normal, fussy, and given to shrieking and crying.

Jackie reminded Rose that she had herself hired a girl to care for Jackie, but Rose was having none of that. Flossie had been a different story altogether, she insisted. For one thing, Jackie was older by then. For another, Flossie had been affectionate and caring, and willing to take orders from Rose. True, children needed discipline. But that was when they were *older*, not when they were tiny cuddly babies.

Jackie stood firm. She would not go on the road again, at least not while Guy was small, but she did not mean to spend all her time changing diapers and chatting with other mothers and nursemaids in the park. She and Bea had started work on a novel called *Underneath the Pancake*, which was to be an inside look at show business. They had shown some of it to Helen Strauss at the William Morris office, and the reaction had been somewhat encouraging. And there was also the campaign to get her figure back, so she would never have to duck photographers again as she had at the New York opening of *Lovely Me*.

Jackie's willpower always amazed Radie Harris, who said, "No matter what she set her heart on, her mind could master it. She was overweight after her son was born. A few months later she had slimmed down to a model's figure, and she never let up in the discipline of her diet." As soon as the Florence Lustig dresses would fit her again, she wore them, and the rest of her growing wardrobe, almost every night when she and Irving went out to dinner, sometimes at the Stork Club or one of the supper clubs where the comics were playing, sometimes at the place Danny Stradella had opened two years before, Danny's Hideaway, which would become one of their favorite hangouts. Stradella remembers that they were usually with another couple, such as Joyce and her current husband. "They came with producers, writers, stars, Hildegarde, Artie Hershkowitz, and Fred Allen. They liked to talk to comedians like Jack E. Leonard and Sid Caesar at other tables."

But mostly she fussed over Guy, and worried. He was a finicky eater and a bad sleeper, often keeping the nurse

and Jackie up half the night. Jackie came to dread Wednesday, which was weighing day and which often showed no
gain for the baby and sometimes even a loss. They spent
the summer of 1947 in a rented house near Atlantic Beach,
New York, and during their whole stay he gained only
twelve ounces. She began to feel that something was
seriously wrong, but doctors could not tell her what it
might be. And Irving, who saw Guy mostly on weekends,
or in the evenings at bath time, refused to see any
problems. "I felt that Jackie was just doing the kind of
worrying that all mothers do," he said. "I dismissed it."

A few weeks before his first birthday Guy stopped
eating again and lost an alarming amount of weight. Not
long after, Bob had another heart attack and went back into
the hospital. In an effort to drag Jackie from her depression
Irving planted several column items about their son's
birthday, then wangled invitations to a round of glittery
social events. But even flirting with glamorous men couldn't
stop her from thinking of her beautiful baby, who seemed
to be having such a terrible time getting started in life. Bob
had said that, with so many near celebrities in the family—
Jackie and Irving, Irving's uncle the judge, even Bob
himself—Guy should have a chance at making it big. But
sometimes it seemed he could barely make it at all.

Then, early in his second year, more medical problems
beset him. One was a tonsillectomy; another was a hernia.
For the hernia repair she insisted on taking him back to
Philadelphia, where Bob and Rose had connections that
would make it easier for her to stay in Guy's room with
him. It was a radical notion in those days, but she was
determined that her baby would not be left in the care of
strangers. Years later an aging nurse still remembered the
experience vividly: "She was a tigress, nasty and tough
and rude to the nurses. We pointed to her as the worst kind
of Jewish mother; we said she was a bitch. Now, of

course, we *ask* the mothers to stay. We think it's better for
the children and it eases the burden on us." She remembers being pinched by Bob and bullied by Jackie, and she
remembers an encounter between Jackie and another mother who was a former high school classmate: "Jackie pulled
rank on her because she thought she was a celebrity, and
the other mother said Jackie was just the whore of their
school, and the two of them swung at each other with their
pocketbooks." But despite the unpleasantness the nurse
couldn't help being impressed with Jackie's fierce dedication to Guy. "When her books came out I found myself
defending Jacqueline Susann. Really! People in Philadelphia said she didn't care about her child, that she had put
him away and forgotten him. And I knew that couldn't be
true."

Jackie's temper, always volatile, seemed to grow more
so as the frustrating months wore on. It was in April that
she had her much-publicized scene with Douglas Watt in
Sardi's, and there were other incidents Irving began to see
as danger signals. He encouraged her to work again, and
she again prevailed on Bea. The result was a radio sitcom
called *It's Always Albert*, starring the nasal-voiced comedian who had been so successful on Henry Morgan's show,
Arnold Stang. As a shy composer who couldn't hold a job,
Stang held the show together for a time, but it was a
faltering summer replacement whose future did not look
good, even to its producer, Irving Mansfield.

The show was indeed short-lived, for reasons described
in *Variety's* review. "There's something desperate about
the scripting. Save for one funny sequence in a department
store it somehow doesn't seem to have the relaxed light-
hearted quality that it needs."

Irving was growing as a force in his own right, a
producer who would soon be whizzing between California
and New York almost weekly to scout talent and soothe

legendary showbiz egos. The columnists he had once
wooed now called *him* for news about his own activities.
He could afford to produce an occasional clunker like *It's
Always Albert*, but he worried about Jackie. She seemed
constantly harassed now, complaining about Guy's problems and even about his own imagined "casting couch"
philanderings. When she had had too many pills or too
much booze she would send him nasty telegrams or air
mail letters while he was in Hollywood, though she brushed
them aside later. Still, he worried. She had even visited his
office at CBS looking like a total mess, her hair and
makeup a disaster and her push-up bra showing above the
too-low neckline. She had looked like a hooker after a bad
night, and he knew some of his colleagues were talking,
and wondering.

Guy had started to speak, or at least to say "Mommy"
and "Daddy" and "Dammit," his favorite expression.
But he showed little interest in the other toddlers in the
park, preferring to run around in frantic circles by himself
or giggle hysterically. And there were the sudden wild
tantrums that came out of the blue, for no cause Jackie
could see. Sometimes they occurred after he had wet or
soiled himself—he showed no interest at all in toilet
training—and often Jackie would be forced to rush home
through traffic, holding the messy and screaming child.
One man who ran a gift shop near the Navarro says,
"Jackie Susann was a prisoner of Fifty-ninth Street. She
could never take that child more than a few steps from
home, because she never knew what he might pull on her.
But she loved him. Like any mother, she was trying to
give him a normal life. She would come in here every
week, almost, to get little presents for the doormen and the
bellhops because Guy made a mess of their uniforms and
the hotel lobby."

Home was little better. He banged his head against his

crib by the hour, often bloodying himself, and when she tried to pick him up he fought her. And he was terrified of the living room, refusing to go there at all. It wasn't much better during their summer, which they spent in a rented house at Atlantic City, on the Jersey Shore. Rose was there, and so was Grandma Ida, and Thelma came with her little girl, Nina, who was slightly younger than Guy. "Nina was fat and lazy but she was very social, and she was starting to talk," Thelma remembers. "And when Rose saw Guy and Nina together, her eyes would fill up with tears. She knew that her grandson was handicapped." But Rose was little help to Jackie, advising only that she take Guy to a "good doctor." Jackie asked, "Who, for example?" and Rose was stumped. Her own uncle, Dr. Kaye, the only physician she really trusted, had long since died. Bob, on the other hand, assured Jackie that the boy was very smart, and he reminded her that creative geniuses were seldom average children. Jackie wanted to believe him, but watching Guy with other toddlers made it nearly impossible. It was Grandma, feeble though she was growing, who made sad sense. "He doesn't eat and he screams a lot, so he could have trouble in his stomach and that could be fixed. He acts like he doesn't hear you, and maybe he's hard of hearing, which also is not the end of the world. What I don't like is the way he looks right through a person, through you but not *at* you."

It was in many ways a dreadful summer. On the fifth of July Jackie got up and turned on the radio, to learn that Carole Landis had died of an overdose of pills the previous afternoon. Rex Harrison found her. Carole had never been able to overcome her aging-sex-queen image, and even her affair with Jessel had not got her decent parts. (She and Jackie had compared notes on Jessel's sexual performance, a game Jackie would make use of in *The Love Machine*, where "celebrity fucker" Ethel Evans keeps a score sheet on her many lovers.) At last Carole's failing career, mounting debts, and perhaps Harrison's refusal to leave Lilli Palmer for her had just been too much. The news left Jackie depressed for many days, and before she had fully recovered Fate dealt an even crueler blow. On August 15 her beloved "Aunt Esther" Weinrott was found dead, hanging by two belts from a bedroom door in her home. Esther had spent the last ten years in and out of hospitals, and Jackie had known the woman was deeply troubled, but still—she had respected and cherished her, as she had respected and cherished Carole.

Irving cast about for projects that would divert Jackie from her grief. She did a sketch on Milton Berle's show, playing his wife, and she got a running part on a daytime soap opera called *Hearts and Harmony*. She did volunteer work with Ed Sullivan to raise funds for the Community Chest, and her name began to appear again in the columns. And then Jackie got a real break, again through Irving.

It was a major part on a new show which would try out on radio beginning in July and then would move to television in December, premiering on the sixteenth. It was a "sustaining" show, which meant it was still unsponsored, and it was to star a cello-playing comedian named Morey Amsterdam, who had been doing guest appearances on a number of variety shows and who, Irving was convinced, was a natural for television if he could just be packaged properly.

The package was called *The Golden Goose Café* and was described in a publicity flyer as a new format: "The show will use outside guests but present them in a cafe setting. More than that the show will establish Amsterdam, Art Carney and Jacqueline Susann as permanent characters with a continuing plot line, giving the show a situation comedy pitch. Irving Mansfield, producer, is also co-authoring the show with Amsterdam." In early ads Morey stood between Jackie and Carney, both of whom towered over him. Jackie wore a very short strapless dress with lace about the bosom and hem and a pair of those high-heeled, open-toed, ankle-strapped shoes.

The show was an odd hybrid of sitcom and variety, with Morey—known as the "push-button comedy machine" because of his vast joke repertoire—playing a nightclub emcee who opened the show with "some fast balling of gags, a buck-and-wing," perhaps a straight rendition of "Dark Eyes" on the cello, and the introductions of guests from the "audience." Jackie played Lola, the wide-eyed cigarette girl, a klutzy/sexy sidekick and foil who wore the shortest of skirts and lowest of necklines. Her routines were straight from vaudeville and, as a deadpan "dumb doll," she handled them to perfection. For example:

[Jackie comes through the nightclub calling, "Cigars! Cigarettes!" She is shaking her entire body, breasts and hips jiggling frantically.]

MOREY: *Wait a minute, come here, hold on a sec, what are you doing? What's all this jumping?*

LOLA: *I just took some medicine and it says on the bottle shake well before using and I forgot to shake it.*

Lola then explains that she isn't feeling well and she thinks it is because of the oysters she ate last night.

MOREY: *Well, maybe they weren't any good. How did they look when you opened them?*

LOLA: *Oh. You mean you have to open them?*

The program was reviewed as "good low- and middle-brow comedy," and Jackie was called "highly decorative" and "droll." She did get a fair amount of attention and

Nick Kenny, the poet laureate of the daily press, even penned a verse to her in his *Daily Mirror* column: "The newest thing in your TV life/Is Irving Mansfield's lovely wife." Amsterdam got his share of good reviews, too, though he was not to have a solid television success till he became a fixture on the long-running *Dick Van Dyke Show* more than a decade later. The real hit of *The Golden Goose Café*, however, was Art Carney, who was deemed "the funniest and most refreshing stooge now operating," and predicted to have a bright future.

For reasons perhaps understood by insiders only, despite the accolades for Carney and the generally good reception the show got, it failed to attract a sponsor at CBS. It was picked up by the DuMont network. The mythical café of the show was changed from the Golden Goose to the Silver Swan, Carney became Newton the Waiter instead of Charlie the Doorman, and the cigarette girl's name was changed from Lola to Jackie, which must at least have been easy to remember.

She didn't have to remember it long, though. She had a baseball skit on DuMont's opening broadcast, April 21, 1949, but that was to be her last appearance. After the change of networks Irving no longer had anything to do with either the production or writing of the show, so there was evidently nothing he could do to save her job. Though she got a gratifying batch of reviews for her last skit and a nice stack of fan letters, she was dropped. The show itself continued for some time and did well, but without help from either Mansfield. Irving was philosophical about it all. "Morey Amsterdam made about four hundred thousand dollars on account of me," he said later. "He was playing a cellar nightclub when I put him on TV." Then he added, "Of course, Morey has talent."

Jackie was less philosophical. Success had been so close and then was snatched from her. She would record 1949 as one of her bad years; in fact, it and 1962 are written in much darker numerals than the other years, and there is something like an asterisk next to 1949. In the spring she and Irving went to the Long Island home of a rich advertising mogul who was rumored to be "running guns to Israel." Jackie was much interested in the man, partly because of the rumors but also because she was now turning her attention—and her charms—toward those who controlled the advertising on television. The agents had failed her, and so had the columnists and even the producers, including her own husband. Maybe some sponsor would discover her and push the magic button that would open the door to television stardom.

Several guests at the party were Lola fans. Each time one of them complimented her, she celebrated with another heavy scotch on the rocks. At last she found herself in a small group that included the host, and she was sufficiently uninhibited by then to ask if he could get *her* a gun. "Maybe I'll kill a certain son of a bitch," she said. Or maybe *herself*, thought one of the people who overheard the exchange. She was insistent, and at last she grew so loud and insulting that Irving had to hustle her into her new fox jacket and take her home.

The next day he was so upset he left his office early and rushed back to the Navarro. What he said to her then is only conjecture, but Irving may well have once again quoted his uncle Sam Mandelbaum, the judge. He was fond of one aphorism in particular, and used it often: "Don't get mad, and don't get even. Just be so successful that your enemies will die of envy. Success is the best revenge." And he was successful, he often reminded Jackie. With only a little optimism, he could foresee a six-figure income for 1949. And it was all for her, and to a large extent *because* of her. Without her prodding he would still be a press agent, hustling his tail

off for a fraction of the income and prestige he now
had.

Jackie didn't go for it. "You don't need 'mass love,'
Irving, and I do. That's the difference between us, and if
you don't understand it, you can get the f— out of this
f—— apartment. And I don't want your money, I want my
own. You may be a brilliant producer, but you are a very
simple man." She picked up a convenient ashtray and
hurled it at his ear. Incredibly, according to a witness,
Irving began to cry. Jackie rushed to her closet "like a
madwoman" and pulled out a box from the top of an
out-of-the-way shelf. "Look at this coat, Irving." she
screamed at him, unwrapping the package. He looked and
saw a nondescript cloth jacket. "You don't even remember
this coat," Jackie continued. "A fan of Lola's sent it to me
from a little town in California. She said she didn't need it
as much as Lola did. She was worried Lola would get into
trouble, riding home on the New York subways in her
cigarette costume."

And then Jackie also started crying, and the two of them
were bawling like babies when the visitor tiptoed out.

Soon after, Irving was sitting morosely on a bench in the
park when a friend from his bachelor days came by. "What's
the matter, old buddy?" the man inquired, and to his
astonishment, Irving told him. The friend remembers that he
was almost crying, just talking about it. "She needs that kind
of love from the public," he said. "And she feels everyone
has let her down, including me. *Mostly* me."

Jackie made only about four thousand dollars for all her
show business work in 1948, but at least appearing on the
Amsterdam show had made her feel like an actress again—
even, for the first time, like a star. "In radio you are only
a voice to people," she declared, "and on stage you are

seen by a limited number, but on television you have a large audience, and you have the added thrill of playing on a stage.'' (Actually, the television audience was not so large then, at least not compared with the gigantic numbers reached by a popular show today. In the early fifties there were only 108 stations across the nation, and the networks were still pouring more money into the new medium than they were taking out. It was not until the late fifties that television really exploded across America. Still, Lola was seen by hundreds of thousands at least, if not millions— and some of them seemed to love her.)

Jackie wore her season of celebrity as she thought a star should do, graciously and with modesty. In February she and Irving attended the opening of a play, and she noticed that everyone was craning to look her way. She turned to the woman next to her, whom she didn't recognize, and asked, ''Are all these people looking at you or me?''

''I don't know,'' Margaret Truman answered, though she must have thought her leg was being pulled by this perfect stranger.

——17——

Giving Up on Guy

> *And it was noticed that if a baby is continually unresponsive to its mother, the mother becomes discouraged and then appears to the observer as cold and unfeeling. . . .*
>
> ——Herman Roiphe, M. D., and
> Anne Roiphe, *Your Child's Mind*

*I*N 1949 Irving was riding high, largely because of the phenomenal success of the show he had created, *Talent Scouts*, now entering the beginning of its television run. The show had been suggested by the old *Amateur Hour*, hosted on radio by Major Bowes and later by Ted Mack, but Irving's version featured professional performers who had not yet made it, rather than amateurs. He had hired Arthur Godfrey off a morning radio show, charmed by the freckle-faced redhead's easy style and ability to relate to an audience, but it was not to be an easy association. Apart from Godfrey's arrogant anti-Semitism ("He bought a restricted hotel in Miami *while* I was his producer," Irving said), there were other day-to-day frictions that marred the relationship. It would end the following fall, when Godfrey returned from vacation in time to attend a birthday party Irving had arranged for him at the Stork Club. At the party he snubbed Irving completely, and from that time on he refused to speak to his producer at all. By December Irving was off the production entirely, though he continued to receive a royalty and a credit at the end of each show—except on those frequent occasions when Godfrey "accidentally" ran over and the credits were cut short. "I hated him," Irving said in 1981. "Godfrey was not a very nice man. I wasn't responsible for all of his wealth, but I gave him the vehicle." And he added that it was Jackie who had discovered the clause in the contract that got him the royalty.

In any case, *Talent Scouts* solidified Irving's position with the network. If one retired executive remembers that "he was largely at CBS as a payoff for his ownership position on *Talent Scouts*," Irving did go on to produce a number of other shows, including *The Stork Club*, *The Sam Levenson Show*, and briefly, Frank Sinatra's show. His personal favorite was a television panel show called *This Is Show Business*, hosted by Clifton Fadiman and featuring Sam Levenson, George S. Kaufman, and a roly-poly humorist named Abe Burrows. The show was at least partially the brainchild of Maurice Zolotow, a youngish celebrity reporter who had been Margie Hart's press agent and who would go on to write a number of successful biographies in later years. *This Is Show Business* was a *succès d'éstime* for the network, lasting until 1956 and providing the stock excuse for college professors to buy television sets.

"Mansfield was an important man in early TV as a

producer, but then he was frozen out," that same retired
executive recalls. "He was not popular because he was
ascerbic, anti-establishment, and Broadway oriented rather
than Madison Avenue oriented. . . . He built his life around
Lindy's cheesecake and late-evening poker games. He was
not popular with CBS because he was thought to have too
much contractual control. He extracted a lot of money
from CBS, and really did not deserve it because he was
not that creative." But creative or not, Irving did exercise
power and muscle, as noted by Richard Gehman in an
Esquire article: "A single telephone call from Mansfield
can start a chain reaction that will move an entertainer
from obscurity to stardom almost overnight."

Irving's colleagues recall being dragged to Lindy's and
regaled with the place's lore, from Runyon's special corner
to Joe E. Lewis's barstool from which the comic liked to
pronounce, "One drink always makes me dizzy: The
twefïth." Irving told them about a musical his Navarro
neighbor Frank Loesser was trying to put together based
on Runyon's Broadway stories, claiming that he, Irving,
had fixed Loesser up with both George S. Kaufman, who
would direct, and Abe Burrows, who would co-author the
libretto. Others doubt that Loesser needed Irving to get to
Kaufman, but many do credit Irving with bringing Burrows in, and with a general involvement, though unpaid,
in the production of *Guys and Dolls*.

Some of this same cast would figure in one of Irving's
favorite Jackie stories. It happened when Loesser's wife,
Lynn, came to borrow all their ice for a little gathering
they were having. Jackie handed over the ice, and then she
and Irving did a slow burn all evening while a procession
of people they knew well trooped into the Loesser apartment. The party broke up around midnight, and at three
A.M. Jackie, still furious, pounded on the Loessers' door
and coldly demanded the return of her ice trays.

In January of 1949 Irving received the Silver Mike Award for his achievements, and attended the dinner in a light silk suit and an overpowering necktie with huge squares, a snappy handkerchief protruding a bit too far from his jacket pocket, still looking "like he should have a piece of cheesecake in his mouth," as a colleague recalls. Irving's co-workers may have found him a bit jarring, but then many of them found the new medium itself perplexing, balanced as it was between show-biz razzle-dazzle and the lower-keyed, one-to-one nature of radio. It was perhaps natural that such a Broadway-oriented type would fill the gap, "a wise guy, knowing all the angles and playing them, playing for the main chance, looking down on yokels, cutting corners, fast-dealing, but up to his ears in show business and able to seize the opportunity and the moment." So he was seen by a colleague, who adds, "A lot of fringe people were coming into television then because it was a new terrain. By the end of the fifties when TV was really established, Irving was getting very little work commensurate with his early success. Part of his later downfall was just that his time was over, part was that he was basically not a producer in temperament but a publicist or flack, and part was that he relived a scenario, over and over, again and again, of pettiness in his personal relationships. He developed a reputation for being litigious. He would work with a person and as soon as they fell out he would run to his lawyers."

In pictures taken that night Jackie has her hair pulled back to show the drop earrings Carole Landis had given her. She looks elegant, somewhat Spanish and rather like Rose Susann, the respectable wife of a man being honored. But her face is drawn, and one can almost see the pain behind the mask, an expression perhaps of Lola's clouded future, and certainly a reflection too of her life at home, with a child whose behavior was drifting further from the

"normal" every week. Irving had bought Guy a little
tricycle. He would spin the wheels by the hour, defying all
attempts to distract him and throwing a tantrum if the bike
was taken away.

By April, when she was written out of *The Silver Swan
Café* Jackie was taking Guy from one doctor to another,
not only for his physical problems but in a frantic effort to
have his slow development and strange behavior explained.
She got little help, though a child psychiatrist, Archie
Silver, consoled her for a time, enough so that she referred
friends to him and years later playfully named a fictional
character Dr. Archie Gold. Dr. Silver remembers her
fondly: "Mrs. Mansfield was a bright, sensitive, determined woman with great concern for her family and
loyalty for her friends." And then he added, "Mothers are
no longer blamed for early mental illness in their children."

They were then, however, and Jackie had been getting
more than her share of suspicion and implied blame. Had
she somehow failed to give Guy the warm mothering he
needed? It seemed to her that he frustrated all her attempts
to hold and cuddle him, but why? Had she somehow
caused him to behave so abnormally? Maybe she shouldn't
have taken so many pills while she was pregnant, or gone
to Philadelphia with *Lovely Me*, or returned to New York
when she was already beginning labor. Maybe she shouldn't
have left him so much with the nurse that first month while
the play was struggling in New York. Maybe she should
have breast-fed him. Maybe the nanny really was too strict
and unloving, as Rose had argued. Maybe, maybe, maybe . . .

And Irving insisted the baby was fine. He was concerned about *her*, of course, but he tended to dismiss
Guy's problems as temporary or trivial. Irving himself,
with his high-pressure job, complained of stomach and
heart symptoms so often that Jackie wisecracked, "When I
was pregnant I was opening doors for Irving."

It was a strange, divided life Jackie led. They were spending around two thousand dollars a month on entertaining, making the rounds of Toots Shor's, "21," El Morocco, Sardi's, the Stork Club, the Little Club, Danny's Hideway, and others. They were out so much at night that Irving figured it cost him close to a thousand dollars a year to check his hat, yet her days were spent worrying over Guy and dragging him to doctors. And mostly what she got was confusion, contradictions, implications that she had somehow caused his problems, or that she was failing to solve them. Irving's young assistant, a girl named Penny Morgan, recalls: "Guy was the most beautiful baby, and Irving just thought he was different. He had a face like sunshine. Jackie . . . focused all her energy on getting him well. She never stopped hoping that he would recover; she had constant anguish over it. Outwardly she coped with it well, but she would have traded anything she accomplished in life in return for Guy being normal."

In December of 1949 Guy turned three, and then his small vocabulary almost disappeared. Friends remember him screaming "Goddammit! Goddammit!" One afternoon the nurse brought him home from the park screaming, as had often happened before, but this time the blood-curdling screeches continued throughout the day and the following night, with breaks only when Guy gave in to exhaustion and slept fitfully. Irving questioned everyone in the park and even hired private detectives, but there was never a clue as to what had provoked the child. The screaming stopped in time, but Guy continued to withdraw. And now his condition was given a name: autism.

The word was used by Dr. Lauretta Bender, to whom Jackie's psychiatric journey had taken her. Dr. Bender was a petite and earthy woman who had originated the Bender Visual Motor Gestalt Test, a tool still in widespread use today as a means of evaluating "maturational levels of

children, organic brain defects and deviations in function." She stood somewhat apart from her psychoanalyti-
cally oriented colleagues in that she was more inclined to
look for physical, neurological bases for such disorders.
She thoroughly disagreed with those colleagues who blamed
the mother and "poor communication within the home"
for autism. "I've had mothers come to me weeping and
saying, 'I can't reach my child. I try every way I can but I
can't reach my child.' Of course the mothers are very
upset," she says, *"because* of the child's behavior. I have
never seen one single instance in which I thought the
mother's behavior produced autism in the child."

Dr. Bender was interested in Jackie's Uncle Pete, the
meshugge dentist, and also in Irving's "peculiar" uncle,
believing that there was often a pattern of schizophrenia in
the family history of the autistic child.* She saw Guy's
case as classic in many aspects, including his indifference
to affection and his failure to communicate, his fascination
with spinning objects, his rhythmic rocking and head
banging, and his general withdrawal. She was not very
encouraging, but she suggested a controversial approach—a
series of shock treatments that might jar him out of his
silent world enough so that he could benefit from therapy.

Shock treatments for a three-year-old? It seemed cruel,
yet no one had offered anything hopeful as an alternative.
Reluctantly, Jackie and Irving agreed to leave him in the
Bellevue children's ward in Dr. Bender's hands. They
compared notes with other parents whose children were
there, and were somewhat reassured to find them mostly

---

*Others, then and later, are less sure, and in fact so little is really known
about autism that experts even now disagree about whether or not it is a
form of childhood schizophrenia, from which it differs in several crucial
ways.

upper-class people who, like the Mansfields, sought only the best for their kids. One unhappy father, a physician, told her, "This is the last step before putting my little boy away for good."

Irving long regretted the shock treatments. "I think they destroyed him. He came home with no expression, almost lifeless." And now the doctors advised that Guy be placed in an institution. Perhaps he might have a remission at puberty, Dr. Bender declared, but for now he needed the special care and supervision of an institution.*

They agreed, in the most heart-wrenching decision of their lives, and Guy was taken to his first of many institutions, a Rhode Island facility surrounded by rolling lawns. They left their son there, in one of the red-brick buildings of this strange place where he would be cared for but probably not loved. It was a decision they knew many among their relatives and friends could never understand or accept, so they agreed to keep it from all but a few of the people closest to them. To others, then and for the years that would follow. Guy was said to be attending a special school in Arizona because of a serious asthmatic condition. Jackie's explanation to those who knew the truth was that Guy might recover in his teens, and if so, she didn't want him "stigmatized."

The experience—not only the difficulties with Guy himself, but the grinder she'd been put through by the "experts" —took a harsh toll on Jackie. Autism, which afflicts about three hundred fifty thousand people in the United States,

---

*Even today, institutionalization is necessary for fully two thirds of all autistic children, for whom no chemical or psychiatric therapies avail. Behavioral techniques have had limited effectiveness, particularly in cases where some language skills have been developed and retained, but the prognosis for the majority of autistic children is as bleak now as it was in Guy's infancy.

most of them male, had first been described only a few
years earlier, in 1943, by Dr. Leo Kanner of Harvard. At
first he and most of his colleagues had blamed the condition on mothers: "refrigerator mothers," "schizophrenogenic
mothers," or even—conversely—"smothering mothers."
The influential Dr. Bruno Bettelheim had even gone so far
as to advocate radical "parentectomy"—the complete and
premanent separation of parents and child—as the autistic's
only hope. In the intervening decades the tide has turned,
and in 1975, a year after Jackie's death, Ruth Sullivan,
director of information for the National Society for Autistic
Children, would state: "There has probably been no group
more crucified by the mental health profession than the
mothers of autistic children. It is my own personal belief
that it will rank high among the scandals of the twentieth
century."

Dr. Bender had been the first to absolve Jackie of
blame, but Jackie could not entirely absolve herself. The
guilt persisted, along with the worry about Guy and about
the massive expenses that lay down the road if he required
long-term institutionalization. She and Irving went to visit
him on weekends and found him in good physical health
and even gaining weight. He seemed to recognize them
and to understand some things they said, but he never
talked again.

In Jackie's depression, the pills became more crucial.
She hoarded them, hid them, and increased her intake. She
and Irving disposed of Guy's possessions, but she could
not dispose of the guilt, the terrible conviction that she had
done something wrong, or that she had failed to take other
measures that could have saved her son. There were times
when she could hardly bear to leave her bedroom, and the
days passed in a fog.

Bea tried to help, though she had herself retired from
the theater and had married a European-born engineer

named Roubicheck—nicknamed Roubie but secretly called Rommel by Jackie. The two women led very different lives but remained staunch friends. As Bea explains, "Jackie and I wanted to stay close and we worked at it, although I developed into more of a stay-by-the-fireside type. My husband and I did not fit into the Mansfields' high-powered social life."

Jackie and Bea began to talk of writing again, and they launched another collaboration, *Cock of the Walk*, a sometimes funny and always venomous play with a central character based mainly on Cantor, but with bits of Godfrey thrown in. They worked on it over the summer, and by fall Jackie was announcing the play's completion and the signing of James Dunn as its star. *Cock of the Walk* would start rehearsals in October. In it the hero, a comedian called Jimmy Grant, is a shameless publicity hound of whom one of his employees says, "If there was a big train wreck, Jimmy would rush to the spot and mingle among the dead bodies just to get his picture in the paper." A second employee says, "Yeah, but first he'd wire Mary and the kids to join him."

The play contains a version of Jackie's affair with Cantor as well as a description of the Freedman-Cantor conflict. The "Jackie" character is an innocent young actress named Jennifer Welles. Jennifer's husband, a composite of Freedman and Irving, is holed up in Atlantic City, ghostwriting Jimmy's autobiography. Jimmy seduces Jennifer. As she and Jimmy make love, Jennifer bewails the fact that she has fallen for "America's most married married man."

Jimmy assures her, "Rules weren't made for people like us. Rules were made for people who live in houses, who get up in the morning and go to work, who have kids and go to the movies every Saturday night. We're not people.

I'm Jimmy Grant. . . . You're the girl I love. . . . And there ain't no rule in the world that can fit us."

Jennifer, swayed, says, "I've got a wonderful husband . . . yet this seems right. Jimmy, have I lost my sanity?"

On December 6 Guy's fourth birthday was hailed in some of the columns, which noted that his mother's latest play was "in rehearsal at the moment" with James Dunn as leading man. Dunn was a veteran actor who had made a number of movies with Shirley Temple and had won an Oscar for his role as Johnny in *A Tree Grows in Brooklyn*, so things sounded auspicious indeed. Sometime later a Philadelphia opening was announced.

What happened next remains mysterious to this day. The play was complete. Jackie and Bea took out a copyright, and Dunn was committed, yet the opening never occurred. And the next year Dunn filed a bankruptcy petition, reporting that he had "lost $40,000 in a stage work that failed to reach Broadway." Why was it withdrawn? Perhaps because it was, on second look, thought to be libelous, its characters too thinly disguised? Or perhaps because Cantor intervened to suppress it? Or possibly because Irving, ever aware of the gossip that still clung to Jackie and Cantor, decided production was unwise? Whatever the facts are, in later years Jackie and Bea never mentioned the play, and Irving's memoir, *Life with Jackie*, contains no reference to it.

——18——

The Hockey Club

She could be very warm and very wonderful, but there was this awful abrasiveness that she had. I knew the evil parts of Jackie and I felt that I could turn them into fun.

——Jean Harrison

*I*N early 1951 Irving was doing so well with several new shows that he took out a large ad in *Variety* to celebrate. It featured a picture of Guy, with copy that read: "This Is Show Business conceived by Irving Mansfield, the new Sam Levenson Show, conceived by Irving Mansfield, The Stork Club, conceived by Irving Mansfield, Guy Mansfield, conceived by Irving Mansfield." There was an asterisk next to Guy's name, and below was the line: "*In association with Jacqueline Susann." Considering the problems Guy was having, the ad seems incredible, but perhaps it was done in an effort to deny

those problems, or simply in the hope it would cheer
Jackie up.

It undoubtedly failed. Sending Guy away was something
she had finally come to see as inevitable and necessary, but
it left her in a deep depression that the pills and gin did
little to dissipate. What did help to pull her through those
dark days was work—writing *Cock of the Walk* with Bea,
going through the preproduction hassles that so mysteriously
fizzled, and then throwing herself into a new assault on
television, the medium for which she felt herself a natural.
In May of 1950, after months of professional and emotional seclusion, she gathered her forces and began anew as, of
all things, a disc jockey. She made a deal to take over the
mike for half-hour intervals every night on a show broadcast from the Hickory House restaurant, tackling interviews in a confrontational style that was then unusual, and
probably unique for a woman. *A New York Post* columnist
said: "Jacqueline Susann, lady disc jockey who is as
brassy as a Sousa march, is worth listening to after
midnight." Another observed that she "delights in nothing
more than cutting down inflated egos to proper size,
possessing plenty of 'guts' (admittedly her favorite word)."
Female disc jockeys were virtually unheard of at the time,
but even so a competing station offered her a program.
Guy's worsening condition forced her to decline.

She often complained that Irving's position was more
hindrance than help ("You're Mansfield's wife; you don't
need the job"), but by January of 1951 she had joined
forces with Joyce—now divorced from Berle for the second time—and they plunged into the growing electronic
marketplace with a series of live television commercials
for which they often wrote their own material. The first
job, in January, was Jackie's fifteen-minute, three-
times-a-week interview program for Quest-Shon-Mark
bras following Faye Emerson on ABC. It was short-

lived, but it was a launching pad. By February they were being described by columnist Sid Shalit as two of the latest glamour girls who have "joined Telly's rapidly growing list of commercial stealers. Their chatter was amiable and they looked like a million on the Somerset Maugham Theatre last Wednesday."

By March Jackie was on the air so much that at least one critic—Jack O'Brien in the *Journal-American*—was already tired of her, complaining that too few girls were monopolizing too many shows. "They can't be blamed for their popularity," he wrote, but he felt they might be "pushing their careers too far, or anyway too often." He named Joyce and Jackie, along with Betty Furness, Faye Emerson, and several others, and complained that their contributions were limited to "conversations about innocuous topics treated as if they were epic events couched in Bernard Shaw dialogue."

The epic events featured in her short-lived *Shopper's Corner* show were fumble-fingered demonstrations of sponsors' products, such as replacement-head mops, vacuum cleaners, pressure cookers, and automatic irons. Between these commercials celebrities played a game in which they tried to identify star photos as Jackie removed strips of tape, but as one critic wrote: "The show had possibilities but scant time was left from the plug-spiels to develop them."

That was April. In May she premiered a heart-tugging weekly half-hour written by Bea, *Jacqueline Susann's Open Door*. On the show, which was designed to "open the door for unfortunate victims of circumstance," guests from all walks of life would air their problems for viewers to solve and celebrity would offer words of wisdom based on his or her own experiences. The show undoubtedly did help some people, especially those seeking jobs, but its tastefulness was questioned. *Cue* magazine wrote that

Jackie "impresses us as being a warmhearted outgoing girl who has an awful lot to learn about the art of interviewing. She's never at a loss for words but some of the words would be better off lost. When a recent guest declared she was on relief, Jackie said, 'Goodness, then you don't make much money, do you?'' The show was sponsored by Sunset appliances, whose commercials led another critic to complain: "We are constantly reminded by Miss Susann, the most loyal girl an advertiser ever had, of the generosity of the sponsor. 'Sunset is opening the door for these people, so you got to open the door for Sunset,' is the way she generally puts it." But critic Harriet Van Horne, David Lowe's wife and presumably a friend, may have stung her the worst, advising that Jackie "might also tidy up her speech a bit. . . . Slovenly speech grates on the ear just as much as off-key singing." So much for friendship.

Jackie next adopted a more demure image, with high-necked college-girl-wholesome outfits and innocent curly locks suited to her many charitable activities, including appearances at benefits for the blind and the handicapped. In the fall she would be chosen queen of the Christmas Seal Carnival at the City College's School of Business Administration, and also queen of a television carnival benefiting tuberculosis patients. By now she was appearing on various panel and quiz shows, including a local game show called *Ring the Bell*, and later an audience participation show called *Your Surprise Store* on CBS.

In July she got a terrible shock. On the fifteenth Joyce's pictures were all over the papers as she was carried from Billy Rose's apartment, where she had tried to commit suicide by slitting her wrists. At the hospital Joyce assured Jackie that it had not been a serious attempt, but that she had wanted to convince Billy that she loved him. She showed Jackie the slashes, which did seem superficial, and she jokingly explained to the press that she had been shaving her wrists when the razor slipped. Reassured, Jackie kept her appointment to lecture at a Long Island University actor's lab on "graceful body movement," demonstrating how to walk with a book on her head.

Joyce's experience must have shaken her, though. As one of her intimate circle of women friends, Joyce was becoming central to Jackie's life, perhaps filling the gap left by Guy's departure. The group, which also included Penny Morgan, television producer Jean Harrison, and cover girl Gladys Faye, called itself the Hockey Club, for reasons none of the members can agree upon. Penny remembers that the word "had something to do with the Yiddish word for banging," though she also thinks it might have been chosen for its resemblance to the men's "Jockey Club." (In fact, the Yiddish *hok* does have a resemblance to the English word "bang," in both literal meaning and sexual connotation. *Hok nit kain tchynik*, which means roughly "Stop banging on a teakettle," is a colloquialism used to turn off gossip or idle chatter.) Jean Harrison has another explanation: "It was because of the pucks, the hockey pucks. That was supposed to be a joke. If you had a good puck you could get into the club. It was a play on the word 'fuck.' " Gladys recalls that "we were sitting at a table thinking of ourselves as sort of a team, and we were trying to figure out what sport had five players. And I think I said hockey. I didn't know if that was true, but they didn't either so they accepted it." (Ice hockey has six players on a side; field hockey has eleven.) Gladys later made the five members little round Hockey Club badges.

However it got its name, the group in time became sufficiently legendary in New York to make the columns with fair frequency and to be immortalized, sardonically, as "The Bluebells" in Jules Feiffer's novel *Harry the Rat*

with Women. Feiffer had learned about the group from
Alexander King, the professional raconteur who met Jackie
through Billy Rose and who regarded Jackie as one of
New York's more unforgettable characters. The women
met at Danny's Hideaway or Sardi's for lunches that
could consume an afternoon, and their various relationships with men were the chief topics of conversation,
though they did from time to time venture into shopping
notes and even schemes for self-improvement. Gladys
recalls that Joyce once came up with a young ballerina
who conducted exercise classes at ten every morning.
"Jackie was totally inflexible," she remembers. "She
was terribly stiff, but she would climb into her leotard
and do her damnedest."

They also helped one another through medical trials,
such as Penny Morgan's cosmetic surgery, and through
countless love affairs over the next few years—many of
them Jackie's. Those, too, helped fill the gap left by Guy,
and they seem to have begun again soon after his departure. There was Joe E. Lewis, of course, though Jean
Harrison recalls that by then Jackie's relationship with him
was not really heated. "She was no longer sleeping with
him on a regular basis but whenever they ran into each
other or it was comfortable to do so. The last time she
slept with him she told me that he was very drunk and he
wanted her to treat him like a woman. He wanted her to
call him by a lady's name, and it upset her very much
because she thought it might have been his whole thing all
those years."

Jean recalls another affair with the head of a cosmetics
firm for which Jackie hoped to become the television
pitchwoman, one later with golfer Jimmy Demaret, and a
crush she had on Frank Stanton, though Jean is sure
nothing ever came of that one. But she doesn't feel the
affairs were primarily sexual. "Jackie didn't go to bed

because she had to go to bed," she says. "It was power and the guy had to be big time. Except for Joe E. she was not in love with any of those people. It was the challenge, to get them where they would say, 'I'll marry you,' or 'I'll make you my TV spokeslady,' or whatever. That was the big thing, and when that didn't happen it wore off. Power was what got to her."

Often she used the apartment of her neighbor Jean Bigelow for her trysts, unbeknownst to Jean's husband, Joe, who was Irving's friend. She did so, at least, until the night when Joe Bigelow went to bed, felt a hairy thing against his leg, and pulled out one of Jackie's falls, which had somehow got separated from its owner in the course of an afternoon's dalliance. He was furious, and evidently the incident stayed on his mind for some time. Later on, when Jean caught him cheating on her and threw a rock through his girl friend's window, Joe supposedly snarled, "If your friend Jackie does such a great blow job, tell her to blow this broken glass back into place."

But despite the growing circle of female friends, Joyce was still closest to her, so much so that tongues wagged when Jackie gave Joyce a gold bracelet with two lovebirds on it. Then there were what seemed like contrary rumors, fueled by Billy's sometimes paranoid jealousy, that Joyce and Jackie maintained a room at a Park Avenue hotel where they entertained men, for money. There is no evidence that this was so, although Billy once went so far as to hire a private detective, and Jackie did give precisely this avocation to her Jennifer character in *Valley of the Dolls*. Jennifer's goal was to bolster her wardrobe, a feat that Jackie herself sometimes accomplished by swapping pills with Joyce in return for designer clothes. Joyce had ample access to her own pills, Jackie explained, but Billy was always searching out her supply and getting rid of it.

Jackie's secret poker winnings may have gone into the clothes budget as well. Curiously, Irving remembers her as a poor player who lost consistently, while others who sat in games with her recall that she played well and frequently won. She loved to gamble, staying up all night at the tables in Las Vegas on at least one occasion, Warren Cowan recalls. She and Irving went to the races with Jack Amiel, owner of Jack Dempsey's restaurant, riding in Amiel's Cadillac convertible and carefully noting his insider tips. Amiel owned his own horses, including the winner of that year's Kentucky Derby, Count Turf. But poker was a special love for Jackie, who then often played in a game that included Dave Garroway and Lee J. Cobb and who would later join a game in the Stuyvesant Town apartment of *Galaxy* magazine's legendary editor, Horace Gold. Gold was agoraphobic, so the magazine's business was done almost entirely in his apartment, which he had not left in years. The poker regulars included a number of well-known science fiction writers. The noted avant-garde composer John Cage was frequently in the game, and so was Robert Stein, then an editor at *Argosy*. They, and others, often adjourned to the Village for breakfast when the games broke up, and Stein recalls Jackie as "tough and bright and funny. I had no sense that she was married at the time, although I knew she was an actress. Most of the regulars were single."

Most of the Hockey Club crowd acted single, even though several married, several times apiece, during the years they maintained the circle of friendships. Their loyalty to one another was almost frightening. Jules Feiffer described a fictional group he based on the Hockey Club in his novel *Harry the Rat with Women:* "Their single interest lay in the area they liked to describe as 'The battle of the sexes.' They fought it well and for good reason. . . . To all of them . . . men were a social convenience: things to date when they went out with the girls at night. Marriage was condoned as either an early mistake, a career necessity or a financial arrangement. As a group they lived for themselves. . . ." He describes how they dealt with a straying male considered property of a group member: "Once the mark was spotted an invisible circle was drawn. . . . The total power of the middle level was directed at them: a call to the phone where an anonymous voice lay down the penalties of trespass—to be gossip-columned, public-relationed and legal-actioned to death. . . . The few men who challenged the circle were laid open to public attack and private harassment; called away from their tables at restaurants to hear the whispered telephone message, 'Get rid of the bitch. Get rid of the bitch.' Or if subtlety were the evening's plan no message at all—only heavy breathing,''

Jackie preserved one press clipping in her scrapbook, undated and unidentified. It described how club member Penny Morgan had observed the boyfriend of another member being driven away from the Beverly Hills Hotel by actress Phyllis Kirk. Penny followed them, and when the man reached New York and phoned his girl friend he was told that she would be late for dinner because she was attending a Hockey Club meeting. "What about, Sweetheart?" he asked. "About you," he was told. "Well, if it's about me then you know I did nothing in Hollywood," he told her innocently. "Yes," she said, "and nothing drove you to the airport, too." The story concluded: "The contrite gentleman soon married the lady." The gentleman was Billy Rose, of course, and the lady was Joyce, whom he at last married in June, 1956.

If Joyce was Jackie's closest friend in the group, Jean Harrison was her chief rival for leadership. A fellow Philadelphian whose family had been influential in local radio, Jean was a woman of great energy who produced, directed, or wrote an astonishing number of radio series, including *Boston Blackie, The Cisco Kid*, and three soaps each week. She wrote Jackie into one of her soaps, schemed to get her other television projects, and acted as her "beard" during her various flings. Jean was herself married—to orchestra leader Hank Sylvern in the early days of their friendship and later to Hank Leeds, who was also a producer—but she understood the ground rules of their crowd, and of Jackie's marriage. "They were an absolute team," she says. "They enjoyed each other. Jackie's respect for Irving was absolutely sincere. I think it was outside of sex. They liked to do things together, they were absolutely webbed together. She thought she was beautiful, and because she thought that she was, *he* thought she was. They conned each other all the time. He thought that she was beautiful and she thought that he was the most important man in the world."

Jean's friendship with Jackie was to end badly a few years later, but in the early fifties they were "living out of each other's pockets," as Jean puts it. "I was crazy about her and she was crazy about me. We had a lot of laughs together. I was with her when she got her driver's license. I had so much faith in her that when I was pregnant and she was practicing I let her drive me like a nut. On the Jersey Shore, to New York and back, driving ninety miles an hour." Jean often wondered if Irving suspected Jackie's affairs. "Of course I never knew whether he knew or not. She was very open, but she would tell Irving that she was with me when she was with a guy. I never knew whether Bea knew, either."

During the worst of her last months with Guy, and during the months after he had been sent away, Jackie had drunk heavily, switching from scotch to gin and grapefruit juice, which seemed to go better with the increasing number of pills she took daily. She began to experience periods she couldn't remember later, blackouts that frightened her enough to get the drinking—and then the pills—in hand. Gambling began to occupy more of her time, and the poker games with the science fiction crowd revived her old interest in that writing genre. She decided to try her hand at it, an effort that produced the interplanetary fantasy she called *Yargo*, in which the heroine, captured by an emotionless race from that world, becomes involved in several implausible escapades on various planets. As romantic fantasy the story is overwrought in style and plot, and as science fiction—which Jackie intended it to be—*Yargo* would have struck her poker cronies as amateurish. Jackie's interest in outer space was sincere and long standing, and she believed in the existence of UFO's. Once before a broadcast of *This Is Show Business* she harangued George S. Kaufman so vehemently about flying saucers that he at last capitulated. "In 1929 I took stock market advice from the Marx Brothers, so there's no reason I shouldn't take science advice from you," he declared.

They continued to visit Guy frequently, though his condition showed no improvement in the years immediately after his hospitalization and would grow worse in the years to come. He would be moved several times for a variety of reasons, and hope would be dangled before his parents only to be taken away. One such instance almost ended Jackie's friendship with Jean Harrison, whom she had taken into her confidence about Guy. Jean's cousin, an eminent psychiatrist named Nathan Kline, was developing new psychiatric drugs at Rockland State Hospital, a few miles north of New York City. She arranged for Jackie to consult Kline, who mapped out an experimental three-month drug treatment program for Guy under his own personal supervision, a program he hoped might make the child "functional" enough to be managed at home.

Jackie agreed to get release papers from Guy's present school and deliver them to Kline, but weeks went by with no further word from Jackie. Jean pressed Jackie, who admitted that she had changed her mind but was embarrassed to say so. Jackie of course mistrusted doctors, particularly where Guy was concerned. Even Grandma believed that Guy might be normal if not for that ill-advised ride on the train. Then there were the shock treatments, which could have sealed his doom. How would they ever know? And how could she subject him now to further experiments? True, it was hard to imagine how he could be worse off mentally, but what about his physical health? What if Kline's drugs left him paralyzed or something? But Jean had no patience for Jackie's explanation. Jackie, she says, considered herself the "perfect woman" and didn't wish to live with her own "imperfect child."

Jackie considered having another baby, but Dr. Bender's quoted odds on birth defects discouraged her, and so did the prospect of the pregnancy and birth. She would have to give up pills and alcohol, and maybe cigarettes. Did she want another baby enough to go through all that? Yes, she decided, but then there were her "women's troubles." Intercourse was more painful after Guy's birth, and she now had some urinary pressure as well as sporadic bleeding from her uterus. Something was damaged "down there," she concluded, reaching a decision. Irving deserved another child, but she wasn't fit to bear it. Jackie approached a friend and asked if she would be a surrogate mother, long before the term had come into use. Her plan was that Irving would impregnate the woman, who would then give the baby back to them to raise. The woman declined.

Jackie was always concerned when her friends had abortions, helping them find a "clean" doctor, going to him with them, providing the bankroll if they were strapped.

But twice in the early 1950's she was moved to ask the abortion seekers if they would consider giving the baby to her. One of the pregnant women was a relative, a young cousin from Philadelphia, the other a drop-in member of the Hockey Club.

At first they spent every Sunday visiting Guy, but it became so painful they went less often. Jackie took up golf. She and Irving joined the Alpine Golf Club, a hangout for comedians and other theatrical types seeking outdoor recreation across the river in New Jersey. Regulars remember them there most weekends, Jackie with her hair in a babushka and wearing little makeup, lugging her white leather golf bag around the course for awhile and then settling in for a card game and conversation with the women around the pool. The club would form a significant part of the Mansfields' social life for many years, though there was some crossover—sometimes Hockey Club members would come along as guests, and Alpine members attended an occasional Hockey Club wedding or shower.

She never let up in her efforts to develop a hit TV show. Late in 1952 she did a brief unsuccessful stint on a program called *Fun Time* on WPIX. By spring she was back, this time with a low-budget half hour of variety and fashion called *The Jacqueline Susann Show*, for which she conscripted Sam Levenson as her first celebrity guest. They discussed the sponsor's sewing machines, and Levenson obliged with reminiscences of his mother's skill at converting old drapes into clothing for himself and his brother.

Although Kinsey had just published his startling report on *Sexual Behavior in the Human Female*, in television there was a reaction against sexuality, at least as represented by revealing costumes and the overly generous bosoms of such performers as Dagmar. The unexpected popularity of a show called the *Author Meets the Critics*, and of its conservatively dressed moderator, Virgilia Peterson, who faced the cameras with glasses perched on the end of her nose, prompted Irving to comment that programmers would now be looking for women "with the kind of well-rounded personality turned out by Bryn Mawr instead of Billy Minsky"—personalities like the elegant Jacqueline Susann, who had just been elected to the National Fashion Academy's best-dressed list.

It was an odd list, led by the sweet but frumpy Mamie Eisenhower as Best Dressed Hostess, but Jackie was indeed on it as Best Dressed Television Actress, and she would remain on it for several years. According to Eleanor Lambert, who puts out the real best-dressed-women lists, "The National Fashion Academy was a fake, and was closed by the Better Business Bureau." Fake or not, it helped get Jackie more publicity, and once again she changed her image to suit the times, adopting youthful turtlenecks and poodle cuts. By June, however, when she was photographed in full color for the cover of the *New York Sunday Mirror* magazine, she was back in a low-cut, lace-bosomed, swirly beige silk Florence Lustig number, and she had over-arched her eyebrows. But despite the swings of mood, Jackie was looking her best these days, as if reaching thirty-five and making a list had conferred a certain authority and poise. A friend says, "Jackie was truly beautiful for about five minutes when she was very young, and then she was truly beautiful again in her middle thirties. The prevailing styles were just right for here, although not the ones she would have chosen by instinct; suits that were close fitting and feminine, dresses that were tailored."

On Memorial Day weekend it was the sporty look as she journeyed a hundred miles upstate to the Concord hotel, where Jimmy Demaret was golf pro. She was back there for a week in July, just after playing a role in *Suspense*, the thriller anthology that had moved successfully from radio to live television in 1949. She was bursting with energy, still working on *Yargo* on her portable but taking time off to fool around with the comics and singers, and to have her picture taken with Demaret and Jean Harrison.

Jean remembers those days vividly: "It was all like a big unhealthy family up there, all the screwing and the machinations. There were a lot of big stars, too. Sid and Florence Caesar and Sam and Esther Levenson and Marty Allen, who was married to this woman named Frenchy. It was all kind of fun in a wicked away, and the energy level was high. And we had the run of the hotel. It was very easy to do anything we wanted to do, and Jackie ran off with Jimmy Demaret and once with Joe E. Lewis when he came up." Jean was not much taken with Demaret, but she remembers that Jackie "was absolutely crazy about him. She came on to him like a buddy at first and then she kept after him until he finally went to bed with her. That was her technique."

As the summer wound down at the Concord, Irving was on the verge of a curious triumph of his own, this one involving the plucky Jane Froman, whose show he had been producing for the past year. Miss Froman, the survivor of a wartime plane crash followed by twenty-eight operations and skin grafts, wore leg braces and stammered except when she was singing. She was an American sweetheart and her show, called *U.S.A. Canteen*, had good ratings, but Irving was bored with her theme song, "With a Song in My Heart," and urged her to try something new. She refused, but Irving went ahead and instructed songwriter Erwin Drake to come up with an alternative. He did, and it was introduced on Thanksgiving Day with Miss Froman still objecting. Titled "I Believe," it became one of the greatest hits of the era and remains a standard.

Irving was as proud as if he had written and performed the song himself.

Jackie hustled "Mr. and Mrs." interviews with Irving, one of which appeared in the *New York Post* in November. The story posed the question: "Marriage and career: Can an ambitious girl really have both?" Not surprisingly, "Jacqueline Susann, contented wife, mother and home-maker" assured readers that she could. She posed in a tight dress with lots of pearls and she burbled on about how bad her cooking was and how Irving had accused her of trying to give him ulcers for his birthday. Garlic was discussed, which Irving loathed and Jackie "eats raw like candy," and readers were told that "whenever the actress ventures to feed garlic to their son Guy, 6, Irving complains that the boy smells like a salami."

But despite the Concord adventures, the minor television jobs she hustled, the poker games, and even the fashion accolade, Jackie did not rate 1953 as one of her better years. Among other losses, Grandma Ida had died after a long illness. Guy had been away for several years now, in two different institutions, and was not getting well. Jackie's mind began to turn more and more to religion, and to talks with Hildegarde about the questions that concerned her.

As the new year opened, Jackie's restlessness increased. Irving was traveling a lot, and she was left to spend her time with the Hockey Club or the poker players. With insufficient outlet for what Irving called "her coiled-up energy," she was ripe for what did happen to her next.

And that was—as she described in a letter to Irving—her first meeting with "three exquisite pounds of poodle." This was Josephine, the puppy who had reached out of a pet shop cage and playfully tapped her on the shoulder, and who would one day inspire her first published book.

Irving was not initially charmed by the puppy, but of

course she would in time win his heart as well. Later, when Josephine had become famous, he would tell a reporter, "I like her better than Jackie. She's easier to get along with."

---19---

Conversion

But I knew I wasn't really good. I was doing fairly well. Every year my agents would say "This is going to be your big year."

—Jacqueline Susann

IN the middle 1950's, Jackie spent much of her time training Josephine, a process that seems to have required great patience and a strong stomach, according to her later accounts. There was a momentary time out for her cousin, Bob Jelinek, who had finished Harvard Law School, joined the Coast Guard, and was now stationed in New York. He was very presentable, someone to introduce around to her single friends.

Jackie was still playing golf at the Concord whenever she could, teaming up with Jan Murray and occasionally Milton Berle. The Concord had become her favorite retreat, as Gladys Faye remembers. Gladys advised her on how to dress before her first visit there. . . . "Take the most elegant clothes you have. Everybody changes every two hours and it's like going to the Waldorf-Astoria right in the middle of the Catskill Mountains. Take sequined dresses, gloves up to your armpits; put sequins on the frames of your glasses." She remembers that Jimmy Demaret, who had interested Jackie in golf among other things, gave her a hole-in-one pin that summer. "I've always wondered if she really earned it," she says.

The Concord weekends left Jackie plenty of time for massages and facials, and for letters to Hildegarde in Florida. "I sure envy you," she wrote. "Right now you are probably tan and lovely . . . while I am gray and yellow." She mentions further writing efforts and a television guest spot, but there is an air of dissatisfaction in the letter. "I am up to my neck in painters and wallpaperers and rug men . . . and my French poodle in the midst . . . and my French lessons. But I am thinking good thoughts."

She still rode herd on the affairs and mishaps of the Hockey Club. At Billy's she met the composer Gian Carlo Menotti and she invested in his new opera *The Saint of Bleecker Street*.

The Saint had a powerful effect on Jackie. She wrote glowingly to Hildegarde: "I just can't wait until you get back to see it. . . . The music is fantastic . . . and it is religious. . . . It is about a girl who sees visions and wants to become a nun. . . . To me it was a beautiful thing for the church, but many people felt Menotti was speaking against it. He is a Catholic of sorts. . . . The tears ran down my face and Irving asked me if I was crazy. I want to see it again with you. . . ." Hildegarde was not yet convinced by Jackie's fervor. "She was always shopping around for religions, Episcopal, Jewish, Mohammedan, Catholic . . ."

For all the time she spent in the Borscht Belt, Jackie didn't know any serious Jews. Cantor professed to be one, and so did Jessel, but Jackie wondered. Grandma had faith of a sort, and Jackie remembered how Grandma and the others had stood up to God at her grandfather's funeral. Jackie was always standing up to God herself; but not in the way of someone with deep roots in a religious tradition. She often felt empty inside, hollow, like those humanoid balloons at which, as a child, she'd thrown brickbats in the amusement park. You hurled a bat at the silly balloon and knocked him over, and then he popped right back up on his flat cardboard feet, his painted smile unfading. As Jackie kept popping back up after each blow of fate. Why did God treat her like this? What had she done wrong? Why couldn't he at least have given her a normal child?

And now God was about to take her father, too. "Don't leave me," she whispered to the failing Bob. "Please don't ever leave me." But she knew he would. He was almost seventy, and his heart was giving out. She wished she were still a little girl who could climb into his arms. She remembered the summer when she had been twelve years old. Rose went off to Europe and Jackie had him all to herself. He'd toasted her, pouring her first champagne, saying, "Here's to my lady, the only lady I'll ever love." All her life she had tried to memorize him, to etch him in her mind: the way he held his brushes, his smile, the smell of his cologne. "Mental and spiritual incest"—she admitted it. She couldn't have him as a lover, so in a way she'd tried to *become* him, to emulate his wit, his creativity . . . even his philandering. She was like Diana Barrymore, she said, drinking herself to death in imitation of John; or that daughter of Errol Flynn, who became a stunt flyer. And Jackie had been certain she would make Bob proud of her. "The whole idea," she often said, "is to show the father what he has missed by ignoring the daughter."

In July, 1956, Jackie got a rare opportunity to go on the

stage again, this time playing Janice in *Anniversary Waltz* at the Long Beach Playhouse. She was listed third in the program, after Martha Scott and Donald Woods, and the *Playbill* bio made her sound like a major television personality. A friend who drove out to Long Island to see the performance was disappointed: "I had helped her rehearse for the audition, and I realized that for Jackie the challenge was in getting the part—that's when she did her best acting. Once she was in it, she was quickly bored. She lacked the concentration."

Shortly after the play's brief run, the Mansfields went to Europe, with Jackie lugging the manuscript of *Yargo*, on which she hoped to do further revisions. They had some difficulties with return passage, so she made one of her "deals" with God: If He would get them on a boat, she would give up smoking for the voyage. She desperately tried to keep her bargain despite what she described to Hildegarde as the "agony of withdrawal."

To take her mind off cigarettes, she discussed *Yargo* with George Chasin, an agent with MCA, the west coast giant. Chasin was interested enough to shop the manuscript around Hollywood on his return, but science fantasies were not then in vogue and he got no takers.

Jackie also told Hildegarde about another experience on the boat, one she felt guilty about but attributed to her frayed nerves caused by nicotine deprivation. It was an affair, brief but scorching, with a macho character actor and film star. It was to be one of her last great sexual flings.

She discussed the affair compulsively with Hildegarde during the fall, feeling that this time it really had been a betrayal of Irving. Hildegarde was concerned for her friend, who seemed to be suffering physically as well as emotionally during those days. Her mouth was falling apart, Jackie complained, and she was again "going steady" with her dentist, Dr. Goldberger, in an effort to get her darkening caps replaced and her "gummy" smile repaired.

Jackie had recurrent nightmares about Bob's death. She told Hildegarde that she had to believe he would watch over her from heaven. ("How we talked about God and spiritual things when we got going!" Hildegarde recalls.) The singer had been Jackie's friend for a decade, but now they were drawing very close. Hildegarde was breaking up with Anna Sosenko, her friend and manager of twenty-three years. Starting over in middle age after a series of disastrous relationships with men, she was achieving serenity that Jackie envied. She even became a lay nun, committed to a life of celibacy and religious devotion. Jackie often went with her to Saint Patrick's Cathedral now, lighting candles for Saint Andrew, the least popular saint there, who she hoped "might have more time to heed the prayers of a Jewish girl."

Jackie asked Bob if he was still an atheist and he said yes, but she seemed so disappointed that he went on to tell her something he'd often heard from his sister Rosa: The Susan bloodline had a lot of mystics and religious scholars, he said. That's what Vilna was known for; it was the seat of Jewish mysticism. If she felt a pull toward religion, it might be in her genes.

At the end of March, 1957, he was back in the hospital, still making playful passes at the nurses. On April 2 he called his student Pearl to confirm that he would keep his appointment for a lesson on Saturday. But then on April 3, just two weeks short of his seventieth birthday, Robert Susan gave up the fight. In the funeral parlor Rose whispered, "Good-bye, Mookie," with "the greatest sadness and sweetness" a friend had ever seen her convey. Rose had been forced to rely on herself but she would miss him.

Jackie claimed his body like a trophy. She wrested him

away from Rose, and buried him in a plot that Irving owned in Queens, New York, where she could easily visit the grave. But his grave was insufficient comfort. Jackie dug dangerously deeper into her cache of pills. Twenty years later, after she had died, the film critic Andrew Sarris would write with uncanny perception: "If there is any single key to the oeuvre of Jacqueline Susann it is to be found in an extended Electra complex afflicting little girls who grow up wanting to go to bed with their daddies, and failing that, begin to pop pills as a consolation. From the *Valley of the Dolls* through *Once Is Not Enough* it has been one long refrain of 'My Heart Belongs to Daddy or His Equivalent in Drugs.' From the drug counter where dreams are dispensed to the drug rack where Susann sells so well is but a short step between the writer and the reader. Jacqueline Susann did, as they say, touch a nerve out there."

A few months before Bob's death, Hildegarde walked Jackie to the Catholic Information Center at Fifty-ninth Street and Columbus Avenue, in the heart of a dangerous neighborhood. The center was connected with the parish of Saint Paul the Apostle. Hildegarde introduced Jackie to Father Justin J. O'Brien, a jovial man in his early sixties, long experienced in instructing potential converts, especially actors, writers, and Jews. The Paulist order had been founded to "make America Catholic," O'Brien said. Jackie was given a book called *The Grace of God* to study and began a course of private instruction.

Jackie became certain she would meet Bob in heaven. He couldn't have left her for good. Dazed and drugged, she repeated a poem Aunt Esther had taught her: "Serene, I fold my hands and wait,/Nor care for wind, nor tide, nor sea;/I rave no more 'gainst time or fate,/For lo! my own shall come to me."

She caught herself unaware in the bathroom mirror,

looking as batty as Aunt Esther had become. She was frightened at the way her mind leaped about, but she was coming to understand God was not a "short-order cook," as she and Aunt Esther had imagined Him, trading His rewards for trivial good behavior. God demanded obedience, and love. He might "turn his countenance upon you, and give you peace," the way he had for Hildegarde, if you served Him and followed His discipline. If Jackie took God more seriously, He would do the same for her. He would become her Father.

O'Brien cautioned her to make sure she wished to become a Catholic. Jackie said she was.

But she didn't tell Rose, who was having troubles enough of her own in adjusting to Bob's death and to the paltriness of his estate—a mere five thousand dollars, much less than had been anticipated and barely enough to pay for his last hospitalization. And now that she no longer had to remain strong for him, Rose's own sturdy sixty-five-year-old body was failing.

Jackie did tell Irving of her plans, and for once the easygoing, permissive, anything-you-want-is-fine-with-me man she had always taken for granted was truly appalled. But she worked on him, and by late May Hildegarde would write in her dairy: "Jackie called. She has talked with Irving and he doesn't mind her becoming a Catholic. Our prayers are answered. She has longed for this to happen and wants me to stand up for her."

The date was set for June 18, a Tuesday. Hildegarde remembers that Jackie was nervous but that she looked radiant in a Chanel-style suit as they walked together up the aisle of Saint Paul's beneath the remarkable cerulean-blue ceiling, an exact replica of the constellations of the midnight sky on the day the church was dedicated in 1885. They crossed the marble floor with its two circular mosaics, following Father O'Brien to the baptistry. There they waited while he arranged the bottles of chrism and picked up a small shell. Hildegarde felt tears sting her eyes as the priest turned to Jackie.

"Do you believe in the Father Almighty?" he asked her.

"I do," she said, her voice husky.

"Do you believe in Jesus Christ, the only son of our Lord?"

"I do."

"Do you believe in the Holy Spirit, the Holy Catholic Church, the Communion of Saints?"

"I do."

"Do you wish to be baptized?"

"I do."

The priest motioned to the font, and Hildegarde placed her right hand on her friend's shoulder as Jackie lowered her head toward the holy water. She saw a painting of John the Baptist baptizing Jesus in the river Jordan, then felt the drops of water splash against her skin.

And, as though far away, Jackie heard the voice of the priest: "I baptize you in the name of the Father and of the Son and of the Holy Spirit."

He helped her to stand straight again, then said, "I now anoint you with the oil of salvation." Jackie said to herself the words she had learned would calm her spirit: "Let nothing disturb thee. Let nothing afright thee. All things are passing. God remains the same and patience gains all things."

"Receive the light of Christ," Father O'Brien said, and he handed her a candle.

"Thank you," she said, beaming at the priest and at her friend, who was now crying openly. And then it was over.

Hildegarde's diary for June 18 records: "Met Jackie at 3:15. To St. Paul's to see Father O'Brien. She is so thrilled and happy she is to become a Catholic today. She was baptized in St. Paul's and I stood up for her. . . .''

They went to the Waldorf for cocktails, and Jackie raised her daiquiri in a toast.

''Well, here's to Jesus,'' she said.

20

The Schiffli Troubadour

Even if a rich man is short, fat and ugly, he always convinces himself that his money has nothing to do with women liking him.

—Jacqueline Susann

JOSEPHINE had filled some of the void left by Guy's institutionalization, and her newfound religion had helped, but Jackie was still drawn strongly to children, although she had decided that she would never bear another child herself. She showered attention on the small daughters of friends. And then, sometime during 1957, while dining with Rose in a West Philadelphia Chinese restaurant, she was struck by the charm and beauty of the owners' four-year-old daughter. She would thereafter become "godmother"—unofficially but quite seriously—to the little girl, Karlina Chau, and would even at one point approach the child's parents about the possibility of adopting

her. The Chaus declined, but over the next fourteen or
fifteen years they would welcome Jackie's doting quasi-
parental attentions to their daughter. She would spend
countless weekends with the Mansfields in New York,
would even appear with Jackie on several television commercials for Schiffli embroidery, and would become in
many ways the daughter Jackie had always dreamed of
having.

Jackie's involvement with Schiffli had begun in 1955.
She was at the Alpine Golf Club sitting around the pool
and shmoozing with Jean Harrison, Jean's husband, Hank
Leeds, and others, including Judge Milton Rosenblum and
his wife, Fran. Jean recalls, "Hank thought it would be
fun to do an all-night show for insomniacs. Judge Rosenblum
also thought the show was a good idea. Hank would be the
producer, I the director, Jackie the fashion commentator."
Rosenblum was connected with an organization called the
Schiffli Lace and Embroidery Institute,* which provided
the backing on WOR-TV.

Night Time, New York went on the air September 21,
1955, with Milton Ford, a Washington disc jockey, as
emcee. "It was," Jean says, "a hodgepodge, running
weeknights from one to seven A.M., with music, games,
quizzes, auditions for amateur songwriters, interviews with
celebrities, and even a parrot. Ernie Kovacs would watch
and then call in and kibitz, do some shtik on the air. We
had a contest every night, and about three in the morning,
when the interviews and shtik were over, we would put on
movies, and then at six Milton Ford would come back
without Jackie and do a kid show, from six to seven, which

---

*Schiffli is a machine process for making embroidery and lace, and is not
a brand name. The Institute was a group of manufacturers who pooled
their resources for generic promotion.

was very cute." But if Kovacs was laughing, Jackie was not. She felt she was not being given enough to do, that she was the one who through her friendship with Rosenblum had raised the backing, but that now Jean was trying to cut her out. Those celebrity interviews were the major sticking point, as Jean recalls. "Jackie's interviews were hostile; she gave them too much muscle, and she wanted to do interviews that were inappropriate for her."

Others, such as Candy Jones, a famous model, agrees with Jean that Jackie could do a most peculiar interview. "It was hard to get a word in," Candy recalls. "I remember it distinctly because I have never had anyone else interview me and then answer the questions for me. Jackie asked a question—let's say, 'How tall does a girl have to be today to be a high-fashion model? It's five-eight, isn't it? Shouldn't she be a size eight or ten? That's correct. What is the most difficult thing in the life of a model? She has to go to bed early, she has to stay in shape; she always has to look her best. She doesn't have much of a social life.' All I could do was nod my head. I was in accord with everything she said. I was wishing she'd say something inaccurate."

About six weeks into the program the judge called for a meeting. "I think he wanted us to drop Milton Ford and make Jackie the star," Jean says. "It would never have worked because it was Ford who was bringing in the audience. At the meeting Jackie got very excited. She accused me of extorting free meals from the kiddie segment in the morning, and of taking home the prizes that we offered during the night and selling them. She accused me of bizarre, terrible, chintzy things and that's when I realized it was impossible; *she* was impossible. I knew she was a very difficult lady but I thought it was going to be different with me. I knew the evil parts of Jackie and I thought I could turn them into fun."

After the meeting things got worse. Jean describes threats on her life, strange phone calls in the middle of the night, calls so frightening that a policeman was stationed near her on the studio floor at WOR. "It wasn't worth all the agonies, and so the show went black," she says. But the phone calls continued, and there was even a late-night visit from Jackie in person: "She pounded on our door at three or four in the morning and ran in and took the picture off the wall, the beautiful Bob Susan still life that he had given me." Thirty years later, Jean's voice still shakes when she talks about it. Now the head of a successful television-commercial production company with such major clients as Bloomingdale's as well as Procter and Gamble, she regards those weeks as "the most bizarre, dramatic time of my life. I never had that bitter an enemy, never. . . . She went to all my friends and told terrible stories and I really felt my career in New York was over. She knew a lot of people." Years later Jean found herself seated in front of Jackie at a movie premiere. "We didn't say hello," she remembers. "I squirmed all through it, and I was positive my hair wasn't combed."

Judge Rosenblum continued his association with Schiffli and his interest in making Jackie the spokeswoman, but it would be another year before a deal was set with a specific show. That was *Night Beat*, the tough, confrontational local interview program on WABD that brought Mike Wallace to sudden stardom in late 1956. Wallace left the show for a network position in June, 1957, to be replaced by John Wingate. Jackie had a crush on John Wingate for a time. A bachelor, he was from the South and was in his late thirties. A Hockey Club member recalls a strange evening with Jackie and Joyce at the Billy Rose mansion on East Ninety-third Street. Jackie wrote Wingate a mash note, which she kept revising and rereading to her girl friends, who finally convinced her not to send it. Another time, Candy Jones was present when Jackie and Wingate had an argument. "He came into her dressing room. She seemed crazy about him, and he had obviously been drinking. I got up and walked out. The fight had something to do with him seeing her after the show. She said something like he had 'promised,' or 'We're expected.' "

Jackie's contract called for two live Schiffli commercials, every night, five nights a week, written and produced by her. She often brought friends and even Karlina on with her to model Schiffli products, and occasionally she also used Josephine, the two appearing in their famous mother-and-dog outfits.

On *Night Beat* Jackie first became aware of a pony-tailed New Hampshire housewife named Grace Metalious whose new novel, *Peyton Place*, reached number four on the bestseller list a week before its official publication. Metalious, six years younger than Jackie, had spent several years writing her story of the sexual entanglements in a small New England town, and it had been turned down by at least seventeen publishers before being picked up by a small and unlikely house called Julian Messner.

Jackie was not much impressed with Metalious herself, but she became almost obsessively fascinated with the success of Grace's writing. *Peyton Place* was a gossipy, soap-opera kind of a novel written from a woman's point of view—the very sort of thing Jackie felt she could do herself, and probably just as well. And think what *she* could do on television to promote a book! Grace, in person, was chunky, depressed, and colorless. And yet the book was selling, almost in spite of the author's publicity efforts.

When Grace arrived for her *Night Beat* interview, Marlene Sanders, the associate producer, took her to the makeup room. "Make me beautiful," Grace pleaded. Makeup did what it could. The program started, and Wallace took the offensive. "What gives you the right to pry and hold your neighbors up to ridicule?" Speechless, Grace seemed on the verge of weeping, and Jackie felt so sorry for her that she offered God a deal. "Don't let this poor woman cry in front of millions of people. Get her through the show, God, and I won't smoke another cigarette tonight." Grace found her voice but not her composure. When Wallace said, "I thought your book was basic and carnal," Grace lamely answered, "You did, huh?" But *Peyton Place* would soon sell more copies than *Gone With the Wind*.

Jackie's connection with Schiffli was by now providing her with another kind of celebrity, however. After *Night Beat*, she moved to WABC-TV, where, as *Variety* put it, "for twenty weeks she was the Schiffli voice on the Ben Hecht show," a program that was canceled rather abruptly on February 21, 1959, when Salvador Dali used the word "orgasm" on the air, one of the unspeakable words at that time. Mike Wallace later referred to it as "Ben's orgasm-and-out show." Ben had not been overly impressed with Jackie in the beginning, mainly because he disliked the commercials she did. He disliked *all* commercials, in fact, and was quite outspoken about this on the air, stating at one point, "I've seldom met any human of any age group who didn't wince when a commercial whoop-dee-doo'd on the screen and who didn't curse the sponsor for interrupting his diversion." After which Missy, the weather-girl announcer, appeared on camera and said, "Please be attentive to the bitten hand that feeds us," as Jackie waltzed out in a Schiffli-embroidered dress.

Hecht's opinion of Jackie changed after an incident involving eight somewhat fragrant Bowery bums who had been rounded up by producer Ted Yates for a group interview "in the interest of sociology." Jackie strolled into the studio, recoiled from the collective smell of eight unwashed and wine-soaked bodies, then draped her arm around Hecht's shoulder and said sweetly, "Ben, why didn't you tell me you had your fan club with you tonight?" After that, though he still thought she looked like "an imitation Hedy Lamarr," Hecht had a bit more respect for Jackie's wit. Eventually he christened her his "Schiffli Troubadour" and even composed a verse in her honor: "Here's to Jackie Susann/Come rain or come snow/ The backbone of my TV show." Such a family feeling developed between them that one evening he interviewed Jackie's friend Billy Rose while Jackie brought Joyce— currently Mrs. Rose—on camera to help with the Schiffli commercials.

On the Hecht show, in October, 1958, Jackie encountered Grace Metalious again. Grace had developed a trifle more confidence and had also put on more weight. Somewhere in the middle of the program Jackie became aware that she was having a strange problem with her clothes. For the occasion, Grace had bought herself a panty girdle, which suddenly went *whang* and dissolved into shreds. Jackie was beginning her commercial when she saw Grace, clutching her stomach oddly, waddle off toward the ladies' room.

When Ben Hecht went off the air, the Schiffli Troubadour returned to Mike Wallace for a reprise. He had left the ABC network, and was again doing local interviews, now on Channel 13. He continued the confrontational method he had pioneered, a style Jackie felt she herself had invented on her disc jockey show and on *Night Time, New York* in 1955. She felt that she and Wallace, who were the same age and who actually resembled each other physically, were practically twins. And in truth, they did look remarkably alike. Both had the Oriental eyefold (in school Mike had been nicknamed Chink), and both had the flat cheekbones and brunette coloring with light skin that recurs now and then, through the generations, in certain Russian Jewish families. Once when they were putting on makeup together she looked at their faces in the mirror and said, ''I think our great grandmothers must have been raped by the same invading Mongol.'' Mike didn't get the joke. Nor was he impressed with the fact that they were both somewhat overaged out-of-town Jews trying to make it on camera in New York.

Mike's lack of interest stung her, as did his success with a kind of interview she felt she, as a woman, had not been given a chance to do. Certainly she said in later years that ''every show I was on made someone a star—and it was never me.'' Marlene Sanders, the beautiful redhead who had been production coordinator at *Night Beat* and who later became a CBS news correspondent, recalls: ''Her style struck us as funny and ridiculous. It was not treated with a lot of respect. For one thing commercials for embroidery itself seemed like a crazy idea. She was very heavily made up. She was skinny and brassy. It all seemed so out of left field. . . .''

Ridiculous as the ''crazy idea'' might have seemed, by 1959 there was no doubt that it was working. The Schiffli Troubadour was unsinkable, popping up for personal appearances constantly at shopping malls, department stores, community centers, even churches and synagogues. She persuaded Chet Huntley to wear a lace embroidered shirt for his sign-off speech at the Emmy Awards. And she made her own sign-off line so familiar that it began to turn up in the routines of several comics whose work she had previously admired. Throughout that spring Jerry Lewis opened his nightclub act wearing a Schiffli embroidered shirt and explaining, ''Schiffli adds beauty to everything it touches. See how beautiful I am?'' Another of her slogans was less famous but just as quotable: ''Lingerie without Schiffli is like Amos without Andy.''

The campaign was so successful that by the spring of 1959 *Women's Wear Daily* reported in a front-page story, that Schiffli was having the biggest year of its history, with deliveries of the products running four to seven weeks behind. In May *Variety* also acknowledged the phenomenon, explaining: "Much of this is attributed to the video commercials delivered by Miss Susann, who both writes and transmits the messages on Mike Wallace's nightly program over WNTA-TV." The story added: "Since TV means Miss Susann and no one else the impact of her video message has evidently struck a responsive chord."

Jackie gave her all to those commercials. John Wingate recalls them as "high camp before the days of Andy Warhol," but he also remembers how professional she was about the job: "She did at least two commercials per show and she took pride in doing them well, writing and producing as well as pitching them. Obviously, she had to work very hard preparing them, with different apparel and household furnishings and models every night. She had to deliver commentary and give the prices and store credits, all in sixty seconds."

Irving, meanwhile, was still quite busy. He had produced Polly Bergen's NBC show for a few months in early 1958, an experience she would recall fondly. "I don't remember him doing a bad job and I don't remember him doing a good job. I remember him as a nice man." By late 1959, he was producing Dick Clark's *The World of Talent* in New York and *Take a Good Look* starring Ernie Kovacs, Edie Adams, and Cesar Romero in L.A.

Despite the bicoastal schedule, Jackie was a bit concerned about Irving's status as a producer. He was no longer the power he had been in the early fifties, when he and his friend and colleague Lester Gottlieb were referred to as "the one-two-programming punch in CBS radio and TV." Now sometimes it seemed he was scrambling to stay in the game. She was beginning to see that he might not always bring in the sort of money needed to keep everything going. Yet he was important to her emotionally as well as economically. She realized more than ever how much she depended on him.

True, he remained opposed to her Catholicism, which hurt and angered her at first. As the months went by she began to have some doubts herself about the course she had taken. And as the doubts grew, her devotion to Hildegarde weakened, perhaps because of the guilt she must have been feeling at letting her friend down. John Wingate remembers the change: "We were always running to see Hildegarde perform. But then Jackie turned her sights more toward Anna Sosenko, Hildegarde's ex-partner."

Sosenko was, in fact, an original, a raspy-voiced, unstylish woman whose intelligence and creativity more than made up for her lack of chic. Anna was launching Jackie on a great books program and trying to clean up her language. "I got her away from the Broadway idiom," she says now. "I started her on the French storytellers—Flaubert, de Maupassant, George Sand. She went on to Nietzsche. This was in the late fifties. Later her taste changed dramatically, in clothes as well as books. She began to wear more subdued clothes and she 'moved' to the other side of Broadway. It was now Park Avenue, Fifth Avenue." Anna adds that Jackie had "a first-class imagination, first-class descriptive powers, and almost total recall," though those descriptive powers often utilized a vocabulary-that would have made a longshoreman blush. "This was an exciting woman; this was a colorful woman; this was a woman with ideas—and don't let anyone tell you that Jackie wouldn't have made it without Irving," she says. "They had a fine symbiosis, but Jackie would have made it without him."

That fine symbiosis was often sorely tested, and not just by Jackie's dalliances with comics and golf pros and Irving's commuting. In June she went to Paris as Schiffli's representative at the spring fashion shows, and Irving went along. They dined with Maurice Chevalier, but she was even more taken with the woman whose wool knit suits were the epitome of style, Coco Chanel. And Coco took a fancy to her, too, though no one is certain how far the relationship may have gone. Undoubtedly Coco made sexual advances, and Jackie did return from the trip with at least one magnificent Chanel original, a suit Coco had given her. But whether there was a romantic involvement or not, Jackie took away from the confrontation a new conviction that those who were successful could make their own rules. Coco Chanel's bisexual affairs were well known, yet she had the high-fashion world at her feet.

Back from Paris, she returned to her Schiffli chores, making public appearances to describe the new Paris lines and presenting endless "Schiffli Fashion Awards" at endless creamed chicken dinners. She was still doing commercials for Wallace on Channel 13, and by now she was also doing them at least occasionally on David Susskind's *Open End* and on *The Play of the Week* on the same channel. In the summer she signed for a role in a new play. In September she was a guest on *The Jack Paar Show*, and was reviewed as "one of the best talking women the show ever had and gor-jus too." And she was busy with Josephine and with Karlina, who was now seven and a beautiful, doll-like little girl for whom Jackie had high hopes and a constantly open checkbook, about which Irving was beginning to complain.

Irving was complaining of other things, too, one of them being Jackie's "star-crush" infatuation with Ethel Merman. She had met "the Merm" earlier, but she had not really gotten to know the reigning queen of Broadway musicals—the latest being *Gypsy*—until Ethel's best friend, Benay Venuta, moved back to New York. Jackie and Benay had met during the war, when Benay was married to

Armand Deutsch, the Sears, Roebuck heir. Deutsch was a cardplaying pal of Irving's, and the two young couples often dined together, at "21" or the Copa or the Stork Club's intimate and exclusive Cub Room. One day Benay, an actress and singer, mentioned that she needed a novelty song for an appearance she was making at Loews State. Jackie wrote a hilarious lyric in no time flat, and Benay says she recognized that Jackie was creative and smart, despite her showgirl looks and garish tastes. Benay urged Jackie to concentrate on writing. "I knew Jackie way before she started any relationship with Ethel," Benay says now. "And I believe Jackie's warmth toward me, like mine toward her, had nothing to do with Ethel, although I certainly have had people in my life who felt they could get to Ethel through me. She was such a giant star. . . . People are intrigued with the kind of magnetism Ethel had."

Jackie certainly was. She knew Ethel was coarse and vulgar, a woman who described Benay's important Jewish society friends as "dull as pig shit." When she starred in Gypsy, Ethel was turning fifty, overweight, physically unappealing, and an intellectual lightweight to say the least, yet she was a major presence in the world Jackie inhabited. She drank too much, and she was often abusive when she'd had too much to drink, but she emanated the kind of star quality Jackie had aspired to and now doubted she'd ever have. Merman could belt out a song like no one ever had, a talent that had brought high praise from Irving Berlin, among others. "She's the best," Berlin had said of her. "You give her a bad song and she'll make it sound good. Give her a good song and she'll make it sound great. And you'd better write her a good lyric. The guy in the last row of the second balcony is going to hear every syllable."

Rose couldn't understand Jackie's admiration for Ethel, and listening to her records didn't help. Jackie tried to explain that Ethel was a "performer's performer," and that you had to be in the theater to fully appreciate her genius. Ethel was a total professional, she said, and totally in control of everything she did. If someone upstaged her, that performer was out. If she demanded 10 percent of the gross, she got it. She even insisted on house seats for every performance so that she could resell them to scalpers. She had once boasted, "Broadway's been very good to me, but then I've been very good to Broadway." Jackie insisted it was true. Dumpy and vulgar though she might be, and bigoted as she certainly was about "niggers" and "commie Jews," she was the undisputed star of the musical stage, and Jackie worshiped that talent and was proud that Ethel considered her a friend. The two even shared similar dental problems, including a "gummy" smile that had to be concealed when posing for photographers.

Gypsy was a smash from its opening on May 21, 1959, when Walter Kerr called it "the best damn musical I've seen in years." Directed by Jerome Robbins, written by Arthur Laurents, with music by Jule Styne and lyrics by a young Stephen Sondheim, *Gypsy* was based on the autobiography of Gypsy Rose Lee, whose mother, Rose, played by Ethel, had pushed her two daughters relentlessly onto the stage and eventually into burlesque, where Gypsy gained fame as a "ladylike stripper." Jackie had been fascinated with the coincidence of her own performance as Fudge Farrell, a character based on Gypsy, and Ethel's performance as Gypsy's mother. She became a fixture backstage while the show was in rehearsals, and when Ethel admitted she was having trouble with the bumps and grinds she had to do in one scene, Jackie dug out her infamous bikini from *Between the Covers* and put it on under a button-down dress. She wore it to Ethel's apartment at the Park Lane Hotel, and once inside dropped the dress and gave a private performance of everything she had learned from Margie Hart, Christine Ayers, and even Dovita, though of course without the doves.

It was a highly erotic performance, and whether it taught Ethel how to strip or not, it certainly turned Jackie on. Ironically, Ethel became the central passion of her life from that moment, a fixation that would become the subject of much gossip in their Broadway world. Most thought the crush was one-sided, but Anna Sosenko believes that Ethel had a crush on Jackie, too. They attended a party together at Lynn Loesser's in the Beresford on Central Park West, and both had quite a lot to drink. As Benay Venuta recalls the evening: "Everybody was very drunk. Jackie and Ethel were very drunk, and there was a big wild thing of Jackie and Ethel on the couch."

Jackie pursued Ethel with undiminished fervor. They were photographed together at a birthday party for Polly Bergen. They were photographed together again at Radie Harris's big birthday party in October, where Ethel sang "Everything's Coming Up Roses." She was even helping Ethel think up quips for the press, such as the famous answer to "Why did you change your name from Zimmerman?" Jackie's inspiration, which Ethel used: "With a name like that in lights, people would die from the heat." Jackie seemed to follow Ethel almost everywhere, in fact—so much so that it was beginning to get on Irving's nerves. After all, Jackie was past forty now, a bit old for those adolescent "star crushes" she'd had on Margalo and Hildegarde. It just wasn't right for her to be tagging around after Merman so blatantly.

And Irving had another reason to be disturbed about Jackie's emotional state. Guy was doing no better. He was beginning to feel sexual urges and would rub against her when he had erections. Assured by the doctors that this behavior was "normal" and probably healthy, she permitted it for a time and even tried to make jokes about it, calling him "you incestuous little motherfucker." It may have been the closest thing to affection he would ever show her, and it must have been painful indeed, since he still gave no signs of regarding her as anyone special in his life. Jackie continued to take him on excursions even though he wasn't entirely toilet trained and sometimes wet himself in public. According to a confidante, "When people stared, Jackie's attitude was 'Fuck 'em.' It was her kid and she was not about to apologize for him, she said." One day she broke down before her friends Sheila and Fran at the Alpine and sobbed that she knew now Guy would never get well. She had kept on hoping for an improvement when he reached puberty, but if anything, his condition seemed to be growing worse.

Miraculously, through all this Jackie kept her sense of humor according to Penny Morgan, who was with her when she made the often-quoted remark to Irving, "Don't interrupt me when I'm eavesdropping." Penny remembers another time when a streaker ran nude through the dining room of the Beverly Hills Hotel. Straight-faced, Jackie turned to the hotel's owner, Ben Silberstein, and said, "You told me men had to wear ties."

In December, Irving joined Jackie at a midnight supper after a performance of *Gypsy*. Benay was there with her date, and Ethel was there with a friend, and there were perhaps one or two others. Benay recalls that the atmosphere got very tense. Irving wanted to take Jackie home, and Jackie was having none of it. Benay's date got nervous at the tension and said, "Let's split. There's going to be a fight." And there was—between Jackie and Irving. Benay recalls that Jackie screamed something like "Fuck you! Get the hell out of here!" Her face was contorted with rage, and she turned the table over on Irving as she screamed at him. More clearly than the exact words,

Benay recalls "the hatred of their faces. Jackie's and Irving's. It's very strong in my mind, the hatred. It was a terrible night. It was terrifying."

Jackie later remembered Ethel saying, "I don't ever want to see you again. You're as crazy as your son." Benay doesn't recall that remark, but she does remember Ethel leaving the restaurant with Jackie following her. Jackie followed her all the way home and then stood outside her apartment, banging on the door and yelling, "Ethel, I love you!" Ethel said later that this went on for hours, until she at last threatened to call the police.

Soon after, in January, Jackie was admitted to LeRoy Sanitarium for about four days. There were stories that she had pneumonia, and Irving says she tripped on a telephone cord, but several of her friends believe—and Ethel believed— that Jackie either had a breakdown or threatened suicide over her. Ethel told Benay that Irving had called her up and begged her to visit Jackie, but she had refused. (In later years, when Benay protested that Ethel had hurt Jackie very badly, Merman retorted, "That woman is a dyke." Oddly, for one so vehement against homosexuality, Ethel was squired around town mainly by homosexual men, listed in her address book under *D* for dates.)

Jackie's stay in the sanitarium made Dorothy Kilgallen's column, a first for Jackie and therefore something of an achievement, also a lesson. "Publicity doesn't kiss back," was the way she put it then. She did paste the clipping in her scrapbook, however, and later on, when she was feeling somewhat more philosophical about it, she said, "Live by gossip, die by gossip." If you spent so much of your time trying to crack the columns, it figured that once in a while it would backfire.

In February, Radie Harris's column carried a grim item: "Jacqueline Susann had to cancel her Beverly Hills Hotel stay with her TV producer spouse Irving Mansfield and put off several commitments of her own to rush to Philly to be at the hospital bedside of her wonderful mother, felled by a heart attack.'' This attack, from which Rose would recover, may have been hastened by the terminal illness of her cherished younger sister, Isabel Jelinek, who would die of lymph cancer later that year.

By spring the atmosphere was improving again between Jackie and Irving. In May they were at the Beverly Hills Hotel together, where Cary Grant complimented Jackie on her tan. Irving bragged that it cost him two hundred dollars in phone bills for her to tell all her friends about it. On Father's Day, the hottest day of the year, he gave her a full-length sable coat, and in July he was trying to sell a show called *Face the Facts*, on which Jackie would have a role. In the summer of 1961, things were returning to something like normal in the Mansfield household.

21

Rose's Turn

To Jackie it was very important that I have twenty-room houses, a rich husband, twelve mink coats . . . her values were a little bit different from mine, but I knew in her heart all she wanted was what was best for me.

——Lily Cates

JACKIE would later rate 1961 as one of her "in-between" years, but it had started out horribly, with the Merman breakup, Rose's heart attack, and her own hospitalization with its attendant publicity. Her chubby Bronx housewife, the president and sole member of her fan club, was so alarmed at the Kilgallen column that she picked flowers from her garden and sent them to the hospital. They arrived too late and were relayed along to the Navarro, but by then they were already dead. At least *she* wasn't, Jackie said in her thank-you note.

In late February she was back in again, spending three

days in Doctors Hospital under the care of gynecologist Arthur Davids. By then she was becoming quite fascinated with the newly inaugurated president, John F. Kennedy, and especially with his glamorous wife. She identified totally with "the other Jackie," with her brunette beauty and elegance, her tragedies with children, her commanding rascal father, her determination to keep personal sorrows private, and most of all her aura of sadness mixed with strength. The fascination with Jacqueline Bouvier Kennedy Onassis would endure, and years later a magazine editor's offhand suggestion that she do a "Jackie on Jackie" piece would result in one of the fastest and easiest bits of fiction she ever wrote. The novella *Dolores* would appear in the February, 1974, issue of *Ladies' Home Journal* after much cutting, and would be reissued by Irving after Jackie's death, with the cuts restored.

But that was years later, when her success as a novelist was established. In 1961 her success was not established in anything, though she was still under contract to Schiffli and still producing those commercials. True, they were making her the butt of jokes in nightclub acts, and for once her comedian friends and lovers seemed to be laughing *at* her instead of *with* her. Even so, it might have been endurable if her next contract renewal had been secure. But she and Judge Rosenblum both had enemies at Schiffli, including executives who felt she was under contract only because of her friendship with the judge—a relationship they viewed in the worst possible light. Her role as the Schiffli Troubadour seemed headed for the rocks, and at a time when Irving's career was also a bit shaky. They were committed to more new expenses with Guy, who was being moved to an institution in Winston-Salem, North Carolina. Their financial needs loomed larger than ever, and their prospects seemed to be diminishing.

In her doldrums her friends coaxed her to try writing

again. They brought books—Harold Robbins's gossipy, showbizzy novel *The Carpetbaggers* for one—and suggested that she could do it better. She had talked about a novel for some time, and she even had the title chosen: *The Pink Dolls*. It would be written from a woman's point of view and would deal with the drugs her show-business crowd indulged in so freely. And there were all her stories about her dog, too, which she'd been writing in letters to Bea and Joyce. Her friends encouraged her to do something with them, several later taking exclusive credit for the idea. Only Anna Sosenko was dubious. "Who wants to read a book about a poodle?" she asked.

Rose was slowly recovering and Jackie felt despair about her mother's physical and economic frailty. Rose, "the rock against which I have been banging and bloodying my head all my goddamn life," now seemed so mortal in her hospital bed. "Mother, you can't go and die on me!" Jackie told her. "I'm too young to be an *orphan*!" "Jacqueline," Rose replied, "you're too old to be an ingenue. Go and do what you were meant to do. Write a book."

Bea and Joyce gave back Jackie's witty Josephine letters, and Bea even offered to reconstruct her own letters to Jackie, written while she was dog-sitting. She also helped Jackie cull some of the doggie jokes from *Lovely Me*, particularly those about paper training. Jackie listened to all the talk for months, reluctant to face further rejection, but by early 1962 she was pulled into the project and working at that typewriter again.

But there was time out for dinners at Danny's Hideaway with old friends and some new ones, including Lee Reynolds and her husband, David Begelman, a poor boy from the Bronx who had become an influential agent with MCA and who had recently left to found his own agency, Creative Management Associates. The friendship between the

Mansfields and the Begelmans would be short-lived, ending after Jackie put pressure on David to help Irving's career, but Jackie would watch Begelman rise to power in Hollywood with great fascination and would use his much publicized affair with Judy Garland in her first novel.

It was during one of those dinners with Lee and David that Jackie's famous temper flared up violently. A member of the party, attorney Morton Mitosky, had been an arts critic in Philadelphia in his youth. "It was a warm and friendly dinner," Mitosky recalls. "We had all probably had cocktails and maybe more than one each, but I have no recollection of Jackie being drunk. She was boasting about her father, and I said jokingly, 'Oh, Jackie, he wasn't that great an artist,' and she became incensed and angry and hostile and she and Irving got up very suddenly and walked out. . . . My remark was not made with any seriousness, but neither Jackie nor Irving ever spoke to me again." And Lee Reynolds, who recalls the episode vividly, says, "It was a terrible thing. She was going to kill him."

Jackie was in a most explosive state, and had, in fact, assaulted someone a good bit more famous not long before. It was also at a restaurant. Johnny Carson was at the bar amusing onlookers with card tricks. Joanne Carson recalls that Jackie said, "You're not that great a comedian," or something like that, and he insulted her back and she threw a drink, a black Russian, in his face. And that was the end of it, according to Joanne. In other versions of the story, the fight escalated, with Johnny all but assaulting Jackie, being evicted from the restaurant, coming back and yelling, "Let me at her!"

Another of the Danny's Hideaway dinner group was television writer Joe Cates and his beautiful Eurasian wife, Lily, who remembers that Jackie walked up to her at a party and announced, "I have a godchild and when she grows up she'll look just like you." Lily was pregnant, expecting in the summer, and Joe was about to go off on assignment in Copenhagen. Lily was determined to join him there, and Jackie was determined that she get safely back to New York before she had the baby. To ensure that Lily took care of herself on the trip, Jackie decided to go along. She spent six weeks with the Cateses in Denmark, looking after Lily with time out for elaborate shopping expeditions. "She just kept coming home with these packages and she wouldn't show them to me, but she was positive I was going to have a girl and it was nothing but dresses," Lily remembers. "Jackie took it on herself to deliver me to Copenhagen, stay with me and sort of see me through, and literally bring me back to New York. She would not let me get on the plane without someone, just in case something should happen."

What happened, not long after their return, was another of Jackie's showers for a few intimate friends. "These two hundred people I had never seen before in my life came bearing gifts," Lily recalls. The baby was indeed a girl and was named Valerie Natasha, much to Jackie's chagrin. She had hoped the child would be named after her, and she didn't buy Lily's explanation that children should not be named after people who were still alive, a part of the Jewish tradition. "It so happens I'm Catholic," she answered huffily. Lily's second child was named Phyllis Bell, which Valerie couldn't pronounce and corrupted to "Peegee." This in time turned into "Phoebe," the name by which she would become famous years later in Hollywood. It was not until 1968 that Jackie finally got what she had wanted all along: Lily's third daughter, born that year, was named Alexandra Jacqueline.

Around the time she went to Copenhagen Jackie did get something she wanted—a face-lift. She was forty-three. After that she always claimed to be "around thirty-nine. . . . If I told you my age I would tell you *everything*." On the subject of cosmetic surgery she said, "I'm a realist. I think we have to accept the fact that one of these days everybody will have their face lifted just like everybody now goes to the beauty parlor. Women can all have bazooms whatever size they want, and wigs, and contact lenses in different colors." Later, when she was a famous author, a reporter pressed her for her birth date: "Just say I was born in November, 1963, because that's when my first book, *Every Night, Josephine*, came out."

The Copenhagen trip was not the last Jackie would take with Lily, whom she came to call the "original Ori-yenta" and whose beauty she greatly admired. She lavished great affection and much attention on Lily, providing a cream for her to rub on her belly during pregnancy to avoid stretch marks and buying her hats to keep the sun from damaging her creamy complexion. The Cateses and the Mansfields took summer vacations together at the Beverly Hills Hotel for years, and they usually spent Christmas together at a Miami motel. It was during one of these trips, when they were staying at the Thunderbird Motel, that Jackie conned the Cateses into adopting a large pregnant poodle with blue-painted toenails. When Lily protested, Jackie said, "You've got a big house and a garden, and I think it would be good for the dog." Joe returned to New York with it, and Jackie made frequent visits during the dog's pregnancy to be sure all was going well.

Like many in the circle of friends, Lily never knew that Jackie was Jewish. Ironically, years later Lily said, "I think that Jackie, if she converted, would probably have converted to Judaism, because she always thought it was a very civilized religion." In 1962, as work progressed on the poodle book, Jackie continued her friendships with the Cateses and with the Begelmans, who had also produced a daughter for her to fuss over. And she found time to become involved in the problems of yet another new friend, as recorded in Leonard Lyons's column: "Bobo Rockefeller is quite busy these days, financially that is, not socially. She spends much time at the bank and with her brokers checking on her investments in the stock market. Social engagements are hampered by the suspicion that her suitors might be interested primarily in her millions. 'But men in a similar spot never think that way,' said Bobo's friend Jacqueline Susann. 'Even if a rich man is short, fat and ugly, he always convinces himself that his money has nothing to do with women liking him.'"

As Jackie put the final touches on her poodle book, she was often interrupted by desperate late-night phone calls from Arlene DeMarco, whom she had known since Arlene was a child singing star in the 1940's. The DeMarco sisters were regulars on the Fred Allen show. Arlene, called "Granny" because she was the youngest, was now married to a self-styled actor-writer-director-producer named Keefe Brasselle, a Hollywood original who billed himself as "Mr. Fabulous." He had played the title role in *The Eddie Cantor Story*, about which a reviewer said, "If you think Brasselle is awful, the supporting performances are worse." The Brasselle marriage was becoming violent, and Jackie often acted as mediator, rushing over to calm Arlene after beatings in which Keefe broke her pelvis, jaw, shoulder, and collarbone, always reminding Arlene of the luxurious lifestyle he was providing.

Keefe was the best buddy of James Aubrey, president of CBS, who was nicknamed "The Smiling Cobra," and who was known to be rough with women himself. His two main girl friends, a "hot model" and a socialite, often appeared with arm bruises and blackened eyes. Jackie listened to Arlene's fears that Keefe was procuring girls for Aubrey, which turned out to be true, according to a later investigation by CBS. Ralph Colin, the investigator, said he didn't know why Aubrey needed help. "All he had to do was throw back the blankets, and they'd have jumped into bed.'' Aubrey's star would rise even further in the next few years as the network's ratings continued to dominate the field, but it was his relationship with Brasselle that would contribute largely to his downfall. Brasselle had produced a high-budget series for CBS called *Beachfront*, starring himself, which quickly vanished after a reported $430,000 of network money was lavished on it. He made a reappearance in *The Keefe Brasselle Show*, another klunker, and in 1964 his company, Richelieu Productions, would be given a virtual blank check to produce several series for CBS: *The Cara Williams Show, The Baileys of Balboa*, and *The Reporter*. All three bombed and in 1965, Aubrey was himself canned amid rumors involving his dealings with Keefe.

Arlene says that it was because of her husband that Irving was given the chance to put on yet another variation of *Talent Scouts*, this one called *On Broadway Tonight* and hosted by Rudy Vallee. It would run as a summer replacement on Wednesday evenings from July through September, 1964, and would return the following January for another three-month run on Friday evenings. It would be Irving's swan song as a producer of network television series, although it would not be his last attempt. An item in *The New York Times* on March 9, 1965, reported that ''Irving Mansfield, independent package producer, brought suit yesterday against the General Artists Corporation and the National Broadcasting Company charging a conspiracy to deprive him of property rights in the television program entitled *Hullabaloo*.'' According to Irving, General Artists had granted him the concept, title, and format of *Hullabaloo* as part of an inducement to become his agent. Later, he charged, they took the show to NBC without his knowledge and arranged for a different producer. Irving asked for over a million dollars in damages, and did collect a substantial sum, perhaps a quarter to a half million. His old colleague and crony Lester Gottlieb was one of Irving's antagonists in the suit, even though they had once been so close that when Irving and Jackie broke up for ten days he had stayed with the Gottliebs, "teary-eyed."

By the fall of 1962, Jackie's poodle book, now titled *Every Night, Josephine!*, was finished, and she was looking for an agent. She tried the William Morris office, but the manuscript was rejected. She then turned to Anna Sosenko for advice. "Why can't I have John Steinbeck's agent?" she asked. Anna sent the manuscript to Annie Laurie Williams, the elderly and quite distinguished literary agent who did represent Steinbeck. Miss Williams loved *Josephine!* and invited Jackie to her office for a talk. As they discussed the manuscript, which Miss Williams had decided to submit to Doubleday, a woman handed Jackie a cup of tea. A bit later Jackie asked for a second cup, and Miss Williams had to explain, *sotto voce*, that the woman making tea was not a maid. She was Harper Lee, author of the novel then up for a Pulitzer Prize, *To Kill a Mockingbird*.

Weeks went by without a word from Doubleday. Jackie grew more and more impatient. She called Annie Laurie Williams almost daily, and she began to threaten to phone Doubleday editor Ken McCormick directly.

One of Jackie's friends came up with a bright idea to take her mind off the waiting. Hattie Eichenbaum, a golf companion, was thinking about joining a package tour of the Middle and Far East. The trip would leave on October 13 and would last for a full month, including stopovers in Austria, Israel, India, Thailand, Hong Kong, Japan, and Hawaii. And it would only cost $1,875 per person, including two meals a day. True, the group would be made up mainly of middle-aged or elderly Jews, since it was being booked through Temple Israel in Philadelphia—about forty-five to fifty of them, in fact.

It didn't sound like Jackie's cup of tea, but then Hattie sank the hook: Wouldn't *Rose* love such a trip? Wouldn't it be a perfect seventieth-birthday present for a retired schoolteacher recuperating from a heart attack? Jackie was dubious, but the more Hattie talked, and the more she looked at the brochures Hattie was carrying around with her, the more interested she became. All right, she agreed at last, she would at least put the matter tentatively to Rose and see if she was interested.

Rose was more than interested. She was delighted, and she accepted at once, almost as if she had been expecting such an offer all along. She wasn't a superstitious woman, but she still remembered a gypsy's fortune back in the first winter of Jackie's life, while they were hiding from the flu epidemic in Atlantic City. The gypsy had made several accurate predictions, and she'd forecast that one day her infant daughter would "take you to see the world." Rose told several friends about it over the years, and now, she reminded them, it was coming true.

Gypsies notwithstanding, Rose's friends were appalled. She was an invalid, they reminded her; she had suffered a very serious heart attack and shouldn't even consider such a long and grueling trip. One friend even called Jackie to protest, suggesting she consider a restful vacation in Bermuda or the Bahamas instead. Jackie told them she hated the "creepy crawlies" she kept finding in her bed in such resorts. Besides, she and Rose were not beach loungers by nature. They needed action, things to see and do and learn. Just sitting around in the sun they'd get on each other's nerves. But she did promise to take good care of Rose, and to keep her from getting overheated or overtired. Also, she agreed to give Rose's doctor the final veto on the expedition. If he thought it dangerous, they would forget the whole thing.

The trip did seem somewhat extravagant to Jackie, the

more she thought about it. Especially with Irving now
pretty much out of work, and with her own Schiffli
contract at an end. (She got even with Schiffli later, on a
popular radio program. "I would sooner wear a salami
around my neck than a Schiffli embroidered collar.") And
there were the expenses of keeping Guy in that new place
down south. It was a lot to spend just to make her mother
happy. Besides, as she wrote in her journal of the trip, she
was a little scared to leave Irving for so long, because he
took care of her so well.

On the other hand, given their lifestyle the trip was
really not all that extravagant. They could easily spend that
much on restaurants alone during a month, not to mention
weekends at the golf club or trips to see Guy. Besides, she
sometimes felt she had much to make up to Rose, who'd
had a lot of heartbreak in her life, some of it caused by her
willful daughter. Perhaps a long trip together would bring
them closer and would help them understand each other
better. Anyway, she'd have Hattie for company, in case all
those old ladies got to be too much.

Maybe this was a turning point, she began to think, like
"crossing a threshold" that would somehow make her "a
grown-up-woman" on her return. It had been twenty-five
years—a quarter of a century!—since she had boarded that
train so bravely to make her mark on the New York stage.

On the day Rose's doctor okayed the trip, Jackie put on
her low-heeled Guccis (how she blessed Jackie Kennedy
for liberating her feet) and went across the street to Central
Park and her wishing hill. Sitting there, where she had
made so many deals with God, she tried to place herself
into the stream of nature, or God, or the universe. She
came home convinced that, if she could only put aside her
obsession with selling the manuscript and give Rose a trip
to remember, "the universe was almost certain to drop a
publisher in my lap."

At Anna's urging, Jackie kept a journal of the trip. "Tourist on a plane is not bad at all if you are a skinny midget," she wrote on the flight to London, their first stop. From there they went on to Vienna, stopped briefly at Istanbul, and continued on to Israel, where Jackie's journal is amusing for its omissions. After an ecstatic description of Moishe, their guide in Israel, a sizable chunk of journal pages has been carefully removed.

The tour group continued on through India, whose poverty appalled Jackie as it had so many before her, and then to Hong Kong and Japan. As tour groups do, they shopped, ate, bickered, and shopped some more. There were quarrels over duties to be paid and suggestions that the tour director was playing favorites. These quarrels led eventually to an outright blowup, which Jackie settled in her usual manner. "He ducked unfortunately and only two of my fingers hit him across the face," she wrote. "Had my arm been good he could have lost his false choppers. . . ."

If Jackie seemed frazzled, Rose did not. She remained immaculately coiffed and girdled, and her fastidiousness amazed Jackie, who recorded in her diary that her mother never let anyone see her undressed and was horrified if Jackie entered the bathroom while she was using it. "I sometimes wonder how in hell I ever got born," she wrote, adding that she and Irving had no such taboos. "Sometimes when I take a leak, he stands beside me and pees in the sink."

She also befriended the tour's wallflower, a woman whose complaints had alienated everyone. The woman became a part of their immediate group for the rest of the trip. "How could I tell her she had a lousy personality?" Jackie wrote in her journal. "I never felt sorrier for anyone in my life."

They visited shrines everywhere, and Jackie bought gold charms for Karlina in every country. "Travel doesn't

broaden one unless one wants to be broadened,'' Jackie
wrote in her journal. ''Most of these dames shop their way
around the world, Me with the total recall and sponge
mind sops it up. In a way I wish I'd been born a man. I'd
make a better writer if I could have signed on as a crew
member of freighters. Sinclair Lewis and O'Neill did it,
along with Conrad and a few others.''

She made a great discovery in Japan. Seconals were
sold over the counter there. Jackie didn't take them herself, but Joyce did, so Jackie stocked up with an eye
toward future barter. ''I'll save these for the desperate
hours—after I see her new outfits,'' she wrote.

In Hawaii, bulging from food and purchases, Jackie
realized that the trip, for all its tiresome aspects, had at
least brought her closer to Rose. ''I just realized you're
very bright,'' Rose told her daughter, who noted, ''Well,
this was a gasser. I think up 'til now she's always secretly
thought I was getting by through luck and charm.''

Jackie's journal entries throughout the trip were in a
handwriting that varied from bold and flamboyant (her
normal style) to a childlike, messy scrawl that is sometimes difficult to read. The variations were not caused by
difficult travel conditions so much as by the time of day,
with liquor affecting some changes and her bedtime Placidyl
tablets causing even more noticeable deterioration. She
was aware of the fluctuations herself, and commented on
them in the journal and elsewhere (''By the time my
writing wavers I know the Placidyl is taking effect''),
though they didn't hamper her output.

Further comment on Jackie's handwriting was made
many years later by professional handwriting analyst Janet
Sachs, who often testifies in legal cases. Ms. Sachs was
asked to do a ''blind'' reading of several journal excerpts,
with no knowledge of the person who had written them
beyond the fact that it was a woman in her forties. She

Jackie's maternal grandmother, Ida Kaye Jans, hoped to attend medical school but pogroms interrupted. She kept meticulous diaries, a habit she passed on to her granddaughter. Here she is holding her diary, or "sentiment book."

Jackie's maternal grandfather, Boris Jans, was blond and dashing. An exquisitely gifted tailor, he serviced the Main Line ladies with two-hundred-dollar suits (as costly as a piano) but, a faithful husband, he did not provide the additional services his son-in-law offered.

Jackie at two.
COURTESY ROBERT JELINEK

Jackie with Bob. COURTESY
ROBERT JELINEK

Jackie, age eight,
at the Latona house.
COURTESY ROBERT JELINEK

Jackie with her doll,
age eight.
COURTESY ROBERT JELINEK

A side of her mother that Jackie never saw. COURTESY ROBERT JELINEK

Bob's portrait of Rose in 1952. In her youth she was more beautiful than any of his models, but she was hardened by the pain of his infidelities. "Oh, Mother," Jackie said toward the end of her life, "how could you have stood it for so long?" COURTESY ROBERT JELINEK

Robert Susan at his
easel in 1938.
COURTESY ROBERT JELINEK

Robert Susan enjoyed
being interviewed
on beauty. Rose didn't
care for the
publicity. COURTESY
APRIL SAUL

PHILADELPHIA RE

Woman's Interests—Society—Music—Art—Talkies—Drama

FOURTH SECTION   PHILADELPHIA, SUNDAY, APRIL

By Their Lips Artist Tells De

irl's Mouth

Jackie in a yellow
dress and kerchief
in her early teens. Bob
called this a sketch
because he never
finished her hands.
COURTESY ROBERT JELINEK

Bob's early portrait
of Rose in her "monkey suit."
It hung over the fireplace in
the Latona house.
COURTESY ROBERT JELINEK

A Bob Susan
nude, now
hanging in a
Philadelphia
restaurant.
BRIAN SPEERS

Jackie, in the center, was the camp hellion. She had a crush on the dance counselor and stole her sandals. COURTESY TYBIE MOSHINSKY

Sweet sixteen. Jackie in Atlantic City. COURTESY ROBERT JELINEK

Jackie, age nineteen, during her first year in New York. COURTESY ROBERT JELINEK

Gallery of Some of Jackie's Special Friends

(Top left) J. J. Shubert. He gave her several parts, and encouraged her to write some new dialogue for *Blossom Time*. THE BILLY ROSE THEATRE COLLECTION, THE NEW YORK PUBLIC LIBRARY AT LINCOLN CENTER, ASTOR, LENOX AND TILDEN FOUNDATIONS *(Top right)* Jimmy Demaret in 1951. He gave her a "Hole in One" pin at the Concord Hotel. *LIFE* MAGAZINE, J. R. EYERMAN *(Left middle)* Vinton Freedley: man of distinction, eminent producer. Their friendship did not affect Jackie's relationship with Radie Harris, Freedley's longtime lover. THE NEW YORK PUBLIC LIBRARY AT LINCOLN CENTER *(Right middle)* George Jessel *(left)* and Eddie Cantor. They both let her down, although Cantor put her in *Banjo Eyes*. Jackie and Carole Landis compared notes on Jessel's sexual performance. THE NEW YORK PUBLIC LIBRARY AT LINCOLN CENTER *(Bottom left)* Dom Pérignon is the best revenge. Richard Allman's parents didn't want him to date Jackie, and wouldn't allow Bob Susan in the house. When she got rich, Jackie patronized his restaurant, spending wildly on her mother's birthday parties. BRIAN SPEERS

The Temporary Mrs. Smith, starring *(left to right)* Millard Mitchell, Howard St. John, Francine Larrimore, Fania Marinoff, Mischa Auer. THE BILLY ROSE THEATRE COLLECTION, THE NEW YORK PUBLIC LIBRARY AT LINCOLN CENTER, ASTOR, LENOX AND TILDEN FOUNDATIONS

Lube Malina, who replaced Francine Larrimore when *The Temporary Mrs. Smith* was retitled *Lovely Me.* THE BILLY ROSE THEATRE COLLECTION, THE NEW YORK PUBLIC LIBRARY AT LINCOLN CENTER, ASTOR, LENOX AND TILDEN FOUNDATIONS

Arthur Siegel, who wrote the show-stopping song "Lovely Me," after which the play was retitled. ARTHUR SIEGEL

Eddie Cantor and Jackie *(third from left, with parasol)* in *Banjo Eyes*. Jackie was always in Eddie's dressing room. THE NEW YORK PUBLIC LIBRARY AT LINCOLN CENTER

Better than college: Ilka Chase *(seated, left)* Margalo Gillmore *(center)*, and others in *The Women*. THE NEW YORK PUBLIC LIBRARY AT LINCOLN CENTER

Jackpot, a Vinton Freedley production. Jackie is second from left. Allan Jones is in the center. THE BILLY ROSE THEATRE COLLECTION, THE NEW YORK PUBLIC LIBRARY AT LINCOLN CENTER, ASTOR, LENOX AND TILDEN FOUNDATIONS

Margie Hart: Arrested for her burlesque act, she found Jackie still more daring. THE NEW YORK PUBLIC LIBRARY AT LINCOLN CENTER

The Incomparable Hildegarde, Guy's godmother, around the time he was born. COURTESY HILDEGARDE

Jackie, Carole Landis, and Christine Ayres in *A Lady Says Yes*. Jackie and Carole loved each other. THE NEW YORK PUBLIC LIBRARY AT LINCOLN CENTER, FRED FEHL

Jackie, age forty, with her goddaughter, Karlina Chau, and Irving. COURTESY KARLINA CHAU

The perfect Broadway couple—with comedian Jack Carter and his date Bonnie Shaw. PICTORIAL PARADE

Irving producing *The Polly Bergen Show* in 1958. He later quit smoking much more easily than Jackie did. COURTESY POLLY BERGEN

At Bob's last birthday party, April 13, 1956. Jackie is blond, temporarily. Bob, wearing glasses, is seated next to her.
COURTESY ROBERT JELINEK

Irving looked like his powerful uncle, assemblyman and then judge Samuel Mandelbaum *(fourth from left),* shown with FDR in 1932. COURTESY FRANKLIN D. ROOSEVELT LIBRARY COLLECTION, HYDE PARK

Jean Harrison. She and Jackie "lived in each other's pockets," but then stopped speaking. COURTESY JEAN HARRISON

Dorothy Strelsin. She looked like Dorothy Lamour and dated Damon Runyon. COURTESY DOROTHY STRELSIN, MURRAY KORMAN

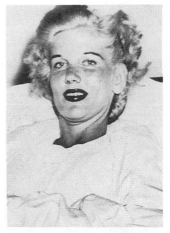

Gladys Faye Walter. Jackie was "everything she wanted to be." COURTESY GLADYS FAYE WALTER

Joyce Mathews in Roosevelt Hospital following her wrist slashing over Billy Rose in 1951. Her ex-husband Milton Berle visited her bedside, as did Jackie. INTERNATIONAL NEWS PHOTOS

Jackie telling Claire Safran and Ellen Peck years later how she set up mirrors to watch Guy's conception. COURTESY CLAIRE SAFRAN

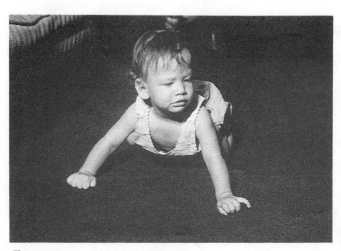

Guy in August, 1947, age eight months.
COURTESY THELMA ROSOFF

Benay Venuta *(left)* and Ethel Merman. Maybe they were talking about Ethel's problems with Jackie. COURTESY BENAY VENUTA

Jackie, with Candy Jones, giving a lecture at Candy's beauty school in 1965. COURTESY CANDY JONES, PHOTO BY ELI AARON

Don Preston, Berney Geis, Irving Mansfield, Jackie, and Letty Cottin Pogrebin. COURTESY LETTY POGREBIN

Jackie and friends in 1973. *NEW YORK POST*

Jackie in 1971 with the wrong J. Lewis—but Jackie said she was "sick for" any Jewish comic. PICTORIAL PARADE, TIM BOXER

In 1969: every morning, Josephine! PICTORIAL PARADE, TIM BOXER

Carol Bjorkman in 1964 showing no signs of her imminent leukemia. Jackie was inconsolable when she died, and dedicated *The Love Machine* to her.
WOMEN'S WEAR DAILY

Girl friends—Jackie with Helen Gurley Brown in the mid-1960's. Jackie sued David Brown, but they all remained friends.
COURTESY HELEN GURLEY BROWN

Helen and David Brown at home with Samantha in 1967.
COURTESY HELEN GURLEY BROWN

Girl friends—Jackie and Anna Sosenko on Central Park West in 1969. PICTORIAL PARADE, TIM BOXER

Girl friends—Jackie and Bea Cole at a party Jackie gave for the publication of Rosemary Wilson's cookbook in 1970. Jackie's friendship with Bea started when they performed together in *The Women*, continued through the writing of two plays and Jackie's celebrity years. PICTORIAL PARADE, TIM BOXER

Girl friends—Jackie and Vera Swift at a backgammon tournament in 1972. Backgammon was Jackie's last new game and she was a winner. COURTESY VERA SWIFT

Johnny Carson, Joanne Carson, Earl Wilson, and Jackie in the mid-1960's. Jackie's will to live helped Joanne regain her own after her breakup with Johnny. CAMERA 5, KEN REGAN

Truman Capote, who said that Jackie looked like a truck driver in drag, and then apologized to the truck drivers. THE NEW YORK PUBLIC LIBRARY AT LINCOLN CENTER

Girl friends—Doris Day and Jackie in May, 1974, four months before Jackie's death. Doris was working on the best-selling autobiography Jackie had persuaded her to write. PICTORIAL PARADE, KENT BRADFORD

Sonia Hamlin, moderator *(left)*, with Jackie, Nora Ephron, and Dan Wakefield on a Boston talk show in 1969. COURTESY NORA EPHRON, PHOTO BY GWENDOLYN STEWART

Jackie with Rex Reed, her buddy, chum, pal, and loyal knight against her critics. COURTESY REX REED

Jackie with Andy Warhol at the 1969 party Earl and Rosemary Wilson gave for *The Love Machine*. (Note the ankh ring on Warhol's pinkie.) PICTORIAL PARADE, TIM BOXER

Enjoying the surf with Bette Davis, Jackie still clutches her cigarette. Bette lost the part of Helen in *Valley of the Dolls* to Judy Garland. JULIAN WASSER, *LIFE MAGAZINE* © TIME INC.

Girl friends—Jackie and Ethel Merman in 1969. They reconciled after Jackie's success was well established, and after Jackie took pity on Ethel, whose daughter died from a drug overdose in 1967. PICTORIAL PARADE, TIM BOXER

John Phillip Law and Dyan Cannon in *The Love Machine* in 1971. Jackie wanted Frank Gifford or Sean Connery to play Robin Stone. She got Brian Kelly, who was injured in a motorcycle accident. John Phillip Law replaced him and inherited Kelly's wardrobe. Note that his sleeves are too short. COLUMBIA PICTURES

The Dolls in the *Valley (left to right):* Barbara Parkins, Sharon Tate, and Patty Duke. Jackie barely missed dying with Sharon on the night of the Manson Murders. TWENTIETH CENTURY FOX

Alexis Smith *(left)* and Melina Mercouri in a lesbian scene from *Once Is Not Enough* in 1975. Joan Collins would make much of this scene when she released the movie for home video a decade later. PARAMOUNT PICTURES

Michael Korda, who edited *The Love Machine* with Jonathan Dolger and Evelyn Gendel. Korda later became a best-selling novelist himself.
SIGRID ESTRADA

James Landis edited *Once Is Not Enough*. When Jackie was dying he reissued *Every Night, Josephine!,* explaining, "I *loved* it, I really did.... It was all the evidence I would ever need that this woman is a writer and was a writer right from the beginning of her career." TOM MONASTER

Jackie found a publisher that treated her like a person when Sherry Arden, then director of publicity at William Morrow, got Morrow's president to meet with Jackie. HELEN MARCUS

Larry Hughes, then president of William Morrow, who gave Jackie three dozen roses in the midst of a publishing lunch.
HELEN MARCUS

Esther Margolis, Arnold Stiefel (Esther's assistant), and Jackie getting off the *Love Machine* airplane. Stiefel, now a Hollywood talent manager and producer, is exactly Guy's age, and Jackie was devoted to him in a maternal way. Jackie once admitted to him that her idea of a perfect day was to "have a headache, take a Demerol, and stay in bed."

The plane was an excellent publicity investment. Irving is behind Jackie in this 1970 photo. ESTHER MARGOLIS

Jackie promoting *The Love Machine* in 1970. She looks tired, perhaps because she is weaning herself off amphetamine shots. COURTESY ESTHER MARGOLIS

Jackie-'n'-Irving, who seemed like bacon-'n'-eggs after their marriage really bonded. GLOBE PHOTOS, JOHN R. HAMILTON

Mr. and Mrs. Mansfield at work. Irving's favorite expressions were "Wanna make a deal?" and "Do I have a deal for you." GLOBE PHOTOS, TOM CAFFERY

Jackie would have been thrilled to sign them all anyhow—even if she hadn't been advised that signed books were nonreturnable.
JULIAN WASSER,
LIFE MAGAZINE © TIME INC.

In 1966. Happiness is being number one.
JULIAN WASSER, *LIFE*
MAGAZINE © TIME INC.

Joe E. Lewis with Lynne Palmer at the Friars Club in 1966. She told him what *Valley of the Dolls* was all about, as he had lost the ability to read after being beaten nearly to death. COURTESY LYNNE PALMER

Jackie with James Aubrey, who seemed proud to be part of the composite that made up Robin Stone, about 1969. (However, Robin had Bob Susan's initials) CAMERA 5, PETER C. BORSARI

The author with Robert Jelinek in 1985, on a mission to restore a Robert Susan painting. JERI DRUCKER

Rex Reed called Jackie's Pucci outfits her "banana-split nightmares," but she went on wearing them because they packed well. COURTESY ESTHER MARGOLIS

At home in the Navarro in the late 1960's. GLOBE PHOTOS, TOM CAFFERY

Where it all happened. Jackie at her typewriter. CAMERA 5, KEN REGAN

A few of her favorite things *(top left)* eye makeup *(bottom left)* wigs *(top right)* caviar *(bottom right)* fur coats

(top) At her wishing-hill. *(middle)* Among schoolchildren at the Central Park Zoo. *(bottom)* Her home away from home, the Beverly Hills Hotel.

Jackie with Joseph Ian, who has gold nail polish on his toes. She collapsed from chemotherapy side effects right after this photograph was taken in 1973.
NEW YORK POST

Jackie as a serious woman in 1973, when she was speaking out against book banning.
PICTORIAL PARADE

Perhaps the last photograph of Mr. And Mrs. Mansfield, at an NBC party in May, 1974, four months before Jackie's death.
PHOTOREPORTERS, PHIL ROACH

Jackie, within months of her death, on the set of "Once Is Not Enough." PICTORIAL PARADE, ROBERT CHIARELLO

concluded that the woman was bisexual and highly gifted, and after the reading she inquired if the subject might be Margaret Mead. A few of Ms. Sachs's comments are worth including here, by way of postscript:

"She's the type of person who doesn't trust too easily anymore. She did when she was a child. Things were catching up with her. She's a person who always tried very hard to control, but I think that what she was fighting was something very deep inside of her, an emotional pull back and forth between male and female. I think she presented to the public a different face than the way she felt inside, a lot of torment inside. The handwriting looks disoriented, it's too full, it's like she couldn't stop, she didn't know where to put the brakes on. It's not clean looking so inside she didn't feel clean, but she had the control, terrific hand control, so talent is also there. . . .

"There are strong oral needs in her handwriting. She never made the proper bond with her mother. She needed other people to fulfill something they could never fulfill. It remained all her life and tore her and it made her narcissistic. She was rejected at the breast, in some curious fashion. . . . Something went wrong and she wasn't held and cuddled enough to make her feel complete. She wanted to be near her mother, and she was torn between male and female, on an emotional see-saw. At times she would go to a woman to 'feed' her.

"She tried in the beginning, when she was younger, to please everybody, and just be the loveliest person in the world. Who could not possibly like her and love her and want her and find her lovely? Then she found out that the real world isn't like that, and people took advantage of her. It tore her apart, she couldn't cope with it, she went into drugs and drinking, and trying to be like a man. And now she is in a passage, and she is trying to create."

* * *

Jackie returned to New York to find the situation at Doubleday even more annoying than when she had left. The editors liked the manuscript, which was gratifying, and they were interested in publishing it—eventually. The problem was that they had committed themselves to Beatrice Lillie's book about *her* dog and had paid a high advance for it. They had to publish that one first, they said, and they couldn't do two dog books on the same list, so *Josephine!* would have to wait. How long? Well, until Lillie finished hers—which she hadn't started writing yet. But that could take years. If Doubleday signed *Josephine!* it would have to wait indefinitely for publication. (As it turned out, Bea Lillie never did finish her book.) Irving felt it was unwise to go ahead under those circumstances, but Jackie had been so delighted when McCormick liked her manuscript that she had told everyone she was to be a Doubleday author. She was almost willing to wait.

"Maybe the theater does that to you," she wrote in her journal. "If you don't make it big the first year you get brainwashed into accepting and living with 'bits' in a show—maybe a 'principal,' but never stardom. You live with it, sit with it in Sardi's, and feel grateful to be acknowledged as part of the 'brotherhood'—a member of Actors' Equity—but in some the dream does not die. It is dormant, festers like a tumor. It's oppressive, but people rarely cut it out. It's there, deeper and deeper in the fat cells of your brain, almost forgotten, driving the hosts to the funny farm. . . . But then in a rare case the tumor gets air, rises to a surface, explodes, and it's good—it's talent released, and suddenly the host is free, the dream is gone. It's a reality."

With the book in limbo, Jackie found herself faced with yet another problem she could not avoid. Toward the end of the tour she had noticed a lump in her right breast, and she was concerned about it. She'd had cysts in the past, and they'd often alarmed her enough to cause a checkup with her gynecologist. Before he'd always been able to collapse them with a needle, but this time he felt the lump warranted a biopsy. He referred her to a doctor who scheduled the biopsy for Christmas Day.

Jackie agreed to the biopsy reluctantly, but she refused to sign the then-customary consent form permitting the surgeon to remove the breast should the lump prove malignant. Given the mood of the time, Jackie's refusal to sign that consent form must be regarded as an act of remarkable heroism. The biopsy was performed, and the tests showed that the lump was indeed malignant. The diagnosis was infiltrating ductile carcinoma, a most common form of breast cancer. Her lymph nodes were entirely clear, which was an excellent sign.

When informed of the test results, Jackie tried to leave the hospital, just as Jennifer in *Valley of the Dolls* actually does. Luckily Irving's response was quite different from that of Jennifer's fiancé, who made her feel that the loss of a breast would render her sexually unappealing. Irving assured Jackie that her breasts were unimportant to him and that it was *she* whom he loved and with whom he wished to spend his remaining years. It seems likely that Jackie believed him. When the resident brought the surgical consent form, she was at last persuaded to sign it— with reservations.

It appears that Jackie was able to put aside her terror long enough to further assert herself with the surgeon. In any case, the following day he performed a somewhat "modified" radical mastectomy, leaving more of the underlying muscle than was then the custom and avoiding the usual conspicuous hollow under the arm. He later told colleagues he was proud of having spared her unnecessary disfigurement.

That December Lily Cates, who was by then pregnant

again, invited the Mansfields to a New Year's Eve party.
Irving came alone, explaining that Jackie was in Doctors
Hospital for "minor surgery." Later that evening Lily
slipped away from the party with a bottle of champagne
and some caviar and went to the hospital, but when she got
there she found a NO ADMITTANCE sign on the door to
Jackie's room. She realized then that the operation must
have been more serious than Irving had told them, perhaps
a face-lift or other cosmetic surgery. She never suspected
the actual truth.

She also did not suspect that the hospital had been
following the doctor's orders to keep the doors and windows locked, a practice usually indicating suspected suicidal tendencies. Although Jackie was released on New
Year's Day, by January 2 she was being treated by Dr.
Arthur Sohval for "reactive depression to a radical mastectomy." Dr. Sohval, who placed great faith in pharmacolo-
gy, would see her five more times in January and February
and several times thereafter, for a total of twenty visits in a
four-year period. By January 18 he noted that she weighed
122 pounds and that she looked and felt well. She was
taking Elavil, an "antidepressant with an anxiety-reducing
sedative component," but on February 8 she complained
of dizziness and that drug was withdrawn. He continued
her prescription for Placidyl, and "oral hypnotic which
induces sleep within fifteen minutes to one hour" with a
duration of five hours, and he also put her on Librium and
Preludin, the former "for the relief of anxiety and tension" and the latter a stimulant "related to the amphetamines," which was used for weight control and added
energy.

In the first week of January, as she was recovering at the
Navarro, the surgeon came to the apartment to dress the
wound. Therese Lasser, founder of Reach to Recovery, an
organization to help breast cancer patients, also came to

teach Jackie exercises for her shoulder and arm. A stunning woman, self-centered and opinionated, Lasser drove her patients through a rigorous series of exercises that were undoubtedly helpful for those who could stand the pain. Many could not, but Jackie stuck stubbornly with the program. She experienced little or no swelling, regained the use of her arm with amazing speed, and showed so few signs of the operation that almost none of her friends ever suspected. At the Alpine, Jackie avoided showering with other women, and often insisted on leaving immediately after her round of play.

Jackie had elected to keep her mastectomy a secret to all but a few close friends, perhaps feeling, as Betty Rollin suggested years later, after she had written her own book on breast cancer, that it would make her seem somehow a loser. "My theory about Jacqueline Susann is that she was a woman to whom success was, if not everything, a lot," Rollin says. "And I think that for a lot of people disease is a failure. . . . It makes you a loser, and I think that's the thing she most of all wanted not to be. . . ." She did confide in Bea and Anna, and eventually she got around to telling Rose, though that was harder. And she told a few others as time passed, swearing each to secrecy and assuring each that she was fine and the cancer was clear. Joyce Mathews was in Switzerland when the operation took place. She learned about it immediately on her return and was horrified, but a year later she was to undergo similar though somewhat more radical surgery herself. "Jackie saw me through it; she was wonderful," Joyce recalls. "But she got very angry when I told my daughter Vicki that we both had breast cancer."

Jackie was recovering physically from the surgery, with the help of Lasser's exercise program and her own tenacity, but emotionally she was doing less well. Her breasts had never been her best feature, and she'd always had to wear uplift bras, but now the right side of her chest was an ugly scar that she could never let the world see.

She was going to an analyst now and would continue this therapy for the next two years, though she had mixed feelings about its worth. And, thanks to Dr. Sohval's handy prescription pad, she had drugs for virtually every hour of the day or night and every physical or emotional problem she might conceivably face. There was still pain, especially in the right shoulder, and frequent numbness in her left hand. The drugs helped with the pain and the depression, though at times they left her feeling confused and disoriented, as if her life was slipping out of her control.

Worst of all, it sometimes seemed, was the lack of any news at all about the manuscript, which Doubleday still had and still refused to schedule for publication. It was frustrating, maddening, and yet there seemed very little Irving or Annie Laurie Williams or anyone else could do about it. At forty-four Jackie felt she had entered a physical decline that would only worsen from that point on, and now it seemed that nothing else was destined to go well for her either. Desperate, she resorted more and more to the drugs for escape, hiding them all over the apartment so Irving wouldn't be alarmed at how many she was taking. It was then, according to Radie Harris, that Jackie went to her wishing hill and made her Faustian pact with God: "If He would give her twelve more years to prove herself the best-selling authoress in the world, she would settle for that." (Irving also remembers that bargain, though he recalls her asking for ten years.)

Then, in February, Irving ran into their friend Earl Wilson at a party. Like everyone else, Wilson had heard that Doubleday was to publish Jackie's book, and he congratulated Irving on her behalf. Irving explained the frustrating holdup, and Wilson mentioned a small but aggressive publisher he knew personally. He suggested that Irving send him a copy of the manuscript. He'd like to read it anyway, he said, and if he thought it workable for the small house he would pass it along.

Irving sent Wilson a copy of *Every Night, Josephine!* Wilson loved it, and he immediately picked up his phone and made the call that quite possibly saved Jackie's life.

PART
FOUR

UP MOUNT
EVEREST
[1963-1967]

22

Berney and Company

I have a beautiful woman in my office and she is in tears because her book about her poodle was accepted by Doubleday and then they changed their minds....

——Earl Wilson *(to Berney Geis)*

IN 1959, three years before Jackie's thoughts turned toward her typewriter, another element of her future was taking shape in a small office on East Fifty-sixth Street, where a new publishing company was struggling to market its first small list. Headed by a former Prentice-Hall editor, Bernard Geis Associates would later expand in size and influence, and would add another floor of offices with a brass fireman's pole connecting the two. Used by staff and visiting writers alike, the pole achieved a certain notoriety during the miniskirt period of the sixties, yet it was probably one of the house's more orthodox features. Berney Geis, who delighted in controversy, was a maver-

ick in the staid and inbred world of New York publishing,
and his operation was to become the yapping little mongrel
in that kennel of pedigreed champions.

The first Bernard Geis Associates list consisted of five
books, two of them by authors of previous bestsellers, Art
Linkletter and Abigail Van Buren. Linkletter's *The Secret
World of Kids* and "Dear Abby's" *Dear Teen-ager* made
the *Times* bestseller list for Geis, as did Max Shulman's *I
was a Teen-age Dwarf* and the first of Groucho Marx's
autobiographical send-ups, *Groucho and Me*. In the following year Geis scored in both sales and prestige with
Harry Truman's postpresidential book *Mr. Citizen*, with a
record-breaking $100,000 first-serial sale to *Look* maga-
zine for good measure. In its twelve-year lifespan the
company would put seventeen books on *The New York
Times* bestseller list, close to a quarter of its total output,
and would harvest more than its share of large paperback
reprint and magazine excerpt sales. It is a record unlikely
to be matched.

The funding for the company was as unorthodox as its
methods, coming as it did from several of the firm's
authors, notably Groucho Marx, Art Linkletter, and Ralph
Edwards. The Diners Club and Goodson-Todman Productions
also invested, as did two magazines that sometimes purchased
first-serial rights to the books, *Look* and *Esquire*. All were
limited partners, their liabilities extending only to the
amounts invested, which were generally small by current
standards. Only Linkletter exceeded his original investment, leaving portions of later book royalties in the pot.

Bernard Geis himself was once described by Dick Schaap
in *The New York Times Book Review* as "a large-sized,
middle-aged cherub who can quote sales figures and Shake-
spearean sonnets with equal ease—and equal passion. [He]
sponsors only ten to twelve books each year, has them
distributed by other publishing firms, and believes in large

print orders, large promotion budgets and, ultimately, large sales. . . . He is a home-run swinger in a league of bunters.''

Geis, whose family name was originally Geisas, was born in Chicago, graduated from Northwestern in 1931, and worked for a time as a newspaper reporter and freelance magazine writer. In 1940, while working as an editor in the New York office of *Esquire* and *Coronet* magazines, he married Darlene Stern, with whom he had two sons. He later moved to Grosset and Dunlap, where he remained as editor in chief until 1953, leaving to form his own company designed to market "talking books" for children. The books, which had phonograph records laminated onto their back covers, did not succeed commercially ("I concluded that God never meant for books to talk," he explained), and Berney moved on to Prentice-Hall as an editor.

Two of the authors on Geis's list at Prentice-Hall were Art Linkletter and Abigail Van Buren, whose books became major bestsellers largely because of their authors' vigorous promotion efforts. What happened next is described by Don Preston, who served as the new firm's executive editor for nine years:

"Berney said to them, 'Look, you make a whole ton of money because of your connections, your ability to promote the books. Prentice-Hall didn't earn any of that money. They don't deserve the profit. What you should do is form your own company, and I will run it for you, and you can invest in it, and we'll publish your books and we'll promote them. Then you'll get the royalties and a share of the publisher's profits, too.' "

The result was Bernard Geis Associates, founded in 1958 and for a time run almost single-handedly by Berney himself. Others joined the firm, and in 1963 two editors were hired who were to figure in Jackie Susann's publishing career, Jackie Farber and Don Preston. A third staff member, equally important in Jackie's early success, had joined sometime earlier: Letty Cottin Pogrebin, who handled promotion, publicity, and subsidiary rights.

Preston is a slim, fair-skinned six-footer with an air of perpetual melancholy that once led a writer to describe him as "looking as if he's always about to suggest that immediate family should ride in the first car." He was born in Louisville, Kentucky, and left there in 1952 for New York with dreams of becoming "the next Maxwell Perkins . . . the image of the editor sitting there, working for writers he really respected . . ." Like Irving Mansfield, Preston was content to discover and nourish genius rather than occupy center stage; always a starmaker, never a star.

Of roughly equal rank with Preston in the Geis organization was Letty Cottin Pogrebin, an acknowledged innovator in modern techniques of book promotion. "Letty was always bright as a button," Geis recalls. "I don't think she was even twenty-one years old when I made her promotion director. I walked into her office and I said, 'You are going to be our new director of promotion.' It was a big job in those days. And she said, 'Excuse me a minute.' She went into the ladies' room, fainted, came back, and said, 'I accept.' "

"Like most of the women at Geis, Letty was five feet three and very pretty," Preston recalls. "The exceptions were taller and very pretty. Letty always looked as if she'd just got off a motorcycle, and she had an incredible energy level. She kept candy in her office—those little pointed Hershey things—and nibbled on them to keep from losing weight. And when *Time* featured her in a general article on book promotion, no one was surprised." Letty has since become a leader of the women's movement, a prolific author in her own right, and a founding editor of *Ms.* magazine. She is still petite and youthful, with a lean figure and long blond hair, and she still looks as if she has just got off a motorcycle, which indeed is often the case, as she uses one to zip around Manhattan. Letty remained with the Geis firm through the birth of twin daughters and a son, leaving only when the birth of her own book *How to Make It in a Man's World* (1970) required more time for promotion than her whirligig job allowed.

The third part of the triumvirate under Berney was editor Jackie Farber, an attractive brunette who also happens to be five feet three. "I had gone back to work when I had a six-year-old and an eight-year-old, as an assistant editor at New American Library in a very lowly capacity. My husband and I were at a Columbia football game with an executive at Random House, and I asked him if he had a better job for me. About six weeks later he called me and said, 'Berney Geis needs an editor, and you'll learn everything you would possibly want to learn about editing. It's a very small publishing house, and we distribute their books.' So I went over." From that time, when she was already in her mid-thirties, she has gone on to a series of impressive positions and is currently editor in chief of Delacorte Press.

Finally, there was Geis's willowy executive secretary, Harriet Blacker, who had joined the company in June of 1962. "I was just out of college, the University of Michigan," she remembers. "An agency sent me over, and Berney hired me in about a minute. He just looked at my legs. I'm serious about this; absolutely serious. No typing test, no nothing. Oh, he knew I could type, and I was certainly bright enough and whatever, and I knew how to use a Dictaphone.

"Anytime someone came in, Berney would have me make drinks," Blacker recalls with a chuckle. "And he had in his office a full wall of bookshelves, floor to ceiling, which had a sliding library ladder. He'd call me into his office and he'd say, 'Hey, could you get me that book all the way on the top there?' And with my little short skirt I'd

go climbing up the ladder, stretching and reaching to get
books for him, and I kind of knew what he was doing. It
was part of the fun. I didn't really mind.''

"Harriet was taller than the Geis average," Preston
says. "She was bright and pretty, and Berney loved having
her around, but she was probably not the world's greatest
secretary. He finally convinced her that she was too good
for the job, but even so I think he was a bit surprised at
how successful she became." Blacker rose to become vice
president and director of public relations for the Putnam
Publishing Group and later established her own public-
relations firm.

"It was astonishing what I got into," she says. "Berney
was clever. The first week he sent me to Doubleday's, the
Fifty-seventh Street store, so I could research what people
were asking for, what they wanted to read. And the second
week Letty—the indefatigable Letty—had arranged for a
bus of sportswriters and critics to go up to Floyd Patterson's
training camp because we had just published his autobiography. It was fun. Groucho Marx would pop in and out of
the office, and Brendan Behan was practically living there.
Letty had to go and get him out of bars in the middle of the
night. He would often come up stinking, stinking drunk,
having pissed in his pants, and he'd go and curl up on the
couch in Berney's office and go to sleep.''

"The girls got quite agile around Brendan," Preston
says. "He was forever grabbing at whichever one was
passing, and they all got so they could dodge without
spilling a drop of the drink they were fetching. And
Groucho once came in, collected every woman in the
place, took them all into Berney's office, and handed out
cigars. They all sat there, puffing away in total mystifica-
tion, and Groucho said, 'You know, I always wanted to see
what a roomful of beautiful broads would look like smoking cigars.'

"It was a certain magic time," he adds. "I really think my brain was working better than it ever did before or after. I remember telling somebody, 'Whatever you say about the quality of the books, the one thing I have to say about my job is that I'm never bored.' I usually went in in the morning with a sense of anticipation. Something interesting was going to happen. And there's no doubt that Berney Geis revolutionized the way people look at books— promotion in particular, advertising and promotion."

"How we came to publish *Josephine!* is that, in 1963, I got a telephone call from Earl Wilson, who was a close friend of the Mansfields' and a friend of mine," Berney Geis recounts. "He said, 'I have a beautiful woman in my office and she is in tears because her book about her poodle was accepted by Doubleday and then they changed their minds. They had signed up a book by Beatrice Lillie about her Pekingese, and they can't have two dog books in the same season. So I told her not to cry, that she was very lucky that Doubleday turned it down because there's only one publisher who knows how to promote books anyway, and that's Berney Geis.' Earl told Jackie that he was going to send her over to me, which he did, and I read the manuscript. And, you know, it sort of told people what it was like to be at the other end of the leash. You could really put yourself in a dog's place. I never read anything so empathetic, and it was charming and I was delighted to publish it."

It's possible that Geis was truly enchanted with the manuscript. It appears at least equally likely, however, that in Jackie and Irving he had sensed a pair of promoters after his own heart. After all, few beginning writers arrive with the blessing of a leading columnist, and few have the muscle Irving could flex in show business. Harriet Blacker remembers thinking it odd that Berney would commit the full power of a Geis promotional campaign to a book about a poodle. "Clearly," she says, "he understood that with the Mansfields he could make out of chopped liver an ice palace."

"Berney knew Irving had clout and commitment," Preston says. "I remember one day, late in the book's run, when Jackie and Irving appeared in Berney's office and demanded he run another expensive ad in the *Times*. He argued that he couldn't afford it, that sales didn't warrant it. Irving pulled out a checkbook and wrote a check for the ad, several thousand bucks. That's the kind of author support that's apt to impress any publisher."

The *Josephine!* manuscript was turned over for editing to Jackie Farber, who says of the author, "She was terrific. She was a cinch. She made changes, she didn't make changes; but certainly there was no restructuring. This wasn't a book that needed real editing. There was very little to do. It was a very cute book."

The fledgling author took editing well for the most part, although she could be characteristically determined about changes that she didn't want to make. "We wanted to change the title to something else, and Jackie played along with us," Farber recalls. "And then, in the end, she said, 'Okay, I still want to call it *Every Night, Josephine!*' That was Jackie."

In the course of producing *Josephine!* the people at Geis got to know the book's protagonist almost as well as its author. But then, everybody who knew Jackie in those days knew Josephine. The Mansfields took the dog just about everywhere—to business meetings, to parties, even to restaurants.

"I was not a poodle lover, so it took a lot for me to like Josephine," Letty Pogrebin says. "But she really was a very personable dog, and smart."

Though they knew virtually nothing about Guy Mansfield,

both Letty and Jackie Farber sensed something of thwarted parental urges in the way the Mansfields treated Josephine. "They were devoted to that poodle," Jackie recalls. "I think that's why we were all so curious about her child. Jackie never said a word, but Irving did. I think he said the child was asthmatic and was in Arizona. I think that was the line."

Every Night, Josephine! was published on November 14, 1963. Letty Pogrebin announced it with a press release that described the book as "delightful enough to capture the heart of even a cat lover." It featured a bit of doggerel and Josephine's personal signature:

Dear Mr. Geis:

If the Nobel Committee
Will just use its noodle
They'll follow up Steinbeck
With Josie the poodle

(Signed) Josephine

---------- 23 ----------

Josephine Becomes Famous

*She had a genius for dominating any conversation.
I'm not saying Jackie was a bad listener, but if you
wanted to finish telling a story it was just as well
not to take any breaths between sentences.*

——Candy Jones

JACKIE threw herself into the Geis promotional program
with a vengeance. She and Irving methodically made
the rounds of bookstores, not only in New York but
in all the cities and towns on her tour. She charmed and
flattered the store personnel. She often bought a copy of
Josephine! and inscribed it for the store owner or manager,
and sometimes she even added a personal gift. In fact, she
quite often autographed every copy of *Josephine!* in stock,
because at that time autographed books could not be
returned to the publisher for a refund. She and Irving even
contributed manual labor, rearranging the store's copies to

better advantage for *Josephine!* and often covering up other books in the process.

Jackie was thorough and relentless. When her tour took her to the Art Linkletter show in Los Angeles, she was horrified to discover that not a single store she visited was carrying the book. Nor, she discovered a few days later, did any San Francisco stores. She sat fuming in her room at the Mark Hopkins until midnight; then she picked up the phone and dialed Berney Geis's home number in New York.

"Do you know what time it is?" he mumbled. "It's three in the morning."

"You son of a bitch," she growled. "I can't sleep, so why should you?" She told him what she thought of his distribution and demanded that he get books to California on the double. "We sent the books out almost instantly by air freight," Berney remembers.

Letty recalls Jackie's skill at promoting with something close to awe. She'd waltz in with the furs and the dog and create a great hoopla, and some of the clerks would stay late, even if their shifts were over. I remember there were a lot of homosexual clerks at Doubleday's and various other stores, and Jackie would camp it up in a way that was sort of a secret code. Stylistically she was good at that. There's a certain high-camp wing of homosexual lifestyle that seems to like that kind of overblown Hollywood, glossy glamour. That's what Jackie was: old-time post-World War II glamour, satin cut on the bias. If she lived in Hollywood she would have had a Russian wolfhound and a white fur rug, that sort of thing."

Irving was as relentless as Jackie in his pursuit of publicity, though his notions took a somewhat different turn. "Some actress died, and he wanted to plant the story that she died reading *Every Night, Josephine!*" Letty remembers. "I talked him out of it on the grounds that you don't want a book to have killed someone. It's almost as if there was no such thing as a bad mention. I think I somehow got one of her books in somebody's hand in a soap opera. That was the kind of exposure they valued.''

Along with the autograph parties at bookstores, Letty arranged a full coast-to-coast schedule of television and radio talk-show appearances for Jackie. However hectic the pace, Jackie seemed to thrive on air time, making the most of her short starring roles in every town. Most hosts were pleased to have her; she was a good interview. She didn't have to be questioned constantly; she was a superb storyteller, and she could pick up a conversational ball and run with it in almost any direction. Nevertheless, she had a way of working all topics back to her book. She never lost sight of why she was on tour.

All the work paid off. According to Berney, *Josephine!* was ''a modest success—number ten on the *Time* magazine bestseller list, which isn't bad. I think we sold about thirty-five thousand to forty thousand copies.''

The sales were arguably at least as much a tribute to the Geis promotional apparatus and the Mansfields' talent for hustling as they were to the book's quality. Moreover, as Rose Susann pointed out to her daughter, *Josephine!* was well timed. ''I will never get a swelled head because of my mother,'' Jackie said in an interview. ''She's a very big realist. My mother said, 'You know why *Josephine!* is a big hit, Jackie? I sit in Rittenhouse Square in Philadelphia and everybody has a poodle, and I look up and there are, like, twenty million poodle owners, and every poodle owner buys your book. And the timing was perfect and right because people have become aware of poodles and you wrote a book about a poodle.' ''

Jackie was convinced that *Josephine!* could stand on its own merit. ''To be successful, the book has to be there,'' she said. ''Many publishers say I have ruined things for them because their writers all say, 'I'll just do what Jacqueline Susann does. I'll do television shows, and look how easy it will be.' Now, many writers when they go on they get so hooked up in theory and talking about how they write that people listening say, 'Oh, I wouldn't buy that book, that guy's dull.' Others can talk about a book well and there can be a big holocaust of people rushing into the bookstore, and they say, 'This isn't what I heard it was.' If the book isn't there you cannot make it a hit."

Her protestations notwithstanding, Jackie was underrating her skills as a promoter. Beyond her energy and her quick mastery of the intricacies of book selling, beyond Irving's press-agent knowhow, Jackie was a media natural. She could tap her flair for the dramatic, even for the outrageous, and make it work to grab attention for herself and her book. And she never stopped perfecting her act. She was laying groundwork for the books she knew would follow.

Crucial to that groundwork were contacts. It was vital to snare the media figures who snared the public who bought the books. While promoting *Josephine!* she snared several who would eventually help make her name a trademark for bestsellers. Chief among them, perhaps, was a forceful, eccentric, late-night New York radio talk-show host named Long John Nebel.

Long John and his regular guests were like family to his listeners. He was a night tripper, a brilliant if eerie personality. In his small East Side apartment the windows were covered with beaver board and heavy curtains. He never bought light bulbs of higher than forty watts. After his death his widow, Candy Jones, found boxes of black candles in his closet.

"In the days B.M.N. (Before Meeting Nebel)," said Jackie, about the night she first met him, "I used to lie in my darkened room and conjure mental images of my

Midnight Guru. . . . I went on in this euphoric state until one day in November 1963 when my publisher informed me I was to be a guest on Mr. Nebel's show.''

Six feet four and blond, Nebel began his radio career at the age of forty-three and reigned on three successive stations—WOR, WNBC, and WMCA—for twenty years. He had an eighth-grade education, a caustic strident voice, and a sometimes hypnotic, sometimes threatening manner.

Divorced from his first wife since 1960, in 1972 Long John married Candy Jones, the model and beauty expert. Jackie had first met Candy in the forties; the women liked each other instantly. Jackie was impressed that Candy was married to modeling impresario Harry Conover. A few days later she announced to Candy that, although she was serious about acting, many people had asked her why she didn't model. Candy had to tell her that at five feet seven she was an inch too short for fashion, and her look wasn't quite right for photographic modeling either.

Candy and Jackie kept in touch off and on over the years, and their friendship was finally cemented in the sixties when both became regular guests on Long John's show. For Candy, the guest spots with her husband-to-be began in 1964 with the publication of her book, *Make Your Name in Modeling and Television*. Jackie became a regular that same year.

On most talk shows Jackie merely acted her role of successful author, but with Long John it was different. There was an intimacy about the show. Maybe it had to do with the way Long John made his regulars feel they were family. Maybe the late-night format gave some guests the cozy, conspiratorial feeling of defying the diurnal order of the rest of the world. Or maybe it was just that the guests tended to get a little punchy in the middle of the night, figuring that no one except kooks were still up. Whatever the reason, on Long John's show Jackie was more herself, saltier, sometimes even a little profane.

One night with Candy, Jackie got a little carried away in her discussion of men she found attractive. "She had a list of men with whom she wanted to have a relationship," Candy recalls. "George C. Scott was one of them, and I sort of think she said Steve McQueen and John Lennon. And then she mentioned Long John." Candy and Long John weren't yet married, but they were definitely an item, as Jackie well knew. Candy was nonplussed. "I was sitting right there and I thought, I can't believe my ears. And then I said, 'Well, it's a good thing he's unavailable.'" Years later, Candy questioned her husband about the comment. "We were just about to go to sleep and I said, 'Remember that thing that Jackie said? Did you two ever make it?' And he said, 'We admired each other. We had a mutual admiration society.' And then he said, 'Wouldn't you rather wonder than know?' And I said, 'That means you did!' And he said, 'No. I didn't say that. You're jumping to conclusions.' So I never did get a straight answer. My feeling on balance is no."

Whether or not they had an affair remains unresolved, but certainly Long John remained for the rest of her life one of Jackie's most ardent fans. His show was her platform whenever she wanted it, and together they sold a lot of her books.

Another supportive couple Jackie became friends with while promoting *Josephine!* were David and Helen Gurley Brown. Helen was also a Geis author; her *Sex and the Single Girl* had been published shortly before *Josephine!* and was a much bigger seller. And Helen was no mean hand at promotion herself, although she did it with a subtlety that was utterly alien to Jackie. "Helen is much more vulnerable," Letty Pogrebin says, "a completely

different person. They both cultivated booksellers carefully, but in very different ways. They both did it by remembering everybody's name and by giving presents, but
Helen did it with tremendous warmth—loving, soft, gentle
gratitude. Jackie did it with 'Us guys together, we're
gonna make a lotta money.' ''

There is a certain demureness in Helen Gurley Brown
that contradicts the iconoclastic quality of her books and
the slick sexiness of *Cosmopolitan*, the magazine she
turned from a tired money loser into a commercial winner.
Helen has been happily married since 1959 to David
Brown, a Hollywood producer with many hits to his
credit, including *Cocoon*. She remembers her first meeting
with Jackie:

"It was on Park Avenue near the Waldorf, and it was
sunny but cold. It's 1963. She and Irving are streaking
across Park Avenue, going east toward the Waldorf, and
I'm streaking across going west toward the other side, and
we bumped into each other on the island there, and she
said, 'You're Helen Gurley Brown,' and I said, 'Yes,' and
she said, 'I'm Jacqueline Susann. Let me tell you about . . . '

"She'd already written her first book at that point, and
was beginning to promote it, and we just stood on the
corner and talked. We were both Bernard Geis authors. I
knew who she was because of her book. David and I were
just newly arrived in New York, so I'd never seen the
Schiffli embroidery commercials. So I didn't recognize
her.

"She couldn't have been nicer. She had that nice, deep
laugh. We never went to their house but they came to our
apartment, and she was thrilled that I had cats."

Helen's own promotion tour had begun months earlier,
and it became something of a model for Jackie's. "I went
everywhere," Helen recalls. "I went to I don't know how
many different cities, and I really hustled. And I was crazy

about it because—like many people who are not in show business—you find it very pleasurable to have people listening to you as you talk. All of a sudden you're a star.

"Soon after that Jackie published *Every Night, Josephine!* and she went out promoting just about every night. We both learned that you really don't say no to anything. You couldn't tell which show was going to sell books. When Jackie found out that some radio station fifty miles outside of Kalamazoo was twenty-five hundred kilowatts, she shouted at Berney Geis, 'Jesus, I've been getting up at three in the morning for twenty-five hundred kilowatts. Did Helen Gurley Brown do that?' And he would say, 'Yes, she did. She did everything. Just go.'

"She and I often stayed up all night together on the Long John Nebel show in New York," Helen remembers. "We went on at midnight. He was on for five hours. Jackie was herself, but she was more of a Tallulah Bankhead person than a Lauren Bacall person because she was tall and skinny and showbiz. She would come in not dragging her sable coat, but wearing it. She had the most beautiful diamond ring that I ever saw. It was absolutely pure. It must have been a hundred thousand dollars in nineteen-forty. I used to wonder where the money came from.

"I loved the way she looked because it was always showbizzy. It was sequins, it was chiffon, it was high heels and ankle straps and lots of jewelry and the beautiful dark hair. I adored her. She was like a role model, almost like a star. She was amusing. When Jackie and I were together I would listen because—I never felt she listened totally.

"Jackie was so shrewd about promotion," Helen says. "She would go in and buy a copy of her book in a store and autograph it for the owner instead of just moseying around and saying, 'How is my book doing?' She always had class about money—and about helping other writers. Like Rex Reed. She told him about promotion, and it helped. She told him everything he needed to know to sell the books. He's a good writer, so the good writing helped, but she taught him what to do on television.

"Jackie had many protégés, Rex and others. But she also helped writers she didn't care about personally. She was honorable. Once we were on Long John Nebel, and there was this girl who'd written a little book. The show was supposed to be about her book, but it was a quarter to three and no one had mentioned it. So Jackie wrote me a note and said, 'Helen, we've got to sell her book!' So then we began. Jackie was darling.

"She was the most generous person. She was so generous financially. She gave Gucci bags and Gucci scarves and jewelry. I have a ring she gave me. You admired something and she would take it off and give it to you right off her finger. It was charming. The ring she gave me is gold. It says, 'Screw you.' It has a corkscrew and a *U*, and you have to look very carefully to see what it is."

Members of the Geis staff unanimously concede Jackie's capacity for hard work and her talent and drive as a promoter. Most of them also experienced her generosity at one time or another. But the Geis people also saw a side of her that appeared utterly egocentric.

About a week after the publication of *Every Night, Josephine!* John F. Kennedy was assassinated. Shortly after, Jackie arrived at Berney Geis's office for a publicity meeting. She found the entire staff, like so many other Americans, clustered around a television set, watching the nonstop coverage from Texas in silent, stunned disbelief. She glanced at the television and blurted, "Why the fuck does this have to happen to me? This is gonna ruin my tour!"

Other writers might have felt like that but only Jackie would have said it aloud.

* * *

Whatever the Geis firm thought privately of its new actress-turned-author, Berney was sufficiently impressed by her book's modest success to offer a second book contract. In 1964 he paid Jackie three thousand dollars for the publication rights to whatever she wrote next, though at the time he had no idea what that might turn out to be.

"Maybe eight months later," he says, "her agent called on me and said, 'Don't laugh, but Jackie Susann has written a novel.' I told her agent to send it over, and I read it, and it was unpublishable. I gave it to Don Preston and Jackie Farber, and they called me together and pleaded with me not to publish it. They said, 'You've already invested three thousand dollars in an advance on this book. Don't throw good money after bad. It's literary trash.'"

The working title of the "literary trash" was *Valley of the Dolls*.

--- 24 ---

A Book Is Born

*I don't think any novelist should be concerned with
literature. Literature should be left to essayists.*

—————Jacqueline Susann

"WE wrote two terrible reports," Jackie Farber
recalls. "We said that there were good books
and bad books, and this was a bad, bad
book. *Valley of the Dolls* was hardly written in English."

Around the Geis firm books acquired shorthand designa-
tions, memos and mailing labels and other uses where full
titles were impractical. *SSG* was *Sex and the Single Girl*,
HAR was *Harlow*, and so on, though no one can remember
how they abbreviated Ellen Peck's *How to Get a Teen-Age
Boy and What to Do with Him When You Get Him*, one of
their more memorable titles. *Valley* was easy. It was
known as *VD*.

Don Preston's report on *VD* was far from gentle. It read, in part:

> It's a publicist's dream. If it hadn't been, I doubt very much if any of us would have bothered with fifty pages before giving up in despair... because she is a painfully dull, inept, clumsy, undisciplined, rambling and thoroughly amateurish writer whose every sentence, paragraph and scene cries for the hand of a pro. She wastes endless pages on utter trivia, writes wide-eyed romantic scenes that would not make the back pages of *True Confessions*, hauls out every terrible show biz cliché in all the books, lets every good scene fall apart in endless talk and allows her book to ramble aimlessly.... If it is compared to the other books in the general area of popular potboilers—such as those of Harold Robbins, Metalious, Rona Jaffe—it falls *far* short. ... It will lend itself to lively promotion but it will be roasted by critics, not for being salacious but for being badly done, dull....
>
> If, however, the decision is to publish this book despite the great odds against it, then what can editing do? If a competent editor is given carte blanche to cut, compress, and edit (interlinear as well as surgical), some of the faults of organization can be corrected and the story can be given greater pace and sharpness. This would mean drastic cutting, since most of the first 200 pages are virtually worthless and dreadfully dull and since practically every scene is dragged out flat and stomped on by her endless talk. Some whole scenes should be dropped, a few characters should all but vanish... many drawn-out explanations would be compressed into paragraphs.... While

doing this the editor would labor mightily to
eliminate a few dozen of the more hopelessly trite
scenes and to keep the characters in character. . . . I
really don't think there is a page of this ms. that
can stand in its present form. And after it is done,
we will be left with a faster, slicker, more readable
mediocrity. . . .

Respectful as he was of his editors, Berney Geis was
shaken by their unqualified distaste for the manuscript.
Nevertheless, he decided to get one last opinion, this time
from an editor for whom his esteem was boundless. He
took it home and asked his wife to read it. Darlene Geis
was a very highly regarded editor at Harry N. Abrams, a
highbrow publisher of art books, and if Darlene agreed the
book was unpublishable trash, then so be it.

"She read it and she said, 'You've got to publish this
book,' " Berney reports. Darlene told her husband that
Valley made her feel "as if I'd picked up the telephone and
was listening to two women telling how their husbands are
in bed. You can't hang up on a conversation like that. And
once this book is edited and straightened out, you can't stop
reading it." His mind made up, Berney took the manuscript
to Preston, the more experienced of his two editors. "We're
going to publish this book," Berney told him.

"And he went home for six weeks and worked on it,"
Berney says. "He did a tremendous amount of work. And at
that time, of course, Jackie, not yet being a success, was very
cooperative. She did almost everything we asked for. She
followed directions, and we told her she had to cut, and
some things she cut; and we let her put some things back in.
This was not normal editing Don did. This was reconstruction."

"There was an enormous amount of work done on it,"
Preston confirms, "including an enormous amount of cutting. I spent six weeks at home on the thing. I worked like

hell, cutting and restructuring, rewriting in spots, moving things around. Scenes weren't in proper order. A couple of key scenes weren't there at all, and I had to block them out and convince her to write them.''

One example is the pivotal scene in *Valley* where two female antagonists, Neely and Helen, get into a cat fight in the powder room of a chic nightclub. At its apogee, Neely yanks off Helen's wig and tries to flush it down a toilet. Preston rough-drafted the first version of the scene. Jackie rewrote it, drawing heavily on a similar episode from *The Women*. Preston rewrote her rewrite, she rewrote him, and so on. The scene was one of Preston's many contributions toward focusing *Valley's* action and strengthening its plot. Nevertheless, his scorn for the book is vast enough to encompass his own work on it, which he still views with obvious aversion.

''Later on my wife said, 'Don, do you realize she made millions of dollars on that book, and what did you make?' I told her I don't really give a shit what I made,'' Preston says, ''because the contribution was a mechanical, technical one. There's *nothing* of me in that book.''

If Jackie's unedited manuscript was less than polished, it wasn't for lack of effort on her part. She was, according to Helen Gurley Brown, ''utterly disciplined. She wrote everything over and over again. Sometimes, she said, at night she would go out and just walk. She would be confused about something and she would walk and clear it up. During times like this, when she was writing, they did go out at night occasionally, but she never let anything interfere with daytime.''

As was her habit, Jackie wrote five drafts of *Valley*, each one on paper of a different color, before submitting the fifth draft to the publisher. She must have been somewhat shocked at the extensive editing, but she was canny enough to know when she needed help and to take it.

''Jackie and I got along quite well during the editing of that book,'' Preston says. ''And a lot of what appears in the final version was hers—probably ninety percent of it. It was just a question of making it track, of making some sense of it. She almost wrote free association. Large portions of the thing were just triple dots and phrases strung loosely together.

"She had no sense of how to construct a scene, but she did know her way around show business. What she'd been doing all her life, in effect, was listening outside dressing-room doors. Her dialogue between the Neely character and the Helen character and all those people was good dialogue because she had heard people talk like that all of her life. She never made it as an actress and never pretended she had. It always astonished me that with such a looming ego she was a good listener. In my experience people like that mostly want you to listen to them."

Berney—and Preston—often complimented Jackie on her dialogue, certainly her strength. If Irving was in attendance he would say, "My Jackie has a photographic ear." If no one smiled, he added, "That's funny, isn't it?" Jackie loved to explain, to her editors or anyone around the Geis office who would listen, "I wrote in dialogue without any description on purpose. I wanted to write a novel where the author didn't butt in. It was like writing a play. My forte is dialogue writing. I'd be a playwright except that I want to succeed now. If you write plays you're at the mercy of directors and actors. If critics don't like your play it can close in three days and there goes a year's work down the drain. Take my advice. If you're a playwright, write novels. Novels are the best way to make money."

Berney, like many of the book's future readers, especially liked the salty dialogue of Helen Lawson, clearly modeled on Ethel Merman. "Ethel and I have an old score to settle, but she might not realize it because she doesn't read books," Jackie told him. "Irving says it doesn't matter, though. Everyone else will know."

After that, Berney always thought of Helen as Ethel, and sometimes he slipped and referred to her by that name. When he talked up Jackie's inchoate manuscript for a possible paperback sale to Ralph Daigh at Fawcett or Oscar Dystel at Bantam, he boasted, "Jacqueline Susann has Ethel Merman down to a *T*!"

Then one evening, while Don Preston was still laboring at home with the manuscript, a small crisis occurred. The Mansfields invited Berney and Darlene to dinner at Sardi's, and there, at a nearby table, was Ethel herself. To Berney's astonishment, Merman was no longer the brash brunette whose performances he had admired in *Annie Get Your Gun, Call Me Madam,* and *Gypsy.*

"My God, look at Ethel," Berney exclaimed. "She's dyed her hair. It's almost *red.*"

Jackie grew rigid, and nearly gagged on the piece of veal scallopini she was chewing. She glared at Merman, and muttered, "That bitch. She just did it to confuse my readers."

Jackie was upset all through dinner. She had given Helen Lawson red hair to lessen the physical resemblance to Ethel Merman—a strategem recommended for legal reasons. Now they both had red hair, even though most people still remembered Merman as a brunette. What to do?

When the dinner was over, she hurried home and pulled out her manuscript, the second paragraph on page 421, and pondered for a while. "Indigo!" she exclaimed happily to Josephine, who was sitting at her feet. Quickly she typed a two-sentence insert:

"She had put on weight, and like many brunettes who are fighting gray hair she had dipped into the dye pot. Her hair was now an indigo black that served only to bring out every line in her face."

Jackie appended a note to Berney, which she attached to the insert and delivered the next morning:

> Irving says I'm silly even to worry. . . but you did seem surprised at the red hair on the REAL Helen last night . . . so this is at least a "saver." Unless that bitch goes and deliberately dyes her hair back black and lets it grow. . .
>
>   Love,
>   Balzac Mansfield

The novel that eventually emerged from all Jackie's labors and Preston's belaborings was a slick, fast-moving page-turner about three young women living on the fast track fraught with deadly detours. On one level the "dolls" of the title are the pills that, like childhood toys, lull the heroines to sleep and then pep them up for the new day. On another level, of course, the dolls are the heroines themselves, whose stories intertwine over a twenty-year period beginning just after World War II.

Anne Welles, fresh from Radcliffe, arrives in New York City hoping to put her privileged but sheltered New England childhood behind her. She gets a job with a theatrical producer and a room in a women's hotel, where she meets Neely O'Hara, a freckle-faced young singer who is already a somewhat cynical veteran of the vaudeville circuit. Through her job Anne also becomes involved in the backstage drama of *Hit the Sky*, a musical starring the aging Broadway legend Helen Lawson, and helps Neely get a role when an ingenue is fired for upstaging the star. Another member of the cast is the beautiful, bosomy showgirl who will become the third member of the triumvirate, Jennifer North. The fortunes and misfortunes of Anne, Neely, and Jennifer—involving careers, money, booze, drugs, illnesses, and men—form the novel's core, though a sizable cast of secondary characters come and go during its two-decade span.

The Helen character is modeled on Merman, but Anne Welles, the heroine of *Valley of the Dolls*, is a composite of three people. However idealized, there is a lot of the author in Anne, but upscaled, moved to New England, and WASP. Anne's childhood home, like Jackie's, is furnished with antiques, and there is a Sargent portrait over the fireplace. (Bob Susan considered himself an artistic descendant of Sargent.) Anne has Jackie's difficulty in making girl friends as a child and teen-ager, and like Jackie, Anne finds her hometown boring and refuses to marry her girlhood beau. Like Jackie, Anne defies maternal disapproval and goes to seek her fortune in New York. Like Jackie, she becomes involved in the world of the theater. And like Jackie, though in much grander style, Anne becomes famous doing commercials. Anne's deflowering by Lyon Burke in New Haven, where *Hit the Sky* is trying out, has its parallels in Jackie's liaison with Joe E. Lewis, while *Cry Havoc* was in Chicago.

Anne's parents bear some resemblance to Jackie's. Her mother is a widow, a stiffly proper woman who appears to Anne to be sexually cold. "You're a lady," Mrs. Welles tells her daughter. "That's why you don't like kissing. No lady does." The late Mr. Welles is described as something of a rake who left an estate of five thousand dollars, the same amount Bob Susan left.

Anne also has a lot of Rose in *her*. The central story of *Valley of the Dolls*, the story of Anne Welles and Lyon Burke, is in part essentially the story of Rose and Bob Susan. It suggests that Jackie in the course of the book examines her feelings about each of her parents and their marriage and came down, at last, on Rose's side. Jackie began writing *Valley* shortly after her long trip abroad with

Rose. Although Bob had been dead for six years, his emotional hold on her was still strong, but his death meant an end to the contest between the two parents for Jackie's love and loyalty—a contest Bob almost always won. Rose's obsessive love for Bob is mirrored in Anne's for Lyon—a beautiful, intelligent, resourceful, self-reliant, and dignified woman who turns down desirable beaux because for her there is only one man in the world.

Anne's Lyon and Rose's Bob are both dashing but devilish, compelling but elusive, as are all the male protagonists of Jackie's novels. Anne waits seventeen years for Lyon to marry her. Rose managed to snare Bob much sooner, but she had to wait twenty-three years for him to come home to her in any real sense, as he did after his heart attack in 1938. Both Lyon and Bob are philanderers, selfish and irresponsible. For example, Lyon is away and unreachable when their young daughter gets pnuemonia and is rushed to the hospital in the middle of the night. Bob deserted Rose during her pregnancy—a pregnancy endured, like Anne's, during an awful heat wave—and he deserted both mother and daughter during the early days following Jackie's birth.

In looks, however, Anne is very much like Jackie's longtime friend Bea Cole, a blond, patrician, New England beauty. Possibly to further titillate her gossip-loving readers, Jackie sometimes hinted that Grace Kelly, the princess who came from Jackie's hometown, might be a partial model for Anne. And some observers, including David McClintick in his book *Indecent Exposure*, contend that "there was a good deal of Lee [Reynolds] in the character of Anne Welles." Lee Reynolds, though a brunette, is a beautiful, elegant, and accomplished woman whose ex-husband, David Begelman, the former head of Columbia Pictures, is the subject of McClintick's book.

Jackie's sources for Lyon Burke are clear, beginning with the traits Lyon and Bob share in their relationship with women. Lyon also has Bob's conflict about work. Bob often told his daughter about his carefree and creative days in Europe, his fantasy of giving up his commercial success as a portrait painter and running away to paint masterpieces. Lyon vacillates between wanting to be a serious writer and the glittery high life of a theatrical agent, fantasizes about running away to England to write a novel, and eventually does.

If Lyon is principally based on Bob Susan, for some of his exterior trappings Jackie draws on two theatrical acquaintances, Leland Hayward and David Begelman, taking his first initial from Leland and his second from Begelman.

The belief of most readers that Neely O'Hara is based on Judy Garland is generally correct. "If you're a Judy fan, and you have read all the stuff you could find on her, you would recognize Jacqueline Susann's sources," says John Fricke, of the Judy Garland Fan Club. "I think the most blatant thing I can remember is that one of Neely's suicide attempts in *Valley of the Dolls* was almost word for word the way a movie magazine described a Judy Garland suicide attempt in 1965. Another example: In *Life* magazine in 1961, Shana Alexander quotes Judy as saying her first London Palladium concert was 'a pistol.' Neely uses that expression. Then there was all that stuff about Neely doing a one-woman show, two a day, on Broadway, and of course, Judy did that. Jackie Susann had Neely making her big comeback in 1961, which is right. That's the year Judy made her comeback at Carnegie Hall."

The general similarities between Neely and Judy are obvious: the phenomenal talent, an abnormal childhood and too-early success, an unhappy personal life that created career problems, the battle with weight, the addiction to drugs and alcohol. Neely, however, has other components. As a winsome young gamine in the early part of the book, she resembles Elfie, the ex-vaudevillian who

was Jackie's first friend in New York, including Elfie's
tacky wardrobe favorites, the purple taffeta dress and the
coat with the fox collar. There is even some Jackie in
Neely, ambition and single-mindedness. Neely has Jackie's
bulldog aggressiveness about getting parts, and Jackie's
own experience of being fired at an early rehearsal.

Mel Harris, Neely's first husband, is modeled on Irving:
the nice guy press agent, the dutiful son who goes home to
his parents in Brooklyn every Friday night. Mel writes for
a radio show starring Johnny Mallon (Irving's Fred Allen),
and the supportive and loving Mel spends a lot of time
getting Neely's name in the papers.

Neely's second husband, Ted Casablanca, is loosely
based on various bisexual designers Jackie knew, among
them Coco Chanel, who had an amorous interest in Jackie
herself. During her Schiffli years, Jackie observed a pano-
ply of designers, and often expressed amazement that so
many were "double-gaited."

Jackie gives her own first initial to a heroine in each of
her novels; in *Valley* it goes to Jennifer, the character she
subjects to the most tragedy yet treats most tenderly.
Patterned chiefly after two of Jackie's closest friends,
Carole Landis and Joyce Mathews, Jen exhibits Jackie at
her most vulnerable and intimate. Both have breast cancer
and Jen must abort a child who would inherit mental
deficiencies. Essentially, tragically, both of them must
remain childless.

Jen, who dies of an intentional overdose, most dramatically points up Jackie's moral about the dangers of drugs.
Jackie had twice come close to OD-ing, after Guy was put
away and then—like Jen—at the time of her mastectomy.
On two other occasions, around Bob's death and after
Ethel's rejection, Jackie's consumption of alcohol and pills
produced terrifying blackouts. She said she wrote *Valley* to
warn people away from drugs. All three of her heroines

deliver the message. "A question I get all the time is 'What kind of a girl takes pills?' You hear people say 'If she came from a good background she wouldn't do that.' Then you hear 'If she really had talent she wouldn't need pills.' Finally you hear 'If men liked her better she wouldn't be insecure.' Anne came from a fine family, Neely was burning with talent, and Jen could have had almost any man." Describing the lure of pills, Jackie continued, "I thought I was a realist. We all control everything with pills—weight, depression, pregnancy. Pills aren't taken to escape reality at first. They're taken so a person can cope with reality. Alcohol ruins careers, but the pills can help for a long while. They induce sleep, so you can wake up refreshed. Add Dexedrine and you can actually sparkle. But loneliness or failure can bring on more pills, and more of the drink that speeds the pill's effects. One drink becomes three, two pills become six or twelve, and then there's the night when you don't know how much you had, and you can die, as I've seen happen to several friends."

Indeed she had. An astonishing number of women she cherished were suicides; Carole Landis, her lover; "Aunt" Esther Weinrott, to whom she had dedicated so many childhood verses; Judy Shinn, her old pal and partner on *The Children's Hour,* whose sudden death in 1958 was rumored to have been an overdose. And others, like Joyce Mathews, had barely survived repeated attempts.

For public consumption Jackie usually implied that Jen was based on Marilyn Monroe and/or Jayne Mansfield, giving her Mansfield's awesome bosom and Monroe's sensual allure. Jen's engagement to a senator echoes Monroe's rumored romances with John and Robert Kennedy; even the suicide is somewhat similar to Monroe's. But for Jackie herself, Jennifer was most truly Carole Landis. The sweet vulnerability, the money-hungry mother, the impoverished childhood, the sensational looks—all recall

Landis, as do Jen's "warmth and easy interest in everyone she met." Like Landis, Jen is bisexual; like both Landis and Joyce Mathews, she believes she has no talent, but only an all-too-transient physical beauty.

Many of the minor characters are based on people Jackie knew; some emerge as friendly tributes, a few as small acts of revenge. The childlike singer Tony Polar is based partly on Dean Martin. Jackie had a crush on the singer for years; when she finally met Martin, he was too engrossed in a comic book to pay her much attention. The often harsh depiction of the "funny farm" where Neely and Tony are incarcerated, and the unflattering view of the personnel who treat them, are drawn from Jackie's own agonizing experiences with the people who treated her own child.

Jackie certainly capitalized on the human appetite for gossip by incorporating notorious aspects of celebrities' lives in her characters. As Letty Pogrebin puts it, "What people already knew about these characters helped them care what happened in this book. . . . You feel you're getting a very forbidden glimpse at the way those people lived. And Jackie's theory was that people wanted to believe that they weren't missing out on much. That's the theory that formed the way she wrote and why, she believed, she was successful."

Yet Jackie was inclined to dismiss the roman à clef aspects of *Valley*. "Many people say that half the fun in reading *Valley* is the show business guessing game, and I say I don't think so," she said in an interview. "To people who don't know about show business or aren't interested, the characters become very real anyway—people from places like North Dakota who aren't interested in the inside gossip. It really warms the cockles of my heart when someone tells me that they don't follow show business but that they personally can identify with even the wildest character in my book, with the drives and feelings of my characters.''

Much of *Valley*'s later notoriety—and, some say, its success—stemmed from its explicit sexual scenes. Though fairly mild by current standards, they were considered salacious at the time. It is ironic, that these very scenes were among the least convincing in Jackie's original manuscript.

"She had the most trouble with her so-called sex scenes,'' Preston recounts. "The book got a reputation—an undeserved reputation, I think—for being raunchy. It actually has almost no graphic sex in it at all. I don't think Jackie understood sex, even if she slept with a hundred men, and I don't think she knew how to write about it. I mean, she knew the facts; she knew all the four-letter words. She just didn't understand what the hell people were doing and why they were doing it.

"Some of the sex scenes were added after the book was written,'' he recalls. "There's the one with Lyon and Anne in a hotel. The original scene had one of those dot-dot-dot things, and the strategic light, and the old-fashioned stopping at the bedroom door. And we said, 'That isn't acceptable. It doesn't work in terms of the kind of novel and kinds of characters.' And she reluctantly wrote a sexual experience into the thing." Anne's deflowering hurts her physically, as Jackie's had: "When the pain came, she clenched her teeth and made no sound. . . . She took a hot bath, and when the water penetrated the soreness within her, it became a tangible memory of him.''

"Anne hadn't come to terms with sexuality yet,'' Preston reflects, "but I think Jackie had not either. She couldn't write a romantic sex scene between a woman and a man. . . . Her lesbian scenes were more tender. She was more free then to romanticize and idealize.

"Her references to sex were always very graphic. 'He was humping her,' things like that, always in animal, physical terms. She always used words like 'fucking' and 'humping.' It wasn't making love; that concept seemed foreign to her. And to be fair, it may have been foreign to most of the people she wrote about, too. 'To be a showgirl in Las Vegas,' she once told me, 'was to be made available to whoever was the high roller at the moment. That was part of the job.' And when she described those things it was always with an air of 'Well, that's the way life is.' She never seemed to feel that sort of thing was at all unusual."

Despite her use of graphic language, certain words offended her and she stubbornly refused to use them. "She hated the word 'nipple,'" Preston recalls. "I was editing one of the sex scenes and I inserted a phrase about 'nipples growing erect'—a rather clinical reference. She didn't object to it as bad writing, which it undoubtedly was, but she came back and said, 'I think the word "nipple" is disgusting. I don't want it there. It sounds like an animal. All I can see is baby pigs hanging on to nipples.' But she used words like 'tit' all the time—not in the book, but in conversation. 'Boobs' was another favorite word."

What Preston termed the "so-called sex scenes" remained the thorniest issue between author and editor. By now it was late May, and Jackie was getting impatient. Rewrite as she would, she could never bring the scenes to life for Preston, who was still holed up in the country. Berney was the intermediary, trying to handle Jackie tactfully, like a jockey gentling a racehorse in the derby. He sugar-coated Preston's more acidic instructions and memos.

In particular, Anne's defloration scene with Lyon flew back and forth between author and editor. One day in Berney's office Jackie's eyes fell on a memo from Preston that was sitting on Berney's desk. "I still don't feel she has gotten all she can out of the scene. Anne is nearly an opaque character, masking her feelings from the reader through much of the book or simply not feeling at all. But in this scene her guard is down, and the reader should get more of a feel of her. Character, that is—emotional response. Maybe this is as far as she can take it, but I still wish she would give it some thought.'' Jackie made no comment, but the disdainful tone of the memo did not escape her notice.

June came, and Preston still wasn't satisfied with either his rewrites or hers. She could hardly believe it. Over two years of dogged work and all those drafts on all those different colors of paper! On the fourth of June, Jackie brought Berney her third rewrite of the aforementioned powder room fight. Jackie had had it. As far as she was concerned her rewrites were finished, done! It was a great book. "The day is over," she said to Berney, "when the point of writing is to turn a phrase that critics will quote, like Henry James. I'm not interested in turning a phrase." And then, as if to underscore her faith in the vulgar, she appended the following note to her third rewrite of the wig-pulling scene.

Dear Don and Berney,

I'm most eager to read Don's completed script . . . so as Helen Lawson would say . . . "Get the lead out of your ass," and hurry up!

Jackie

Preston accepted her third rewrite as the final one, though forever after he thought it wasn't quite good enough. Jackie, on the other hand, thought maybe it was a little *too* good. She always resented the many compliments it brought, galled by the knowledge that it wasn't pure

Susann being praised, but something that was at least one-third Preston and one-third Clare Boothe Luce.

Although he never credited her with talent as a writer, Preston did develop a grudging respect for Jackie's toughness, her basic instincts, her drive to succeed. "When Jackie really liked a phrase she wouldn't change it," he says. "We went back and forth on the opening, where she calls New York an 'angry concrete animal.' It stayed in." Neither would she give way on the title, though it seemed that everyone at Random House, the book's distributor, hated it. "They kept arguing that bookstore personnel might put the book in the children's section. But she said, 'No, that's the title and nobody's changing it.' And I guess she was right. If a book is a runaway bestseller, how can you say it's a bad title?"

Her stubbornness extended beyond titles, Preston recalls. "It did not pay ever to cross Jackie unless you figured a way that you could kind of go around her. If you had a way to make her think that she herself had come up with an idea, then it was all right. But to tell her that an idea she had was not good and had to be changed—she would just dig in and fight like hell. Still, she was always willing to talk.

"And even if I put her down now, I also have to admit she did have a sense of what those people in her book were all about. When it came down to writing a scene that didn't ring true, she would quite rightly say no. There was a lot of talk about the dreary ending in *Valley of the Dolls*. It was such a downer. Everyone wanted to change it, and Jackie absolutely would not do it. 'I'm not going to put a fucking happy ending on this book,' she said. 'That's not the way life works for these people. These are people who have bad lives, whose lives are screwed up by pills and the kind of pressure that show business puts on them, by the buying and selling of "meat" in the world they live in. It does this to them.'

"We got along because she wanted to have a big book, and she saw that Berney was the vehicle by which to do that," he says. "If she could get it published by a big promoter she could make it; and she knew, I think instinctively, that no other publisher would want to do it. And she was driven by ambition.

"It wasn't the money, really, but she said to me one time, 'I want to walk into "21" and I want everyone in the room to turn and say, "That's Jacqueline Susann, the author."' She had wanted originally for them to say, 'That's Jacqueline Susann, the actress,' and when she realized that wasn't going to happen she was determined it would happen to her one way or another. And, boy, was she tenacious and tough and mean as hell. If she hadn't made it as a writer she would have figured out something else to do. Her drive was to be successful."

Hardly anyone knowledgeable about the publication of *Valley* denies that Preston's labor on the book was Herculean and contributed immeasurably to its success. Leona Nevler, editor of the Fawcett reprint line, saw the unedited manuscript when Geis was hoping to make an early sale on the paperback rights. Nevler, the discoverer of *Peyton Place*, did not like *Valley of the Dolls* in its original state. 'The roman à clef aspects of it seemed packageable and there was an energy to it, but it almost seemed like an amateur job. 'Bad' is really not the word. It just wasn't good enough," Nevler recalls. "Authors do not like to feel that someone else is responsible for writing their books, or rewriting their books. Editorial help is one thing, but I really think that Don did a thorough line rewrite, almost, of the book."

Fawcett offered no bid on reprint rights then, and even after the book had been edited Nevler still was skeptical,

as were the other reprint houses to which the final manuscript was submitted. In fact, one of the most surprising
aspects of *Valley*'s history is the failure of so many
professionals to sense the book's potential. When the time
came for the five or six major reprinters to enter their bids
for rights, in the auction that was customary then and
remains so today, Berney Geis was in for a shock. Preston
recalls the day vividly:

"Since we lived from one big reprint deal to the next
economically, they became dramatic events for all of us.
So when the deadline for bids on *Valley* came and Berney
began to make his calls to the paperback houses, we all got
a sinking feeling. No one was bidding. Finally Bantam
entered a bid, a complex thing with clauses that provided
for extra payments if the book made the *Times* list and that
sort of thing. I don't remember what the actual cash
advance was to be, but it wasn't very much. We were all
pretty depressed.

"Berney went back to the other houses to report the bid,
hoping it would inspire someone to get into the act, but no
one did. So he went back to Bantam, implying that there
was other bidding action and that they would have to up
their offer to get the book. He didn't actually lie, but he
was good at giving the impression that things were hap-
pening when they weren't. And Bantam did up the bid, to
something like a hundred and twenty-five thousand cash
advance with those escalator clauses for the additional
payments. Berney was delighted with the deal, and so
were the Mansfields, and I don't think anyone at Bantam
knows to this day that they were bidding against themselves."

"I'll never be a Jacqueline Susann fan," Preston con-
cludes. "I never liked *Valley*, even after we were finished.
I really thought the thing was just an absolute mess. And
later, when I heard those rumors that I had written it, I

almost had the feeling I should sue someone for defamation of character."

Whatever its dubious beginnings, *Valley* did have one ardent supporter at the Geis firm. Letty Pogrebin got the finished product, and she sensed immediately that it was commercial and promotable. "I just knew," she says, "that it was going to sell and sell and sell."

25

The Selling
[and Buying] of
Valley of the Dolls

*Being number one on the New York Times bestseller
list, that's what she cared about, that was the "review"
she wanted. Naturally, she would have liked to have
been adored by the critics, but she knew that the quid
pro quo for this kind of bestsellerdom was that everyone
else would put you down and be jealous and all that
sort of thing. "Number one on the New York Times
'bestseller list, hardcover and softcover," that was'
Jackie's credo. She was the first of the ladies who were
motivated most strongly by mass popularity. As far
as she was concerned her "reviews" came from bookstores.*

——David Brown

E VEN Letty could scarcely have imagined just how
Valley of the Dolls would sell. It would sell beyond
the rosiest imaginings of Berney Geis and the
shrewdest projections of Irving Mansfield. It would sell

beyond the wildest hopes of Jackie herself. The "literary trash" so narrowly rescued by Darlene Geis would become nothing less than the best-selling novel of all time.

The book's commercial beginnings were more auspicious than its artistic ones, but not by all that much. The prepublication Bantam deal buoyed spirits at Geis, as did a subsequent movie sale to Helen Gurley Brown's husband, David, then executive vice president of Twentieth Century-Fox. Berney himself helped nail down the movie deal, using a ploy not unlike the one he had used with Bantam. Brown and other Fox executives had read a copy of the manuscript sent to them by Annie Laurie Williams, and they were interested. "But what pushed us over the edge was a telephone call from Berney Geis," Brown reports. "He said the paperback sale was for two hundred thousand dollars, or something like that, which seemed like an enormous sum because *Josephine!* had not been a raging bestseller." Fox paid $80,000 for the option to make *Valley* into a movie, with escalators that would bring the total up-front money to around $200,000.

That no book club bid on the book was disappointing; a book club deal could have boosted prestige and sales. Still, there was the money from the paperback sale and the movie option, which was substantial if not dizzying. Both Geis and the Mansfields were enormously pleased. *Valley* had brought in over $200,000 and it wasn't even published yet. There was backing for the book and money in the pot for the major advertising and publicity campaign that could now be mounted.

In one sense a book's sales campaign begins months before publication, when the book is presented to the salespeople who will see that it is stocked in the nation's bookstores. Because Geis books were distributed by Random House, *Valley* was part of the presentation made by

the Geis staff at Random's sales conference. The meetings
went on for days and covered extensive lists from several
affiliated companies, so the salesmen had an understand-
able tendency to drift away while editors droned on about
their books. The Geis staff knew this, and always looked
for ways to liven up their presentation. In this case Berney
decided his best shot was the author herself.

Don Preston remembers. "I said a few words about the
book, Letty made her usual pitch about advertising and
publicity plans, and then Berney showed everyone the
paste-up of the dust jacket and introduced Jackie to the big
roomful of bored salespeople. Jackie and Irving took a
look at the jacket, which they hadn't seen before, and then
Jackie did her thing. In a few minutes she had them all
wide awake and interested as hell."

The sales force left the conference with vivid recollections of a stunning jacket, an even more stunning and
charming author, and Geis promises of a publicity and
advertising campaign to rival that of the memorably successful *Sex and the Single Girl*. The Geis staff returned to
West Fifty-sixth Street confident that the books would at
least get onto bookstore shelves. Seeing that they moved
off those shelves and into the hands of readers—and even
nonreaders, they hoped—was the next order of business.

The stops were all pulled out weeks before, although
the official publication date was set for February 10, 1966.
Already famous for her blizzards of prepublication gim-
mickry (tins of fried grasshoppers, swizzle sticks with messages on them, keys, even a little mortar and pestle to
announce a cookbook), Letty Pogrebin cast about for something that would get reviewers' attention—something like
the doggerel and pawprint used for *Josephine!* As usual,
the idea came from the book itself: the "dolls" consumed
incessantly by the principal characters.

The result was an official-looking prescription blank

advising: "Take 3 yellow 'dolls' before bedtime for a broken love affair; take 2 red dolls and a shot of scotch for a shattered career; take *Valley of the Dolls* in heavy doses for the truth about the glamour set on the pill kick." That was followed by a second mailing to the media containing a single sheet with a sugar-filled red capsule taped to it and the message: "This is an imitation 'doll.' But *Valley of the Dolls* is no imitation! Watch for the sensational truth about the glamour set on a pill kick."

These teasers were followed by a press release that accompanied advance galley proofs—which went to every important book reviewer—and the astonishing fifteen hundred free copies of the book itself that were sent to virtually anyone who might help publicize it in any way. The gimmicks worked: Weeks before the book's official publication, mentions of it began to appear around the country, most of them inspired by Letty's efforts.

A few, however, were the work of Cy Presten, a "column-planter" in the mold of the early Irving Mansfield, who had been enlisted to help fuel the flames. Presten, no relation to Don Preston, was a Runyonesque diamond in the rough who believed that *any* mention in gossip columns was better than none. He and Irving were made for each other, and as the publicity heated up Presten's calls to the Geis office were almost as frequent as Irving's. "You got anything? Want me to plant something?" he would ask, and a day or two later one-liners about Jackie or Josephine began to pop up in the columns, sometimes related to *Valley* and sometimes not.

Publication day was marred for Jackie by the death early that morning of her old friend Billy Rose, but there was no time to indulge in grief. She and Irving, in collaboration with Geis and with additional help from Bantam, were about to put on a promotional campaign that would become a publishing legend.

She began by going to her files. While promoting *Josephine!* she had kept careful notes on every book distributor and bookstore clerk and talk show host and reporter she met. She not only knew their names; she knew the names of their spouses and kids and grandmothers. She knew their special interests and their vulnerabilities. She had been careful to write flattering, personal thank-you notes to every one of them who had ever helped her in the slightest way. Every handwritten note was different, although certain phrases recur. "I laughed out loud at your story. . . ." "It was so nice of you to . . ." "Josie has given us so much happiness, and I'm really thrilled when I learn her escapades have contributed to someone else's pleasure. . . ." Now she wrote them again, reminding her contacts that she had a new book out, a really big novel, and asking for all the help they could give it.

Her meticulous spadework helped Letty line up a nationwide tour that featured scores of television appearances and countless radio shows, along with autograph parties and print media interviews. Letty had raised the major book tour to a level of success few could match, but Jackie was determined to outdo them all.

In Los Angeles the Mansfields occupied their customary suite in the Beverly Hills Hotel, a suite that, Irving informed reporter Jane Howard, had previously been tenanted by Princess Margaret, Johnny Carson, Carlo Ponti, Prince Philip, and the maharajah of Jaipur. "Just imagine how many deals have been signed right in this suite!" Irving exclaimed, adding that it was costing them $112 a day.

Although Irving had many contacts in Los Angeles and the Geis firm had its own modus operandi there, they jointly decided that Geis should hire an expert to aid in the west coast publicity tour. The man Berney hired was Jay Allen, who, although he had handled only show business figures in the past, came highly recommended by someone whose judgment Irving trusted—the columnist Louella Parsons. "I met Jackie about four months before Geis released *Valley of the Dolls*," Allen remembers. He worked for her on all her books until she died, hired by successive publishers at her insistence. "Any success I have had in the business I owe to her," he adds. "She taught me how to do book publicity and I just let her lead me, and from that time on I have done nothing but book publicity. I gave up all my show business clients." They were replaced in part by writers Jackie referred to him, including Noel Behn, Helen Gurley Brown, Rex Reed, and even Clifford Irving, though Allen declined to work with Irving.

Allen began to sense that the book was reaching out to the non-book crowd, as did others such as Nick Clemente, advertising and promotion director of the B. Dalton chain. Allen recalls Clemente's telling him: "You know, starting with Jackie we began getting new customers in this door. People that had never been in this store before were coming in to buy Jackie Susann's book. They buy one book and they think, 'Hey, I haven't read a book in years, and I enjoyed this.' And then they'll read another book, and it'll really build the audience for book buying."

In Miami the Mansfields and Geis took on Jim Montgomery, an executive in a local public relations firm, to help with the publicity. His firm had handled the opening of the Fontainebleau Hotel and worked for Dean Martin and Frank Sinatra, but Montgomery and Jackie had yet another interest in common: He was from Philadelphia, too, and he had once dated Grace Kelly, whose father had supposedly been a friend of Bob Susan's. There was Bryn Mawr:

"She told me she went to Bryn Mawr . . . and her mother was a teacher there. . . . Well, she knew all about Bryn Mawr, I guarantee it. She knew the names of the halls, and the area that it was in, and the places that the Bryn Mawr girls habituated. . . . We talked about it on many occasions—Gerrytown Friends, and Wooster Academy and so forth. That had been my life, and I had no reason to question it because I liked her.''

One of the things Montgomery liked about Jackie was her *joie de vivre*. ''She was on a roll when she was down here,'' he says. ''She was in high spirits and she thoroughly enjoyed the interviews that I lined up for her. Maybe that was why she confided in us,'' he adds, referring to the medical problems whose existence was known to so few. ''That, and the fact that we were down here, and the chances were we wouldn't be mixing with their friends up there in New York all that much.''

One of the interviews lined up for Jackie in Miami was with Larry King. ''At that time he was—and still is—probably as fine an interviewer as I have ever heard,'' Montgomery says. ''And he told me that in his opinion she was one of the best interviews he ever had. She was very bright. She could talk about a lot of subjects. She was funny. She was able to carry the interview, and didn't just sit there and wait to be asked questions. She volunteered information. Larry did Jackie two or three hours one night. He was very impressed with her.''

No matter how impressed he might have been, King must have noted the talk was never allowed to stray far from *Valley of the Dolls*. As Jackie told Jane Howard, ''No matter what an interviewer may bring up, I can work the conversation back to the book.'' Howard recounted Jackie's interview with the gossip columnist Dorothy Manners. Jackie ''listened politely as Miss Manners pointed out a poster in her office that had been designed by Her Serene Highness Princess Grace of Monaco. Very nice, Miss Susann agreed, and what's more, 'Her Serene Highness, if she'd take off ten pounds, is exactly the sort of girl I'd like to have play Anne in *Valley*.' ''

Howard also reported the grave temptation that faced the

Mansfields in Atlanta, where they made a pilgrimage to Margaret Mitchell's writing desk and to the street corner where the author of *Gone With the Wind* had been fatally struck down by a car. "Irving said I ought to stand right here on the street, and, just for a gag, have a car come by and just give me a *little* bump," Jackie told her. "I said no, enough is enough."

Jackie always seemed to be at her high-spirited best when she was on tour. She never seemed to tire. She was generous with her time, granting interviews to almost anyone who asked for one, letting them run on as long as the interviewer cared to keep talking. And she never seemed to lose patience with the endless sameness of the questions, or with giving what soon became her stock answers. ("Ethel just doesn't speak to me louder. . . . If Goodman Ace had given me a piano I'd probably be playing in Carnegie Hall by now. . . . To be a writer you have to have a divine conceit. . . . I write five drafts. . . . I don't care what the critics say. I was trying to tell a story. . . .")

If her publishers came up with some new idea to step up the pace, she never complained. "A new book," she said, "is just like any new product, like a new detergent. You have to acquaint people with it. They have to know it's there. You only get to be number one when the public knows about you." When the time came to publicize the paperback edition of *Valley*, Jackie pitched in just as cheerfully. "We always invented things for her to do at the American Booksellers Association," says Esther Margolis, then at Bantam. "With *Valley* we came up with a gimmick that we subsequently used a lot. We had Jackie photographed with booksellers at the Bantam booth, and we sent the glossies to the bookseller's hometown newspaper. We must have taken four hundred pictures in an hour, and I don't think her pose changed. In almost every one of those pictures Jackie is smiling.''

Jackie could, however, turn acidic at a hostile question, and there was no shortage of those. There were interviewers who wanted to know why she wrote such a dirty book, or such a shallow one, or, for that matter, such a ghoulish one—capitalizing on the tragedies of real-life people and all. Typical was a Detroit interviewer who noted that her book had been called trash and asked, ''How does that make you feel?'' To such queries Jackie was apt to respond with ''Way back then they didn't think Shakespeare was a good writer. He was the soap opera king of his day.'' Or ''They called Zola a bad writer. Everything changes in writing. I think James Joyce is a bore. *Ulysses* is a bore.'' If anyone had the temerity to suggest that perhaps she wasn't in the same league with Shakespeare, or even with boring old Joyce, Jackie's attitude was why the hell not? She was, by God, outselling them.

Doubtless she was sometimes roused to real anger, but it is also probable that she knew full well that a feisty Jackie made an interesting show. On Toronto television a hostess asked, ''Don't you ever wake up in the middle of the night and realize that you haven't done anything that is really artistic?'' ''You're sick,'' Jackie retorted. ''Do you wake up and think you're not Huntley-Brinkley?''

She discovered something of a geographical component to hostility levels. Interviewers in the East seemed to find her an interesting personality, but made it clear that no sane person could take her book seriously. In the West, however, there were reporters who gushed that she was ''America's best writer.'' Not best seller, best *writer*. Jackie came to like the west coast quite a lot.

If hostility irritated her, it never slowed her down. A sip of iced tea and a bite of salami and she was off to another bookstore, another show. She did local shows, syndicated shows, national shows. She did Virginia Graham and Merv Griffin and Mike Douglas. She galloped through as many as thirty interviews in a week. When she couldn't get on a show her friends improvised for her. She and Noel Behn, for example, devised a method of plugging each other's novels. For print interviews, Jackie insisted on being photographed in front of her bookcase, where Behn's *The Kremlin Letter* was prominently displayed. In return, Behn helped salve her frustration at being rejected for *The Today Show*. When *he* was booked, he managed to tell a story about identifying himself to a stranger he was meeting at the Plaza Hotel, as "a man who would be carrying *Valley of the Dolls*."

Behn notwithstanding, it galled Jackie that Barbara Walters, daughter of her old pal Lou, the owner of the Latin Quarter, didn't want her on *Today*. Jackie took off after Barbara with a bit of doggerel: "When my disposition falters/I think of Barbara Walters." After a few such jabs, Irving says, "Barbara crawled up to Jackie on the dais of a banquet and said, 'For Christ's sake, will you give up already? I want to be friends with you.' " Barbara has no recollection of Jackie's attack. She says they became friends after a woman they knew smeared them both, implying they were two cats whom she "wouldn't want to see in the same cage." Jackie telephoned Barbara, "and there certainly was a bond. We both laughed at it. Then she volunteered Irving, who walked me through the stores and showed me how to promote my book."

Jackie's old feud with Johnny Carson was now a terrible frustration to her. Carson rarely gave authors the limelight, usually holding them until the closing moments, but his program still aired on 220 stations and was believed to sell a lot of books. Jackie couldn't get herself on so she used Bette Davis as her vehicle; Bette was hoping to play Helen Lawson in the movie. "You know, Johnny," Bette said early in the show, "I just read the most marvelous book. It's called *Valley of the Moon*." Johnny, who had sworn to boycott Jackie, fell into the trap. "Don't you mean *Valley of the Dolls*?" he asked.

"Of course, *Valley of the Dolls*—and it's a terrific book," Davis said, driving it home.

Jackie could cram an amazing number of activities into one day without ever becoming disorganized, and she managed to ride herd on all aspects of her book's promotion, not just her own frenzied schedule. When she saw that Geis was advertising *Valley* only in newspapers' book sections, which was customary, she insisted that he place some ads on the entertainment pages as well. Like most of her ploys it was effective.

In mid-March, five weeks after publication, Jackie began to reach her goal. *Valley* made *The New York Times* bestseller list. She said that staying on the list was more important than climbing to number one. "Look at Rona Jaffe," she often remarked. "*The Best of Everything* never made it to first place, but it's a famous and successful book. It hung in around number five for a long, long time, and everybody read it."

Clearly *Valley*'s momentum was largely due to the publicity. However, there was a second factor that inflated the early sales: a book-buying campaign apparently orchestrated by Irving and possibly financed in part by Bantam and Twentieth Century-Fox, both of which had much to gain if the book could be made a success. And a book's placement on *The New York Times* bestseller list—determined by sales reports from key bookstores around the country—has become not only a measure of success, but often a spur to greater success. "People just look at the list and buy the book," Jackie told a reporter. "It's the 'in' thing to do. And when a book hits a hundred thousand, it will do two hundred thousand because now you're reaching people who rarely buy books.''

Exactly how buyers in key cities were recruited and financed remains a secret. However, Letty Pogrebin says that in those days the names of the specific bookstores reporting to the list were ''common knowledge.'' It was also not uncommon for movie companies to back a book-buying campaign, so they could advertise that a film they'd purchased was based on a bestseller. The value of appearing on the *Times* list is so great that it has tempted many to try the same sort of manipulation. How it works is described by producer Bud Granoff, whose wife was another successful Philadelphia girl, Kitty Kallen:

''I used to spend a lot of time at the Beverly Hills Hotel when the Mansfields were living there. We were always around the pool together. Irving gave me the key to how to make a book successful. I was associated with Chuck Barris, who had a book out, and we didn't know what the hell to do with the book. And the publisher didn't want to promote it. So Irving said, 'Why don't you buy the books?' I said, 'What do you mean, buy the books?' He said, 'Yeah, go into the store and buy the books. It will make it a bestseller.' I had my son in a van. I formed a caravan of young kids buying books in ten cities, and in eight weeks we had a bestseller on *The New York Times* list. . . . We spent about seventy thousand dollars on books, but we sold the paperback for about a hundred fifty thousand.''

In any case, Irving kept an eagle eye on the stores. In every city they visited he checked personally to see that the book was in stock, that it was selling, that it lay on top of Robbins's and Michener's latest efforts and not under-neath. Jackie spent another fortune buying her book retail and presenting autographed copies to the store personnel. ''Salesmen don't get books free,'' she explained. ''I tell

them 'be my guest,' and then they can honestly recom-
mend it to their customers. A clerk won't really push a
book if he hasn't read it himself.'' For all her pains, she
was sometimes disappointed. At Carson Pirie Scott, a
Chicago department store, she discovered that *Valley* wasn't
on display at all. The book department's management
considered it too racy for display, she was told, and it was
being sold only on customer request, ''under the counter.''
Saying she was ''shocked and hurt,'' Jackie sued the store.

''The store has a perfect right to decide whether or not it
wishes to handle the book,'' Jackie told *Publishers Weekly*.
''But I think Carson's should be completely true to whatever standards they live by. Otherwise they are playing a
game of bigotry and hypocrisy that is unfair to the reading
public and to the authors whose books they handle. They
should either display and sell my book in the normal
manner or stop handling it altogether.'' Carson's agreed
out of court to stop handling it altogether. If nothing else,
the suit was another ''news hook'' that got Jackie's name
and her book into a few more papers.

Most writers and publishers consider a good month-long
promotional tour a formidable achievement. Not so Jackie,
who never really stopped promoting *Valley* until she began
touring with its successor. After several months, though,
she did cut back a bit, giving up most of the autograph
parties and the kooks who sidled up to say, ''Wanna fuck,
baby?'' She also cut back by slighting anyone who had
ever slighted her. ''She would cooperate with interviewers
and spend a lot of time, and then they would do a terrible
ax job on her, and, I mean, forget it,'' Esther Margolis
explains. ''They could never get the time of day from her
again. She had a fierce loyalty, and if someone was
disloyal to her she was a very fierce animal.''

Jackie handled personal insults better than she did slurs
against Irving. Someone said, ''He's like the husband of

any movie star—he doesn't bring a lot to the party.'' On a late-night talk show another guest wisecracked, ''Jackie sees her husband, Irving, as a necessary personal convenience—like a toilet seat.'' Remarks like that could make her livid.

The only time Jackie folded was when pressed about Guy. Most interviewers could sense her pain, and they usually moved on quickly to the next question. A *Newsday* reporter took the topic of Guy about as far as anyone dared:

''The author is also a mother, although she doesn't mention it. When questioned about it, she said she tries to spend as much time as possible with her son Guy, 16, now at a private school in Arizona because of an asthma condition. She is reluctant to discuss the boy or his absence, but explains that she had a father who was in the public eye—'He was an artist and painted nudes'—and she wants to spare her own child the life of notoriety.''

At other times, Jackie cited Ethel Merman to explain Guy's absence. When Ethel was in *Gypsy*, Jackie explained, Ethel's son was at the Hackley School nearby. He came home weekends and hung around backstage, often playing cards with a homosexual dancer. One day Ethel thought she saw the dancer make a sexual advance. ''If that faggot makes one move toward my boy I'll have him up on Equity charges,'' she yelled. The story didn't explain why Guy was in Arizona, but it brought the topic back to Ethel and Helen Lawson and Jackie's book.

By the summer of 1966 Jackie was one of the most recognizable women in the United States. She was everywhere—in magazines and newspapers, on posters in bookstore windows and in buses, and, always, on television. Along with the talk shows there were panel and game shows and even variety shows. Omnipresent as Orwell's Big Brother was that tough, striking, showgirl's face: the false eyelashes fluttering beneath white eyeshadow; the bright-orange lips and nails; the wardrobe of dark, lacquered, shoulder-length falls; the vivid Emilio Pucci print dresses, which she finally gave up because, although they "packed well," they made her "boobs look too big."

Even if you managed to escape the face, there was her voice reaching out to you from the radio, a voice that was even more theatrical than her appearance—sexy, throaty, cultured, with remaining traces of Philadelphia's "lockjaw" or High Episcopal *a*. Whenever she was home at the Navarro she dropped in to spend the wee hours with her friend Long John Nebel. She was delighted to find that to Long John's listeners she was no longer just another writer pushing a book; *she* had become something of a guru. Callers sought her opinion on all sorts of topics, and she was content to sit for hours and hold forth.

She talked about marital cheating (not such a terrible thing to do, really, provided your spouse was out of town), about wigs ("What I wear now is Wig City's sixty-nine-dollar special"), about nudity ("I'm not a Victorian, but if I were starting out as an actress again they would never get me to do a nude scene"), and even about her age. ("I'm beginning to dread forty," she said. "Forty is Hiroshima. I'll never be forty." She was forty-eight at the time.) She talked about sex in literature ("I can't stand being clinical. You don't have to say, 'Then he took out his thing and put it in her vagina' "), about God ("Irving says I make deals with God as if He were an agent at the William Morris office"), and about her own religious affiliation (she sidestepped the question with "Well, Josephine is definitely a Jewish poodle. She goes mad at the sight of food"). She gave her views on the American male ("I think he's damned attractive"), and the Meaning of Life ("People start out good. Dillinger even was good once. Life and loneliness change people"), and she discussed estrogen injections (she was for them: "Why should you have a uterus the size of a shriveled almond?''), the difference between the sexes ("It's been proven a man can have an affair without being in love at all. Women who do that, of course, are weirdos") and homosexuality ("If two adults fall in love who happen to be of the same sex, then I don't see what's the harm, in anything they do"). She talked, endlessly, about *Valley*—about her motivation for writing it, her methods, the models for her characters, the place she knew the book would earn in American literary annals. She never discussed *Valley* as a "dirty" book because Long John obligingly did it for her, referring obliquely to one salacious tidbit after another, which brought no protests from Jackie. It was good for sales.

Jackie and Long John also talked quite a bit about drugs. Jackie discussed her own practices, admitting that she took an upper every now and then, or popped an amyl nitrite, when her killing schedule left her short on sleep and she had to be fresh for a public appearance. Later they swapped information on the art of staying lucid while taking massive pain-killers, and Long John also would die of cancer.

To the end Long John was immensely supportive of Jackie. He almost demanded that his listeners like her. "Are you for the book or against?" he would demand of a caller in his inquisitorial way. To callers who were "against it" he could be outrageously rude, and he often hung up on them.

"Friends have made my book," Jackie was fond of saying, and she never failed to give Long John credit. She paid him back by plugging his sponsors whenever she could, and by writing the introduction for his book *The Psychic World Around Us*.

Long John was not, however, the only media heavy who lavished attention on Jackie. It seemed that everyone wanted to talk to her—*Life*, *Look*, *Harper's*, even *Wom-*

en's Wear Daily. Being sought after was wonderful, of
course, but there was one thing that bothered Jackie a
little. Practically every major newspaper and magazine had
run a big feature story on her, but hardly anybody had
reviewed *Valley*, despite the massive Geis mailing of
galleys and review copies. *Publishers Weekly* said it was
"poorly written" and Eliot Fremont-Smith of *The New
York Times* said it was like a bad movie re-created in print
form by a bashful Harold Robbins fan, but there were no
serious reviews—none initially and none even after the
book became a runaway bestseller. Jackie couldn't understand it.

In fact, the reason was simple. Most book editors felt
that *Valley* was just another potboiler, if a uniquely successful one. Virtually the only exception in this sea of
indifference was the *New York Herald Tribune*, and it ran a
review not because its editors thought more of *Valley* than
anyone else did, but because they caved in to the nagging
of a young journalist who kept insisting. Her name was
Gloria Steinem. Like Jay Allen, Steinem was perceptive
enough to realize that those who dismissed *Valley* as so
much hardcover garbage were missing the point, that the
book was making literary history. It was turning nonreaders
into readers in a way that no book had ever done before.
Even so, Steinem was not kind to the book:

"I said that compared to Jacqueline Susann, Harold
Robbins writes like Proust and Grace Metalious writes like
Dostoyevsky," she recalls. "*Valley of the Dolls* is for the
reader who has put away comic books but isn't yet ready
for editorials in the *Daily News*—that sort of thing." The
review ran in the *Book Week* section in April of 1966. "I
think it was the only real review the book ever got," she
remembers. "And I don't think it was the wrong thing to
do. I was addressing why the book was going to sell. . . . I
said to the book editor, 'Look, this book is going to be

big,' and he kept saying, 'No, no, no, it's not worth reviewing.' I told him I thought that it was important as the first book for people who don't read books. The book-buying public in this country is a relatively limited one, and *Valley* is simple—like *People* magazine or *True Confessions*. By being so simplified, they all expand the numbers of people who buy printed material." Gloria also noted that *Valley* was "for many months the only book on display at the Sixth Avenue Delicatessen in New York."

Responding to the review in her inimitable fashion, Jackie promised to slug Steinem if she ever ran into her, adding that if Steinem was anyone at all she wouldn't be hanging around the Sixth Avenue Delicatessen in the first place. Jackie began to circulate an entirely false story that Steinem had panned the book only because she had wanted to write the screenplay for the movie and had been turned down. "I could live with the threat of being slugged," Steinem says, "but being lied about I can't stand."

Gloria went to David Brown and asked him to scotch the rumor, which he did, winning her admiration. As she tells the story:

"What really happened was that David sent me a manuscript of *Valley of the Dolls*, and I read it, and I said, 'Look, I'm a beginning writer in the first place, and in the second place I've never written a movie script. And starting with this novel is like starting eight feet underground because every formula applies. I just don't know how to make it come alive.'"

David Brown backed Gloria's version of how she saw the manuscript, but he never agreed with her appraisal of the book. "Jackie was a master," he still insists. "Helen and I have examined *Valley* many times, and it is an almost perfect book in terms of linear storytelling. The reason is it propels you from one paragraph to another. It's written with extreme skill. If you want to see what the construction of the popular novel should be, look at *Valley of the Dolls*. It's a wonderful blueprint of how to get readers involved and keep them involved, and make them feel about the characters.''

The publicity juggernaut continued and began to pay off in massive reorders, which climbed from a few hundred a week to a high of over six thousand weekly, a pace that inevitably sent the book up the rungs of the bestseller lists. *Life* magazine said the sales of the hardcover edition peaked at eighty-five hundred a week, and the *Saturday Evening Post* pegged the paperback's top sale at one hundred thousand a *day*!

At one point reorders were pouring in at such a rate that Geis ran into problems with his printer, who had not ordered sufficient paper. With Random House and the Mansfields breathing down his neck, Berney called to hasten the shipment and was told that a truckload of paper had not arrived. ''Use anything you've got around the plant,'' he told them.

The result was a printing Don Preston refers to as the ''marblecake edition,'' because each signature, or batch of pages, was printed on a different color and texture of paper. ''The thing had stripes when you looked at it edgewise,'' he recalls. ''The first sixty-four pages were white and the next sixty-four a kind of cream color, and then a signature would be tan and the next one white again. It was the strangest-looking book I had ever seen, but the odd thing is that no one ever complained about it. That printing sold out just as the others had, without a single comment from anyone. It's probably a collector's item now.''

After eight weeks of steady climb, *Valley* hit the top of the *Times* list, a spot it was to occupy for a record-breaking twenty-eight weeks. On the day it hit number one, Jackie and Irving appeared at the Geis offices in a limousine, carrying a wicker case filled with chilled magnums of Dom Pérignon. Everyone, from the receptionist to Berney himself, drank toasts to the book's continued success. Old animosities were set aside and bones of contention were buried, at least for the moment. Don Preston graciously displayed the eighteen-karat gold money clip Jackie had given him, the one bearing the tiny pair of gold scissors, which had come wrapped in a note thanking him for "the kindest cuts of all." Jokes were made about the grueling editorial process and the even more grueling publicity junkets. Jackie even suffered some good-natured ribbing. She had wanted a picture of herself in a leotard on the back jacket, to show off her "real good legs." She'd even had one taken, standing on a ladder and stretching for a book on a library shelf. Berney had convinced her it was undignified, and that people would think of her as a showgirl instead of an author. The air was filled with mutual congratulations, and certainly congratulations were in order. They had all done a good job, the best ever, and on that day, at least, they were united in their satisfaction. It was one of the best of the parties connected with *Valley of the Dolls*.

There were, of course, many parties. The Mansfields had a lot of friends, and not a few of them were eager to help Jackie celebrate her success. The official publication party itself had been hosted by Earl and Rosemary Wilson at their large apartment on West Fifty-seventh Street. Jackie and Irving got there early and stood around in the kitchen. Jackie kept nervously spooning up the caviar meant for the party, until Rosemary finally had to ask her to leave some for the guests. But when the guests did arrive, she was in her element—rooms full of people, of "names," and herself the center of attention, the star!

Don Preston attended the party with his wife, Sue. He

recalls, "I talked with Rona Jaffe briefly. And I watched Toots Shor get sloshed, and little fat Marty Allen cram handfuls of food into his face, and various other glittery types doing what people do at cocktail parties." He also remembered the elaborate dog bed that Berney, ever alert to publicity opportunities, presented to Josephine.

Like Preston, Dick Schaap observed the party with mild contempt. "To honor the publication of a first novel, the literati gathered the other day," he wrote in the *Herald Tribune*, "including James Aubrey, Perle Mesta, Lisa Kirk, Rona Jaffe and a one-star general with a First Army patch on his shoulder. . . . The novel is called *Valley of the Dolls*, by a woman named Jacqueline Susann whose one previous book was . . . a tribute to her pet poodle. 'This one is about dogs, too,' Miss Susann said. 'Bitches.' . . . For sheer literary style, the novel certainly ranks with its publication party. It was a very nice party, except that it had almost nothing to do with literature and the crowd would have been more at home at the Copacabana. I'm positive if James Joyce had walked in, somebody would have called him 'Baby.' "

Let those sneer who might, Jackie loved the caviar and comics and glitz and hoopla. She also loved the many dinner parties, including one that Victor and Patti Lasky hosted for the Mansfields and for Cornelius and Cathy Ryan right after *Valley* and Ryan's nonfiction book *The Last Battle* were published. Victor proposed a toast: "May you both be number one on the *Times* bestseller list!" A few months later, the Laskys opened their Sunday *Times* to find that both Jackie and Connie Ryan had hit the number one spot in their respective categories on the same day.

But of all the parties, the one that must have pleased Jackie most came in June of 1966, when *Valley* was already a blockbuster and didn't really need parties to promote it or well-wishers to toast it. *The New York Times* described it this way:

"Jacqueline Susann, actress and author of the best-selling book *Valley of the Dolls*, was feted at a supper party at Marsal's in the Brevoort last night by Joe E. Lewis, the nightclub comedian. About 200 guests assembled at 10:30 P.M.

"Mr. Lewis said he chose the Brevoort at 11 Fifth Avenue because of its historical association with literature and the arts. The hotel that once stood there, he said, was a meeting place for such notable literary figures as Mark Twain, Thomas Wolfe, Theodore Dreiser, Sinclair Lewis, and Anita Loos."

The *Times* item was only two paragraphs long, and it was way back at the bottom of page 37, next to the movie ads. But that didn't matter to Jackie. Her Joe E. had offered a unique honor. By now, everyone was paying tribute to her celebrity, but he was paying tribute to her worth. He was telling her that she belonged with the best, that for him she *was* the best.

Again Don Preston was there and remembers noticing "Jim Aubrey, the 'smiling cobra' who had been canned as head of CBS. In fact, I passed Aubrey and Jackie at one point, and they were in a corner and she was kissing him. He's very tall, so she had to get up on tiptoes, and it looked like a fairly serious kiss, not just a congratulatory peck."

However nice the parties were, for Jackie the ultimate ego gratification was being number one. As she said in an interview, "A book sticks around at Number Three, Four and Five for twenty weeks, everyone is aware of it as a bestseller. And it can go up and down and you're happy. But when you're Number One everyone is staring, and it's such a drop from One to Two."

It was a drop Jackie came to fear, though she knew it

was inevitable. Her main rival for the top spot was the veteran bestseller Harold Robbins, whose new novel, *The Adventurers*, had shot quickly to the number two spot and was nudging *Valley* for number one. Jackie and Irving raced from store to store on their travels, rearranging displays so that *Valley* would have the favored spot— preferably on top of the stacks of *The Adventurers*. It became a game, and even though it was a deadly serious one to Jackie, it had its comic moments. One occurred at the Beverly Hills Hotel, when the Mansfields discovered that Robbins was also staying there and that he went to the pool every morning at the same time. Irving rushed out and bought forty copies of *Valley*, then slipped out early the next morning to distribute them among the hotel patrons who were relaxing around the pool. When Robbins arrived, all he could see was people reading *Valley of the Dolls*.

Robbins survived the shock, and in time his book did manage to take over the number one spot, though *Valley* hung in and took it back again. The two jockeyed for position for a while, then were both eventually pushed aside by another contender. But *Valley*'s run was phenomenal.

As Jackie and Irving bounced from coast to coast and all points in between, as the ads ran in the book pages and entertainment sections, and as the commotion of success swirled around them, Jackie was in her element. She had written a book about women who "climb Mount Everest" —the metaphor for success she used again and again in *Valley*—only to find that life at the top is bleak and cold. Now this same book had brought her to that same awe- some summit, and as far as she could see the weather was just fine, thank you. If she noticed the irony she never mentioned it.

Her own climb had been long and frustrating and pain- ful, but it had all been worth it! One other dream besides

Irving *had* come true. All of them had, except for the impossible dream of a normal child. When she went to Danny's Hideaway these days she didn't tablehop, she held court. People came to *her*. And when she walked into "21" heads *did* turn, and people whispered together, and no doubt some of them *were* saying, "That's Jacqueline Susann, the author."

Her life had become akin to living inside a drum with the whole world beating on the outside, but she loved the noise, loved being in the center. She was not just a star but a superstar, and it was spectacular, glorious. It was almost everything.

26

Bye-bye, Berney

*He's a fine man. I'm not bitter personally. I just
don't want him to publish my books.*

——Jacqueline Susann

IT seems probable that dear old Grandma Ida would
have spun madly in her grave had someone sat atop
it and read to her the seamier passages of *Valley of
the Dolls*. Certainly, Rose was shocked and mortified when
she first read it. Still, she was much mollified, even
pleased and proud, when her daughter and her daughter's
book became so famous. And once she'd thought it over,
Grandma probably would have been proud, too. After all,
Ida Kaye set great store by a woman's ability to be
independently successful.

Perhaps the greatest testament to Jackie's energy and her
ability to focus it is the fact that she could vigorously

promote one book while writing another. While seeing to it that *Valley* became and remained a raging bestseller, she had already conceived and begun gestating its successor. And for a time it appeared that Don Preston would once again play the reluctant midwife.

"In the summer of 1966 we were, at least on the surface, still friendly with the Mansfields," Preston recalls. "Jackie, in fact, had asked Berney to give her contracts for her next two novels as a sign of faith. He had been delighted to do so, partly because those contracts would also serve as insurance against raids by competitors, a thing he always had good reason to fear. He was working hard to make *Valley* successful, and he knew the sharks would be gathering soon, if they weren't already. The advances were token amounts, under five thousand each, but they were binding contracts, much stronger than a mere option clause."

By early August Berney had 231,000 copies of *Valley* in print and another 123,000 on order, for a total of 354,000. The book was bringing in money as no other Geis book ever had, so his delight at the prospect of another Susann novel was boundless. And the sooner the better, considering the company's always precarious cash flow. "Berney wanted to get a reprint deal early because he needed the cash," Preston explains. "And naturally Bantam was interested. But they wanted to see something on paper before they made the kind of major commitment Berney needed."

Jackie had talked about her second novel, which she envisioned as doing for the television industry what *Valley* had done for Hollywood. Her protagonist was a man this time, she told Berney and his staff—a cad, of course, but a wonderfully fascinating cad whose story encompassed all the seaminess and glitter a Susann reader might hope for. The title was *The Love Machine*, a phrase her friend Jim Aubrey used to describe the television set. As she would

use it, it also described the novel's protagonist, Robin
Stone, who was based in part on Aubrey. "I'm attempting
to get into men's ids," Jackie explained, "as I did with
women in *Valley*. I spent many hours talking to men,
asked about their love lives and sexual feelings. I dug up
their attitudes toward marriage. I spoke to famous
personalities—whose names we won't mention. My theme
will be the hunger for power and the corruption that power
creates. It will be *the* novel about television, East and West,
as I have known it intimately."

"Fine," Berney said. "Boil this all down to a five-page
outline we can show to Bantam." Jackie's answer was not
encouraging. "I don't know how to write an outline."
Berney was undeterred. "Just write down what you've
been telling us, and give it to Don."

Some days later, the document arrived on Berney's desk
with a note attached:

> You see why I cannot write a five-page draft.
> Christ, explaining a bit about nine major charac-
> ters for your sake takes ten pages. And, naturally,
> for me these are just thumbnail descriptions. There
> are many, many other characters that run through
> it, but these are the big babies. See what you can
> do with this jazz. And there are not many typo-
> graphical errors. I actually spell that way!
>
>   Love and kisses,
>   Jackie

Berney Geis couldn't make much sense of her plotless
character sketches, so he tried another tack. "Why don't
you just sit down with Don and tell him what the book is
about?" he suggested.

"So I spent an afternoon with her," Preston says. "She

told me the whole complicated plot she had in mind. I took notes on it and then sat down and wrote an outline, of which I do not have a high opinion. It was in the form of a letter from Jackie to Berney, and after we had got it into the shape we wanted we had it retyped on Hotel Navarro stationery. It ran to eight pages, single-spaced, and evidently it made sense to the people at Bantam."

The outline was a highly competent pulling-together of Jackie's "still-chaotic" vision, and *The Love Machine*, when finished, tracked it closely. Nevertheless, in the memo to Berney that accompanied it, Preston's revulsion at the prospect of editing the book and his disdain for the author are manifest:

> The "flying couch" (described by Irving as an $825,000 converted jet sold by the Lear Company, outfitted with bars, card tables and beds for screwing at 30,000 feet, which is some special kick amongst the real swingers and can get you a badge from Arthur Godfrey) is the thing Robin zips cross country in, from his gleaming Manhattan tower (with angry concrete animals all about) to the other television world, Hollywood, land of competing hostesses, all-purpose sex machines married to producers and disposed to gang bangs, and a version of spin-the-bottle in which you take the girl off to a convenient bedroom and hump her, to quote herself. . . .
>
> Another electrifying scene will be the face-, breast-, thigh- and navel-lift undergone by the lovely social butterfly Consuela Austin (who, incidentally, has a twin sister, just like that Vanderbilt), who is embarrassed at tender moments by hot flushes and sweats brought on by menopause. . . .

This will be a scene comparable in depth and sensitivity to the famous funny farm scene in VD.

Someone in the book is to be a closet queen, as soon as Jackie figures out what that is and who is to be it.

And that's about all folks.

About the time Preston was working on the outline and Jackie was laboring away on the multicolored drafts of her new book, another author was also at work; and what *he* wrote would help cause a rupture that would, among direr things, relieve Preston of the dour prospect of dealing with any more Susann manuscripts.

Walter Goodman was the writer's name, and he was gathering material for an article to be called "The Truth About the Best Seller List." The piece appeared in *McCall's* November issue. It was clear from the article that Goodman had spent a lot of time with Berney and that Berney had talked far too much.

"'A lot of people criticize us for overdirecting authors,'" Berney had said, "'but manuscripts are not engraved in bronze. We feel we have enough taste to guide a writer.'"

Goodman went on: "Mr. Geis and his editors put their taste to Miss Susann's service as they guided her in cutting, inserting a new, key scene and bringing her characters into sharper focus.... To protect their investment in Miss Susann, Geis and his editors have already helped her get through a first draft ... of her next novel.... It will be entitled *The Love Machine*, and we are promised it will do for the TV industry what *Valley of the Dolls* did for show business, whatever that was.

"Miss Susann is not the only novelist in America who is enjoying the assistance of the house of Geis in creating a best seller," the story continued. "Two young writers ... have also contracted to turn out novels to the publisher's specifications. . . . One . . . observes, 'The . . . difference between moderate success and big success is a *schtick*. Jacqueline Susann's *schtick* was pills. When I think of her, I think, If she could do it, why can't I? Then I think, But if she could do it, why *should* I?' ''

The Mansfields were outraged. Goodman's high-hatted attitude toward Jackie's work was insulting enough, but the real object of their fury was Berney himself, for daring to suggest, and none too subtly, that he and his editors were the true geniuses behind *Valley*'s success. Yes, Berney was the main culprit so far as they were concerned and right behind him was that wretched little pipsqueak who had come up with the ''why *should* I?'' remark.

Jackie might have taken her lucrative business elsewhere then and there, but *Valley* was still on the bestseller list and still the object of much media attention. A public break might have hurt distribution and sales. Even so, the Mansfields were mad enough to confront Berney and, for the first time, to threaten to leave the Geis firm.

''Irving and Jackie sat in our office one day,'' Don Preston recalls, ''and Berney asked them what they wanted from him. And they said they might stay with him if he did this and that and the other, and then Irving said, 'What we want from you is that you should bury David Slavitt.' '' The source of the ''why *should* I?'' quote had not been named in the *McCall*'s article, but Jackie and Irving had ferreted it out.

''What do you mean, 'bury him'?'' Berney asked the Mansfields.

''I mean see that no one publishes him,'' Irving said.

''How can I do that?'' Berney asked. ''Even if I agree not to publish him myself, how can I keep somebody else from publishing him?''

''That's your problem,'' Irving said.

Berney did not wrestle with the problem overmuch, partly because Slavitt himself didn't let him. Having heard about the flap with the Mansfields, he called his lawyer and then called Berney.

"You terminate this contract and I will sue you and I will sue her," Slavitt informed the beleaguered publisher, "because one can't do that. It's restraint of trade and it's crazy. It's also illegal."

David Slavitt, then thirty-two years old, had been the movie editor for *Newsweek* and something of a prodigy, having produced a novel, two plays, translations of Greek and Latin poetry, as well as volumes of his own poems. Slavitt was caustic, funny, and very talented, though he seemed to Berney, and no doubt to Jackie, to be an intellectual snob. The Geis staff had invited him to try a popular novel, and the deal had been consummated at Laurent over Dover sole flown in from England. He had agreed on condition that a pseudonym be used, and Berney, who lived on Sutton Place, suggested Henry Sutton.

David was at work on the novel when the *McCall's* article appeared. Slavitt's approach to popular fiction was far more cynical than Jackie's. "You simply write ten pages a day for a month and *voilà*," he says. His string of Henry Sutton novels sold well at the beginning and then died.

The Exhibitionist was published in 1967, accompanied by typical Geis shenanigans including a Times Square billboard complete with a live model in a bikini. The model, who was ostensibly posing for the sign painters (she was also on the jacket of the book), helpfully removed the top of her bikini for the painters—and for the hundreds of spectators gathered below the scaffolding. Berney Geis was arrested on the spot, a "news hook" Jackie herself could have been proud of. "Four million copies were printed," Slavitt recalls, referring to both hardcover and paperback editions, "and it takes a long time to decompose, like plastic in a landfill. It's hip-deep at the secondhand bookstores.''

Another novel published by Geis at about the same time also aroused the Mansfields' ire, *The King* by Morton Cooper. The book had been signed long before *Valley*'s publication, and Cooper had previously written several romans à clef, but that meant nothing to Jackie. Cooper's novel was about show business, specifically it was a roman à clef about Sinatra. Show business was Jackie's turf, and now her own publisher was hiring other writers to invade it.

From October of 1966 through May of the following year, Jackie and Irving quietly shopped for a new publisher. There was no shortage of suitors; after all, she was the hottest writer in America. It was just a matter of finding the best deal. Meanwhile she teased Berney, alternating between new fits of pique and hints that she might let him publish *The Love Machine* after all. The matter of the "imitators," however, and, more important, Berney's implication that he had created Jacqueline Susann were nails in his coffin.

They weren't the only nails, though, or even the biggest ones. There was also the matter of money. Jackie could command big money now, and she could command it from large, well-heeled publishing houses willing to make contractual concessions a smaller house couldn't afford. Perhaps more to the point, these larger houses had no cash-flow problems. By now both Jackie and Irving knew that for all Berney's highly publicized bestsellers, his firm was in financial trouble.

Nobody who knew Berney suggests that he was either dishonest or lining his own pockets. Rather, as Don Preston puts it, "He was naïve about money. He just spent it in all directions, throwing it away on expensive renovations and fireman's poles and the like, including outsized advances to authors.''

David Brown concurs: ''But for Berney, Jackie's books, and Helen's, might never have been launched. But he was strapped. It was never a case of Berney making use of money for any purpose except book publishing. He was running a small business and he was giving advances to authors, he was paying distribution fees, he owed everyone— even President Truman. Nobody had put up a huge sum of money to capitalize Berney; otherwise he would not have gotten into difficulty. He wanted to publish. That's his whole interest in life, but I don't think business was his forte.''

Berney's fiscal faults were twofold. To begin with, financial ledgers were the only books that bored him; he never paid them much attention. He spent too much, and he didn't keep a very close eye on where the money went. ''Once we had an employee who embezzled fifty thousand dollars,'' Preston says. ''Berney was astonished when it came out. He said, 'My God, I didn't think we had fifty thousand dollars to steal.' '' The second problem was Berney's juggling. When a check came in to Bernard Geis Associates, he didn't bother about its intended final destination; he simply used it to pay the firm's most pressing bills.

''He didn't invent the practice,'' Preston adds. ''Actually, every publisher uses its authors' money until the time the contract calls for payment to those authors. It's a sore point with many writers, and with the Authors Guild. But with most houses there's never any doubt the money will be there when payment is due.'' Berney also took advantage of something else common at the time—withholding payments to authors so they could avoid huge taxes when a book sold to a paperback publisher for a large lump-sum amount. Everyone was doing it then, and no one was sequestering the funds withheld from the authors. But there was something about Berney's dealings that made some authors nervous. Helen Gurley Brown was one, and she recalls the situation like this:

"I told Jackie that I had an arrangement with Berney— because I didn't need the money—that I would take fifteen thousand dollars a year forever from my earnings on *Sex and the Single Girl*. It turned out that he was able to just get together my fifteen thousand a year, but God forbid I should ask for another two hundred dollars in expenses for the promotion I was still doing on the book. It wouldn't be there."

The sloppy practices caught up with Berney in 1971, when the firm was forced into Chapter 11. Preston recalls, with a tone of wry sadness devoid of censure, his fondness for his old boss undiminished, "As we got closer to bankruptcy, he'd have me call up the authors I had brought in—Morton Cooper, Stephen Marlowe, Herbert Kastle—a whole gang of writers. There were a lot to whom we owed money. And I'd say, 'Give us two more weeks. There's a cash flow problem.' In the end a lot of people got hurt very badly. R. V. Cassill, an old friend of mine, lost about fifty-five thousand dollars—money from the reprint sale on *Doctor Cobb's Game*. He had hoped to use it to send his kids to college."

"Mort Cooper was owed somewhere around twenty-five thousand dollars, I think, and Berney made a settlement of something like eight cents on the dollar. The covering letter with the settlement check described his and Darlene's recent trip to Europe, and how Darlene went on a buying spree in Paris. How can you hate a man who has so little sense?"

Berney, however, was still very much afloat early in 1967. In fact, he began the year with exceptionally rosy prospects. Somehow everybody seemed to be getting paid. And *Valley* had brought the company money and attention in lavish amounts. Jackie was angry, but maybe that would all work out and he'd get to publish *The Love Machine* after all. There was such a thing as loyalty. How could she leave after all they'd accomplished together? How could any writer leave the house that had made her number one? Besides, they had a contract, not just an option.

Then Jackie dropped her bomb.

SUSANN SUES TO BREAK CONTRACT WITH PUBLISHER, read the headline in *Publishers Weekly*.

"Jacqueline Susann, author of the best selling novel *Valley of the Dolls*, on May 23 brought suit in New York Supreme Court against her publisher, Bernard Geis Associates, charging fraud with respect to royalty payments and requesting a court-ordered termination of her contract with the Geis organization.

"In addition to *Valley of the Dolls*, the contract covers the book which Miss Susann is now completing, *The Love Machine*, plus a third as yet untitled book.

"Miss Susann's complaints alleged that Geis royalty statements were 'false and inaccurate' and that she had not received her full share of payments for paperback rights from Bantam Books and for foreign publishing rights. She charged further that Geis was deliberately commissioning books similar to *Valley of the Dolls* and that it planned to promote these books in the same way that it promoted *Valley of the Dolls*. In addition to termination of the publishing contract, the complaint asked for an unspecified amount of damages." More specifically, Jackie told *Publishers Weekly* that Berney had deferred paying money he owed her. She had received payments of $72,000 for her share of paperback and foreign rights income, she said, and she figured Berney owed her at least $140,000. In addition, she said, during the time *Valley* had been a bestseller, the Geis firm was insolvent and was using money from authors' royalties and their subsidiary rights money as operating income.

" 'If I had walked out then the firm would have gone bankrupt,' she declared, 'but I didn't want to do that because a number of my friends are Geis authors. But I want to get out now.' "

Berney called the charges "completely false and erroneous," and said that Geis royalty statements were based on Random House sales reports. He added that Jackie had gotten "her full share" of income from royalties and subsidiary rights. He said he believed the real reason she had filed the suit was that "she has received several fabulous offers for *The Love Machine* from other publishers, and she would like to get out of her contract with us."

Jackie half admitted he was right. "I don't care for money per se. All I'm interested in is writing. But I'll fight for the biggest price I can get because what you get proves your worth. If Robbins can get one million for *The Adventurers*, then I should ask a million and ten dollars for *The Love Machine*."

The immediate spur to Jackie's suit may have been an offhand comment to her by a Bantam executive about an additional payment Bantam had made to Geis—a payment Berney failed to mention to her. She now suspected that Berney was really out to cheat her, although David Brown believes that "Jackie wasn't looking for money. She was looking for celebrity and achievement. She didn't want anybody, especially Berney Geis, to go around saying he'd 'created' her. Jackie told us that Berney would have had her for life if he hadn't taken the position that he was the brains behind *Valley of the Dolls*."

"Berney did *not* steal money from Jackie," Preston declares emphatically. "What he did do was something he had a contractual right to do, but maybe not a moral right to do. A twenty-five-thousand-dollar payment came in from Bantam. Berney needed it to pay some bills, and he didn't tell her that he had gotten it. By contract he didn't have to give her the money until the next royalty accounting period came around.

"It wasn't that Jackie needed the twenty-five thousand dollars, it was that Berney didn't tell her he had received it. And it *was* a dumb move on his part. He was afraid that they would ask him to pass it through, and he didn't want to do it. They used this later as evidence that he had withheld money. Well, technically he had not. There was no case and the Mansfields knew it. But they were perfectly willing to go public with these allegations, and did."

Eventually, the suit was settled out of court. Berney didn't want to give up Jackie, but neither did he want to continue being called a crook in public. For their part, the Mansfields were happy to avoid long and expensive litigation, provided they got what they wanted: Jackie's freedom, about which she was adamant. "If Berney doesn't release me I'll write *Love Machine* as a movie, direct for the screen, then expand it into a softcover book for Bantam. All Berney can get is the hardcover rights, which won't materialize unless he sees things my way." Berney did. He reluctantly sold her contract to Bantam, obtaining a guarantee of a percentage of the royalties on *The Love Machine* and her third novel.

Berney didn't fare badly financially in the breakup; in fact, he may have netted more than he would have if he had published the two novels himself. "I paid him $250,000 to get out and I'll pay him another $150,000 later on," Jackie said after the settlement. "When you pay someone $400,000 to be free of him, you've got pretty good reasons."

At Jackie's insistence, the agreement contained one proviso that had nothing to do with her own finances:

Berney was to make sure that Helen Gurley Brown got every cent he owed her.

"It didn't mean anything to her except that she was so aggravated with Berney and so fond of me that she didn't want me to get hurt," Helen says. "This is Mafia stuff, this kind of loyalty."

Whether Jackie left Geis because of greed or a bruised ego or some combination remains a matter of debate. David Brown continues to support the ego interpretation:

"I recall that some of us cautioned Berney to be very careful or he would lose Jackie, if he persisted in telling his method of creating bestsellers. She said to him, 'Look at your other authors, see how they do. If you think you can fabricate me, go ahead and try it.' He couldn't fabricate another Jackie Susann, but she was offended at the hint that he even thought it.

"Another thing Jackie mentioned to me was that she didn't want to be part of a list of 'manufactured' exploitation novelists," Brown says. "Berney was starting to build a genre around what he conceived to be the *Valley of the Dolls* kind of roman à clef. Not that Jackie originated the roman à clef, but she felt she was going to be in the company of what she considered to be a number of lesser writers, lesser personalities, and this offended her deeply. She didn't want to be part of his gallery of novels 'created by' Bernard Geis."

"It was the money," David Slavitt contends. "She could get more from Bantam and Simon and Schuster, or whomever it was that she went to, than she could possibly get from Berney."

But there was another reason, which Jackie could never discuss: she was impaled on her own secrets. The richer she got and the more famous, the more certain she became she would die. Four of the ten or twelve years she had bargained for, with God, were gone. Guy might outlive her by half a century. She had to provide for Irving too, and even Rose.

They had once tried a public funny farm when Guy was small, Willowbrook. Then they had hastily pulled him out when they learned that criminals were being transferred into the place. If Berney went bankrupt Guy would lose his inheritance. Even the Bantam money would go down the tubes if Geis held it. Jackie's own position was almost the same as that of Miriam, Tony Polar's sister in *Valley*, who was so single-minded in putting aside the money for Tony's care. Jackie was doing the same thing for Guy.

Don Preston knew she was a liar and he couldn't grasp her reasons: "Her whole life was a lie, in effect," he says, "the mastectomy, the son. She didn't have the guts to say, 'Yes, he is my son,' and tell the world what happened." According to Preston, Jackie habitually took credit for other people's work, or else credited Irving. An example is the jacket cover for *Valley of the Dolls*. "I had what I thought was a great idea for the front-jacket photo," says Preston. "It involved a champagne glass with a string of pearls hanging out of it, next to an overturned bottle of pills. The photographer shot the composition and then, as we were leaving, the jacket designer, Wladislaw Finne, said, 'Why don't you shoot one or two of just a few brightly colored pills scattered on a white background—?' The result was one of the most imitated jackets of all time. My contribution was purely negative, but the Mansfields had nothing to do with it at all. They first saw the cover in paste-up at sales conference, but they were very proud of it and constantly boasted that it was their own design."

Perhaps out of pride, Berney tried to put the best face on Jackie's departure: "I don't think she did anything that a lot of other authors haven't done. Needless to say, it's not all her fault, because publishers are a little bit like wolves.

They were all wooing her and telling her how much more money she could make with them.

"Jackie tended to wear people out," he adds. "She thought the world not only should revolve around J. Susann, but that it *did* revolve around J. Susann. But she also had some very nice characteristics, a very dedicated warmth of personality. If you were her friend you were her friend two hundred percent, and if you were her enemy you were her enemy three hundred percent. She was a little stronger on that.

"On the other hand, Jackie gave a dinner for six of us at '21' which was really magnificent—you know, to celebrate her success and Helen's success because the six of us were pretty good friends. That was David and Helen Brown and Irving and Jackie, and my wife, Darlene, and myself. It was around the time *Valley of the Dolls* got on the bestseller list. It was a very gracious gesture, and it's very seldom an author entertains a publisher on that scale, if at all. Jackie stage-managed that dinner, and they must have worked on it a week. The best wines and foods. Oh, gosh, we liked the wine so much. I think it was a Château Lafite, and my wife thought it was wonderful. The next day she went to a liquor store to buy a bottle, and it was prohibitive. Jackie spent a fortune. Caviar and vodka was standing in front of us when we sat down, and I drank Helen's vodka because she didn't want it. She tried to send it back, but I wouldn't let her. I sacrificed myself."

After Geis folded, Berney continued on a smaller scale, more or less as a book packager. His current star is Father Andrew Greeley, who writes best-selling novels on "weirdness, wickedness, and sex in the Roman Catholic Church."

After the Geis collapse, Preston free-lanced for a time before returning to Prentice-Hall. "I was taken to lunch by everybody in those days, and the question they all asked

was 'Can you do it again?' And what they usually meant
was 'Can you create another Jacqueline Susann?' And I
told them no, because I honestly believed that the combination could never be repeated. Jackie and Irving were the
most phenomenal, tenacious, successful, innovative, and
inventive book promoters who ever lived. And they were
together with Berney Geis, who was no mean shakes
himself, and with Letty, who was as good as anybody ever
got in that job. We had lots of books on the bestseller list,
but with Irving and Jackie there was no limit. They called
in every IOU they had and pulled every trick they knew. I
don't think history has ever seen an operation like that.''

   History in the form of Jackie's later novels did take
some small revenge on Preston. In *The Love Machine* she
named an unwashed writer Preston Slavitt and in *Once Is
Not Enough*, a despicable doctor Preston Alpert. In *Dolores*
she made him the president's assassin, H. Ronald Preston,
a man with a ''greenish white complexion . . . tall and
thin . . . hawk-nosed. . . . Did he think that in his miserable little life this one act would give him a permanent
place in history?''

   While Preston's opinion of Jackie never changed, another critic from the Geis days did have a change of heart.
David Slavitt, whose offhand remark to *McCall's* helped
pull the thread that unraveled Jackie and Geis, still calls
her ''the mistress of shlock,'' but the time came when he
reassessed his earlier judgment of her work.

   ''Thinking back about my Henry Sutton years, I began
to think of Jackie, and the question I had asked Walter
Goodman of *McCall's*. And I thought—hmm, 'Was I
really right in my contempt for her? And how come she
could do this and I couldn't?' ''

   So thinking, Slavitt wrote *Jo Stern*, ''a thinly disguised
novel about Jackie.'' He took the novel to Berney Geis,
who turned it down, partly because he didn't care for the

picture of himself in the book but also because he thought
the portrait of Jackie was insulting.

Jo Stern was published by Harper and Row in 1978. It
depicts "Jo" with some admiration, not for what she
wants to be but for what she is: a tough, ambitious,
relentless woman, valiant in her way, and if she is not
always honest or likable she is, as Preston might put it,
somehow "true on her own terms."

In one scene, set in the Italian Pavillion restaurant,
Slavitt recreates an incident that actually happened between Jackie and Berney. It captures something essential
about them both:

> She had done, was doing, and was going to do
> harm to him, was dumping him, not because of
> anything he had done but only because of what he
> was. And he didn't know it and was being so
> damnably nice. . . .
>
> Also proud. She could tell that he was showing
> her off to these literary types . . . for what other
> explanation would there be for his decision to talk
> about her next book in a room like this with so
> many curious ears straining to catch a few valu-
> able syllables. . . .
>
> Therefore she picked a fight. . . . She could turn
> the damn restaurant to her advantage . . . making
> them all into her audience . . . saying in a voice
> that was not really so loud as it seemed but was
> projected, "Say . . . how about you and me having
> a little peeing contest?"
>
> "A what?"
>
> "A peeing contest. Right here. Let's see who
> can pee higher on the wall!" . . . People were star-
> ing at him. Waiters had stopped, plates of fettuccine
> frozen in midair to witness this extraordinary com-

bat. . . . *Sotto voce*, she suggested, "How about we
tear up the contract? I win, and the option clause
goes. You win, and you get a book for nothing.
Deal?" . . . He felt a pain in his ribs. . . . She had
struck him, poked him with her elbow. "Okay,
kid, but remember the rules. It's got to be fair.
So, no hands!"

And then she started to laugh. And other people were laughing, people at the tables, waiters,
busboys. . . . He felt dizzy. . . . She felt what she
wanted to feel—the contempt that would let her
off without feeling guilty. . . .

"One of the things I finally realized," Slavitt says, "is
that people like Jackie can write what they write because
that's the smartest they are. There's an authenticity to their
doing it, and people like me who condescend to write
bestsellers are a little fraudulent. It was absolutely honest
for her. She used the details of Judy Garland's life, and
dozens of others, and I realized, my God, she hadn't really
invented anything! But why should she; she wasn't an
artist. She was an anthropologist.

"Jackie didn't invent because she didn't believe, or
couldn't comprehend, the truth of fiction. And for America's
most popular novelist to be unable to understand what
fiction is—that says something about publishing, and it
says something about our civilization, if you want to use
that word."

On her part, Jackie's own last word on David Slavitt (a.k.a.
Henry Sutton) was: "When a studio has a Marilyn Monroe,
every other studio is hiring Jayne Mansfield and Mamie Van
Doren. But when your *own* studio does the hiring . . . !"

And then she added indignantly: "I sell because of
what I write—not because I'm wrapped up in a package
and tied with a ribbon."

PART FIVE

VALLEY OF THE SHADOW [1967-1974]

27

Jackie Goes Hollywood

*From the very beginning I knew that
Jackie would not just be my extended
family for this particular television show,
but forever, because Jackie was
a forever person.*

——Sherry Arden

AT her low point, after her mastectomy, on the day
she came home from the hospital, Jackie picked
up her journal, and wrote: "January 1, 1963.
I've never hurt anyone intentionally. I always forgive
people. I go out of my way to be nice. . . . May I say that
this creed is in the ashcan now. I don't say that I'm going
to go around with rocks looking for people to throw them
at, but from now on, I am for me. 1963 is for me, and that
includes Irving who is a part of me. I've looked at the
ledger and it doesn't add up. God, St. Andrew, and the

whole *mishpocheh* owe me more than I owe them. And
since they aren't exactly out beating their brains for me
I'm going to do it. I've got to leave something on this
earth before I go, and I don't want it discovered after I go.
I want to be around to get that Nobel Prize. And I'm going
to start living for me.''

Two years later, on the third of April, 1965, Jackie
reflected on that terrible time in her life. Next to the earlier
comments in her journal she scribbled a postscript: ''So
much has happened. Funny, I was just overdramatic—
rather enjoying the sense of danger that I knew would
never come. But it came, and I faced dying—it's very
lonely. But you lose all sense of fear. It's only anger you
know—that this dare happen. And I've had a dream come
true. *Josephine!* is a jewel—not the biggest best-seller—
but it made it. And it's made so many people happy. For a
while I stopped believing in God too. I believe—oh, not as
I would like to.''

Then in 1967, on July 5, one of her dearest friends,
Carol Bjorkman, died of cancer. She was only thirty-
seven. Jackie and Carol had met when *Josephine!* came
out, and Carol, a columnist at *Women's Wear Daily*, as
well as a former Hollywood actress, came to do an
interview. Jackie was enchanted with her, pronouncing her
''more beautiful than Elizabeth Taylor.'' They often walked
their poodles together; Carol's was white and was called
Sheba. They grew very close. Suddenly, Carol was stricken
with leukemia. ''I'm just fine, a little anemic you know,''
she pretended, and Jackie played along. ''Her hospital
room was banked with flowers and books,'' Jackie recalled
later. ''She even set up a bar. Each day she put on full
makeup and a beautiful hostess gown. When you came to
visit her, she greeted you with her famous smile and told
you how well you looked, and weren't you nice to drop by.
She taught me a lesson in gallantry I shall never forget.

Not once did she ever complain of her illness." Jackie remained at Carol's bedside, helping unwrap her presents, even ghosting her final columns for her. On the night that Carol died, Jackie was on Long John's program. "I felt a strange uneasiness. . . . I began talking about life after death the moment Carol began to sink. And I never stopped talking about it until she went into a final coma. I do think when someone who is very dear to you is in danger, you feel some kind of wave. Perhaps it is love."

Jackie was promoting the paperback of *Valley*, and also writing *The Love Machine*. Instead of stopping to grieve, she poured her affection for Carol into her second novel, basing the fictional character of Amanda on her, and also dedicating the book to her. To Jackie's astonishment, she was rebuked for her pains by some of Carol's other friends. James Brady, a colleague at *Women's Wear Daily*, grumbled, "I sort of resented the picking over the bones of someone I liked so much." These days, the more that Jackie accomplished, the more resentment she drew, something she hadn't bargained for. "How dare you call yourself a writer?" Cornelius Ryan screamed at her one drunken evening when each was number one on the best-seller list, he on the nonfiction side. "Why don't you just roll over and die?"

Meanwhile, Jackie made another friend, Sherry Arden, a book publicist, who was asked to assist with a documentary to be called *Jacqueline Susann and the Valley of the Dolls*. Arden wasn't sure at first that she wanted the assignment. She expected Jackie to be "flamboyant and shallow. . . . I thought, Oh God, is this what I am going to devote my life to? I mean, Jackie Susann. But from the moment I met her, I never felt that way again."

The project took a year and a half. Jackie was at the height of what Sherry calls "all that hoopla," and they were together constantly, in the thick of it, as Sherry filmed her. "I'm from Philadelphia, and you're from Wilmington," Jackie said to Sherry, "so we both have our feet on the ground." Irving had retired from his own career to manage Jackie's, and Sherry noticed that Jackie and Irving tended to play "white hat and black hat. Jackie remained the nice one while Irving attended to the rougher aspects of negotiations." The marriage was so symbiotic now that "if one was on the telephone, people assumed that the other was listening on an extension. They shared a lot of her life. They shared her celebrity and they shared her fame, and Irving was involved even in her clothes and jewelry. He was almost like a girl friend. I think they loved their life. They both loved Jackie's success."

As she became involved in the documentary about herself, she also got more and more absorbed in another movie—the one based on *Valley of the Dolls*, which went into production early in 1967. As the Mansfields and Berney Geis were trading public accusations and legal papers, Jackie was following the casting of *Valley* with fascination. She developed strong feelings about who should play what role in the movie, and told friends that she envisioned Bette Davis in the role of Helen Lawson, Liza Minnelli as Neely, the character obviously based on her mother, Mia Farrow as Anne Welles, Robert Redford as Lyon Burke, Elvis Presley as Tony Polar, and George C. Scott as Henry Bellamy. As usually happens when authors try to cast their own books in Hollywood, she got none of her wishes.

She did, however, strike up a brief friendship with Bette Davis, and when *Life* reporter Jane Howard asked for interviews one was held at Davis's Malibu home, where they were photographed together on the beach. That week also brought another woman into Jackie's life, one who would become a close personal friend. She was Ruth Batchelor, a thirtyish gossip columnist and songwriter who had written lyrics for Elvis Presley and who had made a demo tape of a song she hoped would be used in the *Valley of the Dolls* movie. Ruth dropped by for a swim at the Beverly Hills Hotel. There, walking around in the pool and "bobbing his little head around," was Irving Mansfield.

"He didn't know who I was, and I didn't know who he was," she says. "We were in the shallow end of the pool, and he walked up to me and said, 'What are you doing here?' and 'My name is Irving' and whatever, and I said, 'I wrote a song for *Valley of the Dolls* and I'm taking it over to Fox,' and he said, 'That's very interesting because my wife wrote the book.'" She told Irving about the demo, which was sung by Lana Cantrell, and they arranged for her to come for cocktails and bring the tape for Jackie to hear. She arrived to find Bette Davis also there, invited to dinner with the Mansfields. The demo tape was played, moving Bette to tears and so impressing Jackie that Ruth was invited to stay for dinner. The next day Jackie phoned her with an invitation to the hotel pool, but Ruth's song was not used in the picture, since André and Dory Previn had already been signed for the musical score.

Later that year Jackie attended Ruth's wedding in New York, where she met the actress Carolyn Jones, another cancer victim. Ruth remembers that Jackie was very interested in Carolyn's condition, and in the disease generally: "very obsessed about talking about cancer all the time." She believes, as do others who knew Jackie well, that the mastectomy probably ended her extramarital adventures and directed her energies toward her writing; her "crushes" were acted out in her novels rather than in real life. She and Jackie discussed sex often, and Jackie showed an earthy curiosity about the physical attributes and assumed

appetites of various men, but Ruth knows of no actual love
affairs. Jackie liked Ruth's salty language, which was
much like her own, as was her thirst for adventure and
love of gossip. Jackie, who enjoyed giving her friends
nicknames, opened her letters to Ruth with "Dear Satellite" and signed them "The Sun." Anna Sosenko was
"Earth" in those letters, and Bea was "Gemini."

In April 1967 Jackie was once again in Hollywood, this
time to make her debut as a screen actress at last. The
casting was almost complete, and to Jackie's dismay Bette
Davis had been rejected as too old for the Helen Lawson
part. Instead, Judy Garland had the role, although she was
the model for another *Valley* character altogether—Neely
O'Hara. Even so, Jackie was pleased Judy was making a
comeback, and she must also have appreciated the publicity potential in the casting. The comeback, however, was
not to be. True to form, Judy arrived late, muffed scenes,
held up production for days while she sulked in her trailer.
(Jackie picked up a pill she found in Judy's closet, tasted
it, and noted it was Demerol.) The part went to Susan
Hayward, with Patty Duke playing Neely O'Hara and the
beautiful Sharon Tate as Jennifer. Anne Welles, the character based somewhat on Jackie herself, was played by
Barbara Parkins.

Parkins was making her screen debut in *Valley*. Early in
the filming she met Jackie and found her "a very handsome, stunning woman." The younger actress found Jackie's
personality almost overpowering: "very assured and very
strong . . . with this deep, husky voice . . . very positive,
very excited about the movie, but very apprehensive because somebody was taking her writing and slightly altering
it." Jackie was similarly taken with Barbara, who she felt
resembled an earlier Jackie Susann, dark and intense and
with a distinctive voice. But Barbara was less earthy and

more elegant than Jackie, "the daughter Rose Susann would like to have had," Jackie said.

Lee Grant, who played Tony Polar's protective sister, Miriam, garnered most of the sparse critical praise, though she hardly recalls the movie with much respect or affection. "*Valley of the Dolls* is one of my money movies . . . to pay the rent," she recalls, adding that it was "one of the silliest movies ever made." She also remembers that no one she knew took Jackie seriously. "I think people looked at her like a really pop, trendy moneymaker who cashed in on a lot of fantasies."

After weeks of delays caused by Judy's antics and other casting problems, Jackie at last shot her scene, a mere five-line cameo appearance as a reporter at a press interview. It was not memorable, but it was good publicity for Jackie and the book, which had been Don Preston's intent when he had first suggested it to her back in their salad days. "Her reaction was funny," he recalls. "She said, 'But I'm a professional actress, and I've done lead roles. I don't do *bit* parts.'" Clearly she had changed her mind by 1967, and she did what she called her "Hitchcock" in the later movies based on her novels. It seemed ironic to have made it into a Hollywood movie only after she had put her acting dreams behind her, but she loved the fuss everyone made over her, painting her name on parking spaces and chairs and dressing-room doors, being trailed everywhere by reporters.

One of the reporters was Betty Rollin, a thirtyish senior editor from *Look* magazine who spent ten days around the set doing a cover story called "The Dames in the *Dolls*." Rollin, who would write a book about her own mastectomy, *First You Cry*, was unaware of Jackie's operation, or of the many health problems she encountered afterward. First there were the recurrent and ominous pains in her right shoulder, often acute, though nothing showed on the

X rays. Then she was diagnosed as having a spastic colon, and the following year, at about the time *Valley* was published, she was bothered by numbness and pain in her left hand. Diagnosed as neuritis, or nerve inflammation, it caused her such constant discomfort that Dr. Sohval resorted to occasional shots of Demerol, a powerful analgesic, to give her relief. She also had "pressure pains" in her lower abdomen, which made her doctors fear the cancer had spread. She spent the third anniversary of her mastectomy back in Doctors Hospital for gynecological tests.

But all these problems were part of the "failure" Jackie kept secret from the world. Interviewed in 1981, Rollin said, "When Jackie died I felt so bad that she didn't know she could have unburdened herself and still be glamorous. In those days she probably thought she was the only one-breasted woman alive."

The *Look* story did not flatter the movie's female stars, who were pictured as vacuously vain (Sharon Tate), earnestly featherbrained (Barbara Parkins), or "gutter-mouthed" (Patty Duke's own description of herself). Writing of Tate, who had spent two hours applying makeup for the interview and who "doesn't go in much for underwear," Rollin produced a classic quote. Tate, complaining that people expected too much of her, added: "I'm trying to develop myself as a person. Well, like sometimes on weekends I don't wear makeup." Rollin admits that "the story was very bitchy." She complained that she had "heard more four-letter words in ten days on that set than I heard in four years at Sarah Lawrence," but she had few complaints about Jackie, whom she found somewhat crass but unfailingly considerate. When they lunched together at the Beverly Hills Hotel, Jackie advised her, "Now first write your book and then get your husband. Organize it." Rollin had no book in mind at that point, but she appreciated the well-meant advice. "It was a friendly gesture, an honest gesture," she says, "She was speaking from the depths of her commercial heart."

After filming was completed, Jackie turned her attention to the paperback edition of *Valley*, which was published on July 5, 1967, the day after Carol Bjorkman's death. The first printing was a staggering four million copies, and Bantam chief Oscar Dystel told her she would have to help move them off the shelves by Labor Day. This meant that for every hardcover copy sold in the past year and a half she would now have to help sell twelve paperbacks—and in only eight weeks! She sensed that this was different from the hardcover sales push, where one could sweep into bookstores, autographing books and charming clerks. Paperbacks sold off racks, and more often than not the storeowner didn't have any control over what went onto those racks. The books were dropped off by truck from the wholesaler's warehouse. The problem seemed insurmountable, but Irving flogged her on. He expected so much of her, and sometimes she feared she just couldn't do it. "What Irving needs is five more Jackie dolls," she told a friend after one of their tougher days.

Then it hit her, in Chicago's O'Hare Airport, as she watched paperbacks being dumped somewhat haphazardly on the racks, that the men handling these books were not the pipe-smoking book salesmen she'd charmed at Random House or the cute young queens she had beguiled in the bookstores. These men were truck drivers, teamsters, men much like the ones who had moved her Uncle Harris Potamkin's fish in her childhood. She remembered visiting the fish market with Harris and watching him talking with the foremen and drivers, slipping them little presents or sometimes money, and on Fridays giving them special packages of the first-class fish he'd earmarked for his "tip-top" restaurants. Those men could ruin him, he had told her, if they didn't watch the ice and get his shipments off the trucks in time.

The next morning a historic moment occurred in the history of publishing. Never before had an author—much less a pretty television celebrity—come to the teamsters at dawn, loaded down with Danish pastries. But there Jackie was, contrary to her nocturnal habits, signing books for everyone in sight. "We're in this together," she exhorted the men, there in the warehouse of Chicago's largest paperback jobber. The ploy worked so well that it became a regular event in every city they visited as they moved westward, with Bantam P.R. Director Esther Margolis and Irving alerting the press before each warehouse visit. After Chicago a gaggle of photographers and reporters usually showed up, and as word spread the warehousemen got enthusiastically into the act, turning up clean and camera-ready on the morning of her visit. By California, Jackie was showing the wear and tear of her dawn devotions while the teamsters, in their clean white shirts and polished shoes, looked more like extras on a movie set than truck drivers. "We had a terrific breakfast at five-thirty in the morning in Long Beach, California. A lot of the drivers were from Watts. There were a lot of black men, and many of them wanted to write, so I talked to them about writing."

The paperback moved quickly to the top of the bestseller list and dug itself in for a long stay. Jackie continued her promotion efforts into the fall, with time out for a European tour to promote the foreign editions, now including translations into French, German, Italian, and Spanish. In time, the novel would be translated into virtually every written language, including some as obscure as Icelandic.

The tour began in France, where the prestigious Presses de la Cité was publishing *Valley* under the title *Le Vallée des Poupées*. The Mansfields were invited for lunch at the

Quai Voltaire apartment of the publisher, Sven Neilsen, but when they arrived Mrs. Neilsen at first refused to let them enter. Jackie was wearing a green dress, a color considered bad luck in France. She finally admitted Jackie to the apartment, but Jackie was ignored by her hostess throughout the lunch.

Whether because of green dresses or unimaginative publishing practices, *La Vallée des Poupées* did badly in France. There were few books in the stores, and consequently Jackie saw little point in knocking herself out to publicize it. The sales in France were so bad, in fact, that her second novel was rejected by twelve publishers before being picked up by a small house and becoming a huge success. Somewhat discouraged and more than a little angry, the Mansfields moved on to Germany, where the book was about to be published as *Das Tal der Puppen*.

In Munich they met an attractive, athletic German woman quite important to Jackie's future European success, Dagmar Henne, an agent with the French firm Agence Hoffman. She had handled the foreign rights for many Bernard Geis Associates titles, including *Valley*, and had so impressed the Mansfields that they arranged for her to work along with Bantam's director of subsidiary rights on future books, just as she had worked with Letty Pogrebin on *Valley*. The foreign contracts became so complex and so numerous, involving up to fifteen for each book, that they required extensive review by Dagmar as well as by Mildred Hird at Bantam, the Mansfields' personal lawyer Artie Hershkowitz, and the Mansfields themselves. Huge sums of money were often at stake, and the choice of titles, not to mention cover designs, was debated at length. Wherever they went for promotions, Irving was a tiger over every detail. "There was a press conference at L'Hòtel Intercontinental," a French editor recalls. "Irving came downstairs and made the suggestion that half the chairs be removed so the room would look full."

Irving was much taken with Dagmar at their first meeting, and evidently the feeling was mutual. "Jackie was much more remote and it struck me that she had little sense of humor, compared to Irving's, which was marvelous." Both Mansfields corresponded with Dagmar over the years, and she visited them several times on trips to New York, even being made privy to their problems with Guy.

There was another reception in Hamburg, and afterward Jackie and Irving were taken on a tour of the city's famous Reeperbahn and its even more infamous neighbor, the Herbertstrasse, where whores advertised their skills in store windows. It was a new and fascinating world to Jackie, one she would use in her next novel. They watched naked mud wrestlers in one club, conversed with a nude dancer at another, and marveled at big-breasted female impersonators in Berlin's famous Chez Nous.

In November they were in Venice, preparing for what was intended to be the premiere to end all premieres. They boarded a luxury liner, the *Princess Italia*, for a "junket to end all junkets" that would traverse four oceans and touch three continents. There were to be many showings of the film of *Valley* during the voyage— in Venice, the Canary Islands, Miami, Nassau, Acapulco, and Los Angeles— with grand openings in two New York theaters on December 15, the day after the Los Angeles shipboard premiere. Reporters and critics had been invited aboard for various legs of the voyage, to see the film and to meet the stars who were traveling with it. And, of course, to meet the author of the novel, who had by now become more of a celebrity than any of the actors.

Jackie sat through her first screening of the film in stony silence and then, according to Irving, she nailed director Mark Robson in a corner and informed him, "This picture is a piece of shit." Barbara Parkins, who was ecstatic with the attention she was getting, remembers being astonished at Jackie's reaction. "She was hysterical," Parkins recalls. "She said, 'This is not what I've written. I want off this boat.' She was so angry you couldn't even approach her. . . ."

Jackie felt the cast was ill chosen and inept, and she hated the script, which had been worked on by several writers in addition to the two officially credited, Helen Deutsch and Dorothy Kingsley. She hated the ending (Anne doesn't marry Lyon but instead returns to her bucolic hometown) and the characters who were transformed into caricatures. She and Irving disembarked at the Canary Islands and returned to New York, where, according to Ruth Batchelor, Jackie "stayed zonked out on pills for two weeks." They did rejoin the traveling circus in Miami, and despite Jackie's bitter disappointment they took part in the festivities there. She kept quiet when the press was around, though, and simply avoided discussing the film whenever possible. She did, after all, have a stake in its success, since her contract with Fox called for a percentage of the net profits. When interviewed, she talked about the novel, or dropped teasing hints about her new book in progress, or told stories about Josephine.

She was probably right about the cast, and especially the males in it, who might have been picked for the coincidence of their names. Paul Burke, who played Lyon Burke, had no screen experience, and Tony Scotti, who played Tony Polar, had no credentials at all. Jackie felt her book deserved actors of a somewhat higher order than those the studio had settled for. Barbara Parkins

had only been in *Peyton Place*, the TV soap opera, and
Sharon Tate was veteran of several weird movies such as
Eye of the Devil and *The Fearless Vampire Killers*, in
which acting talent was not of vital importance. True,
Patty Duke had won an Academy Award for her supporting
role in the screen version of *The Miracle Worker*, but she
was still identified with young girl roles such as the
teen-age twins she'd played in her television series. Only
Susan Hayward was a real star, with five Academy Award
nominations and one Oscar to her credit. But even she had
been away from the screen for several years.

The movie did have a lot going for it, though. It was
produced by David Weisbart (who died during the filming), whose credits included *A Streetcar Named Desire* and
Rebel Without a Cause, and was directed by Mark Robson,
noted for bringing other popular novels to the screen,
including *Peyton Place* and *The Prize*. Although not a
musical, it had five numbers by André and Dory Previn
that were considered "integral parts of the dramatic story," with a title song performed by Dionne Warwick. It
had more than 140 costumes by Travilla, most of which
became part of his new line of retail clothing. And,
of course, it had a *big* push from Twentieth Century-
Fox.

The reviews were terrible. One critic called it "Hollywood's first auto-satirical soap opera," and another declared that "no such characters ever existed outside the
overheated imagination of those who made this splashy,
gaudy, and utterly ridiculous film." *Variety*, Jackie's old
nemesis, noted the commercial aspects of the "guess
who" publicity, which the studio was exploiting (the
movie carried a large disclaimer up front before the corporate logo, a clear invitation to play the game), and it had
some praise for the female performers, the songs, the

camera work, and art direction, but little for the movie as a whole, which was described as "a fizzling-out 123 minutes."

Sherry Arden recalls Jackie's reaction to Renata Adler's *New York Times* review: "Jackie called me and she was crying and she said, 'Instead of reviewing the film she reviewed my book again and it was really nasty. Why are they doing this to me?' Irving was on the phone. . . . He tried to calm her down, saying, 'What do you care—you are so successful.' But after we hung up I felt terrible for her because she was so hurt." Jackie, as usual, bounced back. "That night about five o'clock she called me back, and she said, 'I was feeling so poorly that Irving insisted I get dressed. We walked down to the theater on Broadway where *Valley* is playing and there were lines around the block. Sherry,' she said, 'every hooker, every pimp, every pervert in New York was standing on that line, and I looked at Irving and I said, "These are my people." ' "

Despite the reviews, and even despite a script so clumsily pathetic that its most tragic scenes drew laughter from preview audiences, the public loved the movie. It set box office records in many cities and was still doing well in August, 1969, when the news of Sharon Tate's bizarre murder by Charles Manson's gang gave it a second life— just as the movie's original release had given the paperback a second burst of sales. By then Jackie had put her personal disappointment in the movie behind her, but had learned some valuable lessons about how things work in Hollywood. Mark Robson had made more money from the film than she had, due to the provision in her contract that gave her a percentage of the movie's *net* rather than *gross* profits. (Net profits are subject to all sorts of "creative bookkeeping," but a picture's gross is easily determined.) It was a mistake the Mansfields would not repeat.

In January, just as the hullabaloo about the movie was dying down, the television documentary Alan Foshko and

Sherry Arden had been slaving over for long months got its first airing on New York's Channel 7. Several critics reviewed the Mansfields' values and lifestyle instead of the skill with which they had been captured. Marvin Kitman's *New Leader* critique was typical. "Before Miss Susann wrote the book, it was commonplace for agents, studio executives and even critics to take advantage of a girl by telling her they could make her a star. The swine! Today millions of American teenage girls who had read nothing but *Valley of the Dolls* are educated enough to know it is necessary to have talent to achieve lasting success in the movie industry. Sex can help a girl get into a few dozen pictures, and make a few million dollars, but it all turns to ashes."

The film included interviews with, among others, Noel Behn, who declared that Jackie was "damn good." Helen Gurley Brown was interviewed, and so was Rona Jaffe, who had once been told by Jackie that *The Best of Everything* was "her nearest model for the construction of *Valley of the Dolls*, having one chapter from one person's point of view and referring to the other people, and then going to another chapter from another girl's point of view." Rona prepared carefully for the cameras with extreme eye make-up, and she remembers vaguely discussing Jackie's sincerity. According to Marvin Kitman, what she said was "I think her success is a real groovy thing." Another friend, Victor Lasky, added, "A lot of dirty books aren't making the grade like Jackie's."

A touching and sincere moment occurred when Jackie, looking worn and tired, declared, "I can accomplish anything as long as I know Irving Mansfield is my husband. Without him, I wouldn't be a whole person."

The special, called *Jacqueline Susann and the Valley of the Dolls*, went into syndication and was broadcast in different parts of the country over several years. It reached

Philadelphia long after the movie had come and gone, in fact after Jackie's next novel had been published. Reviewer Harry Harris noted that many who appeared in the special had since died or—in the case of Sharon Tate—been murdered, and that other subsequent events had altered one's perception of the show. He mentioned Patty Duke's "peculiar behavior for real, not reel, during last year's Emmy Awards presentation" (she had appeared to many to be on drugs) and Jim Aubrey's discussion of Jackie's work in progress, *The Love Machine*, during which he neglected to mention that the title character was based on himself.

Noel Behn had met Jackie through Aubrey around the time Aubrey was fired from CBS. Behn "hid Aubrey out" from reporters at his place in Westhampton, a cement structure rented from cartoonist Charles Addams, where Jackie and Irving spent many summer weekends. Through Behn and the Westhampton parties, Jackie met a circle of established writers including Paddy Chayefsky, Budd Schulberg, and Elia Kazan. She took delight in coaching them in promotion techniques as she also coached Rex Reed.

Reed became one of Jackie's closest confidants and wrote a number of articles about her. "Her loyalties to other writers were fierce," he said. "For friends or authors she admired, she purchased twenty-five copies of their books at all of the bookstores that reported to the bestseller lists. She phoned columnists and store managers to prepare for a new author's arrival on promotion tours. Nobody asked for these favors. She just did them." In an interview he added that Jackie had taken him by the hand and introduced him to everybody who was important in publishing. She advised him about contracts, about sizes of printings, about the importance of following weekly sales reports, about the necessity of buttering up salesmen and jobbers, about ways of manipulating the media. He followed her advice to the letter, except for those dawn coffee meetings with the truck drivers.

Budd Schulberg, author of the 1940's bestseller *What Makes Sammy Run*, had first met Jackie when she was beginning *Josephine!* "I'd seen her on television and thought she was quite articulate, and . . . when she said that she wanted to write I told her that from the way she talked I thought she could write. Years go by, and then I find her and Irving, too, advising me on how to sell one's book, promote one's book. She thought I was too reticent. She was watching me on some television interview, and I got so involved in my subject that I forgot to mention the title of my book, and she said that's a no-no. So it started with me giving her advice and ended with her in the expert seat."

The Mansfields often met Noel Behn for dinner at an Italian restaurant called Louise's on Fifty-eighth Street, a hangout for conservatives where Roy Cohn frequently held forth at the next table. Behn noted Jackie's sincerity about her books: "I can hardly remember the titles of my books, let alone the characters," he says. "But when you sat down with Jackie she remembered every last one of her characters. They were real to her. And that's the old rule of acting: If you believe it, the audience will believe it. And she believed it." He also listened sympathetically to her problems with Geis, which had become messily public, and he insisted she talk with the people at Simon and Schuster, his own publisher. They had been among the many corporate suitors, but now she was legally available.

Or *partly* available, at any rate. Bantam owned the paperback rights, and Jackie was not interested in giving a hardcover publisher half of her royalties on the reprint edition, as is the customary arrangement. Several hardcover publishers had made offers even before her split with Geis, but none so far had been willing to discuss a deal involving a huge cash advance (reportedly at one point she was asking $600,000) with *no* percentage of the subsidiary rights revenue to offset it. In the 1970's publishers made relatively little profit on a heavily advertised hardcover book, and usually counted on their share of the additional income from subsidiary rights—especially paperback reprint editions. With that lucrative secondary source eliminated, what Jackie wanted seemed like just too much.

However, Simon and Schuster had a special problem. The company's longtime editor, Bob Gottlieb, had moved to Knopf and had taken several key employees and—more important—several valuable writers with him. Simon and Schuster management needed a sure-fire bestseller for an upcoming list, a highly visible book by a highly promotable author who would attract attention to the publishing house. Jackie was made to order. A deal was struck in the spring of 1968, the details of which have never been made public though it certainly involved a substantial six-figure advance and an almost equally substantial amount allotted for publicity and advertising. Promotion budgets are normally the publisher's private domain and are rarely made part of an author's contract, but Jackie and Irving were learning fast.

Simon and Schuster editor in chief Michael Korda was assigned the book, which he would edit with the help of the house's up-and-coming young trade editor Jonathan Dolger, with additional line editing by Evelyn Gendel. They were all set to go, as soon as they had a manuscript to work on. But when would that be? With Jackie caught up in so many promotional activities for *Valley of the Dolls*—the paperback edition, the foreign editions, the movie—when could she actually sit down to complete the final manuscript?

They needn't have worried. Somehow, during the past two hectic years, Jackie had stolen time to shut herself away in her "torture chamber" with those varicolored drafts and blackboard diagrams. She was determined to beat the infamous "sophomore jinx" that plagues so many authors of highly successful first novels. That had become vital, almost as important to her as providing for Guy's future care and Irving's needs—and Rose's. She *must* prove she was more than a one-time media phenomenon, and the only way to do that was to repeat *Valley's* success.

28

The Love Machine

> *Jackie was a very tough, gutsy, funny,*
> *occasionally vicious, but basically*
> *interesting and in some ways rather nice*
> *person. . . . And given that, the one*
> *thing that Jackie wouldn't have wanted*
> *was to be the object of sympathy. . . .*
>
> ——Michael Korda

JACKIE'S medical problems had continued. During the grueling tour for the paperback edition of *Valley*, she complained to Dr. Sohval about new complications, hot flashes or flushes, the beginning signs of a menopause that would prove quite severe and would involve sweats, recurrent palpitations, and sleep disturbances. (The sweating, her friends swore, was exacerbated by the powerful makeup lights in her bathroom, so hot no one could understand how Jackie could tolerate them.) Hormones she was told were contraindicated for cancer patients. Instead she was given Bellergal, a drug combining phenobarbital and belladonna, and was advised to give up coffee, alcohol, and cigarettes—advice she was unable to follow for more than brief periods. The smoking worried her more than ever, because of the chronic cough she had developed and the intermittent sharp pain in the right side of her chest. In typical Jackie fashion, she lied to her doctors and told them she was down to thirty cigarettes a day. In 1967 she got another grim reminder of just how dangerous drugs could be when Ethel Merman's twenty-five-year-old daughter died from a combination of diet pills, Valium, and vodka. (Benay Venuta's account of Ethel's anguish so moved Jackie that she invited her old enemy to the publication party for *The Love Machine*, where the two were photographed together looking older and sadder, if not wiser.)

By 1968 Jackie was seeing another internist, whose records indicate that she had had "no special complaints" for the past one to two months but that she still smoked heavily, slept poorly, and took Placidyl. Her weight was down to 118 and she was in generally good shape, except for recurrent heartburn and her smoker's cough. In March of that year she contributed to a *Cosmopolitan* article on "The Camille Complex," in which several celebrities told readers how to treat a cold. "Take two aspirins and a glass of milk with a jigger of Scotch," Jackie instructed, adding that this worked better than sleeping pills. She went on to advise full makeup, a new nightgown, "something short and mod, so I don't look like an invalid," and perhaps a fall. In the same article, Joan Rivers was more terse: "The best remedy for a cold is death."

While promoting *Valley*, Jackie constantly warned audiences against the combination of alcohol and drugs; at the same time she was risking that combination herself.

Dr. Sohval may have been a bit more cavalier than some of his peers, but many physicians in the sixties prescribed mood-altering drugs for their female patients—especially if they were "housewives" or "menopausal." Elavil, which Sohval gave her in heavy dosage, increases the sedative effects of alcohol and can cause severe nervous system depression, convulsions, coma, and even death. The phenobarbital in Bellergal can be lethal in combination with alcohol.

But if she was having problems physically, she was in great shape economically. *Valley of the Dolls* had sold three hundred fifty thousand copies in hardcover and over seven million in paperback. The movie set box office records that would stand for a year and grossed between seventy and eighty million dollars, of which she and Irving would see far too little. David Brown, the Fox executive and husband of her friend Helen Gurley Brown, had asked her to write the script for the movie's sequel, called for in their contract. As columnist Sheilah Graham noted on March 1: "You can place bets now that *Valley of the Dolls* author, Jacqueline Susann, will have a say in every department of the movie sequel—the cast, the director, and of course the script, which she is writing. And you can bet she will be paid more than the $185,000 she received for *Valley*. This is the most determined, organized and efficient woman I have ever met."

Organized and efficient she may have been, but a screenwriter she was not. After a halfhearted swipe at the script she gave up and returned to work on her novel. The script was turned over to Jean Holloway, though Irving was still to be the producer. The title agreed upon and released to the press had been supplied by Radie Harris, to whom Jackie had sent a check for a thousand dollars in acknowledgment. It was *Beyond the Valley of the Dolls*, which meant that Radie had been paid at the rate of five hundred dollars a word. It was, it would turn out later, a very good investment.

Money was important to her for her mother's care. Never robust after her earlier heart attack, Rose had suffered a stroke that had left her further impaired, although she was still quite alert and very much interested in Jackie's career. She looked forward to the dinner parties Jackie and Irving arranged when they were in Philadelphia, and particularly to the birthday dinners Jackie held for her there every January in the York Town Inn. These events gave Jackie special satisfaction, since the restaurant was owned by her high school boyfriend Richard Allman, whose family had made her feel socially inferior.

Allman remembers the birthday dinners very well: crabmeat or shrimp as a first course, roast beef or sliced fillet for the entrée, with vegtables and salads and all the trimmings. He also remembers the time he suggested serving Great Western champagne instead of Dom Pérignon. "When I order Dom Pérignon I want Dom Pérignon, and that goes for anything else I order," she informed him haughtily. "I don't want any substitutes, period."

In the summer of 1968, working under deadline pressure and with everything riding on *The Love Machine*, Jackie was offered a two-week stint as hostess on *The New Yorkers*, a low-budget local daytime talk show. It made no sense at all for Jackie to give up precious work time for such a nothing show, but she never could resist the opportunity to perform. She gave it her all. "We had no budget," remembers the show's drama critic, Stewart Klein, "so we would take anyone who was pushing anything." One of the fillers was a chef who carried his ingredients in old coffee cans and prepared them on a hot plate. "One day he made matzoh balls and they came out about the size of tennis balls," Klein says. "I said, 'Jackie, you come over here and taste it,' and she stuck a fork in and took a huge bite. And then I did a terrible thing. I started to ask her questions. And she started talking and huge glob of matzoh ball came out.'' Jackie got her revenge, for that and for Klein's bad reviews of movies based on her books: She made him a creepy character in a later novel. ''I felt it was a badge of honor,'' Klein says.

He recalls one incident with something like horror. ''The morning after Bobby Kennedy was shot we go on and needless to say the whole nation is in shock. Kennedy was still alive at that point. I go on and I say, 'Good morning, here we are. Let's go find the latest news about Bobby.' And I described how even if he lived he would be a vegetable, and so on. Jackie comes on and she says, 'Well, now we'll continue with our entertainment. It's difficult, but I know that Bobby would have wanted it that way.' ''

On July 3, she signed the formal contract with Simon and Schuster. No one in the publishing house was told about her medical problems which might have caused some nervousness since her inability to finish the book, or to promote it with her usual all-out flair, could have resulted in a catastrophic loss. Several friends bear out the conjecture that fear of losing those huge advances was at least one factor in Jackie's decision to keep her condition secret to the end.

In the fall she presented the final draft to the Simon and Schuster editorial team, which was standing by for a crash schedule. Company head Leon Shimkin wanted the book out before the May 30 stockholders' meeting, and time was short. Dolger and Korda met with the Mansfields early to discuss the schedule, and Dolger remembers going to the kitchen for more ice. There was nothing in the refrigerator except a bottle of champagne and a jar of capers. ''I'll never forget the capers,'' he says.

"Michael had a bottle of bourbon, I had a bottle of scotch, and we would basically turn pages together and see on a large scale what scenes we would cut," Dolger recalls. "And then it would go over to the Navarro for Jackie to look at." They worked steadily for three weeks, including evenings and most of each weekend, cutting and restructuring, taking out superfluous characters and subplots. "The first week it was fun. The second week it was less fun, and by the third week it wasn't so much fun at all." Dolger remembers Jackie as diligent and cooperative. "She had certainly learned enough to take what we did and go back and do it. She worked very hard." But whatever his opinion of Jackie, he didn't like Josephine. "I couldn't stand her," he says. "Who wants this fucking little dog who is like a child?"

"Jonathan Dolger and I did a terrific job of editing that book," Michael Korda remembers. "We tore it to pieces and put it back together again. We rewrote bits and pieces, put pages through our typewriter, made Jackie rewrite." When asked if he and Dolger did actual revision, he answers, "More than I think that I've done on anything before or since." He goes on to describe the editing as "a lot of line work, a lot of restructuring scenes. . . . We put a heavy pencil to it." And then, considering, he adds, "Looking back on it, we probably did more than we had to. There was an awful lot at stake for everybody because we paid a fortune for *The Love Machine*."

Beyond their connection with Jackie, Michael Korda and Don Preston had little in common. The son of a Hollywood art director and nephew of famed producer Alexander Korda, Michael had grown up in a world of glamour and power he later described vividly in his own bestsellers, *Charmed Lives* and *Queenie*. He was unimpressed by the Mansfields' version. "Their idea of a good time was dinner at Danny's Hideaway with Peter Lawford and some comedian from Vegas, or going to the Beverly Hills Hotel,'' he says. ''Irving's whole life consisted in standing around places saying, 'Jackie will be down in five minutes.' They must have had some kind of genuine private life, but whatever it was I never saw it reflected at all. I mean, to me they were always a corporation, and . . . there never seemed to be the slightest bit of suggestion of a life beyond their appearing on television or visiting bookstores or making deals or taking calls.''

Though Korda did attend one of those dinners at Danny's Hideaway, he let them know that he was not to be co-opted into the Mansfield camp. ''I made it clear to Jackie right from the start that though I would do anything within reason I could for her, I work for S and S, and that I didn't need or want to be invited to dinner or given presents or anything else. . . . They accepted that. I mean, once they were clear about what you could do, they kind of relaxed about it. They had to know how much they could twist your arm, and when they found out exactly what the pain level was, then they would back off and relax.''

The Love Machine was certainly intended to be a major fiction blockbuster, something largely missing from recent Simon and Schuster lists. *The Love Machine* was scheduled for publication on May 14, 1969, with a huge first printing and full-page ads in newspapers all over the country.

The editing had been completed in December, 1968, and in February Jonathan Dolger took a much-needed vacation in Acapulco. With him were his good friends Dan Greenburg, author of *How to Be a Jewish Mother*, and Greenburg's wife, Nora Ephron, then a young reporter-essayist. Also with him—due to the crash production schedule—was a set of the bound galley proofs, the sort sent out in advance to the major review media. Nora was naturally curious. She told Dolger when she had finished that ''it was a

terrific read'' and that she would like to review it, and to
interview Jackie as well.

This struck Dolger as a splendid idea, especially since
Simon and Schuster faced an acknowledged problem with
Jackie's second novel: *Valley* had been largely ignored by
the review media, but after the book's stunning success
and Jackie's leap to celebrity those same publications
could not continue to do so. The prestigious *New York
Times Book Review* and others would be virtually compelled to run reviews this time out, but those reviews—if
written by the serious literary critics normally employed—
could not be expected to help the book's sales. Most of
Jackie's readers would probably buy the book anyway, but
no publisher relishes having his big book of the season
savaged.

Ephron's review started on the coveted page 3 of the
May 11 *Times Book Review.* "There is nothing literary
about Miss Susann,'' Ephron wrote. "Her fictional heroines are ... the most willing group of masochists assembled outside the pages of de Sade.'' ... "I have never met
anyone who talks quite the way the characters do in Miss
Susann's books.'' But she went on to admire Jackie as the
best of the "kitschy'' writers. "And when Jacqueline
Susann sits down at her typewriter on Central Park South,
what spills out is first-rate kitsch.'' She added that she had
enjoyed *Valley* as "a very very long, absolutely delicious
gossip column full of nothing but blind items,'' but she
concluded that "*The Love Machine* is a far better book
than *Valley*, better written, better plotted, better structured.
It is still, to be sure, not exactly a literary work. But in its
own little subcategory of popularly-written *romans à clef* it
shines, like a rhinestone in a trash can.''

Ephron also recalled Jackie's problems with Geis, in
case *Book Review* readers had missed the headlines two
years before, and she pointedly mentioned two of the

writers named in the lawsuit, Morton Cooper and Henry Sutton/David Slavitt—referring to them as "sloppy imitators of Miss Susann's style." This brought Don Preston back into the fray. "What made me mad was the gratuitous attack on Cooper, a good friend." Acknowledging that "common sense dictates silence," Preston tore off a letter to the *Book Review*, which was printed on May 25: "Having spent weeks struggling with Miss Susann's fractured version of our native tongue, I can testify that the one thing no one could ever accuse her of perpetrating was style. There simply isn't any, good or bad. . . . Therefore it is difficult to see how anyone could be accused of imitating it. . . . I am prepared to swear in court that Morton Cooper never saw a word of it (*Valley of the Dolls*) until his own book (*The King*) had been completed. The last thing I would have considered at that time was to encourage anyone to emulate Miss Susann. . . . Show-biz *romans à clef* are virtually a category, like Westerns or science fiction. . . . Morton Cooper . . . had written several of them . . . as paperback originals . . . long before Miss Susann."

Nora Ephron replied that Preston "would have done well to show Cooper *Valley of the Dolls*. If he had, *The King* might have been a better book."

Later Preston admitted, "I'm sure my letter made Jackie crazy, and I've always thought that it accounted for the great animosity she always showed toward me afterward, and the obnoxious characters she named after me. In fact, many people in publishing criticized me for going public like that, feeling that an editor should show more loyalty to his former author. These people obviously weren't aware of just how shabby her treatment of Berney Geis had been. . . . I rather suspect Jackie would have done the same thing in my place."

She might well have done such a thing, or worse, but that certainly didn't mitigate the insult in Jackie's eyes.

Neither she nor Irving ever acknowledged Preston's letter publicly, but those obnoxious characters named after him in *Once Is Not Enough* and *Dolores* no doubt indicate the depth of her reaction.

As for Nora Ephron, she has had something of a change of heart. "I regret it because it's a silly piece," she says now. "It's not anything I look back on and say, 'Thank God I wrote that.' Jackie most certainly did not have the makings of a great writer. I wouldn't compare her to Grace Metalious because Grace was dirtier. She wrote stuff that, when you were in high school, everyone knew what page this was on and that was on. Grace was much better at that.

"But I don't believe kitsch kills," she adds. "It's one of the reasons I wanted to write the piece. . . . I wish it were true that bad books drove out good ones because then it would be very easy to get people to buy good books— you could just stop publishing the bad ones. But it's not true. I mean there are people who want to read trash . . . and there's no point in saying it's not art. It doesn't attempt to be art." But if her feelings about *The Love Machine* have changed, her admiration for its author has not. "I did get to know Jackie and I was crazy about her as a person, and about Irving, too. She was genuinely generous. You know about her getting Helen Gurley Brown's money out of Geis. That was very typical of her."

The daily *Times* regular critic, Christopher Lehmann-Haupt, had little good to say about the book *as novel*, but he did seem to recognize that *The Love Machine* was a kind of anthropological fiction: "Miss Susann is all too sincere," he wrote; "one feels she really believes what she writes. . . . In fact, I suspect it's her sincerity, her complete ingenuousness, that attracts her readers. That and the celebrity guessing game, of course, and the fact that one is always made to feel superior to her characters. . . ." Most reviewers focused on the "ugliness" of the novel, which does contain an unusually large number of truly despicable characters, even for Jackie. *Time* magazine noted that "*Love Machine* lacks *Valley's* primitive vigor, but equals its obsession with pathology: leukemia, gall bladder trouble, heart disease, neurasthenia and nymphomania play important roles. One man is terrified of losing his genitalia: another surrenders them gladly in order to become a woman." In a syndicated column, "The Literary Scene," Alan Pryce-Jones observed: "People come and go: tiny, unpleasant people struggling with their fly-buttons. . . ."

Jackie got some help from her old columnist friends, Radie Harris and Earl Wilson and others, and even from some newer ones such as Joyce Haber, who did a provocative syndicated column on the who-is-who guessing game. Even the two *Times'* reviews were not as bad as she had feared, thanks in part to Jonathan Dolger's influence. She assumed thereafter that a powerful publisher could "fix" the *Times*, and was furious with her next house when a ferocious review of *Once Is Not Enough* appeared.

She was beginning to feel like an insider, and was an avid reader of the industry's trade journal, *Publishers Weekly*. (Jackie Farber, who had edited *Josephine!*, still sounds amazed when she describes her last accidental meeting with Jackie. "I was walking with an author down Fifth Avenue, and there was Jackie who gave me a hug. I introduced my author and Jackie said to him, 'Oh, your book's coming out in September.' And then she said, 'You've got some competition,' and off the top of her head she ran down the list of all the big books coming out in September from every publisher there was.") But Jackie had little time to read books now and depended on Anna to fill her in. Evidently Anna missed Nabokov because Jackie turned to a highbrow agent at a dinner party and remarked that she was quite concerned that *The Love Machine* was

"coming out against Nabokov" the following month. The
new Nabokov was *Ada*, but evidently all Jackie knew was
that he had written a sexy book called *Lolita*, which had
sold to the movies.

The scene in *Love Machine* of which Jackie was proudest
was one in which her heroine, Maggie, sets Robin's bed
on fire in a fit of rage. She bragged to Ruth Batchelor that
it was the equivalent of Puzo's famous *Godfather* scene in
which a character finds his prize horse's severed head in
his bed. She explained to Ruth that every great novel
needed one cataclysmic scene, what she called "a shocker." She believed that the shocker in *Valley* was the scene
in which Tony Polar tells Jennifer to "turn over," leaving
the reader to assume he will force her to submit to anal
sex. She considered the lesbian love scene the shocker in
Once Is Not Enough.

Despite shockers and unpleasant characters, *The Love
Machine* is Jackie's only novel with an ostensibly happy
ending. Robin Stone, a brutal, womanizing television
executive, straightens himself out, and falls in love with
Maggie, a reporter turned movie star who has loved him
throughout the book. She has shared him with a model
named Amanda (the Carol Bjorkman character) and Judith,
the socialite wife of the network head, as well as with
passing strangers including a transsexual. Robin's womanizing
is a sickness, and is cured by Dr. Archie Gold in a
three-hour hypnosis session. On the surface Robin is modeled on James Aubrey, who proudly took bows for the role
at a *Love Machine* party and who had reportedly advised
Jackie to "make me a real bastard." As Jackie reminded
Joyce Haber, Robin was the only son of a prostitute and
was adopted. "Aubrey has three or four brothers and
comes from a fine family," she told Haber, adding, "I
think after this he's going to go around carrying family
pictures in his wallet." But, as usual, Robin is really a

composite, his background as a newsman modeled on Ed Murrow.

Robin Stone's interior, however, is once again Robert Susan's, whose initials he shares, fulfilling her Uncle Harris's prophecy that Bob would one day be the subject of a really dirty book. And she even gives Robin her own traumatic childhood experience: At the age of four he finds his prostitute mother with a man. She was still trying to come to grips with the powerful father-daughter relationship that had so influenced her life. Rose is also in the book, or rather a combination of Rose and Flossie, Jackie's Negro babysitter. Amanda's foster mother is black, and is named Rosie Jones.

A major subplot of *The Love Machine* concerns comedian Christy Lane, another composite character, with bits of Cantor, Berle, Lewis, Jessel, Godfrey, and several others, who allowed her to recycle some of her material from *Cock of the Walk*, her second play. Christy marries the publicist and notorious "celebrity fucker" Ethel Evans, who bears perhaps more resemblance to the early Jackie Susann than to Ruth Cosgrove Berle, who Jackie liked to insinuate was the model.

Robin Stone has a scurrilous sidekick named Dip Nelson, an actor turned producer closely modeled on Keefe Brasselle. Nelson is married to a singer named Pauli, based more loosely on Arlene DeMarco. Pauli wonders if Robin and Dip are "AC-DC." Apparently they are not, although Sergio, a Roman who falls in love with Robin, is the most likable character in the book.

Arlene DeMarco also wondered about Keefe, it would seem who, she says, refused to take her to the hospital when she was in labor, shouting, "If I had to choose between you and Aubrey I would choose Aubrey." If Keefe had a gender identity problem and was a wife abuser, as Arlene claims, his association with Aubrey had certainly made him a wealthy one. According to his former wife, Brasselle's production company, Richelieu, earned an incredible seventy-two thousand dollars a *week* from its prime-time CBS programs. In addition, DeMarco maintains her former husband got kickbacks from other shows. DeMarco left Brasselle in 1967, two years after he and Aubrey were fired from CBS. Arlene got nothing after the divorce.

Jackie had been kind to Arlene during the marriage and even after it. "She'd bring over tuna fish salad for lunch and she'd say, 'Tell me what happened last night. Did he hit you again?' And I'd tell her the really horrible personal things. . . ." She says that Jackie was her role model and confidante, which is why *The Love Machine* came as such a shock. "She picked my brains. She would go, 'Oh, Granny,' and hold me in her arms, and all of a sudden you pick up her book and it's on page fifty-eight." She admits that she was angry as well as destitute when *The Love Machine* came out, and that she wrote to Jackie asking for money. Jackie, she says, sent her a corporate check for five hundred dollars, taking Arlene's "consultation" as a business expense. But Arlene got even, in Jackie's own style, with both Jackie and Keefe: She used them in her own novel, *Triangle*, published in 1971, two years after *The Love Machine* and Keefe's own fictional version of the Aubrey period, *The CanniBalS*. Needless to say, Arlene's characters were not very pleasant people.

Bad or indifferent, the reviews of *The Love Machine*, as before, didn't seem to matter. By June there were three hundred thousand copies in print, and on June 24 the book was number one on *The New York Times* bestseller list, bumping *Portnoy's Complaint* down to second place. As Korda had been quoted as saying in the Ephron review: "It's wild. You have these two giant books out at the same time, and their merits aside, one of them is about masturbation and the other is about successful heterosexual love. If there's any justice in the world, *The Love Machine* ought to knock *Portnoy* off the top simply because it's a step in the right direction." Jackie's own reaction to *Portnoy* was often repeated: When asked what she thought of Philip Roth, she said, "He's a fine writer, but I wouldn't want to shake hands with him." The remark was so well received that she almost worked up an act around it, with Irving as her most appreciative audience. In an interview with *Boston Globe* critic Kevin Kelly she repeated the line, adding the reason it had taken Roth so long to write the novel was that "he could only type with one hand."

To which Irving added, "You said the other one, too, Jackie. . . . 'Philip Roth's started a do-it-yourself club.' "

She hastened to explain that she didn't object to Roth's subject matter. "He can write about anything he wants," she conceded. "What I can't stand is all the nonsense that he's, you know, in quotes, 'literary.' Just don't give me any of that, please!" Her irritation with "literary" writers recurred in the interview, as it did in many others as the reviews rolled in. "What is it? Exactly what is literary worth?" she demanded of Kelly, then hastened to tell him: "What's literary today is stuff we're not able to understand, books that don't make any kind of real connection with their readers, books that the superior double-domed guys push on the public with pretension."

Jackie held forth throughout the interview on the question of literary worth, scorning those critics and most of the writers they considered worthwhile as "cocktail table books that lie there unread." She also had scathing things to say about Nobel Prize committees, who had overlooked Somerset Maugham and the novel she considered truly great, *Of Human Bondage*. Then, turning pensive, she said, "Will Jackie Susann be remembered in 50 or 100

years? Yeh, I think I will, you know that, I think I will! I
think I'll be 'The Voice of the 60s,' that's what I think!''

Double-domed critics notwithstanding, Jackie was all
set for her new publicity tour. In January, while the book
was being typeset, she had gone back into Doctors Hospital. She stayed six days, telling her friends that she was
taking a vacation. In fact, she was having a face-lift—her
second—leaving time for the scars to heal before the May
14 publication date. She rarely admitted to her friends that
she'd had plastic surgery, but her masseuse knew, and
others noticed that when Jackie rode her bike she pulled her
fall into pigtails, revealing scars behind her ears. Ruth
Batchelor recalls that Jackie's face-lift left her smile ever
so slightly lopsided, revealing more gum on one side. ''It
also seemed to have left her with little feeling in her chin,
because she quite often dribbled food on herself and didn't
notice. These were the times when Irving came in handy.
He would give her a look and blink twice and she would
immediately pull out her compact and peer at the face, and
with a flick of her fingers, now loaded with rings, remove
whatever was stuck to her chin.''

Ruth was still a close friend and companion, usually
invited to dinner when Jackie was stricken with a rare
attack of domesticity. The dinners were fixed for a small
group that often included Anna Sosenko and Radie Harris,
with Noel Behn invited, as Ruth puts it, ''so Irving would
have a boy to talk with.'' Jackie always fixed her special
''everything'' meatloaf, with side dishes of potato skins
stuffed with cheese and a salad consisting of lettuce covered with a commercial bottled dressing. There was a
vodka bottle on the table next to the salad dressing, and
dessert was usually Sara Lee cake served on the table in its
box.

Ruth remembers Jackie wearing white vinyl Courrèges-
type boots, her thin wrists and veiny, gnarled hands loaded

with gold rings, including the famous ankh symbol that had appeared on the jacket of *The Love Machine* and had quickly become a virtual trademark for the book.

Jackie had first noticed the ankh on a ring worn by Janet Leigh at a Hollywood party. When she asked about the odd figure—like a cross with a loop at the top—Leigh explained that it was an ancient Egyptian symbol of eternal life. She gave her ring to Jackie, who in turn had Los Angeles jeweler Marvin Hein make up ankh necklaces (small and large), as well as rings and pins, which she would thereafter present to interviewers, booksellers, and personal friends with great abandon. (According to publicist Abby Hirsch, "Jackie insists she didn't give away more than a hundred of the big ones. At eighty-three dollars apiece, that adds up to about three times the money spent on the average book campaign.")

The book's dust jacket was of special concern to Bantam, as well as to Simon and Schuster and the Mansfields. Because Bantam had done so well with *Valley*, using essentially the same design that had appeared on the hardcover edition, it was decided that the new jacket should be handled by the highly respected Bantam art director, Len Leone. He in turn brought in Milton Charles, one of the best-known graphic artists in New York. Both agreed that the same type would be used that had worked so well on the *Valley* jacket (and that would work well on a raft of other Bantam titles thereafter, becoming known for a time as "our big-book look"), but with Jackie's name at the top in large letters, of course. The book title would appear at the bottom, and in the space between would be a photo of two hands, the man's on top of the woman's, with the man wearing the ankh on a pinkie ring. A mock-up was made and shown to Simon and Schuster and the Mansfields, all of whom had jacket approval. Everyone loved it except Irving, who complained that the two hands looked too similar. He was told that they belonged to the best hand models in New York. ''Get the second-best hand models in New York,'' he instructed Charles. The photo was reshot, using a more masculine male model. ''I didn't want any questions about who was holding hands,'' Irving explained later.

29

Jackie Strikes Back

> *Success has not changed me. I've scraped*
> *my ankles climbing, and I want my*
> *next, The Love Machine, to get there*
> *clean. But I was never Grace*
> *Metalious, living out of a little place. I*
> *cut my teeth on Eddie Cantor, and Fred*
> *Allen and Arthur Godfrey.*
>
> —Jacqueline Susann

*T*HE promotion of a Jacqueline Susann novel rested
largely on the personal efforts of Jackie herself, as
everyone at Simon and Schuster was well aware.
"The book would have sold one hundred thousand copies
in hardback, maybe, without promotion," Michael Korda
admits. "That's a healthy figure; but it sold four times that
because of Jackie's personal impact." Planning and managing such an all-out effort would be time consuming,

however, especially because the Mansfields were so de-manding. The publisher therefore decided to take some of the burden from the shoulders of the in-house publicity director, Dan Green, by hiring outside help. In addition to the "stringers" used by Geis in Los Angeles and Miami and other major cities, resourceful young free-lance publi-cist Abby Hirsch was brought in to direct the campaign.

Her first meeting with the Mansfields was memorable. Advised to tone down her appearance to avoid competing with Jackie, she went without her makeup and pulled her hair into a ponytail. During dinner Jackie brought out a detailed critique of her entire *Valley* book campaign, the margins filled with handwritten notes about each inter-viewer. "He is a blintz," she wrote about one, and another she indicated was "nice, but nothing." They discussed the tour, and at the end of the meal a doggie bag was brought for Josephine. As Abby was congratulating herself for having made a good first impression, Jackie offered some advice: "Put on some makeup," she told Abby. "And do something about that awful ponytail."

There were parties, of course. The prepublication bash for the Simon and Schuster staff was held in the publish-er's offices with hors d'oeuvres and champagne from "21" passed around on silver trays. A reversal of the usual publication-day parties held to boost author egos, this gathering is still remembered by S&S staffers as a great boost to their own esprit de corps. Jackie and Irving used the occasion to thank everyone connected with the book for all past and future efforts. This was followed by a cocktail party in Jackie's honor at the American Booksell-ers Association convention in Washington, followed by a dinner at the Shoreham Hotel for 150 of the nation's most important bookstore buyers, hosted by the Mansfields. The cocktail party featured a "Love Machine Cocktail" invented at Hirsch's request: crème de cacao, vodka, Pernod, and papaya juice. "It was dreadful," she says. "It was a liquid laxative. Fortunately, we had even papered the rest rooms with ankh decals."

An even grander party was held at El Morocco, hosted by Earl and Rosemary Wilson, with a guest list of 350, including such disparate personalities as Joan Crawford, Ethel Merman, and Andy Warhol. Ankhs were everywhere, including a six-foot model through which guests could stick their heads through to be photographed. It was, as Hirsch remembers, "a triumph of promotion. Everybody got into the act. The wall-to-wall celebrities were offered caviar and champagne. Standing discreetly by the bar and buffet tables were attractive men in dark suits. As you tried the caviar, one man handed you a card with the name of the company that sold it. Another handed out cards identifying the vendors of the champagne. I'm sure the Wilsons would have been appalled if they had known that public relations people were using their party like a trade show at the Coliseum." The Mansfields might not have been surprised. As Michael Korda says, "Jackie wouldn't buy a pack of cigarettes unless she could get a deal on it. I mean, they were people whose whole life was spent getting things wholesale. . . . They had a deal on everything."

There was yet another party held in the Hamptons later, when the book came out in paperback. Rona Jaffe recalls that "Jackie was sitting on the couch and she never got up. She looked very thin and frail. She had a glass in her hand which maybe had vodka. She sounded really slurry and I thought that was strange. She wouldn't be drunk at her own party; she was far too professional. She was very nice, but she was on something." Rona was shocked at the change, because she had run into Jackie at several parties since the *Valley* documentary, and she had always been struck by the Susann energy and intensity. "We would talk about writing," she recalls. "Shop talk. None of the usual chitchat about the lovely wallpaper in the room. She would dig right in and ask me about my work, how I dealt with certain problems, my techniques—and she'd tell me the problems she was trying to solve. It would be like two academics right in the middle of a big party where everybody is all dressed up."

What Jackie was on may well have been amphetamines, "speed," one of the chief ingredients in the injections administered by Dr. Max Jacobson, the notorious "Dr. Feelgood." Jackie had been seeing Jacobson for some time and would continue seeing him for another year or more, at least until major exposés of his methods began to appear, the first, by Susan Wood, in *New York* magazine on February 8, 1971. Further stories on Jacobson were published in *The New York Times*, *Newsweek*, and *Time*. These, in turn, led to charges of unprofessional conduct by the New York attorney general and to the revocation of Jacobson's license to practice, though the latter did not occur until seven months after Jackie's death.

She first learned about him from Anthony Quinn, who had said the doctor's injections gave him "high-octane dreams." Through the sixties she'd heard much about how Jacobson was helping his patients lead more energetic, productive, and successful lives. As Susan Wood wrote: "With injections in veins or buttocks, his patients swear Dr. Feelgood can cure everything: the common cold, pimples, hepatitis, impotence. . . . He's the Dr. Schweitzer of the urban jungle." Although Jackie never admitted to Wood that she had been seeing Jacobson personally, she was helpful with stories of what had happened to "friends."

Truman Capote had been a patient whom Jacobson had helped to "write faster." In fact, his patient list was studded with celebrities, including Alan Jay Lerner, Tennessee Williams, Eddie Fisher, Cecil B. De Mille, Emilio

Pucci, Otto Preminger, and even President and Mrs. Kennedy, about whom the doctor bragged, "They never could have made it without me." His practice was so popular that it was almost impossible to get an appointment with him unless you were famous, or at least the close friend of somebody famous.

It isn't known exactly when Jackie started seeing Jacobson, though it seems likely that she began shortly after she switched doctors, leaving Sohval's liberal prescription practices for a more conservative internist. She probably concealed her visits to Jacobson from her new doctor, and she may well have concealed her status as a cancer patient from Jacobson. In any case, she must not have been aware of all that his magic injections contained, because the chief ingredients included "cellular extracts," vitamins, amphetamines, and hormones—the latter, as she had been warned, "contraindicated for cancer patients." Jacobson was secretive about his potions—Otto Preminger, who had a two-day dizzy spell after his first shot, says he quit when Jacobson refused to tell him what was in it. Certainly Jackie was enthusiastic about Jacobson in 1969, because she recommended him to Johnny Carson's wife Joanne. Joanne mentioned it to her friend Truman Capote, who warned her that "what he is giving in the injections is very addictive." He added that another friend, Sunny Crawford (von Bülow) had gotten hooked. Capote would later say that he and Jackie had been at war over Joanne's energy and soul.

But then Capote and Jackie had already gone to war by that time, as fans of *The Tonight Show* knew. It had begun on July 23, Irving's birthday, a day Jackie remembered as one of the strangest in her life. Earlier in the day she had gone to tape a David Frost television show, expecting to discuss her book with her friend Rex Reed, her admitted admirer Nora Ephron, and the colorful journalist Jimmy Breslin. She was seated on a raised stage, which forced her to fuss constantly with her short skirt, and she had discovered that Breslin had been replaced with someone she didn't know, a highbrow critic named John Simon.

Ephron and Reed were seated in the front row, facing Jackie, and they spent the first part of the show telling what a "great read" the book was (Ephron) and how Jackie had revolutionized book promotion (Reed). Simon remained silent, and Jackie later admitted she didn't even know who the man sitting next to Ephron was. But after the commercial break Simon came to life, his middle-European accent crackling and his fingers pointing accusingly. "Do you really believe that you are writing art or are you writing trash to make a lot of money?" he demanded, stabbing his finger in Jackie's face.

Jackie may have been confused, and even suspicious that her leg was being pulled by Frost (as she later claimed), or she may have sensed the potential for a publicity-making brawl. In any case, she went immediately into a reasonably accurate imitation of Simon's accent, demanding to know if he were Goebbels or Goering. "I haff heard of Neil Simon and Simple Simon, but vat Simon are you?" she asked him. From there the discussion quickly degenerated into an exchange of insults, with Simon accusing her of "smiling through her false teeth" and Jackie replying that her teeth were capped, not false, but that she knew Simon's hair was real "because it's too thin not to be." Enraged, Simon shouted that *he* would "rather see dogs fornicate than read your love story," which brought a dog trainer rushing down the aisle shouting that *he* would rather see dogs fornicate than listen to Simon talk.

Ephron, who had been attacked by Simon on an earlier occasion, sat in frozen silence during the fracas, but Rex Reed interrupted to say he was too busy to listen to such drivel from a man who spent his time attacking critics and writers and who had no business being on the show anyway, since he had admitted to having read only forty pages of the book. This piece of information naturally infuriated Jackie, who accused Simon of ignorance of both the book and its subject matter, the television industry. And so it went through the remaining minutes of the show, which would be aired weeks later with only the profanity removed.

After the taping, Jackie took Irving out to Danny's Hideaway for his birthday dinner, still furious about Simon but by now beginning to realize that the hubbub would probably sell books. After dinner they went home to the Navarro and took sleeping pills, then went to bed with the television on. Johnny Carson was interviewing Truman Capote, and as Jackie listened, half asleep, she suddenly realized that Capote was talking about her. Suddenly she heard him say, "She looks like a truck driver in drag."

She tried to wake Irving, who had succumbed to the sleeping pills, and finally had to pour water on him to get his attention. She told him about Capote's insults, which had included the opinion that she was "a born transvestite" who wears "sleazy wigs and gowns." Irving was outraged. "To refer to her gowns as sleazy is preposterous," he told reporters the next day. "Here is a girl who was voted one of the best-dressed actresses on television." He added that they planned to file suit against Capote and NBC, whose legal department was "quite distressed." "This may bring censorship to all the nighttime talk shows," he warned the press.

Irving got in touch with Louis Nizer, the famous attorney, who advised against litigation because it would be impossible to prove that Jackie had been damaged, and also because, as he wrote later, such a lawsuit would be "not worthy of the fees, exhaustion of time in extended pretrial deposition, ultimate lengthy trial, and probable

appeals." He was also aware that Jackie had done a rather
nasty Capote impression on a recent radio program, mim-
icking his nasal lisp with deadly accuracy. A judge might
well feel she had provoked Truman's remarks. Discussions
dragged on, and he had just about convinced them to
forget the whole thing, when Capote was quoted at length
in a publication called *After Dark*, as saying that Jackie
had been persuaded to drop the case when Nizer "told her
that all my attorney would have to do was to get a dozen
truck drivers and put them in drag and have them parade
into court and that would be all." Nizer immediately wrote
to Capote, explaining that he had advised against a lawsuit
but that he was now reconsidering, and that "my decision
may well depend on your reply."

Capote replied in a four-page handwritten note. He
reminded Nizer of Jackie's nasty remarks about Capote
himself, including an *L.A. Times* interview in which she
"implied that I am a homosexual (big news!), and a
lazybones jealous of her productivity." Of his *Tonight
Show* remark he said: "That seems to me merely an
aesthetic opinion—a spontaneous observation. Bitchy, yes;
malicious, no." Whether Capote's final word satisfied
Jackie or not, she was by then far too busy with other
matters to pursue the feud further.

But if she was never to cow Capote, she would finally
have her shot at Johnny Carson's show at last, thanks to
network pressure. She appeared on *The Tonight Show* on
September 8, and to everyone's surprise she made no
mention of Capote during the entire chat with Johnny. Just
as she was about to leave to catch a plane Carson
"remembered" to ask, "What do you think about Truman?"

Jackie considered for a moment, then answered, "Truman?
I think history will prove he was one of the best Presidents
we've had." And she departed.

The last act of the feud was particularly bizarre. In a

1985 book called *Conversations with Capote* he was quoted as saying, "I caused Jacqueline Susann's death!" He then gleefully described how she had been lying in bed dying of cancer when she heard his remark, and how she fell out on the floor coughing up blood and never recovered.

Though she had toughed it out in typical Jackie fashion, Capote's remark had hurt her. As she said in a later interview, "I've been a fan of writers all my life. I thought when I became a writer, it would be 'Hello Gore, hello Truman.' I can't understand his jealousy." Gore Vidal also took his shots at her on television, and may have been the first to quip: "She doesn't write, she types." But hurt or not, she could always turn to her sales figures for comfort. "Too many male writers are writing for critics," she told another reporter. "I won't write for men with pipes and leather on their elbows. I write for the public." And with her second novel already topping the bestseller lists, it was clear that the public was responding to her in a way even the publicity-conscious Capote must have envied. As one of the handful of writers in America who had achieved real personal celebrity, he was well aware of the value of controversy in gaining media attention. So was Norman Mailer, and he, too, was on Jackie's hit list. She used him in her third novel, *Once Is Not Enough*, as the basis for macho novelist Tom Colt, who, the heroine discovers, is both undersexed and underendowed. "Tom Colt, the man women worshipped, the man other men looked up to . . . Tom Colt, the living symbol of man—with a boy's penis!" January Wayne muses as she tries to arouse him in bed. "Poor, poor Tom . . . to have to write his sex fantasies because he couldn't live them." (Having at last achieved orgasm with her, Colt confesses, "This is the first time I've made it in ten years.")

Dumping water on a sleeping Irving, as she had during that fateful Capote interview, was becoming a habit. In

Philadelphia that May, while friends were waiting to take
them to dinner, Irving had entered into a conference-call
negotiation with their west coast agent, George Chasin,
and Columbia Pictures producer Mike Frankovich. They
agreed on a staggering $1.5-million payment for movie
rights on *The Love Machine*, a deal Irving failed to consult
Jackie about and did not even mention to her until they
were back in their Warwick Hotel suite. The row, which
brought complaints from other hotel guests about the
noise, featured an entire ice bucket's contents dumped
onto Irving and their bed. In truth, Irving was becoming
something of an embarrassment to her now. She was very
aware of how much she owed him, and she was grateful
for his full-time dedication to her interests. But now that
she was a success, she had begun to wish for a bit more
dignity in her dealings with others. But Irving was still
Irving, still playing the angles and haggling over details,
still making those awful jokes.

She had calmed down a few days later when they went
to "21" to discuss details of the deal with Frankovich,
whose production credits included *Oliver* and *A Man for
All Seasons*. On their way into the restaurant they bumped
into Aristotle Onassis, who asked them if the newspaper
accounts were true. They assured him Columbia had really
agreed to pay them a million and a half, and introduced
Frankovich to vouch for the fact. Onassis shook his head.
"I think I'm married to the wrong Jackie," he said.

"The *right* Jackie" was on the road most of the summer
of 1969, hustling *The Love Machine* with the same ferocious dedication she had given to *Valley*, even though the
new book climbed much faster to the top of the lists.
Writer Sara Davidson traveled with her on the trip to
Washington, where Jackie appeared at the ABA convention and hosted those parties, and then accompanied the
Mansfields on their west coast swing. She describes Jackie

on the 8:00 A.M. Washington shuttle flight: "A tall, slender woman stares straight ahead through a mask of makeup—black penciled brows, heavy false lashes, orange lipstick, and a black shoulder length fall made of Korean hair. Her body is covered with Pucci designs of yellow, purple, and pink."

The article, which appeared in the October *Harper's* issue, was filled with rather catty remarks about Jackie's glitzy appearance and the Mansfields' lifestyle, which Davidson saw reflected in Jackie's books. "She creates a dream world of stardom, money, and power where personal ambition and lust are the only forces," she wrote, adding that *The Love Machine*, though set in the sixties, contained "no mention of Vietnam, the generation gap, racial tensions, urban riots, inflation. . . . When a girl loses her virginity, or a baby through abortion, she gives it no more thought than if she had just lost a tooth."

Davidson followed the entourage to the Beverly Hills Hotel, and watched Jackie hold forth in the Polo Lounge to one reporter after another. Davidson watched Jackie tape a week's worth of *Hollywood Squares* quiz shows and appear on the Steve Allen show, where she did "some sloppy imitations of Zsa Zsa Gabor and Tallulah Bankhead," and where the show's talent coordinator told Davidson, "I hope you're not going to be as kind to her as we were."

He needn't have worried. The article described Jackie as "a national phenomenon, and we are stuck with her" and Irving, she described as a man given to making lame wisecracks and nervously asking "That's funny, isn't it?" Perhaps worse, the article was illustrated with a photo of the two by Diane Arbus that is a classic of tacky tastelessness. It featured the Mansfields in bathing suits, though Irving looks nude and Jackie's suit could as easily be underwear. He is seated in a hotel room chair, wearing an ankh on his bare chest, and Jackie sits on his lap wearing a matching ankh and staring intently at the camera, her long legs looking aggressively naked. It was the legs that upset Jackie most, she told friends later: She thought Arbus had made her thighs look too scrawny.

Jackie was often stung by the press, and the Davidson piece was in some ways typical. As Rex Reed tells it, "Sara Davidson came to interview her... used her phone to call her mother long distance, told her all of her own personal problems, said, 'Jackie, I can't begin to tell you how nice you've been to me,' then murdered her in print." Even Davidson herself has had some misgivings about the article. "I don't consider my piece on Jackie my finest hour."

The article did upset Jackie, as all such pieces did, but what really angered her in this case was Irving's bad judgment. After Davidson approached them for an interview, Irving read a few of her *Boston Globe* features, mostly fan-ish writing on rock groups and the like. He had reported back that Davidson was okay, and Jackie had gone ahead with the interview on his assurance, and look what had happened.

Still, she may have taken some comfort from Rex Reed's explanation. "People cannot stand success," he remembers telling her. "I mean, you are number one. You wanted to be number one, and you also are in the get-famous business. You're not some housewife that wrote a book in some little farmhouse in Vermont. You are in the middle of everything. People resent that." That resentment, though, never ceased to puzzle Reed. "It was open season on Jackie, and I really don't know what she ever did to deserve it. All she did was write her books, and they weren't *Remembrance of Things Past* by Proust. They were Jackie Susann. And they sold, and people wanted to read them, and they didn't hurt anybody. But people were driven mad by her success."

In August the Mansfields were again in California, where the press was generally kinder to her and where Jackie had a circle of friends, among them Joyce Mathews, whom she saw only rarely now.

On August 8 Sharon Tate phoned with an impromptu dinner invitation, which Jackie accepted. She liked Sharon, though she had some misgivings about her husband, director Roman Polanski. It was just a few people Sharon had called when she'd learned Jackie was in town, and it sounded pleasant enough. As Jackie was dressing, Rex Reed arrived unexpectedly. She called Sharon, who told her to bring Rex, but when it turned out Rex was tired, Jackie and he decided to skip the gathering at Sharon's house.

The next morning, Reed remembers, "It was a bright and glorious Sunday. We met at the swimming pool for lunch and Johnny Carson called us both with the news. Sharon had been murdered the night before. Jackie turned white. With the horror of what had happened came the dawning realization that if we had gone to Sharon Tate's that night we might have been part of the headlines." Jackie always credited Reed with saving her life that day, although years later, when she was terminally ill, she told him, "It could have all happened a lot sooner if we'd gone to Sharon's that night."

Ruth Batchelor also joined the group around the pool when she was in town, as did many of her New York friends and even some people she barely knew. One day at the pool Red Buttons' wife Alicia offered to read Jackie's palm, and announced that because Jackie had a short lifeline, she would probably die at about age fifty-six. Buttons said later that she felt terrible about blurting that out, even though she thought Jackie, then past fifty, was in her early forties.

By October, Jackie and Irving were in Europe again,

this time for an appearance at the Frankfurt Book Fair, the annual event attended by publishers from all over the world. Jackie was there to push *The Love Machine*, to which end she autographed books and charmed even non-English-speaking buyers.

A foreign agent recalls that one of the European editions had come out with a jacket the Mansfields had rejected, and now Jackie would see it and be furious. The agent remembers "everyone standing around in terror" as they waited for Jackie, whose sprained ankle would no doubt have put her in an even less receptive state of mind. She surprised them by accepting the rejected jacket with only mild disappointment. The book sold quite well, but Jackie always wondered if it might not have done even better with the jacket design she had wanted.

Much as she fretted over cover designs, and foreign titles, Jackie seemed unconcerned about the quality of her translations. When an agent asked why, she said, "Because I trust you. You've gotten me the finest publishers you could, and they are presumably getting the finest translators. Why should Irving get an ulcer over something we can't understand or control?"

There were other ulcer-making incidents in the Mansfields' life now. On New Year's Day the Navarro apartment had been burglarized. The thieves made off with a forty-pound safe containing jewelry from Cartier and Tiffany and mementos, including an engraved watch Eddie Cantor gave Jackie. In late May, the apartment was hit again. This time the intruders smashed two "burglar-proof" locks and then used the Mansfields' own claw hammer to break open the closet containing Jackie's jewel case. "You'd have thought they could afford their own hammer," Irving told Earl Wilson, who reported the second robbery on May 31. "My wife's going to take out an ad," Irving said. "It will read, 'Dear Jewel Thieves: You've wiped me out. I don't have one piece of jewelry left. Please leave me alone.' ''

Nineteen seventy began with a disturbing incident that involved someone she'd always considered "family"—her cousin, Bob Jelinek. Bob had been working in New York for a decade, a member of the CBS legal department and another link between the Mansfields and Jim Aubrey. He had married a young Englishwoman for whom Jackie offered to throw a baby shower when she became pregnant in 1969. Diana, who found Jackie overbearing, had declined, and Jackie had been disappointed.

Ian Jelinek was born on September 6, 1969, without benefit of one of Jackie's showers for "two hundred intimate friends," but with the benefit of her best wishes until Jackie appeared on a talk show with writer Edie Coulson. During a break Edie mentioned attending little Ian's christening. Jackie wrote Bob a furious note and never saw him after that. At the end of a long list of bequests in her will, drawn in 1974, appears the line: "I make no provision for Robert Jelinek, for reasons he well understands."

With *The Love Machine* selling wildly in America and abroad, with *Valley* established as the all-time bestseller and still going strong in paperback, and with income flowing from movie deals and a multitude of other subsidiary sources, Jackie was well on her way to becoming one of the richest women in America, and one of the few who had started from scratch and made it all herself. A number of women were actually wealthier, but they were either the heirs to great fortunes or old-time Hollywood superstars who had made their money early, when taxes were low, and had invested well. She earned a reported eight million dollars from her first two novels during the six-year period between 1966 and 1972, and she (or her estate) earned

huge additional sums from her last novel, published in
1973.

She invested her money in conservative municipal bonds
and blue-chip stocks and taking chances only in areas
where she had some special knowledge, such as National
General or Columbia Pictures. In a later article in *The New
York Times* she would be quoted as saying: "I've had too
many good friends who've been millionaires and woke up
to find themselves without money. If I felt I could be
worth 55 million, then I would take chances. But to take
the risk of losing all I have to make a half-million is not
worth it. I don't look for angles. I constantly get letters
from people with great deals for me. I ignore them."

She did not, however, ignore the people who had helped
her to become rich. Back in America after the European
trip, she wrote letters to practically everyone she'd met
there. She was, as Irving says, "the ultimate pro when it
came to her career."

Meanwhile, Twentieth Century-Fox had been struggling
unsuccessfully to get a satisfactory shooting script for the
Valley sequel, *Beyond the Valley of the Dolls*. As David
Brown, then the studio's vice president in charge of story
operations, remembers: "We couldn't get something that
we thought worked for us, so we undertook to make what
we characterized as a 'nonsequel' and we engaged Russ
Meyer, whom Jackie regarded as the king of porn, but he's
also a very skillful filmmaker." Many shared Jackie's
opinion of Meyer, whose films included *Eve and the
Handyman*, *Wild Gals of the Naked West*, and *Europe in
the Raw*, but they also recognized his ability to produce
profitable low-budget movies with great speed.

Meyer and Chicago film critic Roger Ebert produced a
shooting script in two weeks and were all set to go. When
Jackie and Irving learned of the planned "nonsequel,"
they were distinctly displeased. On May 22, 1970, Sujac

Productions and Jacqueline Susann Mansfield fired the first shot in what would turn out to be a long war, filing a motion for a preliminary injunction to prevent the studio from using the title on a movie unrelated to *Valley of the Dolls*.

30

Beyond the Valley

> *I hear all those fellas are scared. I mean,*
> *having their books published in the same*
> *season with a new Jackie Susann. John*
> *Cheever on the Mike Wallace show. . . .*
> *You know Cheever any chance?* Bullet
> Park's *his latest. Well, he said it was*
> *murder, plain murder, coming out the*
> *same time against Jackie Susann. I*
> *suppose Nabokov feels the*
> *same way. . . .*

——Irving Mansfield

*T*HROUGHOUT the *Love Machine* tour, Jackie had been
worried over Josephine, now fifteen and still eight
pounds overweight from gorging on "caviar, Bloody
Marys, peanuts, and tangerines," as her mistress ruefully admitted. Jackie's own diets were much stricter now than Josie's,

since every time she quit smoking— which was often—her waist began to thicken alarmingly. On prior tours Jackie had traveled to Eastern cities the night before, to be fresh in the morning for the tough all-day schedules. Now, whenever possible, she commuted there and back in the same day to avoid leaving Josie alone. She'd been praying that Josie would at least make it to her "whelpday," the twelfth of January. The dog received semiannual electro-cardiograms and the best of medical care, but her diet had never been even close to the one recommended. Jackie knew they were spoiling Josie to death with goodies like the chopped-liver birthday cake, but she and Irving couldn't help it. And of course there were those special treats from Danny's Hideaway.

Josie was a good luck charm, like the poodle pin Irving had bought Jackie at Van Cleef the week *Every Night, Josephine!* was published. The pin was small, gold, with ruby eyes, and she always wore it when she was writing, even pinning it to her nightgown if she got up to work in the middle of the night. The burglars missed it—because it was in a desk drawer, under the clutter, rather than in her jewel box. Sitting on her wishing hill in the park, reviewing her deals with God, she decided He had been telling her something by letting her keep the poodle pin when every-thing else was gone.

She worried about Josie, who could no longer go on walks in the December chill—in fact, she sometimes had trouble walking any distance at all now, because of her arthritis and excess weight. She was undoubtedly the most famous poodle in the world, hobnobbing with Richard Burton and Richard Nixon, having a cocktail party held in her honor by the duke and duchess of Windsor, but she was getting feeble, her vision fading and her hearing almost gone. Jackie insisted she had learned to lip-read.

In late December the Mansfields traveled to Miami

Beach, as they had for years, leaving Josie with their
housekeeper, Louise. When they returned on January 5 the
dog was coughing and listless. They rushed her to the vet
first thing the next morning. She died the next day, six
days short of her sixteenth birthday. As Jackie wrote in an
article published the following April in the *Ladies Home
Journal*: "I acted like some of the heroines of my books. I
had a good stiff drink, took two 'dolls' and went to sleep. I
awoke and saw Josie's picture flashed on the television
news. I cried, took two more pills and went to sleep. I
awoke and heard Long John Nebel eulogize Josie on his
midnight radio show. I took two more 'dolls,' and as I
drifted off to sleep I swore there would never be another
dog in my life. I had loved Josie so, and losing her hurt
too much."

The next morning the two proprietors of the Poodle
Boutique, where Josie had always been groomed, arrived
at the Navarro apartment and "thrust one pound of black
poodle with yellow hair ribbons into my arms." A true toy
who would remain smaller than Josie, Joseph Ian (after
Josephine herself, but also after Joe E. once again, com-
bined with Ian McKellen, the British actor whose performances thrilled Jackie) became a bicoastal poodle, traveling
in Jackie's oversized purse on scores of flights to California and leaving "Tootsie Rolls" all over the velvet lawns
of the Beverly Hills Hotel.

She had lost Josie, and it seemed she was in the process
of losing Karlina as well. She'd seen less of the child as
Karlina had grown, and after the Chau family had moved
to New Jersey in 1966, when Karlina was twelve, the
weekend visits had pretty much ended. Jackie had continued to pay for the ballet lessons and had gone faithfully
down to each recital, encouraging the girl to keep working
toward a career in the theater. She had sent presents from

all her travels, or money when she hadn't had time to shop, which happened more after *Valley*'s big success.

In high school Karlina, though, had gained weight and seemed to lose interest in dancing. She switched to an academic program, which prompted Jackie to write in exasperation: "I know you're fat—but are you also some kind of a nut?! College?? An academy to study *after* high school?! What do you expect to be—the only gray-haired ballerina on Broadway?" She advised Karlina to change back immediately to typing and shorthand, always useful for aspiring performers. She planned to have Karlina meet the director of the St. Louis musical festival "the summer after next—if you are not too fat" so that she could get stage experience and earn money for New York. "You should come to N.Y. the day after you graduate—live at the 'Y' and audition for every musical and TV show there is."

Karlina, the letter went on, should become slim "and one hell of a dancer." Karlina couldn't be just *good*, she had to be the best. "I did not hope Valley of the Dolls would be a fair seller," Jackie wrote. "I wanted it to be the No. 1 Best Seller—and I felt I had the talent to write a No. 1 Best Seller. . . . Of course if you run into a millionaire in Phila. who wants to marry you, I'm all for that," she added. "But your chances of meeting one will come out of show business too." She also advised Karlina to consider plastic surgery on her eyes, of the sort Madame Sukarno had undergone. "I saw her the other night. She looks gorgeous—still oriental—but gorgeous. I wouldn't want you *not* to look oriental. It's very big being oriental now!"

Despite the advice, Karlina opted for a career in nursing. Jackie, by now resigned, took the news in good grace. In a March, 1971, letter she wrote: "I was startled when you wrote and said you wanted to be a nurse. It's a wonderful profession, but make very sure it's really what you want to do. Please write and tell me how you arrived at this decision and what caused the inspiration. If you go into it, be sure and keep your eyes open for a nice rich Jewish doctor . . . or a nice rich any kind of doctor." She added that perhaps Karlina's training would not be wasted. "If a male patient gets over amorous, you can always do a ballet leap to get out of his clutches."

But things were never the same between them. "Since nursing school," Karlina remembers, "we were just getting farther and farther apart and I think now that she was just so ill and she didn't have time for anybody." Jackie's last letter followed a mixup over a Christmas gift Karlina had not got around to mailing. "She told me I was terribly greedy and all I ever wanted was her money and she was going to disown me and that she didn't want to have anything to do with me. What started as a beautiful relationship just ended, sort of fizzled out." In her will, Jackie left five thousand dollars to the five Chau children "to be shared equally."

With the loss of Josephine and the slow defection of Karlina, Jackie complained that she felt she had lost *both* her daughters. She still had her son, though in a very real sense she had lost him two decades ago, when he had retreated behind that wall of silence she could never breach. He had adjusted well at first to the institution in Winston-Salem, and he had not seemed to mind that his parents' visits were necessarily fewer. Lately, though, the emergency phone calls had begun again. Guy wasn't getting along with the staff or the other patients; there had been a violent episode and a theft: his treasured television set had been smashed. On their visits—twice a month when they could manage it—they could see the familiar pattern repeating itself, and they knew he would have to be moved again. He was twenty-three now, really neither child nor man but a strange being forever beyond their reach in his incomprehensible private world.

In February, 1970, a few weeks after Josie's death, Irving was operated on to remove abdominal polyps, and Jackie made another deal with God to stop smoking if he survived. She did for a while, but it didn't seem to help the "bronchitis" she'd had for some time. "Ever since I quit smoking I've had this dreadful cough," she complained to friends, only partly in jest. She had complained about the symptoms to her internist months before, also reporting recurrent upper abdominal fullness and difficulties in expectoration. A "bad attack during sleep" had brought her in for the examination. Her weight was 121. In early April she had a fall that left bruises on her chest and tenderness in the region of her fourth rib. Her cough was somewhat better, but now that she was off cigarettes her weight had climbed to 125. She wasn't feeling very well these days, which might have been connected with her decision to stop Dr. Feelgood's shots. Amphetamine withdrawal can often leave one feeling dull and listless.

In March, as Irving was recovering, Jackie prepared to return to the stage in a Robert Henderson Off-Off-Broadway production of *The Madwoman of Chaillot*. Ironically, the play she had elected to "return" to was an anticapitalist piece of whimsy that frankly ridiculed the profit motive. And Jackie herself could honestly deny the profit motive in this case, since she and her co-stars were all being paid the same magnificent seventy-five dollars a week. "I'm back acting and I find it somewhat like group therapy," she told an interviewer. "Hemingway used to hunt big game in Africa between books. And I have a new novel outlined so this is a period for catching up with myself."

Madwoman played two weekends to humiliating reviews. Her friends told Jackie that she wasn't at her best in the play, and a critic could not restrain himself from saying that "literature's loss had been the theater's gain." None of it seemed to bother her, though. She was delighted to be on stage again, especially with so distinguished a former leading lady as Blanche Yurka. Jackie's chief fan was equally delighted, and from the Bronx came another envelope packed with clippings and a note saying that Jackie had now reached her prime and was more lovely—if that was possible—than she'd been at twenty-five. Jackie replied that she hoped the housewife would stop backstage and say hello in person next time. They hadn't actually met since the night they had done the town together twenty-five years ago, and Jackie must have wondered about the woman's life, and how she herself could still figure so prominently in it.

June was a busy month for the Mansfields. They were moving from the Navarro after twenty-six mostly pleasant years. The two robberies had made Jackie nervous, and Josephine's death had added to her restlessness. The hotel, however, was primarily a stopover for transients. It was time they "nested" at last in a place that was really their own, and one that was larger, which they could certainly afford. Their new apartment was only two blocks west, and with a sweeping park view from the twenty-fourth floor.

"I always swore that if I moved, the new place would have a wood-burning fireplace and either a back garden or a terrace," she told an interviewer sometime later. "As you can see, I have neither." What she did have was a bright and cheerful two-bedroom apartment decorated primarily in yellow. "So I went to this decorator, Steve Gasperecz, and he said if we spent $10,000 we could make it light. So, $50,000 later . . ."

The new place was large compared to their Navarro apartment, but it still seemed small to one refugee from a huge California house who came to spend several weeks there a few months later. She was Joyce Haber, the columnist who had plugged *The Love Machine* and who had become a friend. Haber was in the throes of completing a book of her own, and she needed a quiet place to work, away from the hubhub of her own busy life. The Mansfields were off by then on their European tour, so Haber wrote her final draft on Jackie's typewriter, an aging manual model, at her desk in the den overlooking the park. "The views were lovely," Haber says. "At night it was just absolutely stunning and I lost a lot of work time just looking out the window myself. But it was surprising to me that as a best-selling author Jackie didn't have a larger apartment with a formal dining room." Haber also recalls that oddly empty refrigerator, often containing only suppositories.

The new apartment, with its bright "egg-yolk-colored" walls, struck at least one writer as appalling, Claudia Dreifus, a hip young intellectual who interviewed Jackie for a *Penthouse* piece called "Games Women Play." "It was a garish Miami Beach place with a huge garish bar and what I can only describe as a 'Jayne Mansfield look,'" she says. "Joseph Ian sat on a little bed in the living room. He was a ludicrous dog, and the way she fussed over him was ridiculous. However, Jackie was wholly hospitable and wholly kind. I didn't expect to like her but I did."

June also was the time when Russ Meyer's *Beyond the Valley of the Dolls* opened. On June 17 the preliminary injunction was denied, and the movie was released, to the amusement and/or horror of most reviewers. "Russ Meyer," wrote *Variety*, "who once made low-budget sex pix which had a crude and innocuous charm but not much story, this time spent between 20 and 30 times the money he used to have, and got less for it all." Another review described the movie as "beyond belief, so egregiously awful, whether

intentionally or not, that it shouldn't be missed." And
Judith Crist seemed to sum it all up in her *New York*
magazine review of July 13: "Allegedly the previews of
this one were delayed by an abortive attempt to halt the
opening by Jacqueline Susann, who felt it an infringement
(or possibly a traducement of or, more likely, a cashing-in
on) her *Valley of the Dolls*. Actually she benefits, since
this Russ Meyer movie puts the Susann work on a *War and
Peace* level of intellectual content and artistic mastery."

Although the injunction was denied, the suit for damages continued. It dragged on through the courts for some
years, coming to trial at last after Jackie's death. The
lawsuit was complicated, but its heart was a breach-of-
contract action boiling down to a charge (by Jackie and her
corporation, Sujac) that Fox, having failed to obtain movie
rights to *The Love Machine*, had decided to "cheat" a
motion picture on Jackie's reputation without her coopera-
tion or consent, and without paying her the money for a
sequel stipulated in the *Valley of the Dolls* movie contract.

Jackie argued that the Russ Meyer movie infringed on
her rights to the title, and that Fox had intentionally
confused the public into thinking the film was based on her
work. Through her book and her publicity efforts, she had
established the phrase "Valley of the Dolls" in the public
mind, and she had further paid Radie Harris one thousand
dollars for the use of the word "Beyond." The original
Valley movie contract required, among other things, a
fifty-thousand-dollar payment to Jackie if a sequel was
made, and that Irving be hired as the producer of the
sequel. It also reserved to Jackie the right to use the title in
connection with a television series. But no payment was
made to her: Fox argued that its movie was not a sequel
despite the title, and also despite the fact that it had been
widely advertised as a sequel in the months before its
release.

Jackie testified in a deposition taken in May, 1970, that she believed that the title would be used only on a sequel. David Brown had assured her of that, she said. In response to the Fox attorney's badgering repetitions, she volunteered, "I would punch him in the nose if he ever suggested that he was going to use it for anything else. Are you kidding?" She also testified that Zanuck had told her, "I like the title very much and I think it's a great title for your sequel," adding, "Your sequel, to me, means me, Jackie." Jackie handled herself superbly, though at one point she grew irritated: "I am not a lawyer, but I know it's like nine different ways you are asking the same question," she snapped.

Certain language in the contract, Fox argued, gave Fox the right to use the title or its components for motion pictures independent of the book. The language was of course at odds with clauses concerning payment for a "sequel" and reserving certain rights in the title to Jackie. When the Mansfields' attorneys asked in the pretrial settlement hearing for only $350,000 in damages (a relatively modest sum), Fox felt it had the better of the case and refused to come up with a counteroffer. As John G. Davies of the Mansfields' law firm, Rosenfeld, Meyer and Susman, explains: "Fox claimed that the language in the contract . . . was rather clear. . . . They said, look, read the language. It means we have the right to use the words 'Valley of the Dolls' in anything!" And then he adds, "But we convinced the court that those words really did not mean what they said."

That convincing did not occur until August, 1975, when the case came to trial. The case was tried before a jury that was shown the Russ Meyer film, and Davies sums up the outcome: "The movie was rather offensive. And because of that I think the good people on the jury felt she was treated unfairly." After two days of deliberation they

awarded Jackie's estate two million dollars in damages.
Fox said it would appeal the award, but ultimately settled
for $1,450,000.

Ironically, the Russ Meyer film became something of a
cult classic. In 1975 the Museum of Modern Art's Department of Film's notes for the movie described *Beyond the
Valley of the Dolls* as "an inventive and abrasive soap
opera which neatly kisses the 60s goodbye. Its straightforward approach, the ingenuousness of most of its characters, and its serpentine and bizarre situations predate the
television comedy-melodrama *Mary Hartman, Mary Hartman. Beyond the Valley of the Dolls* is a parody not only of
the genre (complete with sermon!) but of the contemporary
American landscape." That assessment was somewhat at
odds with Judith Crist's review, which called the X-rated
quickie "a teenybopper *Valley*, recounting a girl rock-
trio's encounters with a variety of Hollywood perversions
and freaks, and climaxing with a sex-drug-and-slaughter
orgy that seems to be intended as a great comedy satire of
the Sharon Tate case."

Although Jackie would have been delighted at Irving's
victory and windfall, she was genuinely shocked and
revolted by the film, and upset by Brown and Zanuck's
conduct.

By the time the lawsuit at last reached a courtroom,
Zanuck and Brown were long gone from Twentieth Century-
Fox, fired in December, 1970, by, among others, the chief
executive officer of Fox, Darryl F. Zanuck, Richard's
father. *Variety* speculated: "Rumblings of father-son dissatisfaction in the Zanuck family have been heard for
months on both coasts and may have been climaxed by two
sex features, *Beyond the Valley of the Dolls* and *Myra
Breckinridge*." (Brown denies that those movies were the
cause of his dismissal. "When *Cleopatra* closed Twentieth
Century-Fox, we were all fired, all of us," he says.)

Hollywood executives have a way of landing on their feet, and the Zanuck-Brown team was no exception. The pair immediately formed an independent production company, and within the next few years they produced such blockbusters as *The Sting* and *Jaws*. Jackie was probably the first to applaud their success. Despite their legal differences, the Mansfields and the Browns managed to sustain their friendship although David and Helen differ somewhat on the lawsuit's effect. "Even when we were in the most heated negotiations and there were many differences between us... our friendship was never affected. Didn't even strain it in my opinion," says David. "What happened during those years, it never broke up our friendship, but it strained it," Helen says. The friendship, of course, was never deeply personal but rather a casual bicoastal entertainment-world relationship.

If business had nothing to do with friendship, in the end, it did at the beginning. The whole strange *Beyond the Valley* affair had begun in part because of a confusion of the two. Brown had offered $450,000 for movie rights to *The Love Machine*. Added were "sweeteners," including a share of the film's net profits, a $125,000 payment directly to Irving for producing the film, and a similar sum to be paid to him to produce another unspecified movie. Brown worried about having the offer transmitted through the Mansfields' agent so he called Irving at the Beverly Hills Hotel. As John Gregory Dunne tells it in his book, *The Studio*:

" 'Irving,' Brown said, when Mansfield came on the phone. 'I just wanted to say safe trip. It was good seeing you, Irving. It's always good seeing you and Jackie.' He leaned back in his chair and let a puff of smoke curl toward the ceiling. 'I just talked to George Chasin [the Mansfields' agent], Irving, and made a little proposal to him. I'm sure he'll be getting in touch with you. Well, have a good trip

back, and Helen and I will get together with you and
Jackie in New York. Friends, Irving, friends. It transcends
business, Irving.' "

Shortly after, Mike Frankovich bought *The Love Machine* for $1.5 million plus a share of the movie's gross.
Shortly after that, Fox announced its X-rated "nonsequel."
Business was business.

On July 4, as it had done with *Valley* exactly three years
earlier, Bantam released its paperback edition of *The Love
Machine* with the expected fireworks. At the ABA convention in May, Jackie had posed again for endless photographs
with bookstore buyers. A tour was planned, although
Bantam faced the usual reluctance of talk shows to interview the author of a book already promoted heavily in
hardcover.

The challenge, as usual, was coming up with new ways
to attract media attention the second time around. In this
case the gimmick, arranged by Esther Margolis, Bantam's
publicity director, and Irving, was a seven-million-dollar
Grumman jet that belonged to the previous tenant of the
Mansfields' new apartment. The plane was rented by
Bantam for a week, THE LOVE MACHINE painted on both sides
in huge letters, visible from several hundred feet.

It was a grueling week, but the gimmick paid off. "In
Philadelphia we got them to give us the key to the city,"
Esther remembers. "And then we went to Detroit, where
we gave Jackie a huge celebrity party, so that got covered
on the society pages. We actually took party guests with us
to Detroit. And then we went to Chicago, and to Minneapolis and then on to Los Angeles, with the press meeting us
at each airport." Some interviews were conducted on the
plane between cities. "We used the plane for one week,
and we made *Newsweek* and *Time* with it," she adds,
pleased with the investment.

In Los Angeles, Mike Frankovich and his wife, actress Binnie Barnes, got into the act, giving a huge come-as-you-please party with a star-studded guest list to promote the movie, which was about to go into production. Costumes were on the wild side, though Jackie wore a relatively sedate harem outfit featuring gold chains draped around her torso. There were parties all over town, in fact, to celebrate what was rapidly becoming the fastest-selling book ever and the movie to be based on it. Bantam's initial print order was for two and a half million copies, and in the first few weeks after publication the book was selling at the mind-boggling rate of sixty thousand copies a *day*, outstripping even *Valley of the Dolls*' performance in paperback.

The parties had been going on in Hollywood ever since the movie sale was announced a year earlier, alerting the movie community to some juicy roles in the offing. One such bash, given by Henry and Anita Louis Berger to celebrate the hardcover publication, was described vividly by Joyce Haber in the *Los Angeles Times*: "Forty of Hollywood's Beautiful People came as though they were auditioning. . . . Everyone seemed to be made up to look like the characters in the novel. . . . Joan Collins came looking like Dee (the ex Mrs. Howard) Hawks, who many think is the model for Amanda. Jill St. John was a ringer for the late model, Carol Bjorkman, whom others have likened to Amanda. George Hamilton (with Arlene Dahl, she smoking cigars) might have been playing Keefe Brasselle, if Brasselle was Dip Nelson. Donna Reed or Angie Dickinson could have been reading for Phyllis Thaxter, who people are saying is the original for Maggie. Anne Baxter, with her prep-school accents and her patrician ancestry, might have passed vaguely for Mrs. William (Babe) Paley, who passed vaguely through some minds as Judith." Robert Stack said his wife thought he was "a twin" to Jim

Aubrey, and others insisted that Mike Connors was perfect for the Robin Stone part. Aubrey himself was there, and when asked who should play Robin he replied, "Nobody. Nobody can play me but me."

Jackie was moving in some pretty glamorous company now, as Rex Reed reminded her: "Heads turn when you go anywhere," he said. "You sit in Hollywood, at Mateo's or Chasen's or the Bistro, and Barbara Walters hops over to your table. And Barbara Stanwyck, and Sue Mengers and Bianca Jagger and Moishe Dayan." Joyce Haber had written about Mateo's, an Italian restaurant so "in" that even she couldn't get a table. Then one night Jackie and Irving took her there. "We were ushered in ahead of Henry Fonda, who was still waiting for his table at the bar," she remembers, amazed. "I suppose, in Hollywood, when you're hot . . ."

Jackie crisscrossed the country through the summer of 1970, but by October her attention was turning once more toward Hollywood, where filming was scheduled to begin in November, with Irving as producer. Frankovich had supplied her with special promotional stationery identifying everyone in the usual bewildering studio manner. Across the top it read: "Columbia Pictures presents A Frankovich Production." Along the bottom was the line: "Producer Irving Mansfield. Produced by M. J. Frankovich. Based on a book by Jacqueline Susann. COLOR." In October she appeared on *The Tonight Show* again, this time to introduce actor Brian Kelly, who had been cast as Robin Stone in the movie. Kelly was relatively unknown, but Jackie liked him and had high hopes for his portrayal of Robin.

On Thanksgiving Day, however, three weeks into the shooting, Kelly had a near-fatal motorcycle accident and could not continue. He was replaced by a lean and handsome young actor named John Philip Law, who had appeared as the angel in the infamous Jane Fonda picture *Barbarella*, and more recently as the semiarticulate young lover in *The Russians Are Coming, the Russians Are Coming*. Though tall and strikingly good-looking, Law was too young, and his acting style was too wooden, to handle the older and more complex character of Robin Stone. His screen image of the powerful sophisticate was not helped by the studio's insistence that he wear Kelly's wardrobe, which was inches too short in both arms and legs for his rangier physique.

As she had been with *Valley*, Jackie was disappointed with most of the principals in *Love Machine*, though she loved Shecky Greene as the comic Christy Lane. She was glad, too, that they'd been able to get veteran screen star Robert Ryan, who was brought in late to play network chief Gregory Austin and who gave one of the film's few solid performances. Ryan presented a special problem, since he had recently had an operation for lung cancer and was therefore uninsurable, a requirement the money people were always very sticky about on a major movie. She didn't know how the studio had worked it out, but she was happy to have him.

Ruth Batchelor, whose song "Robin Stone is Moving On" was used in the movie, recalls attending an early studio screening with Jackie and Irving. When Jackie's cameo appearance came on the screen it was roundly booed by the audience, which was filled with friends of the film's director, Jack Haley, Jr. Haley had had difficulties with Frankovich during the shooting and had evidently come to feel that Jackie was having too much influence. If she did have influence, it didn't get Jackie the movie she felt her novel deserved. She hated the final cut, which she viewed in March, 1971, but she managed to hold her tongue for a time, mostly out of a genuine affection for

Frankovich, whom she jokingly referred to as "G.W.W.," which secretly stood for "Great White Whale." A later item in *Show* magazine makes her feelings abundantly clear: "Did Jackie Susann like the film they made of her book, *The Love Machine?* She did not—not even with husband Irving Mansfield producing. Jackie says: 'I'll never understand why people buy a book and then make a movie that scarcely resembles it. It would have been nice if they had at least left the leading lady in. Or given Robin Stone a reason for belting a broad. Oh well, as the saying goes, "If you take the money, don't cry in your beer."'"

Batchelor recalls *The Love Machine* as "one of the worst movies in the world." She also recalls a bizarre fight that occurred during the filming of a party scene, shot at Danny's Hideaway. Frankovich seated her at a table with Dionne Warwick, then told her she should pick a man to walk out with, and they would appear as extras in the movie. Ruth picked columnist Earl Wilson, who happened to be seated nearby. "Irving went crazy, screaming at me, 'How dare you? Don't you dare!' I said, 'Irving, what are you talking about?' He said, 'Earl Wilson can't be in the movie. Are you trying to get me into trouble? Leonard Lyons will be mad that he wasn't in it, and then every damn columnist in this city will want to be in the picture.' Then Jackie got into the fray, insisting that I leave with her and Irving, and whisking me out to the waiting limo. Then she tore into Irving for yelling at me. And they had this huge fight, and there I am in the limousine stuck between them." Ruth remembers that Jackie loved Shecky Greene almost as much as she hated Dyan Cannon, who, she believed, didn't have enough class to play Judith. And Shecky Greene himself recalls a screening he attended with Dyan at which she laughed so hard—at the movie and at herself—that she had to get up and leave in the middle. For Greene, the movie was a disappointment after the book. "I loved the book. It's the first book I read after *Heidi*," he says. "Somebody should have had the balls, if you'll pardon the expression, to say this is the way she wrote the book and this is the way we'll do it. It should have had a stronger script, more sex oriented. Jackie wrote about sex and she wrote about this confused human being, this sadomasochist. But Frankovich was very authoritarian, and I think he was too concerned about his image. Jackie's story was not a picture for the same guy who came out with *Oliver.* . . ." Shecky liked Jackie, who was "very warm, very *haimish*; as soon as I met her I felt like I knew her ten years. She inspired me to write my own little scene, a kind of hillbilly sequence and it was kind of cute; it was what Christy Lane would have done. But they took it out."

Jackie loved celebrities. She wrote to Karlina in March, 1971, about a party they had attended. "Michael Caine was there . . . Diahann Carroll and David Frost . . . (that's a big romance) . . . Frank Sinatra, Burt Lancaster . . . the astronauts and Mayor Lindsay . . . it was like the great old days . . . (old . . . like in the forties . . . when New York was fun . . . post war excitement . . . God . . . just think . . . you weren't even born then . . .)." She mused about the freedom younger people had today, but then added that she was also sorry for them, "because it is a glum life . . . worry about wars . . . about ecology . . . about marching . . . about causes . . . we had more fun . . . there was gaiety and hope then . . . and it spawned actors like Bogart and Rita Hayworth and Grace Kelly and Marilyn Monroe and Tyrone Power and Gable . . . and it sure is a cinch that deep down the kids today want it back that way because they make a cult out of Bogie and Mae West etc."

Irving, though, was giving Jackie some problems. Despite her growing fame and wealth, and the ever-more glittery circles they were moving in, Irving, she felt, still played every situation like a street-tough stickball player from Brooklyn. Rex Reed had wondered about it: "Why does Irving manufacture all these fights and have all these big 'fallings-out' with everyone?" he'd asked her. "He writes nasty letters, he can't take any criticism. There's no telling what kind of demons are in his head." She always defended Irving publicly, but in private she was often angry at him, at his tough-guy mannerisms and also at what she was starting to see as his lack of culture. Everyone else seemed to know about Diane Arbus's reputation for photographing freaks, yet Irving let her take the awful photo for *Harper's* without checking her out. She often wished he would keep his mouth shut. Babbling while she was out of the room, he had told Kevin Kelly of the *Boston Sunday Globe*, "I mean, just see who's written about her, a girl who never went to college, who came to New York from Philadelphia when she was only 16 to make it as an actress. Liz Smith's written about her! *Cosmopolitan!* Rex Reed!"

For all her dissatisfactions, though, Jackie knew she owed Irving too much to even think of breaking up. He had worked hard for her success, and they had made a fantastic team. She could not be disloyal now, when he really had nothing else going for him *except* her career. Whether she loved him or not hardly mattered anymore; the truth was that she needed him, and she really did feel incomplete when he wasn't with her.

The same week Irving had infuriated her with his secret wheeling and dealing on the phone over those *Love Machine* movie rights, she had told a Philadelphia reporter, "I think you can do anything if you're not alone, I mean if there's a person you love with you. Once somebody asked me if I could sum up my greatest happiness in one word, and I didn't even have to think. . . . I said: Irving. I couldn't exist without him. . . ." Maybe she didn't love

Irving in the same way she had loved Joe E., but Irving was a part of her in a way Joe E. could never be, because Irving was always there for her.

Still, Joe E.'s death, in June of 1971, hit her hard. She had visited him in the hospital shortly before he lapsed into a diabetic coma, and as she was leaving he had told her, "Remember how I always said if you played your cards right, once was enough? Well, I was wrong. Once is not enough." The thought touched her deeply, and yet at the same moment the writer in her seized upon the phrase. It would become the title of her new novel, the one she had described to a reporter as a "frankly incestuous" story about a girl's lifelong love for her own father. "I think it happens to every girl who has a great father," she had said, admitting that she had worshiped Bob Susan. She had titled the book *The Big Man* in early notes, but now it would be *Once Is Not Enough*.

Jackie sat with Irving in Riverside Chapel as George Jessel delivered Joe E.'s eulogy. Jackie had known Joe E. better than all of them, and she was undoubtedly the biggest celebrity in the chapel. Still, she must have been at least partly glad they hadn't asked her. If she had talked about the real Joe E., would Irving have understood? She listened to Jessel's banal comments ("Joe E. was a friend to everyone") and his clumsy paraphrase of Joe E.'s trademark song ("Unlike Sam's pants, Joe E.'s life was too short"), and she remembered the kind and funny man who had given too much of his life to smoky gin joints and bottomless bottles. The McCandlish Phillips obit in the *Times* had caught Joe E. better: "His business was high comedy for low pay," Phillips had written, adding that Joe's fans had included "princelings of the underworld, ordinary nightclub patrons, bookies, jockeys, hotel keepers, showmen and cronies, as well as an impressive sam-

pling of persons of wealth and social standing, John Hay
Whitney among them.''

Jackie had given Joe E. a copy of *The Love Machine*,
but she knew he hadn't read it, just as he hadn't read
Valley of the Dolls, though he faked it beautifully at that
Brevoort party he gave for her in 1966. She hadn't known
it at the time, but he had asked his devoted girl friend,
astrologer Lynne Palmer, to read it and tell him everything
about it. Ever since his gangland beating, Joe E. had great
difficulty reading anything, it would take him weeks to
struggle through *Valley*. Palmer sat with Joe E. at Toots
Shor's, telling him the plot in full detail while he waved
friends away from the table and listened in fascination. She
still has the book Jackie gave him, inscribed: ''To Joe E.,
All my love—from your buddy—chum—pal—Jacqueline
Susann.''

Lynne heard a lot about Jackie, from Joe E., and from
her astrology client Billy Rose. She became so curious
about Jackie that she tracked down her correct hour and
date of birth, and prepared her chart. The following
paragraphs, edited and condensed, are derived from Palmer's reading of Jackie's horoscope:

> Born August 20, 1918, at 7:25 p.m. Eastern
> Standard Time, Jackie was a Leo with Pisces
> rising and her moon in Aquarius. Mars was her
> most ''elevated'' planet in Scorpio, so she was
> seen as an aggressive person. She had seven
> planets in ''fixed'' signs so she was stubborn, but
> she did have adaptability in her mar— riage
> house. As a Leo with four Leo planets in her
> chart she was ''the Queen Bee'' and difficult to
> please. Pluto is trine the Ascendant so there was
> happiness in her home, especially after she got
> fame in her career. Mars ruled her money house

which made her a big spender. She could be mean
and bitchy but she was generous with money,
loaning it and giving it to others. She could have
sex with men for money too. She kept sex and
love as two separate things.

Venus rules the house of children. Her child
would cost her a lot of money. She would get
angry about it, loving him but resenting his being
like that. She couldn't take pride in her child
which would have really bothered her. And Venus
ruled her writing house, so she would have done
the writing to get the money for the child. She
would have wanted the child to inherit money, but
there could have been battles in court. She'd
battle for money, fight for the child and get
published for the child. She was shocked with
how much money she ended up making. Venus
made her good and nice and kind to relatives, and
they would have cost her a lot of money too, but
her whole thing was the child much more than
anything else. Being separated from her child
because of an institution would have bothered her
emotionally very much, although it also gave her
the ability to hide away behind closed doors and
do the writing she had to do. She lived too much
in the emotions and was over-sensitive about the
least tiny thing, but most of the time she hid it
because the moon is in the 12th house.

Saturn rules her house of friends, which means
that she could use people or they could use her.
And the Saturn Pluto could have brought sneaky
unpleasant surprises like robberies in the home.
And visits to the child were always upsetting but
something she felt she had to do.

Leo was Jackie's strongest sign, her Midheaven,

fame and recognition, the strongest points in her
chart. Cancer is her second strongest sign, which
is what made her so sensitive and so emotional.
She could have done some drinking with this
chart, and with the moon-Neptune opposition it
would have been secret drinking behind closed
doors. It was to escape from pain. But she would
have been realistic and her mind would have
pulled her out of it.

She could have lost a lot of friends too with
this chart because she felt so sorry for herself.
Underneath she was a very negative person. The
moon opposition Saturn is real depression and
negativity, the separation from the child, lost
loves, not trusting friends, feeling rejected and
that few people love her. "Why does this have to
happen to me?" She really could not understand
why she was so unlucky.

Jacqueline Susann.   *August 20, 1918*
                              7 h 25 pm EST
                              75° W 10' 39° N 57'

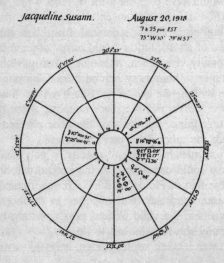

31

Tomorrow and to Morrow

> *Someone said to me, "Lauren Bacall is a star; Jackie Susann is a joke." I told them that Lauren Bacall gets paid to be seen two hours at night. Jackie Susann is sleeping and somewhere in Hong Kong or Germany somebody is buying one of her books. If you can make money while you are sleeping you are a star. Whether she was a joke or not she was a household name all over the world. And nobody can dismiss that.*
>
> ——Ruth Batchelor

JACKIE liked researching her books even more than she liked writing them. Her most amusing project so far had been interviews with men about their sex lives for *The Love Machine*. "Sex," she concluded, "is a thing apart for a man. He can have a devastating crisis one

439

minute and jump into bed the next. But to a woman sex is life, it's tremendously important. A writer must be aware of both sides of the coin.''

Jackie needed to research several topics for *Once Is Not Enough*. As she was now writing the book, her twenty-year-old heroine, January Wayne, a virgin, loves her father, Mike, with an almost openly sexual passion. Mike is a formerly successful movie and play producer, but he is now on the skids. To provide for January, Mike marries Dee Milford Granger, one of the ten richest women in the world, and a secret lesbian. Toward the end of the story Mike and Dee die in a plane crash on their way home from Cannes, where Mike has gone to play at the gaming tables.

For one thing, Jackie needed information on virgins. She tried to interview Karlina, but the girl was reticent. Joey and Cindy Adams gave her the idea of looking for sources at a beauty contest where the girls were coached in answering personal questions and expected them. Jackie signed on as a judge at the Miss Universe pageant. Irving was surprised she took so many notes. "I'm over forty," she told him, "and you still expect me to be a walking file cabinet."

"Over fifty," he retorted, "and a tape recorder."

Jackie's next objective was Poland, where, during World War II, Karla, a Garbo-like film star who is Dee Granger's lover in the book, had grown up. Jackie wanted to get a background as authentic as Tolstoi's in *War and Peace*, and give those double-domed critics something to think about. She enlisted Bea for the legwork; her friend pored over histories and maps, and prepared the material on Poland for Jackie.

Finally, there was Dee Granger's jet-set life. Jackie's old friend Dorothy Strelsin traveled with the ultra-rich, as did her new friend, Vera Swift. Both of them told her to go to Monaco, which worked out beautifully when Mike Frankovich invited the Mansfields to join him and his wife at the Cannes Film Festival. Jackie restrained herself from telling Frankovich how much she loathed his movie of *The Love Machine*; mercifully, it wasn't entered in the festival. Jackie didn't have time to shop. Her "Satellite," Ruth Batchelor, helped her pull together some outfits from her closet, and Jackie wrote to Ruth frequently about the trip.

"Dear Satellite—It's divine—I now play chemin d fer (?) spelling. The G.W.W. is in his element—we see movies—gamble—the silk jersey cape is a smash! Wore it at the Casino last night, with black hot pants (jersey) black jersey blouse—the lion belt—I looked like Superman. A producer wanted to buy it off my back for his girl—Love—The Sun!"

They stayed in a suite at the Carlton Hotel, lunched with Elizabeth Taylor and Richard Burton on their yacht, met scores of people, and threw themselves into the celebrity whirl. But the unquestioned high point of the trip, for an old Philadelphia girl who had always claimed a childhood friendship with Grace Kelly, was an invitation to a party at Monaco's royal palace. She wrote Ruth about it, on Carlton stationery:

I told you, or Earth, or Gemini, that we're going to a gala at Gracie's—(better known as Her Serene Highness). It's black tie—& "gowns"—so I am actually wearing the long black skirt and black jersey top, and doing it up with the lion belt and famous jersey cape. Binnie is also schlepping together an outfit. So far, Irving has been getting by with a bow tie on a business suit—but this great occasion defi nitely calls for an evening jacket. (Naturally the G.W.W. has an evening jacket. He probably has 6—but Irving would get lost in one sleeve.) But our G.W.W. insisted on taking Irving out and buying him a jacket as a gift. Off they toddled—

We all were having dinner—Rosemary and Earl Wilson, Mike and Binnie, Dorothy Strelsin, Irv and I, when the subject of our royal invitation came up. Mike said, "And wait till you see Irving in his white jacket."

Rosemary and I said together, "White?"

Mike insists Everyone at Monaco wears white jackets. I said they went out with high school proms.

Irving says he went along with it because (1) Mike was giving it to him as a gift. (2) Mike insisted white was in. (Mike is wearing blue.) (3) It was the only one in the shop that fits him. (Of course there are other shops, but Mike wouldn't let Irving be seen in anything but a Pierre Cardin jacket.)

So I merely ate my fish, and said philosophically— "Well, we can always tie-dye it."

Right now, hanging in our closet is the biggest most glorious whitest dinner jacket in the world.

We go to Monaco tomorrow and in this big palace will be a sunburned Jew in a white jacket and Grace Kelly will kill herself for having been my friend from Philadelphia.

The letter goes on to tell Ruth to read it to "Earth and Gemini" (Anna and Bea) and mentions one of their mutual friends touching another's "pussy." It is signed "Love, the Sun—Hell—who says I'm just the Sun—Maybe I should be Universe!"

Jackie's fame had cleaned up her language some in public, but even now she still dropped her guard with Ruth. When one of the *Love Machine* actresses appeared in *Playboy*, Jackie phoned to tell Ruth, "The girl has a purple bird!" She used the words "pussy" and "coose," and she always referred to a man's penis as his "cock." (A "prick" was someone she didn't like.) She loved to toss casual references to "blow jobs," "hard-ons," and "cock sucking" into conversations. And once she phoned Ruth to announce, "I think Joseph Ian's a fag—I can only find one ball." For all Jackie's love of vulgar language, Ruth feels, "Jackie didn't see herself as tough, hard, and cold. She saw herself as romantic, good, kind, and generous. She wanted to appear benevolent, strong, advice giving, and omnipotent, but in truth she was vulnerable, insecure in her taste, and obsessed with her age."

Their relationship had its rocky moments, though. In 1972, Ruth—by then a "women's libber"—was also involved in George McGovern's campaign. Jackie, still stinging from Gloria Steinem's review of *Valley*, regarded the Women's Movement as a "a bunch of bull dykes" and she viewed Ruth's involvement in the campaign as a great way to get publicity and refused to take her seriously. "You like guys," she argued, genuinely puzzled. "You like guys all the time. You need a warm body in bed." Yet when Ruth recorded an album of feminist songs, Jackie was instrumental in getting her an interview with Barbara Walters on *The Today Show*. Barbara led off with a question: "It says here you've been married three times. Are you going to try for four?"

Deeply into politics, Ruth was writing McGovern campaign songs and covering the Democratic convention for a radio station. With Bascia Hammerstein and other New York liberals, she decided to organize a kind of ad hoc McGovern club at a restaurant. The proprietor agreed. But Jackie, who had gotten to know Richard Nixon through their mutual patronage of the Poodle Boutique, suddenly became political. "Jackie called me up and said, 'You can't work for McGovern because Nixon is a friend of mine.'" Ruth told Jackie that Nixon was terrible and Jackie replied that he was "better for the Jews." At last Ruth told her in exasperation, "I'm your friend and your camp follower, but I have a mind of my own. I don't tell you what to do and don't tell me what to do."

Jackie settled the matter by calling the owner of the restaurant and telling him that if he went ahead with his plans, she would stay away and so would her celebrity friends.

The owner turned Ruth down even though pamphlets about the club had been distributed. Ruth furiously reported the incident to *Time* magazine, which called to verify the facts. Jackie denied it all, and Irving told Ruth the Mansfields were calling their lawyers. "She was a very generous friend, a wonderful friend," says Ruth, ". . . but if you crossed her . . . She felt that I had crossed her because I didn't take orders. I was the Satellite rebelling against the Sun in her mind. She was a great friend, but she had a gigantic ego."

Jackie's anger was enough that she tried to exorcise Ruth from her life. She threw away or gave away nearly every present Ruth had ever given to her, many to Bea and Anna, but not quite all. Later after Ruth moved to England, and the two made up, Jackie wrote to "Dear Eve," a reference to Eve Harrington, the manipulative acolyte in *All About Eve*. (Jackie had once told Ruth, "I'm Margo and you're Eve, and if anything happens to me you'll get Irving." Ruth had tactfully avoided pointing out that she didn't *want* Irving.) Describing the disposal of the presents, Jackie wrote: "Porky (Anna) asked me if I had given away the bag you brought me from Greece and I said loftily . . . 'Of course!' But I didn't . . . it was too damned attractive to give away and I also kept the Grecian Ankh. About ten days ago, I was having dinner with Melina

Mercouri and she said . . . 'That is a Greek bag you are carrying.' I told her it was a gift from a friend of mine from Greece. I think Melina would have liked it but I clung to it and it is now an integral part of my summer wardrobe . . . except that I can't wear it around Anna.''

Meanwhile, Jackie had acquired a "new best friend," though hardly a "satellite"—Doris Day, whose fanatic involvement with animal welfare struck a sympathetic chord. Their friendship began when Jackie dropped a note to Doris, remarking that Doris's poodle, Bobo, looked exactly like Josephine, whose ashes incidentally were now contained in a paperback book facsimile in her kitchen, Josephine's favorite room. Doris replied, and Jackie soon learned the life story of the wholesome "girl next door," about whom the acerbic Oscar Levant had once said, "I knew her before she was a virgin."

Doris, who told Jackie to call her "Clara Bixby" (she in turn called Jackie "Opal Mandelbaum"), had suffered more than her share of hard knocks. When she was a child, her father had run off with her mother's best friend, her brother was an epileptic after a baseball injury, and she suffered leg injuries in an auto crash at thirteen, which ended her promising career as a dancer. A brief teen-age marriage to an abusive musician left her with a small son, Terry, whom she supported in absentia by touring with a band. There was another bad marriage, followed by a third to agent Marty Melcher in 1951. When he died in 1968, Doris discovered that through mismanagement or outright fraud, he had frittered away over twenty million dollars of her earnings and had left her considerably in debt. Her son, Terry Melcher, gave up a lucrative career as a record producer to help untangle her affairs, and then a year or so later—after Charles Manson murdered Sharon Tate and her friends amid rumors that he had been driven to it by hatred for Terry, who had rejected his music—Terry himself "pressed the down button and went all the way to the bottom" with booze and pills. Then he cracked up his motorcycle, "splintering his legs like matchsticks." Doris prayed at his bedside, and after a recovery considered near-miraculous by the doctors she nursed him through his long recuperation. "Although he is thirty years old, it's the first time I've ever taken care of him," she told Jackie.

By now Doris was practically a recluse in her Beverly Hills home, caring for her son and her pets and venturing forth only to ride her bicycle and to raise funds for her "pet pet charity," as Jackie called it, Actors and Others for Animals. Day once led a raid on a slum shack in the San Fernando Valley, a "tiny Dachau for animals," where more than a hundred diseased and dying dogs were imprisoned. "I stood there, covered in dirt and blood, while they handed each dog to me in a towel," she told Jackie, "and the tears just started streaming down my face."

Jackie became convinced there was a book to be written about Doris Day's life, one that would ease Doris's financial problems and at the same time also inspire readers. "You could help so many people who think life is rotten and without hope," she argued, trying to convince the publicity-shy actress to at least discuss the notion with a publisher. Jackie spoke to her close friend Sherry Arden, now publicity director for William Morrow, who was in Los Angeles for an American Bookseller Association convention. Sherry was understandably enthusiastic, as was Marc Jaffe of Bantam, who was also in town. A meeting followed, and a best-selling book was the result three and a half years later.

Morrow, the publishing house where Sherry Arden now worked, had become Jackie's publisher earlier in 1972. The deal was sealed in April, the same month when the Mansfields moved Guy once again, this time to an institution in Austin, Texas, where he would remain for the next ten years. There is no way of knowing whether Guy comprehended that his mother had died or was moved by her death. Guy is forty years old, and his condition remains essentially unchanged.

The whole industry knew about the big fights at Simon and Schuster. Although Michael Korda still believes, "For the right money Jackie and Irving would have kissed and made up with Heinrich Himmler," others suggest that the rupture had more to do with personality differences. Jackie dreamed of working with a friend, and that meant Sherry, but the meeting with Morrow publisher Lawrence Hughes required some fancy footwork on Sherry's part. Hughes had heard that the Mansfields were "demanding and unpleasant," and was reluctant to attend a luncheon that Oscar Dystel at Bantam proposed. "I was dragged there kicking and screaming a little," Hughes recalls, "but Sherry convinced me that at least I should meet the Mansfields so we could sniff each other out. By the main course I had absolutely fallen for Jackie. She was bright, attractive, and lots of fun. She and Irving knew a lot about the book business—it was obvious that they were professionals."

Jackie continued working on her new novel. After a few months, Sherry tackled Hughes again. Jackie, she hinted, was wondering why he hadn't followed up. "I still had misgivings," he admits, "but in April another lunch was arranged—this time at '21' with Sherry and Jim Landis, the editor who would work on Jackie's book if we published it." On the way up town Hughes purchased three dozen yellow roses, and he left them in the cloakroom just in case—but he wanted to get to the bottom of Jackie's split with S&S. "Why do you want to come to Morrow?" he asked. "*The Love Machine* was well edited, aggressively promoted and advertised. What more do you think we can do for you?"

"I want to be published someplace where I'm treated like a person, and not like a money machine," Jackie answered. Her greatest frustration was that she couldn't get the weekly sales reports that would have enabled her to do the spot promotions she believed in. Jackie confided that things had got so bad at S&S that "some of the people hide when I come into the office." Hughes, satisfied, left the table for the cloakroom. Returning with the armload of yellow roses, he declared, "We think you're wonderful."

No word about money or contract terms passed between Jackie and Larry. That was left to Irving and Artie Hershkowitz. Victor Temkin, Bantam's house counsel, served as go-between in the complex negotiations. The biggest publishing profits were in the paperback edition, and those rights had gone to Bantam at the time of the Geis rupture. "If Morrow had the paperback rights it would have been a gold mine, but I would take a silver mine any day," Hughes decided. The contract between Morrow and Jackie's corporation, Sujac Productions, referred to the book as "Novel 3," and guaranteed an advance of $250,000, payable in five equal installments: one on signing, one on the book's publication, and the remaining three at intervals after publication. Hughes knew he would have to sell 210,000 copies (at a 15 percent royalty on a jacket price of $7.95) to recoup his investment. He was sure he could do it. Jackie's previous sales figures were 350,000 for *Valley* and 250,000 for *Love Machine*.

Hughes successfully argued that he was entitled to some share of the paperback proceeds since Morrow's editing and promotion would lay much of the groundwork for the mass-market edition. Bantam agreed to give Morrow $40,000 if the paperback reached a certain level of sales, which it eventually did. Morrow was also to share in the book-club and magazine-excerpt money. Irving and Artie demanded and got provisions that are seldom given to authors: weekly written sales reports for the first nine months after publication, approval of jacket copy and design, a promotion and advertising budget of $75,000 and five hundred free copies of "Novel 3" for Jackie's own use. In return the Mansfields made an unusual gesture. Sujac would contribute $37,500 toward promotional expenses. (Later, they increased their contribution to $75,000.) Sherry explains that Jackie and Irving "considered themselves partners in a publishing venture." She remembers Larry saying to her before the deal was struck, " 'Look, as publicity director you're the one who's going to bear the brunt of all this. As nice as they are, they are very demanding. You've got a lot of big books coming up; are you going to be able to handle this?' And I looked at Larry and I said, 'Larry, success is easy to handle. It's *failure* that's hard to handle.' "

With so much riding on the manuscript, Landis, thirty years old and not long out of Yale, was somewhat anxious. "I apparently was chosen for class. I had never edited anything like her before, and in fact had disdained *Valley of the Dolls*." Jackie decided that Landis's name was a good omen—although he was not related to either Jessie Royce or Carole. (In a far stranger coincidence, Lela Rolontz, the baby whom Jackie had cared for when she was a child, was now Sherry's assistant.)

Jackie was courted charmingly through the summer. At a party that Sherry gave in the Hamptons, Jackie looked up to see an airplane flying along the beach trailing a long banner emblazoned with ONCE IS NOT ENOUGH. Sherry also promised to cook a gourmet Chinese dinner for Jackie and Irving when the manuscript was delivered. There were delays, caused in part by Jackie's increasing medical problems, but when the book was finished in August, Sherry carried all the ingredients—including salt and pepper; Jackie's cupboards were still as bare as ever—to Jackie's apartment because she didn't feel well enough to come to Sherry's. "They said she had bronchitis," Sherry remembers. "She couldn't get rid of this cough. And she was thin, very thin." But the dinner, which Larry and his wife, Rose, attended, was a great success. It featured marinated butterfly shrimp, spareribs, and "an exotic duck that we hung up for a few days before."

"We were generally happy with the manuscript," Sherry recalls. "Most of it was first-rate Jackie Susann, although there were some problems and Jim would have to do some work on it." In fact, Jim Landis was to spend quite a few long, hard days at the dining-room table of the Central Park South apartment, eating sandwiches and going through the book "page by page, line by line." A lesser problem concerned two characters who, Landis explains, weren't believable. "Linda, for example, was too vulgar. It was fine to talk about fucking this and fucking that, but it didn't fit with her position in the world." Jackie saw his point and rewrote some of the dialogue and several scenes where Linda or David appeared.

The other problem, the *major* problem, had to be dealt with at once. Jim recalls the consternation around the office. "Our antiquated copy machine spewed out pages. People started to read them and they came to the ending, and everybody said, 'Oh, my God!' Larry was especially upset, and so was Oscar Dystel."

Jackie had grotesquely reverted to science fiction, bad science fiction, for the last fifty pages of her spicy roman à clef. Mike is dead, and Tom Colt, her Mailer-like lover, has jilted January. She inherits ten million dollars from Dee, but she is alone except for David, who cares only for her money. She takes a lot of sleeping pills and some sugar cubes laced with acid. Suddenly she finds herself on Yargo, the planet of Jackie's outer-space fantasy written twenty years before. On Yargo, January mates with "the Yargo," the most perfect man in the universe. "If he was the Yargo . . . then she had loved the Yargo all her life and loved her father because he represented the Yargo. And if he was Mike . . . then it was still all right because he wasn't her father now." Ordered to return to Earth, January protests: "No! I can't leave him. Not after just one night. Being happy just once is not enough!"

The book as it stood should not be published, but everyone was afraid Jackie would refuse to change it. Jim drew the assignment of broaching the subject to her. "So Jackie and I had a fancy luncheon alone together at the Russian Tea Room." As he chatted about possible areas to discuss, Jackie said, "Okay, cut the shit. Let's talk about the ending." For about half an hour Landis talked and Jackie listened. "All right," she said finally, "I can't promise anything but I'm going to go home tonight and I'm going to think about it. If I agree with you, then I'll try something. And if I don't, I won't." The new ending, while no longer precisely science fiction, was in some ways as perplexing as the original. As January stands alone on a beach at night, what appears to be a UFO lands. A man emerges who looks like her dead father. He takes her in his arms and says, "I'm not Mike." "Look," January answers, "this is my hallucination. So it's going to be my way." They kiss and sink to the sand, and "she knew it had been the moment she had waited for all her life." They hold each other "until they were united like the sand that joins the wave that draws it back into the sea." The paragraph is followed by an Associated Press bulletin marking "one year since the disappearance of January Wayne, heiress to the Granger millions." January's fiancé, adds the AP story, hopes that somehow she is still alive; her physician theorizes that she probably walked into the ocean and drowned.

Landis questioned Jackie about the new ending: "I said, 'Jackie, I'm still worried about the ending. You don't write the kind of books where people don't even know how the book ends. Is she dead or alive? Even I don't know. Do you know?' She said, 'Well, to tell you the truth, she dies. She's dead . . . but I've got to leave it like this, Jim. My audience takes this book to lunch and they sit at a lunch counter and they've just left their typewriters and they're reading it, and I can't kill her, for them.' "

There were of course lighter moments during the editing, one of which concerned a sex scene in which Linda tells January about the virtues of oral sex, and especially about swallowing semen, "swallowing part of him." January is disgusted, but Linda laughs at her. "It's also very good for you," she assures January. "It's loaded with hormones. It's also great for your skin. I use it as a facial mask whenever I can." She goes on to explain in graphic detail how she catches semen in a glass after "the hand bit," then pours it into a bottle and refrigerates it for later use. "You leave it on ten minutes until it stiffens, then wash it off with cold water. Why do you think I let that jerk from the advertising agency stay . . . I got half a glass from him."

In an earlier version Linda had described this tender scene to January, assuring her that the man had filled a milk carton. Landis had questioned it, and a rather delicate discussion ensued. At last Jackie impatiently asked what he was getting at. "Jackie, men don't produce so much ejaculate," Landis said, which evidently was news to Jackie.

She gave Landis a present, as was her custom (a monogrammed gold key chain), and the two became quite friendly after Jackie's initial wariness wore off. "She later told me she was scared of me, that I had a reputation for liking good books and she was frightened I was not going to like her book, and I think I said, 'If I hadn't liked it I wouldn't be editing it in the first place,' or something like that." In any case, Jackie had learned the value of editing by then. "She said, 'I'm going to be read by millions of people, and I want it to be right, and . . . you're my editor, so . . .' " They took walks together, speculated on whether you could see naked men through the windows of the New York Athletic Club. He worried about her persistent dry cough. Like many others, he was struck by the emptiness of her refrigerator. It contained only a package shaped like an egg carton with one object that looked like a small egg. Jackie explained that it was a Seconal suppository, adding, "You stick it up your ass and then you fall asleep from the tip of your toes." Realizing that only one of the suppositories remained, she rushed to the phone to berate Irving for using up her supply.

She was, at least, no longer hooked on Dr. Jacobson's injections, although she used the experience in her book. Linda convinces January to spice up her sex life by getting shots from a repulsive man whose name (shades of the critic John Simon) is Dr. Simon Alpert. In Los Angeles she must go to Dr. Preston Alpert, who is even worse. "She hated him on sight. He was tall with heavy sandy hair and a hawklike nose. His skin was bad and his long skinny fingers were clean but bloodless-looking. She preferred his brother."

Unlike Preston and Korda, Landis liked working with Jackie. "It was fun to edit her. She inspired you to edit her because she was the most receptive person I ever worked with. . . . If the most popular writer in America meets you and she says, 'I'll think about it,' and she not only thinks about it but she produces an acceptable new ending within two days, then you're more open to doing something."

In October, with the book scheduled for March, 1973, publication, a memo circulated: "Jackie feels strongly that no books should be in the stores prior to two weeks before publication date. She feels Simon and Schuster were wrong in getting a huge advance [early advance orders] and selling, she says, about 150,000 copies before publication date; this she feels, does not benefit a fast climb up the best-seller list." The memo warned that Morrow would have to ship early to California, "before books are shipped to, say, New York City, where she will make frequent trips to the stores to check up." Jackie continued to learn from past mistakes.

There were other memos: Jackie was concerned about the new Philip Roth book due out in May and wanted to be sure to get a jump on it (both books were to be Literary Guild selections in the spring); Jackie wanted no advance galleys sent to the *Kirkus Reviews* or *Publishers Weekly*, both of which had blasted her previous novels; Jackie was in the hospital during the February marketing meeting and could not attend.

Once Is Not Enough was published on March 20, and despite her overwhelming medical problems Jackie hit the publicity trail. In a July *TV Guide* article, she commented that plugging books on the talk shows "ought to rate combat pay." Recalling how no one had wanted her in the beginning, how Long John had taken her only because Letty had "threatened, cajoled and begged," and how she had gotten on Merv Griffin's show only because he was a friend, she wrote, "Almost every city has its own version of *Today*. At that time, there were Roger Grimsby and the late Gypsy Rose Lee in San Francisco, Regis Philbin in San Diego, Marie Torre in Pittsburgh, Tom Snyder in Philadelphia, Irv Kupcinet in Chicago. If you were willing to travel, you got on. I traveled! I made the list without *Today*, without the *Tonight Show*. I kept 'touring.' I went to Detroit, Cincinnati, Dallas, Houston. I developed sciatica from sitting on planes. On the ninth week I got the call. No. 1! . . . But when you sit in the No. 1 spot you're the biggest target of all. That's when I learned that some people were making it a business to Get Jacqueline Susann."

They hadn't gotten her, not yet. In her final illness, she

was facing the greatest challenge of all. But, as she often remarked these days, "there is nothing if you want it badly enough that you can't do."

Jackie went out of the gate like a well-trained filly intent on the finish line, the number one spot on the list she regarded by now as hers by right. Beginning with a first printing of 150,000 copies, and assured that books would be in the stores without four A.M. phone calls to her publisher, she saw a clear track in front of her.

On May 6, 1973, Frederick Forsyth's spy thriller *The Odessa File* relinquished the number one spot on *The New York Times* list to *Once Is Not Enough*, making it an unprecedented three in a row for the undisputed "Queen of Popular Fiction."

-------------------- 32 --------------------

Once Is Not Enough

*Jackie's father is gone now. So is Jackie.
But perhaps the love they shared can be
passed on as a lesson to other fathers—
and other fathers' daughters.*

—*Family Weekly Magazine*, November 3, 1974

"*B*ABY*, you gotta know how to walk away from
the table when the dice are cold," says Mike
Wayne, January's high-rolling father. "Like
all good gamblers" . . . Mike . . . "knew when to push his
luck and when to quit. . . . And if you asked him when
his luck ran out, he could tell you the exact day. Rome.
June 20, 1967."

Once Is Not Enough went to the typesetter in October,
1972. Three months later Jackie's luck ran out. She could
tell you the exact day. New York. January 18, 1973.

She had become aware of breathing problems and a

persistent cough in May of 1971, but had dismissed it as some kind of allergy. By the next year, after periods of seeming improvement, the cough got very bad. By August she was wracked by spasms of coughing, but she went to that party in the Hamptons and later wrote Larry Hughes a cheery note on bright yellow stationery: "Would you believe anyone could be this tardy in thanking someone for a divine dinner party, a beautiful Peruvian necklace—and a banner streaming across the sky?... I have spent every moment at the typewriter.... Again thanks for being so very nice." She naturally didn't add that she was practically living on codeine to control her cough, and that it wasn't working anymore.

Rose was worried about the cough and was pushing her daughter to "get tests." Jackie promised to, then delayed, not really wanting to know. But by January, with Sherry and Lela sending constant memos about promotion plans, she faced the fact that she could no longer procrastinate. Publication date was March 20, and she would have to be in condition to perform. Her first day in Philadelphia was typical of what was to come: A telephone interview at 10:10 A.M., an *Inquirer* reporter at 10:30, which would probably run into lunch. Starting at 1:30 there were book-signing sessions—at Gimbels, Lit Brothers, and Strawbridge and Clothier—where she would meet people she hadn't seen in years who would expect her to remember their names. At 6:30 she would tape *Mike Douglas*. She couldn't get through all that doped up on codeine, even assuming the stuff actually worked. And she couldn't do it coughing her head off.

Jackie called her internist, Clifford Spingarn, who admitted her to Doctors Hospital on January 11. She remained there for five days. X-rays revealed a nodular lesion in the right lung area. Spingarn transferred her, on January 16, to Mount Sinai, a larger hospital with more extensive facilities, for a bronchoscopy and biopsy. She gave her birth date as August 20, 1925, taking seven years off her age; actually she was fifty-four. Her general condition was good, except for her lungs; her heart normal except for mild tachycardia—rapid heartbeat. Her lab tests were normal except for a high sedimentation rate attributable to cancer.

The bronchoscopy, performed on January 17, showed a mass in the right main bronchus. Jackie had "no uncommon reaction" but complained of an agonizing sore throat on awakening, for which she was given ice chips. The diagnosis was "metastatic breast carcinoma," though there was evidently some debate among the doctors about whether it was instead an original and separate lung cancer, requiring perhaps more surgery but fewer chemicals.

The official diagnosis, metastatic breast carcinoma, was delivered to Jackie on the evening of the eighteenth by Spingarn, a stocky, balding, almost uncomfortably candid physician. He gave it to her straight—her cancer was so advanced that she might have only a few months to live. If Irving was present then, the fact was not noted in the records. In any case Spingarn apparently feared Jackie might be suicidal, because he wrote "lock all windows" on her chart and requested that he be notified at once if her private-duty nursing shift could not be covered. At midnight she was still awake but drowsy, with slurred speech, and coughing. At ten the next morning, January 19, she was discharged and left the hospital with Irving.

Jackie knew she would have to tell at least a few close friends, though she suspected at least one already knew the truth. Rex Reed had walked in on her unannounced, something she had tried hard to avoid. As Rex recalls: "Jackie said she had the flu or pneumonia. Betty Spiegel was with me and we walked right into her room with balloons and all kinds of stuff, and we found her in very bad shape with tubes running out of everywhere, Irving looking ashen. So we knew how bad it really was.''

Of course, she had to tell Rose. Irving had explained that Jackie wouldn't be at her birthday party because of a bad cold, but Rose had insisted on talking with Jackie and become so upset that Jackie had finally blurted out, ''My cancer has spread, Mama, and I'm going to die.'' Later Rose said it was the first time Jackie called her ''Mama'' since childhood, and Jackie said it was the only time she ever heard her mother cry.

Jackie was not yet ready to tell any of her friends at Bantam or Morrow, though memos were arriving constantly about publication parties and the New York publicity schedule, which would begin on March 5 with an interview by Rex. Luckily the parties were to be more low key and intimate than the previous great productions. (As Irving would say later, ''The folks at Morrow were practically like family.'') A small celebration lunch was planned for March 4, with only Larry Hughes, Sherry, Oscar Dystel, and their spouses, ''and maybe Jim Landis, too . . . Joseph, of course.'' And there was to be a small party in the Hugheses' apartment on March 14, a few days before the official publication date.

Jackie had begun cobalt treatments and daily chemotherapy injections shortly after her lung cancer was diagnosed, and by early February she was feeling somewhat better, her wheezing and coughing lessened. The powerful drugs* she was receiving though, sometimes made her depressed and agitated in addition to the horrendous physical side effects— hair growth, hair loss, acute nausea and vomiting, fever and chills.

---

*These included Oncovin, derived from a common flowering herb, the periwinkle, which causes sever constipation, abdominal cramps, and loss of neuromuscular control. Methotrexate, with ''a high potential toxicity'' like others, can cause kidney damage, skin ulcers, decreased resistance to infection. Halotestin, a male hormone, can cause ''virilization'' in females.

She was back in Doctors Hospital from February 19 through the twenty-eighth, her condition diagnosed as "weakness, apparently resulting from chemotherapy and cobalt treatment." She grew a beard, which was removed with a six-week course of electrolysis. Then she lost all the hair on her head. Her face was swollen and sore, but when the electrolysis ended her skin was more radiant than ever, and friends commented on her luminous beauty. Her scalp hair started to grow back again and it came in soft and curly, far prettier than before. On tour she performed with only slightly less than her customary vigor, keeping her eye on every detail. A memo from Jim Landis dated March 5 informs the staff: "Jackie Susann has asked that we tell absolutely no one that the blue eyes on the cover of *Once Is Not Enough* belong simply to a model. She feels that there will be speculation about just whose eyes they are and that she will fuel such speculation as a publicity angle. So if anybody asks, we don't know nuthin'."

In March she had a full schedule in New York alone, including interviews with Rex, Gene Shalit, Eugenia Sheppard for the *New York Post*, *Time* magazine, UPI, Barbara Bannon of *Publishers Weekly*, Mort Sheinman of *Women's Wear Daily*, *The Today Show*, NBC radio's *Monitor*, Long John, Dr. Joyce Brothers, and *Midday Live*. In a photo that ran with the Eugenia Sheppard interview in the *Post* on March 13, Jackie looked bloated and unglamorous; an even worse picture of her appeared in the *Daily News* on April 2. By then she was back in Doctors Hospital, where she remained until the fifteenth, suffering from pneumonia, Irving explained to friends. In fact she did have pneumonia, and had spiked a fever of 104 degrees. X-ray treatments were now added to her other cancer therapies and her antipneumonia regimen.

Jane O'Reilly's review of *Once* appeared in *The New York Times Book Review* on April 1, sarcastically subtitled

"A guide to the good parts of Jacqueline Susann." Again it was largely negative, and again there were objections. Larry Hughes's letter complained that O'Reilly had "broken a cardinal rule of book reviewing" by synopsizing nearly "the entire plot of the novel. . . . It is no secret that her novels depend in part for their vast readership on their 'what happens next?' quality. . . . And so it strikes me as terribly unfair. . . ."

Hughes needn't have fretted. An earlier reviewer in *Publishers Weekly* had written: "Our girl has done it again. There is no place for this sensational novel to go but straight up the best seller lists." And so it did. On May 6, its fifth week on the *Times* list, *Once* bumped *The Odessa File* to claim the number one spot, shoving *Jonathan Livingston Seagull* down to number three. It would stay number one for nine weeks. Jackie was in Los Angeles when she got the news, appearing on *The Tonight Show* and *Merv Griffin* and being interviewed by the *Los Angeles Times* and the *Hollywood Reporter*. Jim Landis's telegram to the Beverly Hills Hotel said: "Take nothing for granted, darling. Except publishing history. And my happiness for you and pride in you. Love to you both."

It was probably on this trip that she had her chance encounter with Norman Mailer, supposedly the model for the underendowed Tom Colt. As Mailer recalls it: "I never knew her but I did see her once on the steps of the Beverly Hills Hotel as one of us was going in and the other was coming out. She had already written that unflattering portrait of me but I didn't even know it then. People don't rush up to you and say, 'Hey, look, so-and-so has just done this or that kind of job on you.' So we smiled and said hello. She looked a little uneasy, as if waiting for me to say something, and I was surprised that she was looking uneasy. Of such is innocence. Each to his own heel." Jackie told the story differently. According to her Mailer had whispered, "That's all right, Jackie, I'm taking a swipe at you in my next book."

She had just discussed Mailer in a *Washington Post* interview, in answer to a question about why people called her a commercial writer. "If Norman Mailer after his first book had written three successful books, he would have been a commercial writer," she explained, naming Leon Uris, Harold Robbins, and Irving Wallace as writers whose success Mailer had failed to emulate. "But Norman Mailer wrote one great book and then his next two weren't good and he went into essayism. . . ." She went on to explain why she wrote in simple, straightforward English, which she had learned from Hemingway. "I've always felt that I want to be a good storyteller," she added "If I ever wanted to be literary I could write a piece but I think there are so many fine literary people around who are starving."

She had met the *Post* reporter, Joyce Illig, "wearing a shiny black wet-look jump suit belted with black leather and buckled in large clinky gold. A gold ankh pendant bounces against her bosom. Her hair is neat, she explains it's a Donald Brooks wig." She looked "as if she could use a double order of french fries, cheeseburger and a chocolate malted," Illig had noted, but explained that "Irving thinks Audrey *Hepburn* is fat." She described her research into girlish innocence while judging the Miss Universe pageant in Puerto Rico. "Would you believe that 96 per cent of them were virgins?" she asked, adding that she had made her heroine in *Once* a virgin, because "everybody was a virgin once." She also had some comments on the Women's Movement, having evidently had time to reconsider. "As far as woman's liberation goes, I am for it in certain ways," she said. "I've been woman's lib from way back when I said to Irving before we got married, 'I'm not going to cook. I'm not going to run a house.' I said right away, 'Let me say one thing to you: I love you more than anything in the world but my career is more important than marriage.' ''

Jackie's Los Angeles doctor was Henry Jaffe at Century City Hospital, and she was seeing him daily. She bumped into Susan Hayward outside the lead-lined radiotherapy room, and Laurence Harvey dropped by to talk, complaining incessantly about his imminent death without ever realizing that Jackie was in the same condition. She didn't tell him because she wasn't telling anyone, though she did break her silence with one friend, Joanne Carson, recently divorced from Johnny, still severely depressed and suffering from hypoglycemia. She and Jackie had been friends since the early sixties, and Jackie had counseled her on her marital difficulties, advising that Johnny's infidelities weren't important and that Joanne shouldn't break her heart over them.

Joanne invited Jackie to see her house. They toured the garden and then settled into a love seat in Joanne's little sitting room facing the pool. ''We had a fire going in the room, although it was spring. I had a little Yorkshire terrier named Samantha, and I remember Sam was curled up at Jackie's feet—she had her shoes kicked off and her feet tucked up under her. Animals just gravitated to her. . . . Jackie was wearing very brightly colored silk things and she looked gorgeous, but it was a gray day and I was very sad. I told her I didn't have anything to live for, and she got angry, she jumped on me. 'What do you mean you have nothing to live for? You have your whole life. You don't know how lucky you are.' And then she said, 'I have everything to live for and I don't have a chance. Now *find* something to live for.' ''

Together they went to a small chapel Joanne had set up in a spare room, and they prayed and lit candles to Saint Theresa, the ''Little Flower.'' ''Jackie was a good person,'' Joanne says. ''She really was a great lady for all her temper tantrums and her aggressiveness and her flamboyance.'' At another point they discussed Jackie's conversion, and Jackie joked that ''Liz Taylor or someone had converted *to* Judaism, so that helped keep the balance.'' And she adds, ''I don't know what Jackie prayed, but I prayed that Saint Theresa would take care of her and protect her from pain.''

Not long after their talk Joanne began attending nutrition lectures to deal with her hypoglycemia, which led to returning to college and an eventual Ph.D. in nutrition. ''Jackie was key in my life, a very strong guiding force,'' she says. She remembers Jackie and Irving as ''a perfectly matched pair. Her attitude was 'He takes care of all the problems. Whatever it is, let Irving take care of it—the nuts-and-bolts things.' ''

Irving was taking care of those nuts-and-bolts things, especially those sales figures from Morrow. In one of Landis's later ''Dear Irving'' updates he reported: ''Total sales from the Literary Guild and Bargain Book Club as of January 31, 1974, were 519,742 copies. The earnings on these sales are $117,087.54. We received a guarantee of $75,000 so we are still due $42,087.54.''

Hardcover sales of *Once*, including the book clubs, would total 1,250,000 copies. But Jackie was yet again convinced that her book would have done better had a political disaster not interfered: ''Watergate has knocked off everything,'' she complained. ''When women get home at night they want to turn on the television set and watch the hearings on replay, not read novels.''

Anyone else as sick as Jackie could probably have done little more than watch television themselves. Her treatments were so intense and so debilitating that most patients on her regimen would have thought it a big excursion to go out for dinner. Yet Jackie stayed on the publicity trail from the day she left the hospital in mid-April until she collapsed on the twenty-fifth of the following October. Doctors were located in almost every city, and somehow the veil of secrecy was maintained. A more light-hearted secret was the fact that she often traveled with Joseph Ian, whom she concealed at some hotels. Still harboring guilt at her "neglect" of Josephine, Jackie took her poodle with her frequently. When necessary, she smuggled him onto airplanes in her oversized purse, but she didn't like to do that. Typed in caps on her air travel schedules was the frequent reminder "YOU HAVE PET APPROVAL." This must have irked Irving, who had never felt the same affection for Joseph that he had for Josephine. After Jackie died he gave the dog to Louise, their housekeeper, leading Sherry Arden to observe that "Joseph went overnight from being a rich dog to being a poor dog in Harlem."

With all her physical trials and the publicity demands, Jackie somehow continued to write. She was discussing a musical based on *Valley*, to be called *Helen and the Three Dolls*, and she sold a story about a pigeon named Gwendolyn to *Family Circle*, charging only $2,500 because she was fond of the young fiction editor, Myrna Blyth. In the summer she had lunch at the Four Seasons Restaurant with Lenore Hershey, editor of *Ladies' Home Journal*, and the magazine's managing editor, Dick Kaplan. Jackie was in a confessional mood, not about her cancer but about Guy. Lenore suggested an article, but Jackie decided she wasn't ready to do it yet. The talk turned to Jacqueline Onassis. "How about an article about 'Jackie S on Jackie O'?" Lenore suggested. The result was a novella, which Jackie delivered in the early fall. Kaplan remembers, "The price was twenty thousand dollars for twenty thousand words," but what Jackie actually turned in was around thirty-eight thousand words; it was cut by Kaplan and Mary Fiore. The cuts were restored when it was published as a "novel" by Morrow in 1976, two years after Jackie's death.

Dolores ran as a "book bonus novel" in the February, 1974, issue, the most successful one the magazine ever had. Jackie got the top cover line, and the story inside featured a photo of her, wearing a long dark dress and a large ankh, seated before a portrait that almost resembled Jacqueline Kennedy Onassis. Jackie was proud of the story, and she might have been prouder still if she had seen her fiction proved true. After Aristotle Onassis died in 1975, it became known that his marriage contract—indeed his marriage to Jackie Kennedy—was much like Jackie's speculations. She felt she had captured the sadness of women's lives in the novella; the heroine's very name, Dolores, means "grief." Even the most beautiful and gifted women are torn between love and practical economics, Jackie believed, compelled to sacrifice one for the other. Her feud with Steinem behind her, she was now in favor of the Women's Movement, considering herself a prime example of emancipation.*

When Morrow decided to republish *Dolores* as a novel, there were rumors that Irving had hired someone to finish it. Indeed, there had been rumors all along that Jackie had been getting help from some secret "ghost," and a couple of names were mentioned as possibilities. Don Preston, surely no fan, is doubtful. "The books are just too much like Jackie's letters and even her speech," he says. "I can't imagine any professional writing all those choppy non-sentences." Dick Kaplan believes the book *Dolores* is nearly identical to the original manuscript, before his cuts. In any case, the novel was far shorter than Jackie's

---

*After her death some feminists acknowledged her contribution. A 1986 book called *Remaking Love: The Feminization of Sex*, by Barbara Ehrenreich and others, included a persuasive reevaluation of Jackie and her girl friend Helen Gurley Brown in the chapter called "Up from the Valley of the Dolls: The Origins of the Sexual Revolution."

previous books. It sold close to 175,000 copies and was of course on "the list," but did not reach number one. Morrow declined to publish a second posthumous novel, the early science fantasy called *Yargo*, and Bantam brought it out as a paperback original in 1979.

But back in May and June of 1973 *Once Is Not Enough* was still at the top of the bestseller list, and Jackie was promoting it. She finished her Los Angeles publicity in early May, but a month later she and Irving were back at the Beverly Hills Hotel, with Joseph Ian, for two grueling events. (They'd stopped in Austin on the way, a grueling experience in itself. Guy was handsome now; he looked like both Bob and Jackie but his face was unmarked by the worries of the world. She tried to tell him she was dying, that one day she wouldn't be able to visit him anymore, but there was no response to that.) The first event, a June 3 benefit on the Warner lot in Burbank, was for Doris Day's organization. Jackie had agreed to donate and autograph four hundred copies of *Every Night, Josephine!* and had persuaded her egomaniacal new "friend," Joan Crawford, to donate free Pepsi-Cola and one of her dresses for the auction. "Ethel Merman is a lady and a philanthropist compared to Joan," Jackie said later. "If I had known Joan when I was writing *Valley of the Dolls*, Helen Lawson would have been a monster."

Jackie got through the day somehow, though she felt feverish and faint in the hundred-degree heat. She was in and out of Century City Hospital, disguised in dark glasses and a kerchief, trying to gather her forces for a second party, this one in her honor, at the American Booksellers Association Convention. For the occasion, Morrow presented her with a five-foot-high reprint of its full-page newspaper ad mounted on cardboard: "May 6, 1973. Jacqueline Susann makes publishing history... only one, man or

woman, has ever had three No. 1 best sellers in a row.''
The party, in the Beverly Hills Hotel's Maisonette Room,
was being paid for by Morrow and Bantam. Doris had
agreed to be there as an added attraction, and although she
didn't know it, as a backup hostess because Jackie was
very weak. The day of the party, Doris tried to beg off.
Sherry Arden recalls that Irving had to get tough with her,
and that he sent Jay Allen to pick her up and make certain
she got to the hotel.

Jay Allen and Doris arrived at Jackie's suite about a half
an hour before the party. ''I didn't know how sick she was,
but I knew that something was very wrong and she was not
discussing it,'' Allen recalls. ''She was very pale, and I
said, 'Are you sure you can go through with this?' '' Jackie
insisted she could, but she asked Allen to find a tall
barstool and place it next to Bantam's Marc Jaffe at the
head of the receiving line. He did, but he worried that she
was in too much pain to attend.

One of the guests was Gerold Frank, who was in Los
Angeles researching his biography of Judy Garland. He
had interviewed Jackie for the book during the winter, and
he was struck by the change in her. She wore a long full
skirt, and she half sat, half leaned on the stool. ''My
overriding memory of her is at the party, sitting there on
the stool just high enough so she could sit with one leg
touching the floor and the other dangling, and shaking
hands with people and smiling and being, obviously,
someone in pain.''

In addition to a raft of celebrities, the guests included
hundreds of booksellers who had been shuttled over on a
bus, compliments of Simon and Schuster, from a gathering
at Irving Wallace's house. Jackie amazed Jay Allen by
greeting most of the booksellers by name before they were
introduced, her uncanny memory undiminished. *New York
Times* reporter Martin Kasindorf described Jackie that

evening as "an ageless pop-culture queen . . . raven-haired, deeply tanned and radiant. . . . [but] suffering from a mild flareup of the double lobar pneumonia, brought on by years of overwork, which nearly killed her in New York last winter. . . ." Eliot Fremont-Smith was in a corner watching, and Kasindorf recalled that the *Times* critic had asked, in a review of *Valley*, "Why should Jacqueline Susann pick up all the marbles?" Reminded of the comment, Fremont-Smith admitted that now he had the answer: "Her formula is action, movement. Her books just zip along. . . . Others try the same formula but their stories don't go anywhere. And she's a total professional. . . . Look at her over there. She's not drinking. She's working."

Jackie worked for two hours, then asked Doris to take over for her and retired to her suite. She was exhausted and began to doubt that she would keep up the schedule over the summer. Her new French publisher wanted her to come there in late June to promote *The Love Machine*, and she was tempted. France had been a thorn in her side since the poor showing of *Valley*, especially because she loved Paris as Bob had before her. Bob would have wanted her to go, she decided, to bring glory to the family name in France. She would do it.

After numerous rejections, *The Love Machine* had finally found a home in France with Pierre Belfond, a small publisher of serious books. He had originally bought the rights from a con artist who'd had no valid claim on them but who had passed himself off as a personal friend of Jackie's. The mess was straightened out, and Belfond acquired the French rights legitimately. His editor, Sylvie Messinger, recalls their excitement: "We wanted to make *The Love Machine* a bestseller. It was our first such attempt. But everybody told us, because of what had happened with *Valley*, 'Don't ask Jacqueline Susann to come to Paris, she is so difficult.' We were really afraid,

and we were afraid of Irving, who might think that our
first printing of twenty thousand copies was too small.

"We kept the English title because the word 'Love' is
very well known in France, and 'machine' will be *machine*," Sylvie explains. The book became the company's
first big commercial success, leading Belfond to refer to
his company as "the house that Jackie built." Sylvie
thinks she knows why the book outstripped others of its
kind: "When you read *The Love Machine*, after you have
finished you'll know very well how the TV business
works. A novel like *Lace* is not the same kind of book.
The details about the fashion industry are false."

Sylvie, like Dagmar Henne, Jackie's overseas agent,
maintains that her books are not considered "trash" in
Europe. Instead, as Dagmar explains, they fall into an
intermediate category, sometimes called "entertainments,"
which is below "literature," but well above such mass-
produced fiction as the Harlequin romances. In Europe,
writers of "entertainments," are respected for what they
are—not artists but storytellers—and the Europeans are
puzzled that we do not make a similar distinction. "Jackie
had a great gift for conveying glamour," Dagmar adds.
"That was very new to us."

Sylvie was impressed and amused with Jackie's own
glamour and had no idea she was ill. "She looked like an
old star," Sylvie says. "She looked like she was coming
from Hollywood, not from New York." *The Love Machine*
became a bestseller in France and is still selling there
today, outstripping *Valley*.

Jackie sparkled, charming the French press with sincere
and intelligent questions about their country. But she was,
in fact, fatigued, and at one point she had to cancel a party
in her honor. Pierre Belfond stopped by her Ritz hotel suite
to see how she was, and he was shocked to see in her
bathroom an elaborate array of medications, including

syringes for self-injection, and an assortment of "*flacons*" containing unidentified potions.

June was an exhausting if exhilarating month. *Once* was sold to Paramount in a deal involving no up-front money, but a straight 10 percent of the movie's *gross*, an arrangement normally offered only to top performers. In fact, the deal had another *raison d'être*: It would avoid inheritance taxes by deferring payments, in case Jackie died before the movie was earning money. She had faced the fact that she might not live to see the movie's release.

Also in June, just before she left for Paris, the U.S. Supreme Court extended the right of local communities to ban books, magazines, plays, and motion pictures that a jury of "average persons applying contemporary community standards" found obscene. Despite her case against *Beyond the Valley of the Dolls* (which really had to do with unfair business practices), she had no hesitation in making her anticensorship position known. She gave interviews and appeared on panels, sometimes being quoted with such heavyweights as John Updike and Joyce Carol Oates. She was witty if often earthy ("Think of how many girls in the Ozarks went wrong without any books or movies at all. With only Uncle Clem to misguide them"), but her concerns were practical: "They didn't even have the guts to make a real ruling," she fumed. "How dare they leave it up to local community standards. Why one nut who owns a drugstore can blossom overnight into a big-time book banner now. And don't think he won't." It was not, she hastened to point out, a matter of her own personal writing style being cramped. "I'm going to write as I always did," she said. "What's terrible is the new talent coming up. Will they get a chance?"

The campaign seemed to transform Jackie herself. Gone— for a time, at least—were the flashy "wet-look" jump suits and her other jazzy costumes. For at least that summer she

wore classic suits and dresses, her wigs and makeup subdued and quietly elegant, her image more Clare Boothe
Luce than Broadway Doll, as if she wished to be remembered as a serious, intelligent woman with something of
value to contribute.

In August she celebrated her fifty-fifth birthday, feeling
lucky to have made it after the doctors' predictions. She
had still not put her affairs in order, and she was still
putting off the question of her will. She knew it was
important. There were friends to whom she planned to
make bequests, some of them substantial. Bea and Anna
could both use the money, as could her housekeeper,
Louise. And so could her faithful masseuse, Roberta,
whose eyesight was now failing. She had promised to
"take care of" Roberta, and had even told the Witkins,
also Roberta's clients, that she would do so. Most of all
there was Guy—and Rose, whose care was also expensive.
Who knew how long Rose might go on, despite her strokes
and her heart condition? (Rose died in 1981. Her obituaries listed Guy Mansfield as her only survivor.)

There also were charities Jackie felt strongly about, the
Damon Runyon cancer fund, research into autism, animal
care. She had inquired about the cost of funding a research
chair at Rockefeller University, written to Jacques Cousteau
to ask about his upcoming projects, talked about a "Jacqueline
Susann Ambulance Service" for New York's stray animals.
There was so much to do, and even though she knew money
would keep coming in, she couldn't really know how *much*
there would be and whether it would cover all the things she
had in mind. Always nervous about money, she had squirreled
away as much as she could in cash, at least $50,000 in one
safety deposit box, according to friends.

In September she was off to London to promote the
British edition of *Once*, and this time she had an entourage. Doris Day's friend Racque Rael was going at the

same time, and they persuaded Doris to join them. The party stayed at the Dorchester with mountains of luggage, Doris remembers, but the clothes came in handy in London, where "we went out every night."

One of those nights proved embarrassing because Jackie was in a foul mood. The Harley Street physician who treated her mentioned that her mastectomy might not have been necessary. They were having excellent results with simple "lumpectomies" in England, he said. All that mutilation for nothing! And they hadn't even stopped the cancer. That night during dinner at Les Ambassadeurs she made a scene over what she thought was an overcharge on the bill. The incident was picked up by the seamy London press, which had also salivated over some ill-considered photos Jackie had permitted of herself, supposedly exercising in a shiny black romper suit with her bottom thrust out toward the camera. The tantrum at Les Ambassadeurs would have repercussions the following January, when John Mills, the proprietor, encountered the Mansfields at New York's Raffles disco. Mills made obscene gestures at Jackie, Irving objected, and in the fracas, Mills clamped his arm around Irving's neck and Jackie screamed, "Let go of my husband's neck! You're choking him!" This incident also made the papers.

Her British publisher, W. H. Allen, held an elegant black-tie dinner party on September 24, shortly before the altercation at Les Ambassadeurs. The party, held on the terrace roof of the Dorchester, was attended by "all the film industry of England," as one publicist put it. Certainly celebrities abounded, including Carroll Baker, Melina Mercouri, who was to star in the upcoming movie of *Once*, and Mercouri's husband, Jules Dassin. Jackie worked the party as she had worked the press, according to Margaret Gardner, who was hired to help with the publicity in England and France. But during the trip, Jackie and

Doris grew much closer. In one of their long, midnight talks, Jackie revealed that she had cancer but she minimized it. "She told me that the doctors had found a couple of little spots on her lungs. She said, 'Everything is fine now.' She didn't even hint that it was terminal."

Back home in October, Jackie took a short vacation in Palm Beach and returned with a fever that sent her back into Doctors Hospital. She was there from the twenty-fifth to the twenty-eighth, treated for a respiratory infection and suspected hepatitis, but hospital notes commented that she was doing "relatively well" on radiation and chemotherapy. She left the hospital somewhat depressed, but then she was always depressed these days when she returned to New York from Europe or Florida or California. New York looked so dirty and seedy now. In November, when the *Times* asked what advice she would give to the next mayor, she said, "Take care of the traffic, make Broadway clean and beautiful and clean up the massage parlors." She added that he would need "a hell of a good public relations man. Unfortunately, I can't lend the mayor my husband Irving."

In November she had a liver scan, which was repeated in California in December. The cancer had spread to her liver. In February a bone scan revealed it had spread to her spine. The will, she knew, could no longer be delayed. She signed it on February 6, 1974. And, considering the intentions she had so often expressed to friends, the document, drawn up by Arthur Hershkowitz, is a peculiar one indeed.

It begins conventionally enough, directing that her debts be paid and protecting property that had already passed to Irving. Irving is given the car and household furniture, while Bea Cole Roubicek gets Jackie's sable coat. All her other furs and clothes are to be shared equally by Bea and Bonnie (Bonita) Silberstein, her close friend from the Beverly Hills Hotel, and all of her jewelry goes to Anna.

She had not worn the furs much since her involvement in Doris's animal crusades, and at one point she had casually offered them to Sherry Arden, who had declined.

In the next item, fifty thousand dollars was placed into a trust fund for the "Guy Mansfield Scholarship trust," the income and principal of which, until exhausted, were to be used for the education of minority students. A second bequest of fifty thousand dollars was left for Rose's care; whatever remained in that fund at the time of Rose's death would revert to Jackie's estate. Irving was then left "an amount equal to one-half of my adjusted gross estate."

Following these major bequests there is a list of twenty specific bequests, ranging from $1,000 to as much as $25,000 (Anna and Bea). The list includes individuals— the Chau children, Louise Valentine, Jackie's housekeeper, and her two daughters, Margaret Roberts ("Roberta"), and several friends and relatives. A final item concerns "Robert Jelenik," for whom no provision is made "for reasons he well understands." The bequests, in addition to her works of art and books (all left to Anna) and Joseph Ian (left to Bea, with an additional $5,000 for his care), total $159,500, including $5,000 each to The Fund for Animals, Bide-A-Wee Home Association, and Actors and Others for Animals, "in the name of Doris Day."

The list is not surprising, since it includes charities and people Jackie often said she meant to provide for. What is surprising, even mysterious, is the wording that precedes the list: *"If my husband does not survive me, I give and bequeath:"* The effect of those eleven words, because Irving outlived her (a near certainty under the circumstances prevailing when the will was drawn), was to render all of the twenty bequests null and void. In short, no one on that list—including the animal funds and her close friends Bea and Anna—would get a single penny—or book, work of art, or dog—under Jackie's will.

It is pointless to speculate about how or why this result
came about, or whether Jackie intended it. How much
attention she was paying to the details of a legal document
by then can't be known, but it may be noted that the name
of her cousin Robert Jelinek is misspelled in the document,
an error Jackie would not have been likely to make herself.

She then bequeaths "all the rest, residue and remain-
der" of her estate to a trust fund, the income and principal
of which are to be paid to Irving and/or to Guy "in such
proportions as the Trustees may determine in their absolute
and unreviewable discretion. . . ." Whatever, if anything,
is left after Irving and Guy are both dead—but not until
then—is to be divided among several charities, including
funds for research into autism, cancer, heart disease,
multiple sclerosis, muscular dystrophy, and "the protec-
tion, care and welfare of animals." Irving is named execu-
tor and Irving and Arthur Hershkowitz the trustees, with
power to invade the principal of the trust fund "in their
absolute and unreviewable discretion."

After Jackie's death, the obituaries made much of her
bequests to charity. *The New York Times* reported, "The
family has established the Jacqueline Susann Cancer Research Fund at Rockefeller University." The *Philadelphia
Inquirer* stated, "Jacqueline Susann has left half her . . . estate
to charity, and the rest to her husband." As noted, though,
none of the charities mentioned was slated to receive any
money at all from Jackie's estate until after Irving and Guy
were dead, and if the trust was exhausted—which, as also
noted, could be at the trustees' absolute discretion—the
charities would receive nothing from the estate at all.

Irving was of course free to make charitable donations
in Jackie's name. A friend is reported to have said,
"Irving gave Jackie what she wanted while she was
alive—why should he let the money go to the dogs?" He
did encourage friends to contribute to Rockefeller Univer-

sity, and a small amount of money was received, according to a source in the development department. A year after Jackie's death, Irving made a donation on her behalf to a Catholic priest, Father Joseph M. Champlin, the author of several books on sex and marriage who had corresponded briefly with Jackie earlier. Champlin admired Jackie and her work, and had said so to his brother, Charles Champlin, entertainment editor of the *Los Angeles Times*, who mentioned the priest's feelings to Irving. Father Champlin then received a gift from Irving, a scarf Jackie had in turn been given by Coco Chanel.

Father Champlin's thank-you note was answered with a check, "a small donation to your church to commemorate my sadness." In response the priest conducted a mass for Jackie in the Holy Family Church in Fulton, New York. Though Father Champlin never knew Jackie personally, he feels that "obviously, there was some religious depth in the woman, even though, perhaps, she didn't remain faithful to it. She certainly was a person who was seeking for spiritual realities and was trying to make contact with God. My understanding is that the Jewish tradition does not have a strong belief in something more afterward. . . ."

There seems little doubt that Jackie was becoming much concerned with that "something more afterward," and especially with the possibility of a reunion with her beloved father in the afterlife. She talked about Bob often in interviews, speculating on the father-daughter relationship that had obsessed her for so long, and she seemed eerily bent on reuniting with Bob as her physical deterioration progressed. As she grew thinner and frailer, she became childlike at times, especially with Roberta when she was taking a massage. "Awent I a pwetty, pwetty baby?" she would ask.

It happened that the priest's brother, critic Charles Champlin, had been with Jackie during one of the most gallant moments of her life, her last free public appearance for a charity. At the urging of Joyce Haber and her boss, Buffy Chandler, Jackie had agreed sometime before to join a panel on "public taste" for the Amazing Blue Ribbon 400, Buffy's own pet cause. The event, held at the Chandler Pavilion in Los Angeles on April 1, was a huge and star-studded affair. Jackie was in no condition by then to make such a demanding appearance, but she couldn't make Joyce look bad with Mrs. Chandler, she said, and she couldn't resist the opportunity to take one more shot at that Supreme Court decision. On the panel with her, in addition to Charles Champlin, were Garson Kanin, William Friedkin (director of *The Exorcist*), and Helen Gurley Brown. Helen remembers that Jackie, whose weight had dropped below a hundred pounds by then, "seemed very frail, but even at that point I thought it was the old respiratory problem. She was just so fragile, but she got through the morning. She was practically carried off."

Jackie tried not to be alarmed about her weight loss. At least she liked the way she looked in bathing suits, and friends remember her in them often at the Beverly Hills Hotel pool, where she even took some diving lessons from the lifeguard a few months before she died. She favored one-piece suits with a single strap, and she had developed the trick of carrying a towel draped over one shoulder, covering the breast prosthesis.

One person even remembers her in a bikini, which she rarely wore because of the surgical scars. Dick Kaplan of *Ladies' Home Journal* was lunching in 1974 in the Polo Lounge with the magazine's art director, Herbert Bleiweiss, and Doris Day, whom they were trying to persuade to do an article for them, when Jackie appeared. "She is wearing a tiny little yellow bikini and a transparent robe and clogs and she is smeared with Coppertone," he recalls. "She comes clippity-clopping across the room and plumps herself down and starts to talk and sits there for twenty minutes. Now they had a dress code and here she was half naked, but she was Jackie Susann. They left her alone, after they tried to make Herbie put on a tie.'' He remembers that she ''looked pretty damn good, a little bony . . .''

She returned to New York and reentered Doctors Hospital on April 8, complaining of ''cough and chest pain and fever of two weeks duration,'' the record notes. She was in the celebrity room, 911, the one with the sweeping river view, though she was signed into the hospital as ''Phyllis Mandelbaum.'' And as she lay there for three days, gathering what strength remained to her, the cast of the *Once Is Not Enough* film was moving around Europe for location shots from Spain's Costa del Sol to Geneva and Montreux.

The movie was being produced by Howard Koch, with Irving listed as executive producer. It was directed by Guy Green, and it starred Kirk Douglas as Mike Wayne, with Alexis Smith as Dee, David Janssen as the Mailer-inspired Tom Colt, Melina Mercouri as the Garbo-inspired Karla, and Brenda Vaccaro as the sexually adventurous magazine editor, Linda. Jackie had secretly hoped to get Ava Gardner for the movie, but when Gardner was approached, she reportedly asked a quarter of a million dollars just to read the script. Paramount had held a competition for the role of January, and the finalists were Jane Seymour and Deborah Raffin, who won the role. The shooting schedule was set at sixty days. Julius Epstein, a most distinguished screenwriter whose credits went back to *Casablanca*, had written the script. Clearly he found the novel distasteful. When asked by *Times* reporter Nora Sayre if the father-daughter relationship was ''literally incestuous,'' he shook his head and said, ''I've got lesbianism. But I draw the line at incest.''

The movie drew the line at too many things, according to critic Andrew Sarris, who reviewed it in 1975. Calling it ''inexplicably timorous,'' he added that Epstein had ''lacked the nerve to take the late lady novelist on her own

outrageous terms. . . . The lesbian encounter between Alexis
Smith and Melina Mercouri is performed on tiptoe as if the
Screen were taking a Giant Step Forward to Maturity.''
Jackie lost on another scene she very much wanted, one
between Karla and her retarded daughter. It was cut.

Jackie was good-natured about the filming, horsing
around with Kirk Douglas on a bed for publicity shots and
doing her ''Hitchcock'' as a television reporter, but between the lack of harmony on the set and her own
problems, her heart wasn't really in it. Jackie grew fond of
Raffin and her husband-to-be, Michael Viner. She attended
their engagement party at the end of May. ''It was one of
the last parties she attended but she looked terrific,'' he
says. ''You wouldn't have known for a second that anything was wrong.'' She couldn't make their August 4
wedding but she sent *two* sets of china, along with a note
that said: ''One is not enough.''

Brenda Vaccaro had almost turned down the role of
Linda Riggs, January's ''lewdly liberated'' friend, and had
only been persuaded to take it by her ''father-in-law-to-
be,'' Kirk Douglas. Although she was never satisfied with
Epstein's script, she won an Academy Award nomination
as Best Supporting Actress for the role. She remembers an
improvisation, a temper outburst that Koch permitted over
Epstein's objections. ''I almost broke my goddam foot on
the banister because I kicked it, and I think that's what
probably won me the nomination,'' she says.

During filming in New York, Jackie had been a witness
to yet another of those bizarre moments of violence that
seemed to jinx the stars of her movies. While they were
shooting a night scene in which Deborah was crossing a
street near the UN, a car came careening along and
appeared to try to run her down. The mood of the cast
went from sour to explosive.

Jackie was in Los Angeles during May and June for the

film's wrap-up, and in June she was back in Century City Hospital to have fluid drained from the sac around her heart. Malignant cells were found in the fluid. A few days later she was back again, with a fever and an allergic reaction to the chemotherapy. She missed the booksellers convention that summer, giving the movie as an excuse, and Esther Margolis came up with an alternate idea for promoting the paperback of *Once*. Unaware of the real reason for Jackie's absence, Esther was "privately relieved because I was having trouble coming up with a new gimmick. We couldn't just have Jackie wandering around at ABA, and I had an idea I thought was delicious that didn't require her presence. We held a drawing for booksellers, with the winner to be flown to L.A. to appear in a scene in the movie." Esther telephoned Irving, and "I picked up from his voice that something was really quite wrong, really bad," she says.

He asked if Esther could fly out to Los Angeles, and she was on the next plane, accompanied by Bantam chief Dystel. What they learned was that Jackie would not be able to promote the paperback of *Once*, to be published, as always, on July 4. "We had dinner with them on Thursday night in the hotel restaurant," Esther remembers. "And Jackie, who looked fabulous, told us herself. She was quite thin but she was all made up, and truly radiant. They told us who knew at this point—it was a very small group—and they said they didn't want anyone else to know." They discussed the new novel Jackie still hoped to write called *Five Foot Two*, about a show business character who was a combination of Cantor and Billy Rose. She also still wanted to do a sequel to *Every Night, Josephine!* to be called *Good Night, Sweet Princess*.

They attended a party, and Jackie tried to fix Esther up with composer Marvin Hamlisch, who had also appeared briefly in *Valley of the Dolls* as Patty Duke's accompanist.

Jackie sent Esther out to buy a special dress for the occasion. "Marvin Hamlisch was on my right, Irving on my left, and Jackie on Hamlisch's right. He never talked to me the entire evening. He only talked to Jackie. Jackie kept talking over him to me so I would be included; it was very sweet."

Jackie and Irving had stopped off in Austin on the way home, to visit Guy. He was busy with a jigsaw puzzle, at which he was very adept. He was proud of the puzzle, but Irving remembers that when Jackie tried to hug her son he wriggled away. The trip marked Jackie's last visit to her beloved Beverly Hills Hotel, and it was also to be her last visit with her son, who had caused her so much pain and bewilderment in the twenty-seven years of his life.

Jackie entered Doctors Hospital at three-forty in the afternoon of July 1, complaining of a pain in the chest. Her temperature was 103, and the diagnoses were pneumonia of the right lower lobe and metastatic cancer of the breast, which had now spread to the liver, lower spine, pericardium (the sac that surrounds the heart), and right bronchial region. She was treated with antibiotics, while "multiple drug chemotherapies" and cobalt treatments to her liver were continued. On July 3 she was notably depressed, and on the fourth she complained of a dull headache, though the paperback's official publication cheered her somewhat. Esther was calling daily with news, and found her "fabulous on the telephone." Her temperature dropped for several days, then shot back up to 103 on the eleventh. She went home on the morning of July 16 on two antibiotics and cortisone, still running a fever of 100, her pneumonia improved.

She was home for less than two weeks, during which she tried to tell Joseph Ian that she would be leaving him soon, though of course he understood even less than Guy did. She talked to Bob's statue in her living room, a habit she had fallen into, and wondered again about the afterlife and what it would be like.

On July 18 she learned that dancer Betty Bruce had just died, also of cancer, in Roosevelt Hospital. Bruce was only an acquaintance, but Jackie had been preoccupied with her illness, even helping her financially. Bruce had developed her cancer after a particularly nasty and public divorce, which led Jackie to wonder if there might be some connection between Betty's life and her condition. "Sorrow can do that to a woman," she said. Betty's death hit her hard, as if it were an omen.

Jackie wrote veiled farewell notes to friends she hadn't seen and friends with whom she had had misunderstandings. Her insomnia was worse than ever but Anna had it too, and they spoke on the phone for hours in the middle of the night. Jackie, in her nightgown, fell near a window in their apartment, and Irving feared that she was trying to jump. He bought a pair of handcuffs and cuffed her to him for a while, but Jackie said, "I'm not your prisoner of Zenda," and he set her free. She denied that she was suicidal but said that the medications—so many of them now—often scrambled her brain. Sometimes she felt like a walking test laboratory for every new anticancer drug, antibiotic, hormone, and pain-killer.

She was far too ill to go on television, but she granted print interviews to *Family Weekly* magazine and the *Philadelphia Inquirer.* She owed it to Bantam, she said. *Once* was number one on the paperback bestseller list, but two and a half million copies seemed too much for Esther to move all by herself. Jackie's last interviews were laced with childhood memories, perhaps slightly laundered: "I saw my father in daily, ordinary ways. Then Saturday was our day to go out together. He'd take me to see Betsy Ross's cottage, to the waterfront for Italian ices, even to the prizefights. Mostly he took me to the theater and then we'd go backstage to visit his actor friends. He was a very successful portrait painter and many of the big names in the theater sat for him.'' She talked about writing in a more thoughtful way than she had before, describing not multicolored drafts of paper but her own imagination and experience, even her tactile senses and keen memory of smells. Talking about the conception of her character Ethel Evans, the promiscuous publicist in *The Love Machine*, she said: ''I would almost get the smell of the street when Ethel sat on the stoop at night. I could smell mashed potatoes, boiled cabbage and onion, so I wrote about them. The boy with the protruding ears had to have a boil on the back of his neck. I saw him. He became a character. . . .''

She mustered her strength for a final drive to Philadelphia to visit with Rose and her friends Isabelle and Harry Biron. Isabelle had often asked about Rex Reed, so Jackie brought a copy of Rex's latest book in which she had written, ''To Isabelle and Harry Biron with all the best wishes from Rex Reed and Jackie Susann.''

After barely two weeks at home, Jackie returned to the hospital on July 27. The admission notes described her as ''acutely ill''; ''staph pneumonia,'' usually fatal for someone in her condition, had driven her temperature to 104. She had a large open ulcer on her left hand. Her fever was brought down at last, but the fluid accumulation in her lungs could not be controlled. Determined to celebrate her birthday in her own apartment, she checked out on August 18. On the nineteenth her friend Vera Swift dropped by, but stayed only half an hour because Jackie said she was ''getting a little tired.'' They did not play backgammon, which Vera played at the tournament level and which she had taught to Jackie. Jackie had become so proficient that she, too, had entered some tournaments, and after her death some of her friends established a Jacqueline Susann

Backgammon Championships tournament in Las Vegas, with a thirty-thousand-dollar purse intended to lure players from all over the world.

On the morning of the twentieth, her birthday, she woke with a racing heart and pulse and labored breathing. Irving loves to tell the story of what happened during the ambulance ride to the hospital. At Seventy-second Street, she noticed a blue Cadillac and said, "Look at that car. It's the same color as ours." Then the Cadillac pulled ahead and she saw the license plate: JSM 5. "My God," she said, "it *is* our car." Evidently garage attendants were renting it out on the sly—something that probably didn't bother Jackie much. Success hadn't spoiled her, it made her better than she was. It made her, in Joanne Carson's words, "a great lady—the last of the sweet, swinging broads. She loved to be called that. She lived and enjoyed her celebrity life to the hilt. She was laughing, generous, earthy. When she got those first two bestsellers, back to back, she bragged to me that she 'had life by the short hairs.'" And Jackie became forgiving, more or less. Speaking of Ethel Evans, she explained to that last reporter, "Ethel was hateful only because of how she had grown up and what had happened to her."

On the last of eighteen admissions to Doctors Hospital, at 1:45 P.M. on her fifty-sixth birthday, Jackie acknowledged her age as fifty-four. She was given the corner room again, the celebrity room she had been sharing alternately with Lyndon Johnson's brother. Spingarn noted that her deterioration was most likely related to her metastases, compounded by the effects of medication. Jackie said to one of her nurses, "Don't tell my husband, but I am going to die in here." An antidepressant, Triavil, was prescribed along with Demerol. On the twenty-fifth she became "delusional and confused." She said she was going to see

Josephine and Bob Susan. She was also calling for "someone named Miriam," according to a nurse.

Her condition vacillated over the next several weeks. Irving sat with her each day until about eight P.M. and then went to dinner with Esther Margolis or with Artie Hershkowitz and his wife. Esther still called Jackie daily with sales figures and press notices, but so few people knew of Jackie's condition almost no one visited. Vera, who didn't know the full truth, believes Jackie was trying to spare her the pain of those last days. Doris and Racque Rael flew in for a brief visit, along with Muriel Slatkin from the Beverly Hills Hotel. Irving recalls that they all cried afterward in the corridor. Doris stayed in New York with Jackie for eight days. "I wanted to be at Opal's side until the end, but I was called back to Los Angeles to testify in court."

On the eighteenth of September at 3:45 A.M. Jackie awoke in extreme pain and with labored breathing. The nurse was so alarmed she rushed to get oxygen and called for the resident, who gave her extra Demerol. The nurses' notes record Jackie as tense and moaning, "Everywhere, I ache." Her blood pressure was perilously low.

Irving told Esther "it was quite near the end," and she prepared a lengthy obituary in the form of a press release. She also drafted a eulogy for Oscar Dystel to deliver at the funeral. Irving wanted no cause of death given, but Esther finally persuaded him to reveal the truth.

On the nineteenth and twentieth Jackie rallied. She seemed more comfortable and alert and was taking fluids. She called Long John Nebel and Candy Jones. "She was saying good-bye and we didn't know it," Candy says. "She was always quite breezy, though, and now she sounded in awful, dreadful agony. She had never called me darling before, but her last words were 'Good-bye, my darling.'" But by the morning of the twenty-first, a

Saturday, she was described as "stuporous. Condition terminal."

Irving was having dinner with the Hershkowitzes that evening when the telephone rang, but it was not the call he feared. Instead it was from Austin, where Guy had suffered a fractured jaw in a fight. Irving had barely hung up when the phone rang again; this time it was the hospital to say that Jackie had died.

The first person Irving notified was Esther, who drove in from the country and on Sunday sent out the obituaries and photographs by messenger. "I expect it was shocking," she says, "because nobody knew she was ill."

The service at Campbell's Funeral Home two days later on the twenty-fourth was conducted by a rabbi from Temple Emanu-El. The mourners went back to Irving's apartment, Rose accompanied by the Birons and her nephew Bob Jelinek, who had asked Irving's permission to come. Isabelle remembers that Rex Reed was there, and that "he got down on his knees and put his arms around Rose. The way he spoke to her was just beautiful."

After the service Jackie's body was removed to Westchester for cremation; her ashes were placed in a bronze container resembling a book, which Irving put on a shelf in his library. On Irving's orders, the container carries 1921 as her year of birth, instead of 1918.

Epilogue

Yeah, I think I'll be remembered....
I think I'll be remembered as the voice
of the 1960s ... Andy Warhol, the
Beatles and me....

—Jacqueline Susann

JACKIE Susann was nowhere at the age of forty-four. Her looks were fading; her health was gone; the best of her dreams seemed dead. But instead of languishing, she shut herself up alone in a room with a typewriter to make one last grab at the brass ring.

The result was a record that had never been equaled: three consecutive books at the top of the bestseller list, one of them—*Valley of the Dolls*—officially credited by the *Guinness Book of World Records* as the best-selling novel of all time. And, finally, the closest thing to happiness Jackie would ever see.

* * *

Jackie Susann's life was a story of appearances. She appeared to be the most favored of children, bright, pretty, financially secure in a time when many were not, cherished by a dashing father and a beautiful mother. In fact, she was a miserable little girl, confused by her father's adulteries and her mother's bland acceptance of betrayal, always the bewildered war prize in the pitched battle that was her parents' marriage.

She appeared to be the young Philadelphia aristocrat, daughter of a well-known artist, product of Bryn Mawr College, a person bred to familiarity with good books, the theater, music, and art. In fact, her father was an immigrant, and she barely made it through high school.

She appeared to be a Christian, for a time an ardent Catholic who prayed to her own patron saint. In fact, she was born a Jew and knew the sting of anti-Semitism early.

She appeared to be destined for success as a dramatic actress. In fact, she never progressed beyond bit parts, and as she entered middle age she remained one of the theater's hungry waifs, her nose pressed against the glass behind which the truly talented earned their celebrity.

She appeared to be happily married and in the end she was content. Before that, she was habitually unfaithful to her husband, just as her father had been to her mother.

She appeared to be a doting mother, sending her son off to the best prep schools to give him every advantage. In fact, the institutions were of quite a different sort.

She appeared to be a man's woman, a seductress. In fact, although many men passed through her life, her books suggest that her strongest allegiances were to her own sex. "What I call a nice girl is a girl who gives of herself," she once said, "not physically, but to friends with love." And she could be almost grotesquely macho,

swearing like a sailor, and even slugging men. At times
she assaulted her own husband, who, at times, cried.

She appeared to be a healthy and vital woman. In fact,
her life as a celebrity—the only life she ever wanted to
live—began just as the cancer that would kill her started its
inexorable spread through her body.

She appeared to be the most public of figures, everything about her open to view. In fact, almost everything
about her—her age, her background, her countenance—
was altered to suit the image she wanted to project. Even
her death. Her final days, while exhibiting great gallantry,
were lonelier and far more barren than they had to be. She
would have liked to die like Carol Bjorkman, in makeup
and a five-hundred-dollar dressing gown, a bar in her
room, and friends unwrapping gifts. But she traded that to
hold on to her pride and to her record-setting book deals.

How should Jackie Susann's life and work finally be
assessed? As for her work, what her books lacked in
literary value and graceful prose they made up in raw
reader appeal. Critics sneered, yet those books entertained
millions, and continue to do so today. Dismissed when
they were published as "fairy tales for adults," they now
seem in some respects almost prophetic. Jackie explored
the emerging themes of the 1960's—the drug culture, the
acceptance of homosexuality, the changing aspirations of
women. The bleak picture she painted of love and marriage seems less jarring today as more and more women,
like Jackie's heroines, are self-supporting and alone. The
posture of her tough ladies, secondary but successful
characters like Miriam Polar in *Valley*, Ethel Evans in *Love
Machine*, and Linda Riggs in *Once Is Not Enough*—women
who were unsentimental and frankly seeking financial
independence—seems far less cynical, almost ordinary,
when we read her novels today.

Jackie changed the face of book publishing, taking

power from the critics and giving it to authors who, like herself, could be convincing on television. She likened the selling of a book to the selling of detergent, and, as she often said, "Why the hell not? It works." Aided by her husband, she also broke new ground for authors in dealing with their publishers, securing rights and privileges and percentages of the profits that had never been obtained by an author before. The enormous sums she earned for her publishers were, like the hordes of nonreaders she brought into the bookstores, a shot in the arm for the industry itself.

Perhaps what her life was about was told best at the end. In the face of great adversity and sorrow, she "showed them all." She was, in a word, indomitable. Jackie Susann was not an artist, but in dying she mastered the art of living, if that means making the most of a bad hand that was dealt.

Sources

Preface

Bowen, Catherine Drinker. *Biography: The Craft and Calling*. Boston: Atlantic Monthly Press/Little, Brown, 1968.
"Real Lives, or Readers' Digest?" *Times* (London), Feb. 2, 1986.
Slung, Michele. "Book Report: *Once Is Not Enough*." *Washington Post*, Jan. 31, 1982.

From this point on, important newspaper sources are generally cited in the text, and a number are listed in "A Sampling of Major Sources" below. So many clippings were consulted that sheer volume precludes mention of them all. The clippings that come from Jackie's own scrapbook are not usually identified by exact date. See also "Selected Interviews" below.

Night Thoughts (Chapter 1)

Sources include Jackie's diaries and Dr. Arthur Davids and his staff.

Part I: The Early Years (Chapters 2–6)

Sources include Richard Allman, Evelyn Rubin Arnold, Sylvia Babbitt, Selma Rosinsky Belchic, Mildred Berkowitz, Isabel Biron, Harry Biron, Esther Broza, Charles Diletto, Reba Potamkin Elkoff, Bertha Miller Gershenfeld, Elliot Green, Ackey Harris, Samuel Heller, Louis Hirschman, Frances Hirshenhorn, Robert Jelinek, Rosalie Johns, Kitty Kallen, Rita Weinrott Katten, Jack Kelly, Jr., Pearl Sklaroff Krekstein, Arnold L. Landesberg, Dr. Charles Lee, Helen Gansberg Lilienfeld, Herman Mandell, Samuel Marcus, Tybie Moshinsky, Sally Olds, Meyer Potamkin, Lela Rolontz, Thelma Schonholz Rosoff, Frances Sacks, Florence Birdie Schklowsky, Sophie Schlein, Francis Spade, Cynthia Wolfe Sills, Walter Smith, Flossie Potamkin Stern, Carol Stoner, Doris LeSavoy Watter, Esther Weinrott II, Joel Weinrott, Isaac Witkin.

Major written sources, besides newspaper and magazine clippings, include the following:

Crosby, Alfred W., Jr. "The Influenza Pandemic," in *Symposium on the History, Science, and Politics of Influenza in America: 1918–1976 in Madison, Wisconsin*, edited by June E. Osborn, pp. 5–14. New York: Prodist, 1977.

Goodman, Philip. *Franklin Street*. New York: Alfred A. Knopf, 1942.

Sharrar, Robert G., M.D., et al. "Some Aspects of the 1918–19 Influenza Epidemic in Philadelphia and the United States." *Philadelphia Medicine*, pp. 454–462.

Wolf, Edwin, II, and Maxwell Whiteman. *The History of the Jews of Philadelphia from Colonial Times to the Age of Jackson*, pp. 7, 374–376. Philadelphia: Jewish Publication Society of America, 1956.

Liberties were taken with conversations on art attributed to Robert Susan. The exact words were taken from newspaper clippings. Susan had a habit of rehearsing his pronouncements on art in front of his family first.

Part II: The City (Chapters 7–15)

Sources include Goodman Ace, Jack Amiel, Gertrude Bain, Miriam Bertell, Bill Burnham, Arlene DeMarco, Arlene Francis, Beatrice Freedman, David Noel Freedman, Betty Furness, Ann Thomas Gierlach, Margalo Gillmore, Helen Harris, Radie Harris, Margie Hart, Lillian Hellman, Hildegarde, Celeste Holm, Sandra Klewan, Lawrence Langner, Marion Lulling, Florence Lustig, Judge Abe Marovitz, Joyce Mathews, Joey Nash, Candy Jones Nebel, Marcella Palmer, Margaret Roberts, Betty Rose, Beatrice Cole Roubicek, Claire Safran, Maxine Stuart Shaw, Arthur Siegel, Dorothy Dennis Strelsin, Harriet Van Horne, Benay Venuta, Douglas Watt, Rosemary Wilson, Kate Witkin, Miriam Witkin, Mary Hunter Wolf.

Sources regarding Irving include Goodman Ace, Polly Bergen, Bill Burnham, John Peter Cowden, Arnold Forster, Ed Gottlieb, Lester Gottlieb, Elizabeth Forsling Harris, Eddie Jaffe, Walter Kirschenbaum, Ted Klein, Robert Landry, Irving Mansfield, Joey Nash, Bernard Wilson.

Lovely Me and *Cock of the Walk*, the "lost plays" of Jacqueline Susann and Beatrice Cole, were obtained from the Copyright Office by Michael Patrick Hearn.

The following books were used:

Atkinson, Brooks. *Broadway*. New York: Limelight Editions, 1985.

Berle, Milton. *An Autobiography*. New York: Delacorte Press, 1974.

Cantor, Eddie. *Caught Short!* New York: Simon and Schuster, 1929.

Cantor, Eddie, and David Freedman. *"My Life Is in Your Hands."* New York: Harper and Brothers, 1928.

Carnegie, Dale. *How to Win Friends and Influence People*. New York: Pocket Books, 1981.

Clark, Tom, editor. *Romance in the Roaring Forties*. New York: Beech Tree Books, 1986.

Cohn, Art. *The Joker Is Wild*. New York: Random House, 1955.

Harris, Radie. *Radie's World*. New York: G. P. Putnam's Sons, 1975.

Hayward, Brooke. *Haywire*. New York: Bantam Books, 1980.

Jessel, George. *The World I Lived In*. Chicago: Henry Regnery, 1975.

Mansfield, Irving. *Life with Jackie*. New York: Bantam Books, 1983.

Sanders, Marion K. *Dorothy Thompson: A Legend in Her Time*. Boston: Houghton Mifflin, 1973.

Sheed, Wilfred. *Clare Boothe Luce*. New York: E. P. Dutton, 1982.

Stagg, Jerry. *The Brothers Shubert*. New York: Ballantine Books, 1968.

Terkel, Studs. *Working*. New York: Ballantine Books, 1972.

Zolotow, Maurice. *It Takes All Kinds*. New York: Random House, 1946.

Part III: The Schiffli Girl (Chapters 16–21)

Sources for this section include many of the ongoing sources mentioned earlier. The specific persons will be self-evident from the quotes. Other sources include Isaac Asimov, Katharine Balfour, Anita Bayer, Don Beddoes, Dr. Lauretta Bender, Polly Bergen, Penny Morgan Bigelow, Joanne Carson, Lily Cates, Betty Chau, Erland Chau, Karlina Chau, Arthur C. Clarke, Ted Cott, Warren Cowan, John Peter Cowden, John Crosby, Dr. Charles Debrovner, Eleanor Fields, Mary Flanagan, Horace Gold, Sheila Bond Goldberg, Lester Gottlieb, Gloria Hailey, Helen Harris, Jean Harrison, Robert A. Heinlein, Diana Jelinek, Margie King, Hillary Knight, Julius LaRosa, Dr. Nils Laurson, Morton Mitosky, Al Ramrus, Lee Reynolds, Al Robison, Dr. Herman Roiphe, Janet Sachs, Marlene Sanders, Seymour Schwartzberg, I. Leonard Seiler, Dr. Archie Silver, Joan Castle Sitwell, Robert Stein, Danny Stradella, Ruth C. Sullivan, Emily Toth, Mike Wallace, Gladys Fay Walter, John Wingate, John Woestendiek, Charlotte Zolotow, Maurice Zolotow.

The following books were used:

Charles-Roux, Edmonde. *Chanel*. New York: Alfred A. Knopf, 1975.

Feiffer, Jules. *Harry, the Rat with Women*. New York: McGraw-Hill, 1963.

Gottlieb, Polly Rose. *The Nine Lives of Billy Rose*. New York: Crown, 1968.

Hildegarde. *Over 50—So What!* New York: Devin-Adair, 1962.

Metz, Robert. *CBS: Reflections in a Bloodshot Eye*. New York: New American Library, 1975.

Toth, Emily. *Inside Peyton Place*. New York: Doubleday, 1981.

Wallace, Mike, and Gary Paul Gates. *Close Encounters*. New York: William Morrow, 1984.

With the assistance of David Zimmerman the literature on autism was searched and reviewed. Special thanks to the Academy of Medicine Library in New York, Mary Flanagan at the National Society for Children and Adults with Autism, and Ruth C. Sullivan at the National Society for Autistic Children. A sampling of book and article titles includes the following:

Hoffman, Lois Wladis, and Martin L. Hoffman, editors. *Review of Child Development Research*. Russell Sage Foundation, 1966.

Lee-Dukes, Gwendolyn, M.D. "Infantile Autism." *American Family Physician* (June, 1986), pp. 149–155.

Mussen, Paul H., editor. *Carmichael's Manual of Child Psychology*. New York: John Wiley and Sons, 1970.

Roiphe, Herman, M.D., and Anne Roiphe. *Your Child's Mind: The Complete Guide to Infant and Child Emotional Well Being*. New York: St. Martin's Press, 1985.

Unger, Michael, "Autism." *Newsday*, Oct. 23, 1984.

Wing, Lorna, M.D., D.P.M. *Autistic Children*. New York: Brunner/Mazel, 1972.

I would also like to thank the current staff at St. Paul the Apostle Church in New York who helped with the conversion material, and especially Father Diskin, who took me around the church.

Jackie's journal of her trip around the world with her mother in 1962 exists in two forms: the edited one she gave her mother, and the original handwritten journal itself. Two separate sources provided access to them.

Part IV: Up Mount Everest (Chapters 22–26)

Again, sources for this section include many of the ongoing sources mentioned earlier. Others include Jay Allen, Noel Behn, Harriet Blacker, David Brown, Helen Gurley

Brown, Bette Davis, Jackie Farber, John Fricke, Bernard Geis, Patti Lasky, Esther Margolis, Jim Montgomery, Leona Nevler, Bertrand Pogrebin, Letty Cottin Pogrebin, Dick Schaap, Budd Schulberg, David Slavitt, Anna Sosenko, Gloria Steinem, Barbara Walters.

There are hundreds of print interviews with Jackie from this period, but a more revealing source of her attitudes is the tapes of her Long John radio interviews, provided by Candy Jones Nebel.

Books used include the following:

Cerf, Bennett. *At Random*. New York: Random House, 1977.

Daigh, Ralph. *Maybe You Should Write a Book*. Englewood Cliffs, N.J.: Prentice-Hall, 1977.

Frank, Gerold. *Judy*. New York: Harper and Row, 1975.

McClintick, David. *Indecent Exposure*. New York: William Morrow, 1982.

Slavitt, David R. *Jo Stern*. New York: New American Library, 1978.

Part V: Valley of the Shadow (Chapters 27–32)

Again, sources for this section include many of the sources mentioned earlier. Others include Sherry Arden, Ruth Batchelor, Pierre Belfond, George Bellak, Irwin Berg, Myrna Blyth, James Brady, Kathy Brady, Joyce Brothers, Alicia Buttons, Charles Champlin, Rev. Joseph M. Champlin, Paddy Chayefsky, Sara Davidson, John G. Davies, Mallen DeSantis, Jonathan Dolger, Claudia Dreifus, Nora Ephron, Leslie Fiedler, James Finkenstaedt, Alan Fushko, Gerold Frank, Margaret Gardner, Lee Grant, Shecky Greene, Joyce Haber, Dagmar Henne, Mildred Hird, Abby Hirsch, Jane Howard, Chauncey Howell, Lawrence Hughes, Rona

Jaffe, Richard Kaplan, Stewart Klein, Michael Korda, James Landis, John Lennon, Norman Mailer, Jean Majors, Sylvie Messinger, Madonne Miner, Barbara Parkins, Rex Reed, Betty Rollin, Paul Rosner, Andrew Sarris, George Stravropoulos, Vera Swift, Brenda Vaccaro, Michael Viner, Susan Wood.

Books used include the following:

Alpert, Hollis. *The People Eaters*. New York: Dial Press, 1971.

Brasselle, Keefe. *The CanniBalS*. New York: Bartholomew House, 1968.

Bugliosi, Vincent. *Helter Skelter*. New York: W. W. Norton, 1974.

DeMarco, Arlene. *Triangle*. New York: New American Library, 1971.

Ehrenreich, Barbara. *Remaking Love*. New York: Anchor Press/Doubleday, 1986.

Grobel, Lawrence. *Conversations with Capote*. New York: New American Library, 1985.

Hirsch, Abby. *The Great Carmen Miranda Look-Alike Contest*. New York: St. Martin's Press, 1974.

Korda, Michael. *Charmed Lives*. New York: Avon Books, 1979.

Nebel, Long John. *The Psychic World Around Us*. New York: New American Library, 1969.

Rollin, Betty. *First, You Cry*. Philadelphia: Lippincott, 1976.

Zec, Donald. *Some Enchanted Egos*. New York: St. Martin's Press, 1973.

Elkoff, Reba Potamkin
Ephron, Nora
Farber, Jackie
Fiedler, Leslie
Fields, Eleanor
Finkenstaedt, James
Flanagan, Mary
Forster, Arnold
Fushko, Alan
Francis, Arlene
Frank, Gerold
Freedman, Beatrice
Freedman, David Noel
Fricke, John
Furness, Betty

Gardner, Margaret
Geis, Bernard
Gershenfeld, Bertha Miller
Gierlach, Ann Thomas
Gillmore, Margalo
Gold, Horace
Goldberg, Sheila Bond
Gottlieb, Ed
Gottlieb, Lester
Granoff, Bud
Grant, Lee
Green, Elliot
Greene, Shecky

Haber, Joyce
Hailey, Gloria
Handemann, Barbara
Harris, Ackey
Harris, Helen

Harris, Radie
Harrison, Jean
Hart, Margie
Heinlein, Robert A.
Heller, Samuel
Hellman, Lillian
Henne, Dagmar
Hird, Mildred
Hirsch, Abby
Hirschman, Louis
Hirshenhorn, Frances
Holm, Celeste
Howard, Jane
Howell, Chauncey
Hughes, Lawrence

Israel, Lee

Jaffe, Eddie
Jaffe, Rona
Jelinek, Diana
Johns, Rosalie

Kallen, Kitty
Kaplan, Dick
Katten, Rita Weinrott
Kelly, Jack, Jr.
King, Margie
Kirschenbaum, Walter
Klein, Stewart
Klein, Ted
Klewan, Sandra
Knight, Hilary
Korda, Michael
Krekstein, Pearl Sklaroff

Lambert, Eleanor
Landesberg, Arnold L.
Landis, James
Landry, Robert
Langner, Lawrence
LaRosa, Julius
Lasky, Patti
Laurson, Dr. Nils
Lee, Dr. Charles
Lehman, Ernest
Lennon, John
Leopold, Lee
Lilienfeld, Helen Gansberg
Lulling, Marion
Lustig, Florence

Mailer, Norman
Majors, Jean
Mandell, Herman
Mansfield, Irving
Marcus, Samuel
Margolis, Esther
Marovitz, Judge Abe
Mathews, Joyce
Messinger, Sylvie
Miner, Madonne
Mitosky, Morton
Montgomery, Jim
Moshinsky, Tybie

Nash, Joey
Nevler, Leona

Olds, Sally

Palmer, Lynne
Palmer, Marcella
Parkins, Barbara
Pickman, Milton
Pogrebin, Bertrand
Pogrebin, Letty Cottin
Potamkin, Meyer

Ramrus, Al
Reed, Rex
Reynolds, Lee
Roberts, Margaret
Robison, Al
Roiphe, Anne
Roiphe, Dr. Herman
Rollin, Betty
Rolontz, Lela
Rose, Betty
Rosner, Paul
Rosoff, Thelma Schonholz
Roubicek, Bea Cole

Sachs, Janet
Sacks, Frances
Safran, Claire
Sanders, Marlene
Sarris, Andrew
Schaap, Dick
Schapp, Mattie
Schklowsky, Florence Birdie
Schlein, Sophie
Schmale, Arthur
Schoenstein, Ralph
Schulberg, Budd
Schwartzberg, Seymour

Seiler, I. Leonard

Shaw, Maxine Stuart

Siegel, Arthur

Sills, Cynthia Wolfe

Silver, Dr. Archie

Sitwell, Joan Castle

Slavitt, David

Smith, Walter

Sosenko, Anna

Spade, Francis

Speers, Brian

Stiefel, Arnold

Stein, Robert

Steinem, Gloria

Stern, Flossie Potamkin

Stern, Gloria

Stoner, Carol

Stradella, Danny

Stravropoulos, George

Strelsin, Dorothy Dennis

Struber, Jan

Sullivan, Ruth C.

Swift, Vera

Toth, Emily

Vaccaro, Brenda

Valente, Renée

Van Horne, Harriet

Venuta, Benay

Viner, Michael

Wallace, Mike

Walter, Gladys Faye

Walters, Barbara

Watt, Douglas

Watter, Doris LeSavoy

Weinrott, Esther, II

Weinrott, Joel

Weiss, Marvin

Wilson, Bernard

Wilson, Rosemary

Wingate, John

Witkin, Isaac

Witkin, Kate

Witkin, Miriam

Woestendiek, John

Wolf, Mary Hunter

Wood, Susan

Zolotow, Charlotte

Zolotow, Maurice

A Sampling of Major Sources in Newspapers and Periodicals

Bannon, Barbara A. "Jacqueline Susann." *Publishers Weekly*, Apr. 2, 1973.

Bender, Marylin. "Guessing Game from Jacqueline Susann's Typewriter." *New York Times*, Apr. 26, 1969.

Davidson, Sara. "Jacqueline Susann: The Writing Machine." *Harper's,* Oct., 1969.

Donnelly, Tom. "Jacqueline Susann on the Supreme Cop Out: 'I'm Wildly Upset.'" *Washington Post Book World*, July 22, 1973.

Dorsey, Helen. "Eavesdropper Jacqueline Susann, the Writing Machine." *Philadelphia Inquirer*, Sept. 8, 1974.

"Fathers, Daughters, and the Lesson of Love: A Last Interview with Jacqueline Susann." *Family Weekly*, Nov. 3, 1974.

Gehman, Richard. "Irving and the Cave Man." *Esquire*, July, 1952.

"Girl Quits Broadway Show to Be Near Dying Father." *Philadelphia Inquirer*, Dec. 10, 1938.

Gross, Ben. "TV Girl Makes Million out of a Sexy Novel." *New York Sunday News*, Dec. 11, 1966.

Haber, Joyce, "Beautiful People Love Jacqueline Susann." *Los Angeles Times*, June 29, 1969.

Hamilton, Alex. "Jacqueline Susann: Behind Every Poodle Something More Formidable." *Times Saturday Review* (London), Jan. 20, 1968.

Howard, Jane. "Happiness Is Being Number 1." *Life*, Aug. 19, 1966.

Hurley, Kay. "Susann on Sex." *Newark Evening News*, July 20, 1969.

Illig, Joyce. "Everybody Was a Virgin Once." *Washington Post*, Apr. 8, 1973.

Kasindorf, Martin. "Jackie Susann Picks Up the Marbles." *New York Times*, Aug. 12, 1973.

Krymer, Murray. "Her View from the 'Valley' Is Dizzying." *Newsday*, Jan. 22, 1968.

Michaelson, Judy. "Woman in the News: Jacqueline Susann: Her Friends Tell Her Everything." *New York Post*, May 17, 1969.

Nachman, Gerald. "That's Show Biz." *New York Post*, Feb. 23, 1966.

Prevor, Gabriel. "A Pair of Pretty Playwrights Who Say

They Simply Didn't Know They Were Supposed to Have Stage Fright." *New York Sunday Mirror Magazine*, Sept. 17, 1950.

Purdy, Ken W. "Valley of the Dollars." *Saturday Evening Post*, Feb. 24, 1968.

Reed, Rex. "Jackie Susann: The Writing Machine." *New York Sunday News*, Mar. 18, 1973.

Safran, Claire. "Drugs and Your Daughter." *Pageant*, Feb., 1967.

Silverman, William A. "What Kind of a Woman . . ." *Detroit News Magazine*, July 6, 1969.

Susann, Jacqueline. "Along Came Joe." *Ladies' Home Journal*, Apr., 1970.

Susann, Jacqueline. "Footlights: Autobiography of 'an Actress' Who Became a Playwright." *Philadelphia Inquirer*, Dec. 1, 1946.

Susann, Jacqueline. "The War of the Words." *TV Guide*, July 7, 1973.

Susann, Jacqueline. "Why Women Are So Much Smarter than Men." Publication unidentified, undated.

Tallmer, Jerry. "Jacqueline Susann." *New York Post*, July 8, 1972.

Taylor, David. "Passing Through: Jacqueline Susann Talks to David Taylor." *Punch*, Oct. 3, 1973.

Torre, Marie. "Cupid Pooled Their Talents." *New York World Telegram and Sun Magazine*, Nov. 7, 1959.

Wilson, Earl. "It Happened Last Night: The Year with Too Many Dogs . . ." *New York Post*, Sept. 23, 1974.

Wilson, Earl. "The Lady Protests." *New York Post*, July 24, 1969.

Index

By the year 2000, 2 out of 3 Americans could be illiterate.

It's true.

Today, 75 million adults… about one American in three, can't read adequately. And by the year 2000, U.S. News & World Report envisions an America with a literacy rate of only 30%.

Before that America comes to be, you can stop it… by joining the fight against illiteracy today.

Call the Coalition for Literacy at toll-free **1-800-228-8813** and volunteer.

Volunteer Against Illiteracy. The only degree you need is a degree of caring.

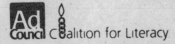

Ad Council Coalition for Literacy